Gender, Sex and the
Shaping of Modern Europe

Gender, Sex and the Shaping of Modern Europe

A History from the French Revolution to the Present Day

Annette F. Timm and Joshua A. Sanborn

Oxford • New York

English edition
First published in 2007 by
Berg
Editorial offices:
First Floor, Angel Court, 81 St Clements Street, Oxford OX4 1AW, UK
175 Fifth Avenue, New York, NY 10010, USA

Berg is the imprint of Oxford International Publishers Ltd.

Library of Congress Cataloging-in-Publication Data
Timm, Annette F.
  Gender, sex, and the shaping of modern Europe : a history from
the French Revolution to the present day / Annette F. Timm and
Joshua A. Sanborn. — English ed.
    p. cm.
  Includes bibliographical references and index.
  ISBN-13: 978-1-84520-356-6 (cloth)
  ISBN-10: 1-84520-356-9 (cloth)
  ISBN-13: 978-1-84520-357-3 (pbk.)
  ISBN-10: 1-84520-357-7 (pbk.)
  1. Sex role—Europe—History. 2. Sex—Europe—History. 3.
Europe—Social conditions—1789-1900. 4. Europe—Social
conditions—20th century. 5. Europe—History. 6. Social history.
I. Sanborn, Joshua A. II. Title.

  HQ1075.5.E85T56 2007
  305.320973—dc22   2006037868

British Library Cataloguing-in-Publication Data
A catalogue record for this book is available from the British Library.

ISBN 978 1 84520 356 6 (Cloth)
ISBN 978 1 84520 357 3 (Paper)

Typeset by Avocet Typeset, Chilton, Aylesbury, Bucks
Printed in the United Kingdom by Biddles Ltd, King's Lynn.

www.bergpublishers.com

Contents

Preface

The authors of this book met as graduate students in a seminar on gender history at the University of Chicago. An incident in that course guaranteed that we continued to remember each other, despite our differences in speciality and our various post-graduation wanderings. One steamy day in late spring, what had been a collegial, interdisciplinary atmosphere erupted into a dispute between students in the class about whether scholars could ever break free of their own gender and racial backgrounds and become thoughtful critics of others with different backgrounds. The debate quickly turned personal. Pointed questions were raised about the extent to which men could or should participate in certain areas of class discussion (and indeed in the class itself) and whether white, middle-class women and men could or should critique positions taken by women of colour. Both of us left that seminar with scars. The details of the incident are unimportant, and our memories of it differ. But the experience left a lasting impression of what it means to be an apprentice in a fledgling field fraught with political and personal tensions. It was no accident that emotions exploded on a day when the assigned readings dealt with extremely personal stories of gender and racial oppression. The politics and emotions of the present intertwined with these stories of the past, and the question of who had the right to speak for oppressed minorities provoked angst and indignation. The dispute revealed that the ground rules of studying gender in a scholarly way were not entirely clear to any of us. We were acutely aware that the older categories of women's history and women's studies were being challenged and revised. We were also aware that new perspectives from cultural history, the history and theory of race, post-colonial theory and theories about masculinity should inform our understanding of gender. But at least for the two of us, the explosion of that day proved that numerous scholarly currents had collided around the term 'gender' and that establishing our own identities as scholars would involve a very careful balancing act.

Scholarly discussions about the meaning of gender continue, of course. But the participants in that graduate seminar have gone on to employ 'gender as a category of analysis' (Joan Scott) with self-confidence and the support of a burgeoning theoretical and empirical body of literature. It is a category that we can, for the most part, take for granted in our daily lives as researchers. There are, of course, still theoretical disputes about how gender should be approached historically. But there is also a vibrant, interdisciplinary and international community of scholars, which has developed a common language of scholarly reference points. While there is certainly still resistance from some quarters – one hears the grumbling in the hallways at large multi-speciality and regional history conferences about how the 'trendy' panels have pushed out 'traditional' subjects – historians who 'do' gender can generally rely on a respectful reception from the larger discipline. But being tolerated and having found comfortable niches are not quite the same thing as having been entirely integrated into the master narratives of our respective historical sub-disciplines. Most of us have developed scholarly identities based primarily on our geographic specialities, and we are comfortable in these academic homes. But scholars trained in gender theory and research methods can still find themselves frustrated by a lack of understanding in the larger historical discipline about what 'doing gender' actually means.

The degree to which gender still operates as a sub-speciality of historical practice is perhaps most evident in the structure of undergraduate history surveys. Even historians very amenable to gender approaches to history find it difficult to integrate these perspectives into the overarching narratives of their national survey courses or their broader overviews of European history. Throwing in separate lectures on family or on women's rights (the 'add women and stir' approach) has proven unsatisfying both for instructors and for students. Many instructors, including the present authors, have even taken lectures focused directly on 'gender' themes back out of their repertoire because they proved unpersuasive and confusing to students. Either students could not understand how these 'episodes' fit into the larger subject matter of the course, or they expressed resentment at the apparent attempt to 'indoctrinate' them with a 'feminist agenda'. It is our conviction that finding a way of integrating gender perspectives into undergraduate education is a necessary step along the road towards integrating gender into the broader narrative of European history.

As a result, our imagined audience when writing this book was a reader who knew (or was concurrently learning) the standard outline of European history. We expected that readers would know something about imperialism, feminism, fascism and communism, for instance, but we did not expect a detailed knowledge of these or other developments over the past 250 years. We also assumed no knowledge of gender theory. If we have accomplished our aim, the book should be accessible and informative for interested readers of any age, for students in introductory classes in European history, and for a wide range of classes in gender studies programmes. We hope, finally, that the text will also be of interest to specialists in the field of gender history. We wrote this book because though there is now a large specialized literature on gender in Europe, there is a shortage of compact, interpretive works. We are certain that specialists will find much to dispute in terms of our thematic choices, our case studies, and our particular narrative lines. But we are also optimistic that the book will stimulate scholars to see connections where they had not been evident before and to think of European gender history as an integrated whole. That, in any event, is what happened for us as we wrote the text.

The challenge is to elucidate both the gendered nature of politics and the political nature of gender. Our goal in this book is not simply to find areas of European history where gender played a role. Readers looking for an encyclopaedic reference to the history of feminism, the family or the progress of knowledge about sex and sexual difference will be disappointed. We are not looking to recover stories untold, describe a history of oppression, or trumpet a success story of progress in equality and rights. Instead, this book attempts to track key shifts in how the roles of men and women were understood in modern European history. The fact that these key shifts come under the headings that are to be found in many European history survey courses is no accident. We are explicitly arguing that the dramatic ruptures in the political life of Europe in the modern era are incomprehensible without some attention to gender. Political revolutions, economic change and ideas about race and human hierarchy all rely on culturally constructed understandings of gender roles both for justification and for modes of implementation. Our ultimate goal is to make a case for the necessity of including gender in any comprehensive survey of modern European (or any other) history. Our method of achieving this goal relies on the most powerful tool of the historian's trade: weaving a convincing story.

In choosing the elements of the story to be told, we relied on a theoretical understanding of gender that stresses its relational nature. In our view, gender describes both male and female actions and identities and is impossible to understand by studying either masculinity or femininity in isolation. We chose our case studies with this in mind, focusing on moments where the two sexes collided or where the separation of their social roles was particularly important for the formation of broader cultural identities, such as the angel of the household, the mother of the nation, the soldier-citizen or the heroic male conqueror of foreign territory. We were also guided by our conviction that although gender touches on (and is affected by) many areas of human experience and behaviour, it is always, in some way, intimately and centrally about sex. How sexual activity was controlled, defined and scientifically understood had a dramatic effect on individuals' sense of self and their understanding of themselves as citizens. The challenge in a book of this sort is to show the ways that gender is about large-scale social abstraction and individual human desire at the same time, and, most importantly, the ways that these seemingly natural and static forces can change dramatically in a relatively short period of time.

This book contends that gender history is neither a 'women's history' nor a 'men's history', and that to understand the operation of gender in modern Europe one must historicize it rather than trying to find one progressive narrative that explains how life came to be as it is today. The changes that this book describes laid bare the deep historical contingency of European notions of society, sexuality and individual identity. These changes were radical and important, but they were not always 'progressive' or unidirectional. They did not affect every European country equally or at the same time. Telling a coherent narrative about change across Europe runs into problems of definition and comparison. In terms of definition, we understand Europe to include both the central continent and its outer reaches, from Scotland to Sicily, and from Portugal to Russia. Rather than attempting the immensely complex and confusing task of comparing how each shift reverberated across the diversity of European nations or constantly placing each country on some kind of time-line of gender progress, we chose to emphasize what we viewed as especially illustrative moments of gender transformation. This bears the risk of making it seem like a dramatic event in one country can stand as a symbolic representation of change everywhere. We have no intention of implying this. Our goal instead is to provide a narrative that gives enough detail for undergraduates to understand how gender is intertwined with political and social change. This is more easily achieved, we believe, by pausing longer to reflect upon the symbolic meaning of individual cases rather than providing a comprehensive comparative account. Many of the cases we chose are well-studied parts of the standard narrative of European history, like our investigation of gender in France in the revolutionary era. Others rarely appear in textbooks, like our study of Bulgaria after the First World War. Some readers will no doubt wonder why we ignore Bulgaria in the revolutionary era; others will be frustrated that more attention was not paid to France after the First World War. We tried to achieve some balance between east and west, north and south, famous and obscure, but we knew that a perfect balance was impossible to achieve. The choices made here were the result of a productive and extended conversation between two authors with different perspectives and specialities. We hope that the result will contribute to a broader conversation about how European historians can make constructive use of gender in their teaching.

We have been helped by numerous people along the way. Our first acknowledgement is to Leora Auslander, who taught the seminar at which this book in a sense originated. The scholarly rigour of her courses taught us what 'doing gender' can mean both for teaching and research, and her warmth and openness have made the path both more enjoyable and more rewarding. Many others read parts of this manuscript and made comments. Our thanks go out to Andrea Smith, Paul Barclay, Geoffrey Sanborn, Victoria Langland, Beverly Lemire, Till van Rahden, Elizabeth Heineman, Josie McLellan, Martin Staum, Alexander Hill, Scott Anderson and the members of the Lafayette College Works in Progress Seminar. Thanks also to Bob Weiner, who assigned a chapter of the text to his survey course and helped collate the feedback and to Sarah Blair-Miller, a student in that class who agreed to give extensive comments on her impressions. General advice in areas outside of our expertise was provided by Maggie Osler, Chris Archer, Paola Rodriguez, John Ferris and Ken MacMillan. Particular thanks to Nancy Janovicek, who provided extensive and invaluable feedback and moral support. Special thanks are due to our student research assistants for this project: Lori Weaver, Brian Geraghty, Sandamali Wijeratne, Diana Galperin, David Henderson and Leanna Seamans. Financial support for these assistants and for authors living two time zones away to work, on occasion, face to face was provided by the Academic Research Committee of

Lafayette College and both the Faculty of Social Sciences and the University Research Grants Committee at the University of Calgary. Thanks too to Melanie Friesen, who graciously accepted our intrusions into the artistic process and crafted a wonderful image for the cover. We are, finally, much in debt to Kathleen May at Berg, who suggested this project to us and nurtured it along the way.

Last, but not least, our thanks go to our families. Scott Anderson and Kimberly Babcock Sanborn dealt with several periods of mental and physical absence (and, yes, a great deal of increased childcare) so that this project could be completed. We would like to dedicate the book to our children Madeleine Sarah Timm Anderson, Clayton Babcock Sanborn and Grace Babcock Sanborn.

Annette F. Timm and Joshua A. Sanborn

Introduction

The biology of sexual difference has been studied since the time of the ancient Greeks. Aristotle believed that women were imperfect men. Basing his understanding of human anatomy on the concept of a conservation of fluids and heat, he argued that women were cooler: their need to expend fluids in menstruation and in breastfeeding left them insufficient heat to develop exterior genitals and the personality traits associated with them. Galen, writing in the third century BCE, concurred, arguing that female genitals were male genitals turned inside out. This one-sex model, as Thomas Laqueur has called it, had significant consequences for the Western understanding of sexual response, and it prevailed into the eighteenth century, with lingering effects into the nineteenth century and beyond.[1] In the early modern period, the one-sex model helped explain anatomical anomalies, such as hermaphrodites (individuals with ambiguous external genitalia). The sixteenth-century surgeon Ambrose Paré, for instance, recorded cases where 'swift and violent movements' or sexual encounters had caused pubescent girls to spontaneously sprout penises. They had, in his view, generated enough heat to become men.

The one-sex model postulated a vertical hierarchy of sexual difference that emphasized male superiority while still implying a spectrum of biological and psychological variation. The belief that men and women were different versions of the same thing (and the lack of knowledge about the actual biological processes of fertilization) also made it logical to assume that the sexual act was analogous for each sex. If men had to ejaculate to impregnate a woman, it was logical to assume that women also had to achieve orgasm in order to create the heat necessary for conception. In fact, if one expected male and female anatomy to be basically analogous, it was logical to think that the man and the woman would have to climax simultaneously to ensure conception. The fact that science linked the sexual response of both sexes to their ability to reproduce had significant social and political repercussions. Among other things, it fuelled interest in female sexual response and led men who wanted to become fathers to pay some attention to the sexual desires of their wives. But this understanding of reproductive biology also helped fuel the prejudice that women were entirely sexed beings, so controlled by their desires that they could not be considered politically mature subjects.

Since we now know much more about how reproduction works and about the genetic basis of sexual difference, it would perhaps be logical to expect that a shift in

1

understanding about what makes men and women biologically different was the result of a scientific discovery or some advance in medical or anatomical knowledge. This was not the case. Around 1800, the one-sex model increasingly came under attack, but the roots of this shift had very little to do with scientific knowledge of reproductive biology. The first indication that ovulation might occur without copulation arose from Theodor L. W. Bischoff's experiments on dogs in 1843. Extrapolating from this research to humans, medical researchers began to agree that women were 'spontaneous ovulators'.[2] In other words, it was only in the middle of the nineteenth century that there was scientific evidence refuting a one-sex model of simultaneous ejaculation. Female orgasm and conception were now conceptually separated. But arguments that the two sexes were incommensurable preceded these anatomical discoveries by almost half a century. In the absence of new 'scientific' explanations, it is clear that social and political thought drove science rather than the other way around. It was no accident that men and women were found to be biologically opposite creatures at the precise moment, just after the French Revolution, when most Europeans were reinforcing the exclusion of women from the public sphere.

While we focus here on the modern period, our purpose in venturing back to the ancient Greeks is to point out that sexual difference has a history. The fact that Europeans between Aristotle and the nineteenth century could look at a vagina and see a penis turned inside out might well strike moderns as odd. But to dismiss this view as simply foolish ignorance would be a mistake. Bodies are not easily read. Whether male or female or somewhere in between, they harbour no self-evident truths and no obvious clues as to how we should translate their differences into the fabric of our social and political lives. As a result, all aspects of sexual difference – as read in the body and as manifested in society and politics – are subject to historical change. Over the past 250 years, that change has been dramatic. While ancient and early modern understandings of sexual anatomy may seem faintly ridiculous to us today, understanding how definitions of sexual difference were translated into norms of behaviour for European men and women and how these norms changed over the course of the modern period is a vital task for any student of modern European history.

In 1750, patriarchy was the main organizing principle of European life. The word patriarchy derives from the Greek roots for 'father' and 'rule' and refers to those social and political systems in which fathers or father figures exercise ultimate authority.[3] No system of power is ever total, of course, but the conviction that fathers should rule saturated European life from Ireland to Russia and from Sweden to Italy. This conviction provided the glue that held together the hierarchies of authority across the continent.[4] How it played out in practice took many forms. In rural areas across most of the continent, but particularly in the South and East, it was a durable pyramid of power reaching from a male head of household up to male village elders, who in turn owed deference and obedience to local lords and notables, who then swore fealty to kings, who universally promised to govern in obedience to God, the greatest patriarch of them all. In areas where traditional village life was already breaking down, such as parts of Great Britain, greater mobility gave some people, including women, more choices in life. But even in these more robust societies, centuries of tradition, of religious practice and of the consistent application of political power had solidified the theory of father-rule to such a degree that even those who tried to avoid its grip accepted it in principle.

Patriarchy manifested itself broadly, affecting not only the dynamics of family life, but also broader socio-economic and cultural forms. Patriarchal structures were especially well suited to life in the small agricultural communities that predominated throughout the continent in various forms. Eastern Europe, where more than 90 per cent of the population lived outside of urban centres in 1750, was particularly rural in composition, but rural life dominated everywhere. In north-western Europe, 72.2 per cent lived in the countryside, and in central and Mediterranean regions the number was around 65 per cent.[5] In all cases, rural communities were fairly small, which meant that everyone knew everyone else in their primary community. In addition, many rural families lived in compact villages and could hear and observe the behaviour of their neighbours. This intense social intimacy allowed for more comprehensive social control, as village romances and family dynamics in general were carefully observed by one's neighbours.

The economic organization of rural communities had profound effects on family life. In the East, country people were still most likely to be living on large estates, while in western, northern and central Europe, eighteenth-century economic life had been slowly shifting from a system of large manors and estates to an agricultural economy in which small family-based households were the primary economic unit. Those who still lived on estates operated within a very hierarchical universe in which landlords determined the boundaries of work and family life, including whether or not one had the right to marry at all. But in areas already entering the early stages of industrialization, the production of manufactured goods within the home had become more common. Families thus began to function more as independent units, and parents asserted exclusive responsibility for their children, which changed both family dynamics and the meaning of work.[6] These family units had much more autonomy, and their decisions were increasingly governed by the economic needs of the family as a whole. In all areas, a complementary division of gender roles and forms of work was the norm. In other words, all family members contributed their labours to the joint effort of achieving subsistence or sometimes even a family income. The division of labour between the genders was quite strict in some regions and more flexible in others. But women's contribution was crucial everywhere, even as the principle of their subordination to the will of the male head of household was clear and repeatedly articulated.[7]

Beyond the local level, society was structured by patriarchy as well, usually through a formal system of social estates. One's social identity was normally ascribed, not chosen, and it was based on male status passed from fathers to sons and from husbands to wives. One's estate position determined one's economic and political prospects and even, in many areas, the laws to which one was subject. Some especially fortunate individuals rose from one estate to another through marriage or entrepreneurial success. In France, it was possible for wealthy commoners to enter the nobility by purchasing a royal office. In England, industrialization brought various opportunities for enterprising individuals to move up the social ranks. In most other areas, though, even these very limited opportunities for social mobility were distant dreams. A boy born to a serf family in Russia, for instance, would be a serf himself when he grew up. He could be sold by his lord and was forbidden from moving. Religion also determined both social and legal status in many parts of the continent. A Jewish boy in Salonika, a European port city in the Ottoman Empire, would be governed by laws specific to the Jewish community there and would normally aspire to assume control of the family business when his father thought it was time.

In general, social mobility was not unheard of, but its routes were open only to a select few and the distance travelled usually quite small. Even in regions of northern and western Europe where modest degrees of social mobility were possible, most individuals occupied the same social station (and often the exact same job) that their parents had. In one recently studied region of eighteenth-century Scandinavia, half the population passed away in the same farmhouse in which they had been born, and fully 95 per cent died in their home parish. Any social mobility that was achieved was normally a shift from being a farm worker to a farm owner or vice versa – a significant difference for those involved, of course, but hardly the mark of a highly fluid society.[8] Even among a sample of individuals most likely to see social mobility in the period (English writers of autobiographies, who were generally literate and of the 'middling sort'), only 10 per cent saw significant upward mobility and 3 per cent downward mobility.[9] For women, social mobility was equally difficult to attain. A girl born in Europe at this time derived her status from her father up until her marriage, at which point she took on the status of her husband. At all times, she was expected to be obedient to the will of the man in her life. Lived experience was of course not this universal, and plenty of women found possibilities to exert their own will at certain times or on certain issues. They acted as trustees for their sons, for instance, or negotiated with governments in their husbands' absence, sometimes relying on local customs that contradicted written law.[10] To varying degrees in different regions of early modern Europe, certain groups of women (such as those who chose the convent instead of marriage and thereby owed obedience to Church fathers, or those older women who had either never been married or had been widowed) were able to maintain positions of independence from men. The marginality and unique position of these women sometimes afforded them greater opportunities, as it did for widowed noblewomen in Russia, who were allowed to own property and otherwise act in many ways as if they were male householders.[11] Some exceptional women even attained prominence as authors and scientists.[12] But marginal and exceptional women could also find themselves in danger, as the victims of early modern witch trials could attest.[13]

European cultural forms were also deeply patriarchal in nature. Religious teachings, primarily in the form of Christianity, Judaism and Islam, provided a reliable cultural bulwark for male dominance. The doctrinal traditions of all three of these religions were developed among deeply patriarchal societies, first in what is now called the Middle East and later throughout the European continent itself. Religious leaders, as a result, reaffirmed that patriarchy was the natural order of mankind, imposed by God Himself. To take just the most obvious example, Christians across the continent memorized the 'Lord's Prayer', in which the power of God, of political lords and of family fathers were linked together and worshipped. It begins 'Our Father, who art in Heaven, hallowed be thy Name. Thy Kingdom come, thy will be done, on Earth as it is in Heaven. Give us this day our daily bread...'. Obedience to the Father's will, on earth as well as heaven, was connected to the father's gift of economic goods and the ability to survive. There is perhaps no clearer statement of the premises of early modern patriarchy.

Other cultural institutions were also informed by patriarchal principles. Courtship practices were structured around the fact that the consent of fathers was necessary before marriage, even though many Europeans also believed that affection between spouses was desirable. Patriarchy was sustained most clearly in traditions of arranged marriages, which persisted in many regions of Europe, and which occurred not only among powerful elites seeking to build strong political bases, but also among modest peasants seeking good matches in terms of production and reproduction. In early modern Europe, typically, Jewish marriages were arranged, though it was expected that love would follow.[14] Family pressures or the disapproval of the community could take precedence over the desires of the individuals being wed. While love was not unknown in early modern marriage, the choice of partner was vital to one's economic survival, and issues of economic security were at least as important as sexual passion or love in choosing a mate.[15] It is easy to underestimate the degree to which this is still true today. Nonetheless, early modern European societies were more likely to link marriage choice directly to the continuance of the family farm, of the village, of the country and of the monarchy. Inheritance laws in all European countries were generally geared towards preventing the excessive division of property and thus favoured the patriarchal structure. Economic considerations, enforced by fathers or communities, could easily bar couples from marrying, sometimes forcing them to emigrate if they wished to stay together.

The age at which people married affected family life and sexual behaviour in Europe dramatically. In the British Isles, Germany, Scandinavia, France and Germany couples did not marry until surprisingly late. In England, for instance, the average age of first marriage in the first half of the eighteenth century was 27.5 years for men and 26.2 years for women.[16] This age was only slightly older than in other places in northern Europe, where the average for women was twenty-five years.[17] This was dramatically different from the pattern in the South and the East, where couples either married as teenagers and lived in extended families with one set of parents until later in life, or where there was a large age gap between the husband and the wife.[18] These different models of marriage were suited to the specific systems of agriculture and economics, since they ensured that family life would bring economic stability. Extended families could unite their resources to pay feudal dues in areas where these still existed. In areas where marriage was late, households were only founded when a man might reasonably expect to inherit the family enterprise and become economically independent. This late-marriage model, however, was incompatible with the sexual desires of youth. As a result, premarital sex was common, and many local customs developed to govern it. In most rural and working-class communities in north-western Europe, it was expected that a couple would start sleeping together once they were betrothed. If pregnancy resulted, marriage generally followed. There certainly were heated family struggles and assaults upon young men and women who had chosen to ignore family or community standards about what made a good match. Men who were reluctant to marry their pregnant lovers faced the community's wrath, at least until expanding opportunities in the cities provided them with an escape route. But the disciplining of premarital sex in the early modern period was much milder than measures taken against other forms of deviance from the marital norm. Both adultery and homosexuality, for instance, were punishable by death in many European legal codes, though in practice adultery was more usually punished by fines or shaming and homosexuality was punished very rarely indeed. Still, early modern courts were kept quite busy policing sexuality. In Essex County, England, population 40,000, there were more than 15,000 people charged with sexual offences between 1558 and 1603.[19]

The world of 1750 seems very far away now. Almost nothing we have described above corresponds to European life today. By the early twenty-first century, though male power remained vibrant and dominant throughout the continent, the pyramid of early modern patriarchal authority had been utterly destroyed. It was no longer taken for granted that men should rule women or that older men should exercise tyrannical authority over younger men. The tradition of one-man rule was also gone. Though powerful presidents, prime ministers and corporate chief executives still populate the political and economic landscape of the continent, they now nearly always rely on election to their posts and must in any case answer to bodies of representatives in the form of parliaments or boards of directors. And, though powerful fathers still rule families in many places in Europe and compel other family members to bend to their wishes, they no longer have an entire cultural and political system to buttress that power. States will not return rebellious young adults or demoralized wives to the family home if they decide to walk out, and will, if only imperfectly, attempt to restrain would-be patriarchs from the private assertion of their authority by confirming the legal rights of women and adult children as independent citizens.

To the extent that patriarchy still exists in Europe today, it is a mere shadow of its former self. Male power has been forced to assume other forms, female power is much greater, and nearly everyone agrees that, in principle, authority should be based on factors other than sex. While pockets of patriarchal practice still exist, many Europeans consider them 'normatively deviant' and linked to ethnic, religious and regional minorities.[20] The status system that governed the functioning of European political and social systems in the eighteenth century has collapsed. The estate system is long gone, and citizens are now equal under the law throughout the continent, though sex-based distinctions continue to exist in legal practice and in family law. Europeans are no longer predominantly a rural people. To the contrary, where about 20 per cent of Europeans had lived in towns or cities in 1750, now 73 per cent of Europeans do.[21] London, Europe's largest city in 1800, had 900,000 inhabitants, which today would put it in forty-fifth place, just behind Voronezh, Russia, and barely ahead of Turin, Italy.[22] It is now quite easy to move to a city where few people know you and into an apartment block where no one does. The previous forms of social control, based on the surveillance of neighbours, now exist only in small pockets, in some remaining villages and in urban apartment buildings with particularly intimate (or nosy) neighbours. Individuals now have much more freedom to choose spouses, careers, friends and leisure activities.

Similarly, as we noted above, the model of political power has been completely transformed. Monarchs exist largely for the pleasure of tabloid readers, lords seek significance as much in sponsoring strange hobbies as in politics and diplomacy, and sovereign decisions are theoretically made by parliaments, understood as the direct representatives of the people. Though political and economic decisions continue to be made by a small group of elite men, political participation of both sexes is commonplace, and all residents have legal protections.

Alongside the decline of patriarchy and monarchy, the controlling role of religion in the lives of Europeans has also greatly diminished. Church attendance, once almost mandatory for believers (at least on big holidays), has fallen sharply. Just as importantly, the role of religion in public and political life has declined accordingly. In 1750, there was a general consensus about what the Bible instructed men and women to do and an expectation that these religious edicts should be reflected in law and in practice. In 2005, that consensus no longer exists. There are still many Europeans, Muslims and Jews as well as Christians, whose lives are guided by their faith. But religions no longer have the capacity to discipline the behaviour of non-members.

Sexual and matrimonial practices have likewise seen a sea change. In 1750, economic considerations were at least as important as emotional ones when contracting a marriage. Now that balance has tipped towards emotion, in theory if not always in practice. Love was not absent from the calculation in the eighteenth century and money is far from unimportant even now, but marrying for money today is not widely respected. Young men and women are taught by parents and public culture alike to marry for love, and they are expected to find their own mates. Individuals no longer need the consent or the approval of their or their spouse's father, either socially or legally. Except in certain religious communities, European men who ask their potential bride's father for his daughter's hand in marriage are seen either as faintly old school, faintly ridiculous or both. A man who does so without consulting his girlfriend first can get himself into real trouble. There are, of course, more conservative families and cultures across the continent that wish to maintain traditions of arranged marriages and parental control. But their practices now result in significant social and legal tension, a fact that further highlights the magnitude of the shift that has occurred in the dominant cultures of Europe.

Sexual union is now primarily a means of personal expression rather than social reproduction. This shift, whereby sex has been separated from reproduction in much of the public discourse and in the daily practices of Europeans, has had profound implications.[23] On the one hand, exceedingly few people, married or not, expect or desire to conceive a child every time they have sex. On the other, new technologies of fertilization have given new hope to couples who desire children but cannot conceive them through their own efforts alone. Reproduction still looms, dangerously or promisingly depending on one's viewpoint, over heterosexual intercourse, but most sexually active Europeans can conceptually separate the two processes and believe that they can exert a great deal of control over when and if sex will lead to conception.

This now mundane separation of sex from reproduction has also reduced some of the aura of deviance and pathology that has surrounded homosexual activity for much of the modern era in Europe. It is evident that deep antipathy towards homosexuals and unease with the thought of homosexual acts persist for many Europeans, but the shift towards the assertion of individual rights in legal codes and the increased acceptance of varieties of sexual practice have changed much, not only since 1750 but particularly since 1950. Sodomy, once outlawed in most European states, has now been decriminalized throughout the continent. Further, the civil union of same-sex partners is legally recognized in many European countries. Full marriage rights have been granted to homosexuals in the Netherlands, Belgium and Spain and seem likely to gain wider recognition in other European states quite soon. In the arena of sexual practice and sexual regulation, as in all the other areas we have mentioned, the changes of the modern era have been very significant ones.

This book is about how and why attitudes towards gender and its social configuration changed so dramatically over the course of the modern period, and we contend that it is impossible to understand the shape of these transformations simply by tracing the state of the relations between the sexes over time. We agree with Joan Scott's influential definition of gender: 'The core of the definition rests on an integral connection between two propositions: gender is a constitutive element of social relationships based on perceived differences between the sexes, and gender is a primary way of signifying relationships of power.'[24] Scott's definition is important because it insists that gender is constitutive of society, deeply affected by culture, and indispensable for analysing not only sexual politics, but also politics as traditionally understood. Since gender is integral to the construction of political life, it is counterproductive to treat gender and politics in isolation from each other. The large shifts in European political life in the modern period are not completely comprehensible without some attention to changing gender norms. Though a good deal of the change in European gender history was incremental, there were also periods of more visible and dramatic change. Not coincidentally, the five most important such periods we treat in the five core chapters of this book are also the ones that we take to be the major historical ruptures in the larger narrative of modern European history.

The first moment of rupture, which we will explore in Chapter 1, was the assault on inherited status that was initiated during the era of democratic revolutions in the last quarter of the eighteenth century. Though open rebellion against monarchies took place first in the colonial spaces of the Americas, the most significant revolution within Europe took place in France. These democratic revolutions presupposed that sovereignty belonged to the people as a whole, but from the beginning this begged the question of who 'the people' were. Modern notions of citizenship developed precisely in order to answer this question. The revolutionary theory of popular sovereignty derived from Enlightenment beliefs in universal humanity and basic human equality. This notion of equality directly conflicted with the patriarchal model of inequality, particularly between the sexes, that preceded it. The ideas of equality embedded in revolutionary discourse provided a language for various disaffected groups throughout Europe to assert claims for increased political and social rights, but models of patriarchal inequality proved flexible enough to insinuate themselves into new, ostensibly democratic guises. As a result, few of these demands were easily or immediately granted. Even in France, the revolutionary heartland, conservative ideals were able to make a comeback within a decade of the first assaults on the monarchy. The subsequent rise and fall of France's expanding empire in Europe then allowed conservatives throughout Europe to reassert their power following Napoleon's final defeat in 1815.

The political outcomes of the democratic revolutions were therefore ambiguous at the outset of the nineteenth century. The trajectory of economic change, on the other hand, was becoming far clearer. In Chapter 2, we will discuss how throughout Europe, at differing speeds, economic life was transformed by the new practices, technologies and organizational forms that historians lump under the term 'Industrial Revolution'. Over the course of the eighteenth to the twentieth centuries steam power, wage labour and modern corporate structures changed the relationship between Europe's rural and urban regions. This had a more immediate and direct effect on family life and sexual organization than had any abstract discussion of political rights. As Marx and Engels put it in 1848, the new barons of the industrial age had 'put an end to all feudal, patriarchal, idyllic relations' and had 'pitilessly torn asunder the motley feudal ties that bound man to his "natural superiors"'.[25] Improvements in agriculture and the spread of manufacturing, both within homes and in factories, produced waves of migration across the continent. Cities like London and Amsterdam, for a long time hubs of international trade, became even more vibrant cosmopolitan centres, which attracted both internal and foreign immigrants. Elsewhere the change was quicker and more dramatic. A provincial backwater at the beginning of the nineteenth century, Berlin grew very rapidly into a metropolis, attracting massive waves of immigrants from the increasingly impoverished surrounding countryside. By 1875, only about 40 per cent of the city's one million residents had been born in the city.[26] The percentage of newcomers arriving from the impoverished countryside and eastern Europe only increased, and the population grew fourfold by the first decade of the twentieth century. Berlin and other new industrial centres of continental Europe struggled to house and integrate the massive influx.

The emergence of these modern cities created the possibility for dramatic changes in social relations. A combination of industrialization and urbanization eroded patriarchal control by forcing many young Europeans to become dependent upon their bosses rather than on their fathers. These changes took place over the course of many decades. In parts of England they were well under way before the end of the seventeenth century, while in many regions of Russia they would not take place until the 1930s. Still, all Europeans eventually had to adapt to these new economic and social realities. Standards of living increased, but many Europeans at all levels of the social hierarchy felt anxious and insecure in their new world. Insecurities were often dealt with through desperate attempts to stabilize the gender order. These attempts succeeded on the surface, but they only barely concealed the changes that the modern world had wrought.

The transformation of European economies gave added impetus for European states to transform the nature of the globalized economy they had done so much to create in the early modern era. That first global economy was centred around trade; with the support of superior naval and military strength, imperial powers gained profit and influence by creating unequal terms of trade with partners around the world. The Industrial Revolution, however, impelled economic actors to focus more fully on production. This shift of focus helped lead to a wave of European emigration, first to Asia and then to Africa, as trading posts were replaced by growing settler populations engaged both in production and in organizing native societies to restructure their own economic activities to better fit into the industrial imperial system. The larger European presence abroad meant that more Europeans were exposed to societies with different norms and practices. As we will demonstrate in Chapter 3, this more intensive sort of colonial encounter did two things. On the one hand, it provided a space for criticism of the European social order, including its gender relations and norms of sexual behaviour. On the other hand, the fact of conquest and domination solidified a sense of civilizational superiority present in the imperial venture from the beginning. Thus the expansion of European power and people brought about first a new interest in human difference that included an obsession with eroticized foreign lands and then new ways of conceiving of human difference, most prominently race, that were heavily shaped by notions of sexual difference and inequality.

The European civilization that solidified in the imperial milieu of the late nineteenth century was haunted by the fear that some nations, like some species, would not survive in a competition of the fittest. Ironically, this anxiety only hastened that bloody struggle. The aggressiveness and expansion of all European imperial states eventually led to a collision between them. Chapter 4 will demonstrate that the First World War and the Second World War once again transformed gender relations even as European societies relied upon gender as a mechanism for understanding conflict and change. The gender models inherited from the nineteenth century were challenged by the social mobilization for war. Men and women found themselves occupied with different tasks, in different places and with different people than in the pre-war period. The largely male society at the front developed a new set of ethical codes and social practices, while the rapid integration of women into new economic and social spheres transformed the way that both men and women thought about the 'natural' characteristics of the sexes.

These wartime transformations effectively crippled patriarchy for good. Old men were replaced by young men as the icons of European power. This new 'fraternal' system had its roots in the French Revolution, but it came to maturity during the First World War. The fact that this 'victory' of sons over their fathers occurred in wartime made fraternalism even more intensely militarized than it had been before. The fraternal order also relied quite heavily upon the state, which had stepped in to fill important paternal economic and social functions when the dislocations of life on the home front turned the European family 'inside out'.[27] This combination of militarization and increased state power found expression in a wide variety of political systems in the interwar era, ranging from a left-wing dictatorship in the Soviet Union, to right-wing authoritarian regimes in much of eastern and central Europe, to the rise of fascist states in Germany and Italy. These states were aggressive in even more toxic ways than their imperial predecessors had been, and Europe soon found itself in the throes of an even more devastating total war than the one that had just concluded. The Second World War saw the destruction of entire cities and of social populations like Jews and homosexuals. It also showed the horrible potential of the model of militarized masculinity. The post-war period would be marked both by attempts to save this model of masculinity from itself and, eventually, attempts to challenge the very notion of male dominance that underpinned both the new fraternal and the old patriarchal models.

The First World War and the Second World War seemed on the surface to have initiated revolutionary change in the gender order. In particular, the dislocated societies of wartime Europe saw a collapse of social control over sexual activity. The result was a simultaneous increase in individual freedom of sexual choice and a weakening of social protections preventing coerced sexual relations. Rape was a commonplace experience in war zones, and populations threatened by invasion universally feared the sexual violence associated with war. But sexual practices were transformed even in places far removed from the fighting as societies were restructured. On the home front, near the battlefield and within occupied territories, completely new possibilities for the formation of relationships outside of traditional family controls arose. For some, the somewhat freer social environment during the wars provided a glimpse into a future in which individuals could exercise freedom of choice in the sexual realm rather than being controlled by the prescriptions of conservative societies.

The massive disruption that twentieth-century wars produced in European sexual mores was only one stage in a longer transformation of sexual knowledge. In the late nineteenth century, the new discipline of sexology arose in part to explain in a scientific fashion the political and social consequences of human sexuality. By the early twentieth century, as a result, Europeans were convinced that sex and politics were permanent bedfellows. Psychologist Sigmund Freud, the discipline's most famous scholar, made this link clear when he argued that civilized political systems could only develop if individual sexual urges were at least partially suppressed. The concept of sexual identity – the insistence that one's sexual desires and behaviours were fundamental to a sense of self and critical in determining social roles – had been born. Chapter 5 will explore both the roots and the political manifestations of this relationship between sex and politics, placing the famous sexual revolution of the 1960s into the broader context of European modernity. As a result, when student activists proclaimed the beginning of a sexual revolution in the 1960s, they were in fact drawing on a century's worth of social turmoil in the sexual realm, despite their claims to be breaking new ground. The sexual revolution of the 1960s did indeed change the way that many Europeans thought about and practised sex. But the historical roots of this transformation ran far deeper than 1960s activists shouting slogans like 'make love not war' were willing to admit.

As this brief description suggests, we see no clear boundary between a 'history of gender' in Europe and a 'gendered history' of Europe. Determining the relationship between the two is, indeed, the challenge. As the nineteenth-century poet John Keats argued, 'not knowing' is the essence of learning. Gender history takes its power directly from the irresolvable tension between asking both how gender affects history and how history affects gender.[28]

If sex and gender have a political aspect, it stands to reason that they have a history as well. The historical study of gender also has a history. The development of a historical tradition that focused on sex roles and gender structures happened only gradually. In 1929, Virginia Woolf mused about what would happen if female students were to 'rewrite history' or at least provide a supplement to it, 'calling it, of course, by some inconspicuous name so that women could figure there without impropriety'.[29] But it was not until the 1970s that historians really took up this challenge to develop the field of 'women's history'. Before long, women's historians were filling university bookshelves with a wide variety of scholarly explorations about women's lives in the past and present.

Many of these pioneers linked their scholarship to their simultaneous activity in campaigns for political and social equality. In 1973, Sheila Rowbotham wrote a book called *Hidden from History: 300 Years of Women's Oppression and the Fight against It*, and she explicitly stated in her introduction: 'This book comes very directly from a political movement'.[30] Historians and university women of the 1970s were involved in forms of 'consciousness raising', group exercises to increase women's awareness of how society had shaped their own behaviours and their understanding of gender roles. The idea that 'the personal is political' was crucial to these endeavours. Historians and other academic feminists linked personal experiences (such as abortion, rape and workplace harassment) to larger political structures and social systems. Applying these insights to history immediately opened up new vistas of historical research, bringing into view historical subjects that had previously been ignored. This work represented an invaluable contribution to our knowledge about past societies. It revealed the historical roots of present-day social questions and the connections between political oppression in the past and in the present.

By the late 1980s, however, historians were growing increasingly concerned about the shortcomings of a historical approach that assumed sexual identity to be a universal constant. Without allying themselves to factions in the discipline that remained hostile to women's history as a whole, some historians began to challenge narratives that depended upon trans-historical definitions of gender difference and oppression. The writer most associated with this shift is Joan W. Scott, whose 1986 definition of gender we outlined earlier. That definition was part of Scott's broader criticism that the path of feminist scholarship in the 1970s had tended to render male domination as a universal constant, underestimating the historical variation of social influences on gender roles.

Scott, and those who followed in her footsteps, made it clear that the development of gender history represented a challenge to women's history as much as it did an extension of it. It has been a very quiet and civil challenge, however. Both inside and outside of the academy, most observers still think that gender history and women's history are basically the same thing. It is true that, in sharp contrast to the participants of more acrimonious intellectual battles, the practitioners of gender history and women's history tend to frequent the same conferences and panels and generally offer each other mutual respect and support. But despite all this, substantive differences remain. To take just the most obvious example, there is no widespread agreement even about the definition of the term 'patriarchy', one of the central organizing concepts for both women's history and gender history.[31] Those influenced by feminist theories that were developed in the 1960s and 1970s use the term to refer broadly to male power in all its manifestations, both within larger political systems and within the family.[32] Others, including the present authors, prefer to use patriarchy only to refer to social systems based on the authority of a literal or acting 'father' and husband.[33] When used in its most overarching and universal sense, the concept of patriarchy can lead historians to search backwards in history for evidence of male dominance and to present this evidence in a way that makes male power appear universal, almost natural. But gender history has precisely the opposite goal. It seeks to denaturalize the gender roles of any given historical period by revealing how gender relations have changed over time and how they have been influenced by family structure, demographic and social conditions, and the interrelations between society and politics. The specific power relationship between men and women in any given society is formed through a constant process of familial, social and political negotiation. Assuming the universal existence of male dominance does little to explain how it came to be or what its tensions, contradictions and ambivalent effects on both men and women were.[34]

The latest stage in the development of gender history has been quite expansionist. Most recent practitioners believe that gender history should extend not only beyond women's history, but also beyond a narrow focus on explicit discussions of sex roles and sexuality. The past twenty years have correspondingly been rich ones, with many scholars seeking ways to treat gender as a nearly universal (though not all-encompassing) presence in political and social life rather than as a discrete aspect of human experience. Our notes and bibliography include only a fraction of what is now a very substantive corpus of scholarly work, and our interpretations rely heavily on the vibrant dialogues carried on by recent historians of gender. But this book is not a summary of this research. Rather than seeking to include all the key discoveries made in the field of gender history, we instead tried to answer a relatively simple question: how does the concept of gender matter to the study of modern Europe? Part of our answer to this question took the form of an explicit investigation of gender norms and sexual politics, and part of our answer took the form of a demonstration of how a gender perspective can help us see familiar events (like the Industrial Revolution or the outbreak of the First World War) in new ways. Our simple question therefore has quite a complicated answer. We trust that readers will understand that writing a short book with such a broad scope necessitated leaving out a great deal of interesting and important material. We can offer no further apologies. Modern European gender history is an enormous topic. This book is rather small. It is meant as an introduction and not a conclusion.

Notes

1. Thomas Laqueur, *Making Sex: Body and Gender from the Greeks to Freud* (Cambridge, Mass. and London: Harvard University Press, 1990). Laqueur's model has received some criticism. See: Michael Stolberg, 'A Woman down to Her Bones: The

Anatomy of Sexual Difference in the Sixteenth and Early Seventeenth Centuries', *Isis* 94, no. 2 (2003): 274–29. Laqueur replies to this critique of *Making Sex* in: Thomas W. Laqueur, 'Sex in the Flesh', *Isis* 94, no. 2 (2003): 300–30.

2. Thomas Laqueur, 'Orgasm, Generation, and the Politics of Reproductive Biology', *Representations*, no. 14 (1986): 24–27.

3. Some historians use the word 'patriarchy' simply to refer to a hierarchy of the sexes with men at the top. See for example: Merry E. Wiesner-Hanks, *Gender in History* (Malden, MA and Oxford: Blackwell Publishers, 2001), 12–13. We insist throughout this book on this more precise definition of the term.

4. We use 'continent' in this book to refer to the geographical unit, which includes the British Isles.

5. Jan D. Vries, *European Urbanization, 1500–1800* (Cambridge, MA: Harvard University Press, 1984), 32.

6. Heide Wunder, *He is the Sun, She is the Moon: Women in Early Modern Germany* (Cambridge, MA and London: Harvard University Press, 1998), 68–69. Sociologists refer to this new model of family life as 'neo-locality': once married, couples form their own households, which means that they become economically independent. This system was quite unique in the world when it arose in early modern Europe. See: Göran Therborn, *Between Sex and Power* (New York: Routledge, 2004), 144–47.

7. Anna Clark, *The Struggle for the Breeches: Gender and the Making of the British Working Class* (Berkeley: University of California Press, 1995), 14.

8. Beatrice Moring, 'Marriage and Social Change in Southwestern Finland, 1700–1870', *Continuity and Change* 11 no. 1 (1996): 91–113.

9. Michael Mascuch, 'Continuity and Change in a Patronage Society: The Social Mobility of British Autobiographers, 1600–1750', *Journal of Historical Sociology* 7, no. 2 (June 1994): 177–97.

10. Amy Louise Erickson, *Women and Property in Early Modern England* (London and New York: Routledge, 1993); Margaret Hunt, *The Middling Sort: Commerce, Gender, and the Family in England, 1680–1780* (Berkeley and Los Angeles: University of California Press, 1996); and Beverly Lemire, *The Business of Everyday Life: Gender, Practice and Social Politics in England, c. 1600–1900* (Manchester: Manchester University Press, 2006).

11. Michelle Lamarche Marrese, *A Woman's Kingdom: Noblewomen and the Control of Property in Russia, 1700–1861* (Ithaca, NY: Cornell University Press, 2002), 27.

12. Judith P. Zinsser, ed., *Men, Women, and the Birthing of Modern Science* (DeKalb, IL: Northern Illinois University Press, 2005).

13. See for example: Sigrid Brauner, *Fearless Wives and Frightened Shrews: The Construction of the Witch in Early Modern Germany* (Amherst: University of Massachusetts Press, 1995); and James A. Sharpe, *Instruments of Darkness: Witchcraft in Early Modern England* (Philadelphia: University of Pennsylvania Press, 1997).

14. Merry E. Wiesner, *Women and Gender in Early Modern Europe* (Cambridge and New York: Cambridge University Press, 2000), 72.

15. Ibid. Most historians now reject Lawrence Stone's very pessimistic view of love in the early modern period. See: Lawrence Stone, *The Family, Sex, and Marriage in England, 1500–1800* (New York: Harper & Row, 1977). For a more balanced view that takes both economic necessity and the presence of affection into account, see: John R. Gillis, *For Better, For Worse: British Marriages, 1600 to the Present* (New York: Oxford University Press, 1985).

16. Stanley D. Nash, 'Marriage', in *Britain in the Hanoverian Age, 1714–1837: An Encyclopedia*, ed. Gerald Newman (New York and London: Garland, 1997), 439.

17. David Levine, 'The Population of Europe: Early Modern Demographic Patterns', in *Encyclopedia of European Social History from 1350–2000*, ed. Peter N. Stearns (New York: Charles Scribner's Sons, 2001), 2: 46.

18. Wiesner, *Women and Gender in Early Modern Europe*, 71.

19. See here: Jan Sundin, 'Sinful Sex: Legal Prosecution of Extramarital Sex in Preindustrial Sweden', *Social Science History* 16, no. 1 (1992): 99–128; Lawrence Stone, *The Family, Sex and Marriage*, 492, 519.

20. Therborn, *Between Sex and Power*, 130.

21. United Nations Department of Economic and Social Affairs (Population Division), *World Urbanization Prospects: The 2003 Revision* (New York: United Nations, 2004), 173. Christopher R. Friedrichs, 'The City: The Early Modern Period', in *Encyclopedia of European Social History from 1350–2000*, ed. Peter N. Stearns (New York: Charles Scribner's Sons, 2001), 252.

22. Friedrichs, 'The City', 252.

23. There are, of course, exceptions. See for example: Ursula Barry, 'Abortion in the Republic of Ireland', *Feminist Review* 29 (Summer, 1988): 57–63.

24. Joan W. Scott, 'Gender: A Useful Category of Historical Analysis', *American Historical Review* 91, no. 5 (1986): 1,067.

25. [Karl] Marx and [Friedrich] Engels, *Manifesto of the Communist Party*, 2nd revised edition (Moscow: Progress Publishers, 1977), 38.

26. Alexandra Richie, *Faust's Metropolis: A History of Berlin* (London: Harper Collins, 1998), 941, n. 15.

27. Maureen Healy, *Vienna and the Fall of the Habsburg Empire: Total War and Everyday Life in World War I* (Cambridge and New York: Cambridge University Press, 2004).

28. Joy Parr, 'Gender History and Historical Practice', in *Gender and History in Canada*, eds Joy Parr and Mark Rosenfeld (Toronto: Copp Clark Ltd., 1996), 20.

29. Virginia Woolf, *A Room of One's Own* (New York: Harcourt, Brace and Co., 1929), 68.

30. Sheila Rowbotham, *Hidden from History: Rediscovering Women in History from the 17th Century to the Present* (New York: Pantheon, 1973), xxxv.

31. For summaries of the debates see: Pavla Miller, *Transformations of Patriarchy in the West, 1500–1900* (Bloomington: Indiana University Press, 1998); and Karin Hausen, 'Patriarchat: Vom Nutzen und Nachteil eines Konzepts für Frauengeschichte und Frauenpolitik', *Journal für Geschichte* 5 (1986): 12–21 and 58.

32. This definition of the term gained particular currency with the popularity of Kate Millet's *Sexual Politics* (New York: Ballantine Books, 1969). A much more complex picture emerges in later accounts. See for example: Lynn Hunt, *The Family Romance of the French Revolution* (Berkeley and Los Angeles: University of California Press, 1992).

33. For a recent and extremely wide-ranging discussion of family that also takes patriarchy to mean male family power rather than gender discrimination more broadly, see: Therborn, *Between Sex and Power*, esp. 8. Therborn uses 'phallocracy' to describe 'sexual power without paternal significance'.

34. Hausen, 'Patriarchat', 19.

–1–

Liberty, Equality and Fraternity

As the year 1789 dawned, the most powerful person in Europe was a woman. Born a minor German princess in the town of Stettin in 1729, Sophia of Anhalt-Zerbst was sent to be married at the tender age of fifteen years to a distant and cruel man who lived far away. She left for a foreign country where she was expected to learn a new language and adopt a new religion. She would never see her father again. Her new husband held no attraction for her, and his refusal to consummate the marriage for years following the wedding ceremony indicated that the feeling was probably mutual. She had no friends, no family and almost no practical experience of any kind. Virtually abandoned by her husband, she consoled herself with reading everything she could get her hands on, from ancient classics like the *Annals* of Tacitus to recent political tracts of the French Enlightenment like Montesquieu's *Spirit of the Laws*. There was just one redeeming feature of her situation. Her husband Peter was the heir to the Russian throne.[1]

Upon her marriage and adoption of Russian Orthodoxy, Sophia took on a new name, Ekaterina (Catherine, in English), and she seemed destined to be the next in a long line of forgotten women who were wed to the autocrat of Russia. Russia was one of the most patriarchal countries in Europe, but when Catherine arrived in St Petersburg in 1744, the ruler was the Empress Elizabeth, the daughter of Peter the Great (1689–1725), Russia's vigorously reformist and 'Westernizing' tsar. As the third woman to sit on the throne in the past twenty years, Elizabeth was continuing a curious trend of female rulers in Russia. This was a remarkable string considering that just a few generations before most elite women lived in seclusion, away from the gaze of any men but their kin. The rather surprising development of female rule indicated, of course, that elite women in Russia were now visible in the public sphere in ways unthinkable a century before, but it did not mean that women were treated as equals. To the contrary, the choice of women as leaders had occurred precisely because the top Russian aristocrats wanted to prevent the emergence of a powerful autocrat of the type of Peter the Great, who had disrupted their lives and threatened their social position. They expected that women rulers would be dependent upon them and that they could be strong-armed into serving the interest of whichever aristocratic clique had sponsored them. These expectations had not been fully borne out, as both Empress Anna and Empress Elizabeth proved to have stronger backbones than the men who surrounded them had hoped (their predecessor Catherine I

(1725–27) was considerably less forceful). Still, by their very presence, female monarchs did encourage factionalism, and ambitious courtiers were continually tempted to plan coups by selecting politically weak (and thus often female) candidates whose ascent would allow them to be the strong hand directing the puppet ruler.

It was in this way that Catherine would seize the Russian throne. Her husband Peter III was crowned tsar in December 1761 and quickly became as odious to many elite Russians as he had long been to his wife. The marriage that had begun so badly grew even worse over the years. Peter was rumoured to have decided to put Catherine aside and marry a young Russian princess, while Catherine, for her part, was bearing a child fathered by her lover Grigory Orlov.[2] Soon after the delivery, in late April 1762, Peter publicly humiliated his wife by screaming at her at a banquet and even ordering her arrest before being talked down by his advisors. Peter could have easily recovered from a split from an unfaithful wife, but he had also made the more serious mistake of alienating his officer corps. Orlov and Catherine were well positioned to organize a coup with the support of the army, and they did so with remarkable ease in June 1762. When Peter left the capital briefly with his mistress, Catherine was declared the new Empress, a seizure of power Peter only learned of when he appeared at one of his summer palaces for a party to discover it empty. He was soon arrested and then died in custody, almost certainly murdered by Orlov and his brothers. It is unclear whether Catherine knew of the plan to murder her husband, but she benefited from it and likely shed few tears.[3]

Catherine was now the empress of the largest empire on earth, which stretched from the coast of the Baltic Sea to the shores of the Pacific Ocean. Her power was in principle unlimited. She issued law by decree, appointed the people who executed those laws, and was a one-person Supreme Court. She commanded an army that had just defeated Frederick II's Prussian forces on their home territory and would go on to other notable successes. Over the course of her reign, Russia would establish itself firmly on the Black Sea through a series of convincing defeats of the Ottoman Empire and would incorporate much of Poland into its fold, destroying its long-time rival in eastern Europe. Catherine 'the Great' was probably the most competent ruler in Russian history. In addition to her military victories, she regularized Russian administration, set in motion a process of reforms guided by the latest Enlightenment theories, sponsored scholarly and artistic projects both at home and abroad, and presided over what the Russian nobility (though not the Russian serf population) would long remember as a golden age.

When Catherine died thirty-six hours after suffering a massive stroke in November 1796, Europe was roiled by revolution, but Russia remained a conservative anchor in the East. After thirty-four years of rule, she bequeathed to her country a political and military system that proved able to withstand Napoleon's invasion in 1812 and that would establish itself as one of Europe's Great Powers for the next 200 years. One might have thought that with this experience in mind, female rulership would have been even more welcome in Russia than it had been in the eighteenth century. But Catherine was the last woman to rule the Empire. Almost immediately after her death, her son Paul (another disastrous tsar, who would be killed five years into his reign) changed the Russian succession law to formally prevent a woman from coming to the throne.

Catherine's reputation, meanwhile, was subjected to a concerted smear campaign on the part of Russian conservatives. Catherine and the women who preceded her were charged with having corrupted the morals of the whole country through light-minded frivolity, conspicuous consumption and, most damning of all, unbridled sexual excess. Catherine in particular was accused of being unduly influenced by men who sexually pleased her and to have been voracious in her acquisition of new 'favourites'. Like most wise female monarchs in patriarchal systems, she had never remarried after the murder of Peter, as the presence of a husband would have called into question her capacity to rule.[4] Women were expected to be obedient to their husbands, an expectation fully underpinned by all European Christian churches, and this made it very difficult to combine autocratic power with wifely subordination. Not desiring to take a vow of chastity, Catherine continued to engage in sexual and political relationships with members of the Russian elite for the rest of her life in a pattern we would today call 'serial monogamy', and gossip surrounding her bedroom activities and the political implications of her new alliances was the fodder of Russian high society.

The most systematic critique of female rule in general and of Catherine's reign in particular came from one of her former servitors, Prince M. M. Shcherbatov, who wrote a treatise entitled *On the Corruption of Morals* in 1786–87.[5] The manuscript was read only by confidants and family members at first, as the author rightly feared arrest if his scathing criticism were made public, but his views were shared by other members of his set. Russia's moral fabric, Shcherbatov claimed, had been eaten away over the course of the eighteenth century. The original sin belonged to Peter the Great, who in his eagerness to open up the country to Western influence had actively desegregated public life in Russia, allowing women and men to mix freely and encouraging liaisons and marriages based on affection rather than paternal order. The ceaseless attempts to please the opposite sex ruined the familial bond and led to useless consumption of luxury goods. The whole elite had become focused upon individual gratification rather than duty and obedience. This desire for sensual pleasure was, Shcherbatov argued, the main reason for the decline in morals, for it 'gives rise to various violent desires, and a man will often stop at nothing in order to attain their gratification. Indeed, a man entirely given over to his disorderly desires, and worshipping the reprehensible passions within his heart, thinks little of the Law of God, and still less of the laws of the country in which he lives.'[6]

Though a man had initiated these changes, and though it was male morality that had been corrupted most of all, the key to the problem lay with women, who loved both 'luxury' and 'despotism' more than men did.[7] The string of female monarchs, from Catherine I to Anna to Elizabeth, finally culminated in the reign of Catherine

II. Shcherbatov was not blind to Catherine's abilities, but he saw even her political aptitude as essentially corrupt because of her moral degradation:

> It cannot be said that she is unqualified to rule so great an Empire, if indeed a woman can support this yoke, and if human qualities alone are sufficient for this supreme office. She is endowed with considerable beauty, clever, affable, magnanimous and compassionate on principle. She loves glory, and is assiduous in her pursuit of it. She is prudent, enterprising, and quite well-read. However, her moral outlook is based on the modern philosophers, that is to say, it is not fixed on the firm rock of God's law; and hence, being based on arbitrary worldly principles, it is liable to change with them. In addition, her faults are as follows: she is licentious, and trusts herself entirely to her favourites...[8]

In sum, then, it was female sexual excess, in violation of God's law and encouraged by secular Western influences, that was accountable for the state that Russia found itself in, for it encouraged political corruption, loose morals among other elite women and the endless search for private pleasure rather than public good on the part of Russian males. 'By such stages', Shcherbatov concluded, 'Russia has reached the ruination of all good morals.' He begged God to bless Russia with a new emperor, who would be firm and fair in his rule and 'gentle and constant in friendship, showing an example in himself by his domestic harmony with his wife, and banishing licentiousness'.[9] Shcherbatov's treatise linked together many of the main concerns of eighteenth-century European thinkers: the relationship between virtue and good governance, the model of the wise monarch, and the relationship between proper familial order and the social order as a whole. In all these areas, the so-called 'woman question' loomed large.

This explicit connection between conservative politics and fears of feminine sexual excess helps to explain one more legacy of Catherine the Great: the outrageous slur circulated soon after her death and repeated ever since that she had died while having sex with a horse. Presumably she was so debauched and bestial that mere men could no longer please her. This accusation was obviously and demonstrably false, but the popularity and durability of these rumours, combined with the prohibition of female rule, demonstrates that Catherine's reign coincided with real changes in the ways that gender and politics were discussed in Russia.

Catherine's story was, of course, unusual, but her story of gender and power in one of the most patriarchal and conservative regions of Europe is all the more telling because of its setting. It shows in sharp relief the set of changes that rocked the continent as a whole. While such powerful women in Europe were certainly atypical, the discourses surrounding them reveal how gender norms helped shape political norms. Over the course of the eighteenth century, new ideas about citizenship and individual honour emerged that had profound effects upon the public roles of men and women. Politics, philosophy and scientific ideas were intertwined in this process, and ideas about gender were both reinforced and, in some cases, transformed. The

French Revolution (1789–99) represents a momentous turning point in the history of gender in Europe, since new political ideas that might have brought about a shift towards increased political rights for women instead justified a much more strict separation of male and female spheres. Explaining how this occurred requires an examination of how the philosophical flowering known as the Enlightenment (*c.* 1685–1789) prompted European thinkers to place increased emphasis on self-control and the attainment of individual virtue. It also requires an exploration of how the concept of citizenship came to be linked to the glorification of the citizen-soldier over the course of the revolutionary period.

Tracking the interrelationship of gender norms and political ideals from the late eighteenth to the early nineteenth century reveals the degree to which understandings about appropriate political roles for men and women were integral to the debates about the distribution of political power. At the very moment when human equality was being forwarded as a revolutionary slogan and when women were pointedly demonstrating their capacity to think and to be active participants in politics, a counter-current of thought was being promulgated that suggested that women were incapable of self-possession and needed to be protected from the storms of modernity that were building in strength throughout Europe. Explaining not only how this seeming paradox operated, but also how in some respects the very notions of liberty, equality and fraternity depended on a more aggressive subordination of women will be the theme of this chapter.

The Enlightenment

Prince Shcherbatov's dislike of Russia's female monarchs was part of a long tradition in European religious and social thought that saw passion as corrupting and women as too susceptible to the wild extremes of pleasure. The core of this tradition was the story of Adam and Eve in Genesis, in which Eve succumbed to the treats of the devil and then tempted Adam to do the same. Preventing sin and social disorder meant keeping women away from sources of power and firmly subordinate to male control, first in the form of the father and then in the form of the husband. Women had to be obedient for their own sakes. Only the surrender of wilfulness would keep them away from dangerous apples. Given Eve's success in the realm of temptation, it was equally important for male souls that women be kept subordinate. Failing to do so would lead to a 'corruption of morals' identical to that described by Shcherbatov.

This moral outlook was evident throughout the continent in the middle of the eighteenth century. Indeed, in significant respects, the intellectual developments associated with the Enlightenment strengthened these concerns. The assault on traditional religion made by some of the scientific and secular trends of the period is easy to overstate. Instead, as Norman Davies has pointed out, it is more accurate to talk of an Enlightenment ethic against 'fanaticism' or, more broadly, 'enthusiasm'.[10]

Put another way, the Enlightenment was largely about control, beginning with self-control and continuing through control of social systems and ultimately to the control of nature itself. The exercise of reason as a form of external discipline, a check against the ignorance of folk tradition, the self-interested teachings of Church leaders and the dark continent of human nature itself, was a key feature of this search for control.

It is important to note that 'reason' in the 'Age of Reason' was not disembodied. To the contrary, rationality found its power only when it was applied to 'nature' broadly defined. This was especially evident in the dramatic changes in scientific thinking that occurred on the eve of the Enlightenment. In the astronomical observations of Kepler and Copernicus, the physical laws of Newton and the biological classifications of Linnaeus, scientists sought not only to apply reason and (often mathematical) logic to the natural world, but also to demonstrate that the natural world had its own internal logic. Planets moved in regular patterns, gravity exercised its influence everywhere in the universe and species existed around the globe, already differentiated from each other and awaiting only the proper mode of observation. Nature, in other words, had laws, and these natural laws provided the context for everything else, including the behaviour of human beings and the exercise of rationality itself.

This embodiment of reason and inner rationality of nature helped to account for the dualities, even self-contradictions, of much Enlightened thought, including that of individual thinkers who combined the abstract and metaphysical operations of reason with the very concrete and physical observations of natural conditions. Indeed, many of the most heated intellectual debates dealt with questions of 'epistemology', or the study of how we know what we know. Some, like Francis Bacon and John Locke, argued that humans create knowledge by observing and sensing their surroundings and inferring patterns from the data they accumulate. Others, like René Descartes, started from the proposition that only a mind pre-equipped with the capacity to reason could create knowledge and meaning from the sensory stimuli provided by bodily organs.

These philosophical developments had significant implications for the way that human beings studied themselves and understood gender difference. On the one hand, the presence of universal and rational laws led to expectations of a fundamental equality for all human beings. If everyone was a member of the same species and equally subject to the laws of physics, then it followed that at the most basic level all humans were equal. Descartes' philosophy of abstract reason provided for a separation of body and soul that worked in favour of ideas of sexual and other types of equality. If the body did not make any difference to thought, then neither sex could be said to have a greater capacity to reason.[11] On the other hand, the observation of human society revealed a condition of deep inequality. Women throughout Europe (and almost everywhere one looked outside of Europe as well) were subordinated to men, held to be unequal and treated unequally. They were physically different, dressed differently and, many argued, shared sex-based behavioural characteristics. Shcherbatov's claims, for instance, that women loved 'luxury' and 'despotism' more than men were not at all unusual.

The contradiction between equality in principle and inequality in practice was dealt with in two major ways, which roughly corresponded to the 'nature vs. nurture' debate that still rages in discussions of human inequality. Some argued that all humans were *not* created equal and that the observed inequality was the result of natural inequality between men and women. Others claimed that oppressive social systems had thwarted the development of the female sex and deformed the natural order. But discussions on the question of human nature were complicated by confusions regarding the term 'nature' itself. 'Natural' had two meanings that were only rarely differentiated by authors and readers. In the first instance it was descriptive – it described one's surroundings as they were observed. It was in this sense that gravity was a 'natural' law. In the second instance, however, it was normative, that is, it described how things *should be* rather than how they were. In this sense, male dominance was a 'natural' law. Authors appealed to nature, to history, to biology and to logic to defend it, but unlike gravity it was a law that could be broken. It was not that violations could not exist in nature, but that they should not. These were very different notions of 'natural law', but both were treated as if they were scientific propositions of the same order, a confusion that still exists today when politicians or activists argue that specific human behaviours (like same-sex relationships, for instance) should be forbidden because they are 'unnatural'.

This contrast between the descriptive and normative meanings of 'nature' was especially salient in discussions of the 'woman question' in elite European circles in the eighteenth century, most notably in France. Women were becoming ever more educated and visible in aristocratic circles. Social and sartorial fashion became ever more open, as plunging necklines combined with an ethos of flirting to convince social critics that sexual propriety had collapsed. Many condemned what they saw as a rise of adultery and perversion. Similarly, when several important women formed intellectual circles in their salons, they discovered new realms of cultural freedom and influence. Julie de Lespinasse, for instance, hosted a popular salon in Paris that brought together artists, philosophers and scholars to discuss the most important cultural, philosophical and political events of the day. These gatherings were more than merely sociable; they were important spheres of political debate where pre-revolutionary ideas were formulated.[12] Women were playing an important role in public life, a fact that led some contemporary observers like Rousseau to despair, while others proclaimed the eighteenth century the 'century of women'.[13] With some philosophers attacking the underpinnings of social inequality in other spheres and forwarding the notion that it was a 'self-evident' truth that 'all men are created equal', this demonstration of individual autonomy and intellectual capacity on the part of women logically promised to extend the notion of the 'rights of man' to women as well.

The notion that women might gain equality and exercise independence troubled not only conservatives hostile to the emerging order, like Shcherbatov, but many of the men who were leading the transformation in social and political thought as 'enlightened' philosophers as well. Jean-Jacques Rousseau was easily the most influential commentator on gender and proper familial relationships in this respect. In 1761, he published an epistolary novel entitled *Julie, or the New Héloise: Letters of Two Lovers who Live in a Small Town at the Foot of the Alps* that became an immediate and persistent best-seller both in France and abroad in translation.[14] It was the story of a young woman who, in the early chapters of the work, succumbs to passion and finds both fulfilment and unhappiness. In the later chapters, she marries a man she respects but does not lust for and discovers contentment and happiness in domestic life. *Julie* was popular, but it was immediately controversial. On the one hand, it alienated women who sought equality, for Rousseau's explicit message was that women had to submit to the authority of a good man and focus their energies on the household in order to be happy. On the other, it offended conservatives by frankly discussing pleasure, by portraying complex women and by blaming conservative patriarchs rather than free thinkers or lustful women for the moral decline in France. Rousseau insisted that female behaviour had to be viewed as a response to their place within family and society. 'But let us be fair to wives', he argued, 'the cause of their disorder lies less in themselves than in our evil institutions. Ever since all the sentiments of nature have been stifled by extreme inequality, it is from the iniquitous despotism of fathers that the vices and misfortunes of children arise; it is in forced and ill-matched unions that young wives, victims of their parents' avarice or vanity, undo ... the scandal of their original honesty.'[15]

Rousseau's assault both on coquettish adultery and patriarchal arranged marriages through the figure of a flawed but richly drawn and ultimately moral woman struck a chord throughout Europe, especially among women. Female readers identified with Rousseau's characters because so many of them chased the same dreams of loving relationships, meaningful motherhood and happiness in the home. In addition to being happier, women would also be more respected, as the new moral order sketched out by Rousseau would be centred in many ways around the place and behaviour of women.[16]

This new social vision, so attractive to Rousseau's women readers, rapidly became attractive to many men in the late Enlightenment as well. Increasingly concerned not only with the damaging effects of traditional patriarchy, but also with the dilemmas faced by 'new men' in a world of increasing economic, social and political competition, philosophers and social critics alike sought a moral anchor. They found it in the figure of the tamed woman. Women were on the one hand thought to be 'naturally' wild and passionate. Without the guiding hand of man, they were directionless and potentially destructive. On the other hand, when controlled and 'domesticated', they could find their true moral nature and become useful within the order of civilization. This notion had long been a feature of patriarchal thought. What distinguished

Rousseau's vision was the idea that for this new order to be effective, women had to voluntarily choose this path of submission. They had to be moral actors prior to marriage in order to exercise a beneficial moral influence in the household afterwards. This moral core made women fully human, and therefore in a sense equal.

This distinction may seem slight to present-day readers, who could note that both before and after this 'Enlightened' intervention, women were supposed to be obedient to men and to focus their attention on domestic affairs. But in fact the change was substantive. It transformed notions of female education, which now focused even more heavily on the need for a moral education for daughters, and it struck a blow against fathers. Daughters in 'Enlightened' families were now expected to choose their own mates, not on the basis of passion but on the basis of love and respect. By wresting control over sexual reproduction away from their elders, young men and women were also wresting control over a great deal of social power. In family life, the faint outlines of 'liberty, equality and fraternity' were beginning to emerge from the background. As we shall see, all these notions would take on a masculine flavour in the era of revolution, but they also all depended in central ways on a female willingness to serve as obedient moral compasses. This new order was bolstered and replicated not only in sentimental novels, but also in social treatises like the massive *Encyclopedia*, which focused its investigation of the social order on male productive labour in the workplace and on the bodily attributes of female reproduction in the domestic realm. Thus philosophical investigations came to an Enlightenment consensus: humans were equal, but men and women were fundamentally different. This was a formulation of 'separate but equal' that was founded on the proposition that it was nevertheless 'natural' for men to rule and women to obey. At the very moment that the concept of nature was being employed to argue for human equality and freedom, it was also being used to exclude women from the realm of the free.[17] As the 1780s dawned in France, then, an important revolution of moral sensibilities had already taken place, one that promised a new nation based on the principles of liberty and equality, but only if it was run by a fraternity.

The French Revolution

Politically knowledgeable Europeans living at the end of the eighteenth century had many reasons for believing that a realignment of gender relations might be afoot. Women were more active in the public sphere than they ever had been before. While the women of the salons exercised political influence in private spaces, lower-class women were voicing political demands in the streets: they participated (and often led) bread riots across Europe, and in Paris they were actively involved in political associations and revolutionary movements. Meanwhile, Enlightenment thinkers like the Marquis de Condorcet were arguing that women, though physically weaker, were

– like men – perfectible, particularly if they were provided with the education from which they had thus far been barred. While Condorcet agreed with his contemporaries that women were more suited to domestic than to political tasks, he left open the possibility that exceptional women provided with education and opportunity could excel and 'leave behind them the vast majority of the human race', including most men.[18] Enlightenment beliefs in the perfectibility of 'mankind' opened up the theoretical possibility of perfecting 'womankind' too. Condorcet argued:

> The rights of men derive entirely from their status as sentient beings, capable of acquiring moral ideas and reasoning about those ideas. So women having the same qualities necessarily have the same rights. Either no individual of the human race has any real rights, or all have the same. And one who votes against the rights of another, whatever their religion, colour or sex, has by so doing abjured his own.[19]

Condorcet's views on this subject remained marginal, however, and in the course of the revolution, women's rights were increasingly ignored and, in the end, actively denied. Enlightened and revolutionary movements gave women the language to claim unprecedented rights, but the republic that was eventually created not only excluded them as political subjects, but was also 'forged into a myth against them'.[20] The ambivalence of this situation has prompted serious debate between historians about whether or not the French Revolution was an emancipatory moment for women or the beginning of a long period of subordination to the demands of the modern nation state.[21] Rather than taking sides in this debate, we will focus here on how the events of the French Revolution helped to entrench the belief that the genders could only be equal in the sense that they were confined to entirely separate political and social roles. When hopes that women would be included in the definition of universal rights were dashed, the symbolic force of male citizenship took on new power, affecting both the lives of women and men. Traditional forms of patriarchy collapsed in France with the downfall and execution of the King and were replaced with a fraternal order whose foundational concept of the citizen took on an increasingly gendered connotation as revolution turned to Terror and counter-revolution.

The absolutist French state was understood metaphorically as a family. After the reign of Louis XIV (the 'Sun King', r. 1643–1715) in the seventeenth century, the King was almost literally viewed as the father of the French people. Louis reigned over France as a patriarch reigns over his family: the royal family's private acts and their cultivation of personal relationships took on enormous public significance.[22] Taking the sun as his symbol to emphasize that he was anointed by God, the creator of all life, Louis presided over a household of intrigue, nepotism and partisanship. His body was sacred, since it represented the life of the community.[23] Even the objects in his household, the possessions of the royal family, had unique symbolic power.[24] Ironically, given the importance of patriarchy in this system, women in the King's family and social circle played key roles as facilitators of the personal networking that was essential to the attainment of power. Matchmaking and sexual intrigue were often more important in attaining political posts than birth or merit. It was this type of Old Regime patriarchal power that created the space for the role of the women of the salons. The dominant political role of the absolutist monarch – his fatherhood of the entire nation – placed all others beneath him in a similar subordinate position, causing conservative nobles to worry about the 'feminization' of the national body politic.[25] The system held together as long as military, political and social successes were attained. But those successes were costly in financial terms to a public stretched thin by population growth and a series of poor harvests. When Louis XVI (r. 1774–92) took the dramatic step of supporting colonial rebels in North America in their war with Great Britain (1776–83), the corresponding expenditures led to deep fiscal crisis.[26]

French involvement in the American War of Independence also undermined the monarchy in another way, as the connection between liberty, patriotism and military service was strengthened among those who had fought with the American rebels.[27] The war of the American colonies against the British Empire was a crucial step in the transformation of Western ideas about the relationship between soldiering and the rights of citizenship. Beginning in 1775, the success of local militias against English monarchist troops helped strengthen the conviction that military service to protect the homeland was an integral component of citizenship; serving as a soldier became the duty of all virtuous men. With armed conflict looming across the colonies, the duty to protect local communities made abstract patriotic principles much more concrete.[28] But early successes were followed by a series of crushing defeats as the British repeatedly drove back revolutionary forces. With each loss, the voluntary Continental Army suffered a decline of morale and an increase in desertion. Revolutionary leaders finally allowed non-citizens (and presumably unvirtuous men) like transients and criminals to volunteer. The numbers were still too small, and the losses piled up. After a series of setbacks, George Washington, the army's commander, convinced Congress to approve a coercive draft in 1778. No one, Washington included, wanted this institution to become permanent. All saw it as a temporary expedient, and indeed it was abandoned at the end of the war. The idea that the new United States of America would have a full army only in times of war and would rely on state militias to train citizens in military affairs and masculine civic virtue was written into Article I of the Constitution, which prescribed that Congress could only appropriate money for an army for a two-year period and that the permanent military force of the country would be militias regulated by the states. It was further reaffirmed by the Second Amendment to the Constitution, which gave every citizen the right to be an armed member of his state militia.[29] The political system that emerged from war and revolution in the American colonies was one that depended upon the exercise of male civic and martial virtue.

These initiatives in political emancipation were begun by European colonists, and they were part and parcel of the European political and military milieu. These were not exclusively American events. European observers followed the action with great interest, British and French armed forces were directly engaged in the conflict and eager revolutionaries from across the continent (notably from Poland and France) volunteered to be on the front lines of history. As a result, the ideological and institutional legacies of the American Revolution were easily and rapidly reimported back into Europe. This was particularly the case with the idea that martial virtue was inseparably linked to civic emancipation. The Marquis de Lafayette was an important symbolic figure in this process. When he returned to France in 1779 (after escaping the French army at the age of nineteen and fleeing to 'fight for liberty' in the Americas), he was welcomed home by a quickly forgiving king and ecstatic French crowds. Lafayette had been an extraordinarily successful general in key battles of the revolutionary war and had become a close friend of Washington. Granted honorary American citizenship, Lafayette's exploits in America became famous in France and helped to popularize the American notion of 'liberty' and the 'citizen-soldier'. Benjamin Franklin, America's Minister to France at the time of Lafayette's return, helped to orchestrate this fame and consciously fostered the symbolism of American men as the upholders of freedom, truth and natural innocence.[30] As the political crisis at home deepened, the French looked to American notions of liberty as a remedy for corruption and mismanagement. The founding of the American Republic 'captivated European minds and made a powerful contribution to preliminary steps towards social and political reform'.[31] French experience in the colonies was also an important impetus for the formation of new ideas about the relationship between duty, military service and republican citizenship. Martial citizens banding together in brotherhood seemed preferable to courtiers juggling deviously incurred national debts. The seeds of revolution had been sown.

Still, the biggest reason for the political crisis that precipitated the revolution was the disastrous state of the King's finances. Misery in the countryside also played a role, and at key moments demands for bread and lower prices would influence the nature of revolutionary violence and political demands. But it was concern about looming economic collapse that prompted Louis XVI, in August 1788, to convoke the Estates General (an assembly of representatives from the three estates of French society: the clergy, the nobility and everyone else) for the first time since 1614. The meeting of the Estates General, convening in Versailles (the King's palace about 20 kilometres outside of Paris) on 5 May 1789, began with a drawn-out debate about voting that pitted the Third Estate against the nobility and most of the clergy. Fed up with conflict and having invited the other two estates to join them, the Third Estate took independent action and named itself the National Assembly on 17 June 1789.

The National Assembly was suffused with the ideas of civic and masculine republicanism that had been so important for both Enlightened French thinkers and American revolutionaries. In its first meeting, the Assembly swore an oath to defy its opponents until a constitution had been written. The President of the Assembly,

Jean-Sylvain Bailly, led the assembled delegates in their oath by placing one hand over his heart and thrusting his other arm outward and upward like a military commander. 'With right arms outstretched, fingers taut, six hundred deputies became new Romans, echoing the oath' in unison.[32] Having removed themselves from the spaces of royal (family) control, the delegates' appropriation of martial symbolism also helped them to reclaim the roles of men of action, no longer cowed by the feminizing influences of the court. Paris received the news immediately. On 15 July, Lafayette was appointed Commander of the National Guard, a force of 48,000 male citizens charged with the task of fighting for political liberty and protecting the revolution from the King's army. Crowds in Paris rioted, and the royal fortress, the Bastille, was stormed on the fourteenth by a crowd of women and men who had seized royal muskets. Rebellion also raged across the countryside with the sacking of churches and castles, the burning of seigniorial records and attacks on landlords and nobles.[33]

The King did his best to quell the fear and gain the trust of the rioting crowds, and by doing so he unwittingly opened the floodgates to the political participation of women as well as men. On 17 July 1789, he appeared in Paris wearing the revolutionary tricolour cockade and accepted the lists of grievances that the Estates General had been gathering from around the country at the King's request. These grievances provided vast numbers of French men and women from the Third Estate with the feeling of directly participating in the creation of what Rousseau had called the 'general will'.[34] While not all of the written grievances have survived to the present, a few of the 60,000 that still exist were written by women, suggesting that the experience of hoping to become involved in new forms of political participation was not limited to men.[35]

As in grievances authored by men, women requested changes to their immediate social circumstances – flower sellers, for instance, wanted a controlled market that would prohibit interloping female entrepreneurs from underselling them – rather than a transformation of the political system. In January 1789, women of the Third Estate petitioned the King, asking:

> To be enlightened, to have work, not in order to usurp men's authority, but in order to be better esteemed by them, so that we might have the means of living safe from misfortune and so that poverty does not force the weakest among us, who are blinded by luxury and swept along by example, to join the crowd of unfortunate women who overpopulate the streets and whose debauched audacity disgraces our sex and the men who keep them company.[36]

Concerned that prostitutes in the city were besmirching the honour of all women, the authors of this petition mostly sought recognition from the King that would include them in discussions about the reformation of French society. But demands in this first phase of the revolution, including those emanating from women, were made in the language of the Old Regime and appealed to the King to provide in a fatherly way for his people.

This political restraint was short-lived. Newly energized female political activists soon took a leadership role in the deepening crisis. The issue that motivated these activists was outrage over skyrocketing food prices. Over the course of the summer of 1789, daily processions in Paris and repeated gatherings of market women protesting bread prices set the tone in the capital. In October, a group of women marched to Versailles, killed some of the royal guard and forced the King and Queen to return to Paris with them. Upon their return, many of these women swarmed into the National Assembly as it was meeting on 5 October 1789. They interrupted debate with their demands and voted on legislation about grain distribution.[37] At all the key moments in 1789, women were very visible and active. The symbolism of the women's seizure of the King was not lost on a nation that idolized the 'father' of their nation. Women's involvement in riots, their willingness to take up arms and their vocal invasions of the National Assembly and various political clubs prompted some respect for their seizure of the rights of citizenship – they were forging their own identities as female citizens.

These same actions also caused concern among frightened men outside of France that these 'harlots' and 'furies' were out of control. Conservative member of the British Parliament Edmund Burke epitomized these fears when he claimed in his *Reflections on The Revolution in France* (1790) that the Queen had been forced to flee almost naked to her husband and had been sexually threatened by the invading marchers. His description of the marchers' return to Paris displays his general disdain for the revolutionary violence of these days and women's participation in it: 'The royal captives who followed in the train were slowly moved along, amidst the horrid yells, the shrilling screams, and frantic dances, and infamous contumelies, and all the unutterable abominations of the furies of hell, in the abused shape of the vilest of women.'[38] Perhaps influenced by the force of these words, even present-day historians often describe the women as apolitical rioters concerned only with issues of subsistence. But a closer look at the actions of the women as the revolution progressed reveals that they were intimately aware of the political issues at stake and were motivated not only by hunger, but also by the desire to transform their country.[39] Indeed, the fact that male members of the National Assembly became increasingly concerned about the involvement of women in revolutionary violence suggests that these actions carried considerable political weight. They must also be understood with reference to ongoing debates about the very meaning of citizenship.

On 4 August 1789, the National Assembly took the first step to establishing a nation of equal citizens by abolishing feudalism, revoking the nobility's seigniorial rights over peasants and ending the Church's right to collect tithes. On 26 August 1789 the Assembly submitted the 'Declaration of the Rights of Man and Citizen' to the King.[40] Drafted by Lafayette, this statement of principles defined the individual and collective rights of French citizens and insisted on the fundamental equality of all men. Article VI of the French Declaration said: 'All citizens being equal in the eyes of the law, are equally eligible to all dignities and to all public positions and occupations, according to their abilities, and without distinction except that of their virtues and talents.' The implication of this article for female political rights thus hinged upon the interpretation of the word 'citizen'. Many women reasonably hoped that they would now be enfranchised. But the Declaration used only the masculine form of the word citizen – *citoyen* – and insisted that the 'rights of man and of the citizen requires public military forces'. This made it clear that military service to the state would help define the citizen as male. The feminine form of the word citizen – *citoyenne* – later appeared in revolutionary rhetoric, but only as a kind of after-thought. It never carried the weight of political rights.[41]

The definition of citizenship was further refined in the Constitution of 1791, which created a short-lived liberal constitutional monarchy. The franchise was extended to all men over the age of twenty-five who met certain property qualifica-tions. These were considered 'active' citizens, while the majority of French men (who did not own property) and all women were decreed 'passive' citizens. 'Passive' citizens could not participate in political bodies or become members of the National Guard. The authors of the Constitution never seriously considered female suffrage. This was the first time that women had been explicitly excluded from voting rights in France, since they had previously been able to vote for some governing bodies (sometimes by proxy) if they owned property.

The new citizenship laws prompted considerable dissatisfaction, particularly in Paris, where the majority of the working-class and middle-class activists had now been declared 'passive' citizens. Political clubs and organizations proliferated, many of them accepting female members and some supporting female suffrage. In this atmosphere, the question of female citizenship became a central one. Olympe de Gouges, a playwright, responded to the gendered nature of the original Declaration and the Constitution with her own 'Declaration of the Rights of Woman' in 1791. Addressing her appeal to the Queen, de Gouges called for the creation of a separate National Assembly for women, female suffrage, legal protection for illegitimate children and their mothers and a role for women in government administration. To draw attention to women's participation in the revolution, de Gouges alluded to the fact that women had already been executed for their political involvement. 'Woman has the right to mount the scaffold', she argued, 'she must equally have the right to mount the rostrum.'[42]

De Gouges acted on her political convictions by forming and joining revolu-tionary societies. But even this most vocal of representatives of women's rights blamed the 'nocturnal administration of women' in the Old Regime for its corrup-tion and called for prostitutes to be confined to certain areas. Her desire for women's rights, in other words, was balanced by a conviction that traditional understandings of female honour and chastity needed to be maintained and specifically motherly values and behaviours fostered. She asked that men grant women these rights; she saw no possibility of women seizing them for themselves. Like other female activists of this era, her words 'functioned to preserve difference and hence guarantee sexual inequality, even as they were yoked to a universalist, egalitarian protest'.[43] Like many French women activists before and after her, de Gouges was profoundly affected by the rumours of sexual impropriety that circled around the royal family (particularly the Queen, Marie-Antoinette), and her political views were affected by the desire to inculcate the values of republican motherhood as an antidote to royal corruption.[44] Her declaration, then, had a rather specific audience and did not necessarily speak to the majority of women in Paris, whose demands centred much more directly on the needs of everyday survival.

Many of de Gouges's concerns were echoed in a far more extensive analysis of the implications of the French Revolution for women's rights that was written by a woman observing events from England: Mary Wollstonecraft. In *A Vindication of the Rights of Woman* (1792), Wollstonecraft forcefully argued that women too could be virtuous in Rousseau's sense of the word – having the moral fortitude to act in the interest of the polity and to actively care for public affairs. But it was still the production of active citizens through motherhood that would entitle women to a measure of public influence and would remain any woman's most enduring contribution. If European women had thus far failed to demonstrate their virtue, it was only because, like those men who had been denied the full rights of citizenship, the paths of civic action had been closed to them.

But, like de Gouges, Wollstonecraft blamed the frivolous concerns of wealthy women for the poor reputation of the sex. Only a concentrated effort to return women to their primary duties – to motherhood – could prevent aristocratic excess from undermining political freedom. Wollstonecraft's stirring appeal to motherhood as a motivation and justification for women's political involvement assured the fame and enduring influence of her book. She argued that

> If children are to be educated to understand the true principle of patriotism, their mother must be a patriot; and the love of mankind, from which an orderly train of virtues spring, can only be produced by considering the moral and civil interest of mankind; but the education and situation of woman, at present, shuts her out from such investigations.[45]

Failure to grant women the conditions to make republican motherhood possible would 'render both men and themselves vicious'. Men should grant woman these rights and cease impugning and threatening her chastity; women should exercise self-control.[46] In all these respects, de Gouges and Wollstonecraft shared the conviction of Shcherbatov and Rousseau that self-control and virtue were necessary for an orderly society and that women in the Old Regime had exercised neither. They disagreed mainly about the potential of women to develop their own special sort of civic virtue. The tumultuous events of 1792 and 1793 would put many of these ideas about the role of women in politics to the test.

During the summer of 1792, women pressed newly formed political clubs like the Jacobins and Girondins, which were becoming more and more like political parties, to pay more attention to social and economic issues in the capital. Women were particularly active in the Girondist Society of the Friends of Truth, a political organization seeking social reform and the end to patriarchal family relations.[47] In March 1791, the Dutch woman Etta Palm d'Aelders (1743–99) formed a women's section within the Society. This group lobbied for both female political rights and welfare measures for poor families.[48] But Girondin tolerance for these activities left them open to charges from the Jacobins that Girondin ministers were controlled by their wives. The Jacobins also charged politically active women with having morals as loose as those of their aristocratic predecessors. Sexual innuendo thus undercut the efforts of Girondist women to bring about gender equality in the law. While divorce was legalized in 1792, and the age of majority (the age at which one could marry without parental consent) was set at twenty-one years for both sexes, efforts to reform laws on adultery failed.

As the revolution radicalized, so too did revolutionary women. They took part in the arrest of the royal couple, in their execution in 1793, and in the creation and expansion of mechanisms of political terror between March 1793 and August 1794. This 'reign of terror' led to the execution of between 30,000 and 40,000, while civil war in the south killed as many as 200,000.[49] That terror, forwarded by a largely Jacobin 'Committee on Public Safety', was based on the idea that violence would be necessary to create a 'Republic of Virtue'. Under the Committee's reign, denunciation became a civic responsibility. It was the duty of all citizens to display their vigilance of revolutionary values, their virtue and purity by denouncing enemies of revolution.[50]

In this atmosphere, radical women revolutionaries seized the opportunities that the Terror offered them to demonstrate their worthiness as citizens. Pauline Léon (an unmarried chocolate maker) and Claire Lacombe (a provincial actress) formed the Society of Revolutionary Republican Women. The group wanted to be 'armed to rush to the defence of the fatherland' and participated in surveillance measures to help enforce the repressive laws of the Terror. In other words, they hoped to use the weapon of denunciation, now defined as an act of citizenship, to prove that they should be considered fully active citizens of the republic. But their public visibility (they walked through Paris in groups, sporting red bonnets, tricolour ribbons and trousers) irked the Jacobins, who reacted to the women's taunts about insufficient enforcement of the Terror with attacks on female honour. At a Jacobin meeting on 16 September, François Chabot railed: 'It is these counter-revolutionary sluts who cause all the riotous outbreaks, above all over bread. They make a revolution over coffee and sugar, and they will make others if we don't watch out.'[51] In October 1793, market women attacked republicans trying to enforce revolutionary dress codes and later stormed a meeting of the Revolutionary Republican Women, beating some of them. The spectacle of women fighting pushed the National Convention (the constitutional and legislative assembly formed in September 1792 and charged with drawing up a new constitution) towards the Jacobin view that women had to be banished from the public sphere and forcibly returned to their domestic duties. All female involvement in political and popular societies was henceforth banned.

The debate preceding this decree made it clear that the republican camp was deeply divided over the question of whether women should receive equal rights with men.[52] But another event carried far more significant symbolic value: the execution of Marie-Antoinette. The execution was justified in primarily sexual terms. Already before the revolution, pornographic literature and satirical songs about Marie-Antoinette's supposed sexual exploits, adultery and lesbianism had made it almost impossible for her to be seen in public. If she did venture to the theatre, she was often greeted with hisses.[53] When she came before the revolutionary tribunal, her supposed political intrigues (including alleged collusion with the Habsburg Emperor, her brother) were conflated with sexual sins. She was accused of sexual abuse of her own son, the eleven-year-old Dauphin, who had been taken away from her in prison and would soon die of physical maltreatment. The president of the revolutionary Paris Commune charged that the Queen had taught the Dauphin to masturbate in order to 'enervate the constitution of the child in order that they might acquire an ascendancy over his mind'. Marie-Antoinette refused to respond to this charge of sexual treachery, asking only: 'I appeal to all mothers who are present in this room – is such a crime possible?'[54] But her days of representing French motherhood were over, and on 16 October 1793 she calmly laid her head under the guillotine's blade to the joy of cheering and jeering crowds. Nothing better symbolized the degree to which women's sexual crimes had now become political crimes.[55] As in the case of the story about Catherine the Great and her horse, impugning the sexual propriety of a powerful woman revealed itself to be a remarkably effective weapon. In this case, the power of the slur was magnified by its combination with rumours of the King's impotence.[56]

Neither the Queen's attempt to portray herself as a loving mother nor the revolutionary zeal of republican women sufficed to overcome the fundamental dilemma of female citizenship in this era. The virtually universal conviction of the pre-revolutionary era that female power rested on underhanded sexual manipulation presented any woman (or man) advocating full female citizenship with an insurmountable rhetorical barrier. To deny the existence of feminine intrigue at court would have been to undermine a key element in the revolutionary argument about the illegitimacy of monarchical rule. But when women like de Gouges and Wollstonecraft highlighted the frivolity and corruption of elite women in their attempts to define specifically female virtue, they only drew attention to it and left all women open to the charge of unseemly, immoral behaviour. Female political action remained synonymous with sexual desire and depravity. Constant references to the need to control and rehabilitate prostitutes, both in elite writings and emanating from market women concerned about their reputations, did not help matters.

In the end, women seeking increased political rights had, as Joan Scott has argued, 'only paradoxes to offer'.[57] They emphasized their difference by extolling the virtues of motherhood even as they sought to establish equality by appealing to the categories of universal rights and civic virtue. This was an understandable strategy, but it created difficulties. It meant accepting the 'natural fact' of sexual difference even as one was trying to eliminate it as a justification for political exclusion. When they made claims on behalf of women, de Gouges, Wollstonecraft and their like-minded contemporaries helped to reinforce 'woman' as a natural and immutable category: 'To the extent that it acted for "women," feminism produced the "sexual difference" it sought to eliminate. This paradox – the need to both accept and refuse "sexual difference" – was the constitutive condition of feminism as a political movement throughout its long history.'[58] In the atmosphere of a revolutionary regime that strove to balance political change with the destruction of poverty – to achieve both political freedom and freedom from natural necessities – it was almost inevitable that women's insistence on being closer to nature would backfire. Stressing difference helped fuel the arguments that excluded them from politics.

Over the course of the revolution, women mounted an unprecedented challenge to the notion that only men should engage in politics, and they questioned emerging notions of citizenship.[59] While it is important to remember that some of the most radical female political actors – such as the market women of Paris – were not necessarily seeking a transformation of gender norms, their politicization of social issues and their insistence on making their specific concerns heard did in practice challenge that gender order. Elite women like de Gouges saw that hunger and illiteracy among urban women were political questions and hoped that the acquisition of political rights would improve the material well-being of those who received them. This seemed a rational argument to be making at a time when revolutionary events were intertwined with demands for social change. The King's acceptance of grievances from his subjects had been, after all, an important impetus for the growth of political activism. Female activists were thus acting in the spirit of the times when they linked demands for political rights and for social justice. But neither poor women in the streets nor their elite counterparts ever found the means to counter a growing resistance from revolutionary men towards the idea of allowing women a political voice. Since women were not included in the definition of active citizen, they were excluded from the increasingly important public sphere; their concerns were labelled 'social' rather than truly political.[60] This set a precedent for arguments against women's active participation in the public sphere that would grow in strength throughout Europe in the nineteenth century. The public sphere became a masculine sphere in a much more formal way than it ever had been before.

Echoes of the French Revolution

The discussion of women's rights and involvement in the public sphere that emerged in the French Revolution resonated across Europe. Some men of influence began to argue that the new democratic ideals should foster an improvement of women's political position. In Prussia, Theodor Gottlieb von Hippel wrote *On Improving the Status of Women* (1792) in reaction to hearing that women had not been granted the rights of full citizenship in France. 'Do I go too far', he asked, 'in asserting that the oppression of women is the cause of all the rest of the oppression in the world?'[61] But this was a lone voice. Most European philosophers of the period (like Immanuel Kant and Georg Wilhelm Friedrich Hegel) shared Rousseau's opinion about women's place in the home. They 'succeeded in writing women out of the state' in their political philosophy.[62]

Nevertheless, France was far from the only country where the place of women in politics came into question during the revolutionary era. In Belgium, the Dutch Republic and various regions of Italy and Germany women demanded increased political rights. The Dutch case is particularly instructive. Over the course of two revolutions in the Netherlands (the Dutch Patriotic Revolution of the 1780s and the Batavian Revolution of 1795) there was a fundamental transformation in the role of women in political life. As in the French case, this transformation ensured the triumph of a male-dominated public sphere.

In the early modern period, women had enormous influence over community life in urban neighbourhoods and villages.[63] Dutch society gave women responsibility for maintaining community bonds: women controlled household finances, governed relationships with friends and neighbours, organized neighbourhood welfare programmes, and dominated public spaces as market women. Given these positions close to the community, they were prominent in all the riots and rebellions of the early modern period. The Dutch Patriotic Revolution threw the political model that reserved a place for women within the popular politics of the crowd into turmoil. Patriots, who were inspired both by Enlightenment ideas and by direct experience in the American Revolution, reacted to military defeat at the hands of the British in 1784 by joining with Old Regime forces to drastically curtail the powers of Prince William V. William's battles on behalf of the American rebels had led his nation to defeat and economic turmoil. In response (and several years prior to their French counterparts), the Patriots began demanding 'sovereignty of the people'. By 1787, they had gained considerable political ground in the provinces. Women played an important but subsidiary role both in the patriot and monarchist camps. Princess Wilhelmina van Pruisen (William's wife) used her relationship with her brother (the King of Prussia) to secure the Prussian troops who would end the revolution and restore the monarchy in 1787. At the other end of the social spectrum, a female mussel seller named Kaat Mossel was prominent among the monarchists, while patriot women like Betje Wolff wrote political pamphlets. But Wolff confined her agitation for women to demands for improved education for girls, and she did not advocate specific rights for women.[64]

A second revolution began in December 1794, when Dutch Patriots joined with French revolutionary forces to drive the monarchists from power and institute representative democracy. Revolutionaries proclaimed the Batavian Republic in January 1795. The new regime was closely allied to France, and went through several political transformations between 1795 and 1810, when the northern Netherlands were annexed to Napoleon's empire. In the midst of these transformations, Etta Palm d'Aelders, who had been forced to leave France, began to take a prominent role in Dutch political discussions. Signalling a new era of female involvement in politics, she called for the formation of women-only political clubs. 'Batavian Maidens' appeared at revolutionary celebrations and planted liberty trees as symbols of the new republic. An anonymously authored Dutch tract, *A Demonstration that Women should Take Part in the Governance of the Nation* (1795), argued that excluding women from politics was a kind of 'despotism' and that the Dutch could become an example to the world by achieving what the French had not: a true inclusion of women in a new democratic state.[65] The 1790s saw an increase in female voices in political periodicals. In the last years of the century, several revolutionary journals published pieces advocating women's rights, and Petronella Moens founded a journal for patriotic women that advocated better training and education for women.

But these women's attempts to transform female political roles from the leadership of neighbourhood crowds into a considered contribution to political debate foundered upon the new political system that the Patriots were developing. In their desire for a rational, democratic system of government, the Patriots shunned the old model of popular protest and were openly hostile to community activism, which they saw as an expression of the 'rabble' or the 'mob'. They wanted to replace this form of popular politics with a more organized politics from above. Patriots organized local committees and, most importantly, militias on the American revolutionary model. These militias eventually became highly successful in replacing crowd politics with orderly, disciplined political structures that by their very definition excluded women. Since the Patriots followed the American example in linking active citizenship and the right to bear arms, this political order was increasingly interpreted as a male enterprise.[66]

While the exclusion of women from politics in the new Batavian Republic was never openly declared, the success of the militia model of local governance and revolutionary action brought about a decisive shift in Dutch women's political position. Townswomen's role as active organizers of crowd protests disappeared as local dissatisfaction was channelled into organized political committees and through the militias. The informal influence and formal authority of aristocratic women, like Princess Wilhelmina, was curtailed by the replacement of royal privilege with representative government. While women did not disappear from political life – they continued on as journalists and pamphleteers, often writing anonymously – by the turn of the century women's political clubs and the most prominent female publicists had disappeared from Dutch public life. It is difficult to avoid the conclusion that the elimination of traditional female paths to political participation ensured that the revolution represented a decline rather than an advance for Dutch women's rights.[67] But it is most important for our purposes to note that in the Dutch case, as in the French, the demarcation of spheres of activity for men and women was increasingly influenced by the ideals of martial citizenship. The ability to serve as a soldier – as a member of the militias – guaranteed a man's access to the rights of citizenship, while traditional forms of political participation for women, which had been a key force in the life of early modern Dutch communities and had been centred around specific social and economic conflicts, disappeared.

Revolutionary Wars and Revolutionary Nations

Republican ideology was not an invention of the late eighteenth century. The study of classical republics, particularly in Athens and Rome, was part of any elite European's education, and the great political theorists of early modern Europe like Machiavelli had attempted to rearticulate these theories in the new civic conditions that emerged from the sixteenth century onwards. Both the classical and early modern experiences of non-monarchical forms of rule in Italy, England and the Netherlands had demonstrated that republics were particularly vulnerable forms of government. On the one hand, they were prone to the corruption of self-interest, as politicians and potentates jockeyed for power and access to public funds and public projects. On the other hand, the lack of a central, undisputed source of authority meant that it was difficult to organize the coercive measures necessary to raise taxes and soldiers to defend the republic from foreign invasion. It turned out that rule by the 'public' required citizens to repress their selves (or at least their self-interest) in order for the republic to survive. This form of public-spiritedness and enlightened self-control is what republican theorists called 'virtue', a quality that could emerge through the proper training of young men, but not one that could be coerced.[68] This civic virtue was of course seen as an exclusively male trait, a view that was only strengthened by the late eighteenth-century trend we saw above to concentrate on male activities in the public and intellectual sphere and to concentrate on female qualities in the domestic and bodily realm. Thus male virtue was understood as a taming of public passions while female virtue was limited to the taming of private sexual passion.

It was this connection between male civic virtue and the survival of the republic that inspired republican thinkers to argue that a healthy republic required all citizens to be soldiers and all soldiers to be citizens. It also followed that the right to civic participation and to participation in the military should be limited to those capable of exercising virtue, which is to say men who had received proper moral training. In addition, influential Enlightenment figures like the prominent Scottish philosophers Adam Smith and Adam Ferguson felt that service should not take place in a standing army, which both men despised as a tool of despotic monarchs and a dangerous temptation to conduct the sorts of foreign military adventures that had ruined earlier republics. They instead envisioned a militia of all able-bodied men, living and training at home, ready to take up arms en masse when the republic was endangered, but fundamentally unwilling to wage wars of aggression that would take them far from their families and farms.[69]

If there was little disagreement about the principles of military service in a functioning republic, there was a great deal of confusion about how revolutionary republics could build the military force necessary to overthrow existing regimes and then defend themselves from the conservative counter-attacks that were sure to come. After all, training in republican virtue was very weak in monarchical states, so one could not expect masses of men to have the fortitude necessary to fight long battles for liberty and freedom. And masses would be necessary, for the fight would almost certainly take place in conditions in which the enemies of the republic would deploy well-trained troops led by seasoned officers against a very green revolutionary force. Bluntly put, republicans feared, with good cause, that pitting all the virtuous revolutionaries against all the soldiers of reaction on the battlefield would result in defeat.

In their concerns about how to build a loyal army, French revolutionaries were well aware of the American experience. As we have seen, Lafayette had served with American forces and corresponded with American politicians during the 1770s and 1780s. French republicans experienced the same theoretical dilemmas about building loyal volunteer armies, though they ultimately resolved them in an even more extreme way than the Americans had. In France too, coercive drafts were resisted at first because they reminded members of the National Assembly of the methods of the armies of the Old Regime. Only one representative suggested in 1789 that France should consider an equal and universal military levy, and his plan was rejected in favour of supporting local militias.[70] As the revolution deepened, however, the prospect of war became ever more likely, especially after Louis XVI was captured while attempting to flee abroad in 1791 to join counter-revolutionary forces in Austria. Still, the Assembly continued to call for volunteers throughout 1791 and again during 1792, when the expected invasion from abroad finally occurred. The volunteer soldier movement reached its peak in 1792. That year saw both the writing of the French revolutionary (and later national) anthem *La Marseillaise* as an inspirational hymn for volunteers, and then later the Battle of Valmy, at which a French force partly composed of old army regulars and partly of new volunteers defeated Prussian forces and delayed the foreign assault. Those two events played a significant role in the building of French nationalism over the ensuing centuries, but they could not hide the deficiencies of the volunteer levies.

In 1793, as the revolution radicalized and the Terror began, the French turned towards a compulsory draft, tentatively at first, with a call for 300,000 soldiers selected by local officials authorized to use force to meet their quotas. This draft led not only to outright rebellion in parts of the country, but also to widespread tension in virtually every French town and village, as local notables were accused of corruption and other unfair practices in the selection of the young men who were conscripted.[71] Rather than give up on the idea of the draft, the leaders in Paris radically widened it, decreeing the *levée en masse* in August of 1793, which proclaimed that the entire population would be called for national service:

> All French persons are placed in permanent requisition for the service of the armies. Young men will go off to battle; married men will forge arms and transport provisions; women will make tents and clothing and serve in the hospitals; the children shall turn old linen into lint; the old men shall repair to the public places to stimulate the courage of the warriors and preach the unity of the republic and hatred of kings.[72]

This was not simply a crash course in enlarging the army. It was also a deeply political edict, intended to address the unrest that the earlier levy had caused and to radicalize the process of nation building. Above all, it represented 'an essentially ideological measure'.[73] In the first place, the *levée en masse* was based on the recognition of the desirability of universal equality in the field of military service. Many of the problems with the earlier levy had stemmed from the conviction of young men that the process was unjust, and indeed the mass levy in the autumn went far better than the partial one in the spring.[74]

In the second place, it was based on a fraternal understanding of the revolutionary nation. Fraternity (the principle that social and political authority should rest with 'brothers' or 'sons' rather than their 'fathers') is the least studied of the great principles of the French Revolution, but it is impossible to understand fully either modern gender history or modern nationalism without understanding how fraternity was 'revolutionary'.[75] Part of the problem in understanding the phenomenon stemmed from the decision of some practitioners of women's history to define patriarchy as the system of power in which men dominate women. As we argued in the introduction, however, this characterization was too crude, for it ignored the variety of gender orders based on male power. Patriarchy is a specific form of male dominance in which fathers exercise authority not only over women and children but over young men as well. Power and influence in this system increase with age. The gender revolution that occurred in the late eighteenth century was one that did more to transform this generational relationship than to change the relationship between the sexes.

Revolutionary arguments against patriarchy that ignored the importance of generation and used exclusively sex-based arguments, like those articulated by Olympe de Gouges and Mary Wollstonecraft, were doomed to failure. They failed to take into account that traditional patriarchy was in the process of being replaced by a definition of equality linked to fraternity. The ideology of the post-revolutionary nation depended upon a belief in the fundamental equality of citizens. But as we have seen, these citizens were gendered citizens, and the brotherhood that was slowly beginning to replace traditional patriarchy excluded women by its very definition.[76] Nevertheless, patriarchs did not relinquish their authority without a fight. A fraternal gender order was constructed over the course of the nineteenth century, but it would take the experience of two world wars in the twentieth century for 'brothers' to achieve dominance over their 'fathers'.

Before fraternity would rise, it would fall. The *levée en masse* was proclaimed at the high-water mark of revolutionary fraternity, just months after the execution of Louis XVI, the 'father of France', in January 1793.[77] The decree, as we have seen, was insistent on separating adult males into three separate categories (young men, married men and old men) based on age and family status, but it was indifferent to similar distinctions among the adult female population. Furthermore, the decree was notable for placing the figure of the young, unmarried man at the centre of attention. Traditionally, young unmarried men were the ones who did the assisting, working under the authority of older men in family farms or family businesses. Their needs were filled only after those of married men and fathers in the family. That situation was suddenly reversed, as their older married brothers would make their guns and carry their provisions, their fathers would sing their praises in the town square and their women and children tended to their medical and personal concerns. Just as significantly, soldiering was now portrayed as an honourable profession rather than as a trade for social deviants or as the fulfilment of an onerous state obligation.

All this, again, was an ideological proposition that described how the Jacobins hoped that military service would be performed and perceived rather than how it actually was. Systems of familial authority do not change overnight, even if the king is killed and a republic declared. Nor did the prospect of military service suddenly become attractive for young men and their families. The long tradition of hating soldiering and fearing soldiers was maintained in most areas of the country. But ideologies are not simply fantasies. Over time, the repetition of values, the demands of state institutions and the routines of social and bureaucratic life make an impact. In the long run, the figure of the national citizen-soldier would help establish the new political form of the fraternal nation and would remain its most reliable bulwark.

In the short run, revolutionary fraternity met with setbacks. As the chaos and violence of revolutionary upheaval dragged on, increasing numbers of people sought stability. Social stability in particular seemed to depend on solid families, and traditionalists were able to make an effective case that all this newfangled thinking had upset the natural balance within the household. Radicals too were increasingly inclined to look askance at expressions of female independence. As we have seen, the Jacobins themselves excluded women from politics after women's riots in Paris threatened their position. As the 1790s progressed, the trend to look longingly towards the traditional family and away from any stray revolutionary thoughts of female civic equality deepened considerably. Indeed, even fraternal measures were now looked on with some suspicion. Rejecting the proposition that individuals were the building blocks of the national order, some French politicians, like Charles Guiraudet, were persuaded by 1797 that it was a mistake to think of individuals as distinct units and of societies simply as a collection of those individuals. Rather, the building blocks of society were families, and all other divisions could be 'neither elementary nor natural ... only man in the family forms the element of society'.[78]

This domestic conservatism, indeed this widespread reversion to patriarchy, found its leading light in the figure of Napoleon Bonaparte. Napoleon openly portrayed himself as the new 'father' of the nation, and he reinstituted or reinforced patriarchal institutions in many different ways. He portrayed himself as the patriarch of France, made peace with the Pope ('father') of the Catholic Church and personally saw to it that the new comprehensive legal code being compiled in the early years of his reign would ensure the unchallenged authority of the father in French households. The code prescribed that familial rather than individual property would determine the voting eligibility of male heads of household, and it firmly placed women under male control in the family. Divorce, which had been legal for only about a decade, was now made nearly impossible for women. It was somewhat easier for men to dissolve a marriage, however, since men were allowed to divorce unfaithful wives, but women could divorce only if infidelity occurred inside the 'conjugal home'. Fathers, moreover, recovered the right largely lost to them in the revolutionary era to assume judicial authority in many matters concerning minor children, and they could withhold marriage consent from sons under twenty-five years old and daughters under twenty-one.[79] In 1801, the revolutionary journalist Sylvain Maréchal wrote – only somewhat tongue-in-cheek – a 'Proposed law prohibiting women from learning to read'. While clearly satirical, Maréchal's proposal came just at a 'turning point in the history of sexual equality ... following the appearance of revolutionary women as political subjects in the public arena'.[80] Several prominent intellectual women were prompted to respond, and the 'joke' revealed that some revolutionaries fantasized about shutting women out of the public sphere entirely by denying them the key tools of involvement in political debate: reading and writing. Patriarchy was back in style.

But it was a new and modified patriarchy, as Napoleon remained a revolutionary in some respects, most notably in military affairs. France had established regular, annual male conscription in 1798 as a means of preserving the ideological basis of the popular, national army and of replenishing the troops raised five years earlier in the *levée en masse*. Napoleon had no desire to overturn the fraternal institution of conscription upon coming to power in 1799. He had built his reputation and career on the backs of the military that radical revolutionaries had created, and he intended to deploy armed force liberally in the years to come. Indeed, the routinization of military service as a passage to manhood rather than as a devastating imposition took place largely in the Napoleonic era, as acceptance of army service as a duty grew and draft evasion dwindled.[81] Temporary setbacks did nothing to change this trajectory, though the ruinous losses and desperate levies that were occasioned by Napoleon's final campaigns, especially his disastrous invasion of Russia, finally did lead to another small increase in evasion and a short-lived abolition of conscription in 1815. In 1818, the draft was reinstated, and in conditions of peacetime, military service was linked even more inextricably to masculinity and the place of the young man in the civic order than it had been before. By mid-century the popular image of the conscript had been transformed from that of a boy ripped from his weeping mother and stern father to that of a dashing youth whose return as a real man was eagerly awaited by fresh-faced available maidens.[82] This shift of focus from the emotions of the parents to the emotions of the lover was just another sign of the ways that conscription moved social attention to the younger generation.

Napoleon's military success, and then his military failure, did much to export this fraternal model. Virtually everywhere French troops went, they defeated old-style armies, occupied part or all of the conquered country and then struggled to deal with insurgencies that drew, ironically enough, on the revolutionary ideals of the nation, the people in arms and the citizen-soldier. The specific form of the response to Napoleon varied from place to place, ranging from an increased sympathy for 'regular guy' war heroes like Admiral Nelson in Britain to cautiously formed and quickly disbanded popular militias in Russia, but the influence of revolutionary nationalism was visible everywhere.

Perhaps the most dramatic and lasting responses to Napoleon's incursions occurred in Prussia and Spain. Prussia succumbed to France first. In 1806, Napoleon's forces routed the Prussian army at the Battles of Jena and Auerstadt, resulting in a peace treaty the following year that cut the size of the Prussian state nearly in half and mandated that the French had rights of occupation until a large war indemnity was paid. The impact of the defeat was enormous. It led to soul-searching across the country, especially among Prussia's proud military elite. Some, like the future military theorist Carl von Clausewitz, left the country to volunteer with the Russian army, the last intact fighting force on the continent. Others took advantage of the forced dismantling of the old Prussian army (which was cut by more than half by French edict) to suggest that when the time came to rebuild the military, they should do it on a popular basis. When the moment came for the army to be resurrected in the so-called 'Wars of Liberation' of 1813–14, visions of nations, citizens and the 'people in arms' held sway, leading eventually to the establishment of universal conscription in 1814.[83] The new Prussian 'bands of brothers' were a smashing success not only against Napoleon's weakened forces, but against an array of other enemies over the course of the nineteenth century as well.

The same patriotic and national visions that structured the interaction of young Prussian men with the state opened up a temporary space for Prussian women to engage with the authorities too. Female activists from all classes formed a variety of patriotic associations to assist in the national war effort, and they sprang up in 414 towns around the country. This effort was sanctioned by the state, as one such public appeal in 1813 made clear:

> The fatherland is in peril! Thus spoke the king to his loyal and affectionate subjects, and all hurried to remove it from this danger. Men grasp the sword ... But we women, too, must participate, and must help to promote victory. We, too, must unite with the men and boys to save our fatherland. Thus let us found an association with the name of Women's Association for the Good of the Fatherland.[84]

Women's activities were crucial to the war effort, and these civic groups provided many of the necessary auxiliary services, such as nursing, that Prussian troops required in the final spasm of the Napoleonic Wars. By 1815, in direct contradiction to the emerging notion that women could not and should not participate in the public sphere, women's patriotic associations were one of the most extensive and most numerous networks of civic organizations in all of Prussia.[85] In times of brotherhood, there was no logical or practical reason that systems of sisterhood could not emerge to play a visible and public role in civic and national life.

A similar phenomenon occurred in Spain, which came under French occupation in 1808. In contrast to Prussia, however, an anti-Napoleonic insurgency quickly gained an armed following, and the guerrilla war that ensued relied heavily on female participation. As would be the case in virtually all future partisan campaigns (in particular those during the Second World War), the rebels came to rely heavily on women comrades. Women were more effective at smuggling goods and information to partisan units precisely because they were women and raised less suspicion among occupying forces. They were the ones who provided food, animals and even safe houses for the guerrillas.[86]

Nor did some Spanish women refrain from taking direct military action when the opportunity arose. The most famous such warrior was Agustina Zaragoza, who rallied decimated defenders in one besieged town by firing a cannon into advancing French troops while wounded men lay prostrate and defenceless around it. The Spanish held the town for several more months before surrendering. Though Agustina and her four-year-old child were so ill that they were in hospital when the occupiers arrived, the French knew of her fame and ordered her sent as a prisoner back to France, a trip that killed her son. This maternal suffering only increased her popularity at home, and her celebrity reached such heights that she was eventually commissioned as an officer after her escape from French captivity.[87] Nor was she the only active female participant, as other women also took up arms during the siege and many more attacked Napoleon's soldiers when they strayed too far into the countryside. As one French officer remembered, they were 'fighting the entire population; all the inhabitants, men, women, children, old folks and priests, were in arms, the villages abandoned'.[88] In Spain too, women were active and visible in the national struggle.

As politics were transformed across Europe in response to the revolutionary ideas and revolutionary wars, the political form of the nation emerged, based on the idea that all participants (citizens) in the nation should be equal and that they should feel the bond of brotherhood between them. Military action did much to strengthen these inclinations, though the upheavals of both revolution and war left many desiring a return to the relative stability of the past. As was the case in France, the assault on patriarchy left open the question of the position of women in the new political communities forming across the continent in places like Prussia and Spain. Would ideas of sisterhood create the possibility for an alliance between public-spirited young women and young men devoted to challenging the traditional authority of their elders? Would the logic of equality persuade politicians to extend civic equality to women? Would the repeated demonstrations that mass warfare required female participation allow this new ideology, seasoned by the violence of the Napoleonic era, to envision women and men alike as full actors in even the masculine arena of armed struggle?

The short answer to all these questions in all the countries of Europe was 'no'. In every case, these new nations followed the French model, which endorsed male dominance and female passivity and promoted male civic action and female domestic care as both politically necessary and 'natural'. This gender consensus became a fundamental plank of European nationalism. In Prussia, the wartime valorization of female patriotic action ended abruptly, with the remembrances and histories of the wars of liberation focusing on male action. Nearly all the women's associations shut down, with only 10 per cent remaining as charitable organizations. Within a generation, they were mostly forgotten, consigned to historical oblivion.[89]

In Spain too, women mostly disappeared from the narrative of the national uprising. Even in the case of Agustina, a peculiar but telling twist developed. When José Palafox, a Spanish commander, recounted Agustina's feat in his post-war account, he claimed that Agustina had leapt to the cannon after watching her fiancé killed by a French bullet and had fired the gun with the words 'I am here to avenge you!' Agustina, in this account, was acting out her private passions rather than taking up the public and civic duty of defending her city and her country. She was acting, in other words, as women should and naturally did. But Palafox's story was a total fabrication. Agustina was already married and, as we have seen, already had a child. Her husband was not by her side. Palafox's account also contradicted Agustina's own report of her actions. Nevertheless, historians throughout the nineteenth century, and many much later on, believed Palafox.[90] As usual, myths proved more convenient than history in the accounts that nations liked to tell themselves.

Duelling and the Nineteenth-century Fraternity

When the Napoleonic Wars ended, men looked for new ways to express their bellicosity in a 'civilized' manner. One way they did so was by turning in increasing numbers to the practice of duelling. Duelling was transformed as the ethos of 'fraternity' took hold across Europe and the forms of masculine performance changed in response. The duel became a primary arena for the display of masculine honour and the establishment of social hierarchy.[91] Adopting the ethos of chivalry and adapting it to the changed circumstances of post-revolutionary Europe, men fought duels to remove the taint of an insult that had besmirched their reputations, for trivial slights arising from a game of cards or an ill-timed joke, to protect the honour of their women, to avenge an adulterous act and ultimately to establish their firm hold over a position of social standing.

This was more than a case of the new middle class aping the traditions of the aristocracy. Across Europe in the nineteenth century, duelling became associated with the bodily demonstration of masculine strength and social rank and became more and more highly ritualized and specialized.[92] Duelling persisted in aristocratic classes, but it grew in popularity particularly among those who saw the growth of republics and the demise of old political systems as an opportunity for their own advancement. The ancient chivalric code of honour was held up as a defence against the corruption and decay of the republican ideal under Napoleon. Elsewhere in Europe, it acted as a ritual to unite those who sought national unification, particularly in Germany and Italy.[93] Duelling was a way for bourgeois men to establish their honour as citizens through bodily performance, thus legitimating their right to hold the advanced positions that the decline of the aristocracy had opened up for them. It was an act that demonstrated individual skills (the ability to shoot straight or fence well) while still adhering to strict rules of engagement agreed upon by a fraternity, fencing club or honour code. For those who advocated it, duelling thus encapsulated the republican ideal of the individual's ability to act in his own self-interest while still upholding the values of the society as a whole. This was, in other words, a fraternal act. Establishing courage and physical fortitude through duels with pistol, sword and sabre allowed them not only to defend their honour, but also to accrue it, unlike women, whose honour was confined to sexual chastity and fidelity and could only be lost.[94] From famous military generals like the Duke of Wellington, to literary figures like the Russian poet Aleksandr Pushkin and several French prime ministers like Georges Clemenceau (who fought twenty-two duels), duelling struck most famous and not-so-famous men of standing in Europe as a necessary defence of their political and social honour. Since duelling had been prohibited by the pre-revolutionary French monarchs, it also held the attraction of defying royal prohibitions and fostering individual liberty.[95]

In post-Napoleonic Germany, duelling became an essential aspect of university life. Some German student fraternities or *Corps* continued to be dominated by aristocrats and aristocratic traditions. But the *Burschenschaften* (literally associations of lads or guys) were formed out of frustration with the fact that the defeat of Napoleon had not resulted in the unification of Germany. While some of the *Burschenschaften* scorned duelling, many of them encouraged it, transforming an aristocratic practice into an avenue for instilling honourable behaviour and the values of brotherhood in a generation that sought social advancement.[96] Members sparred in ritual fencing matches on the flimsiest of pretexts in hopes of garnering the cherished scar – a slash across the cheek that would thereafter stand as evidence of both their willingness to fight and their involvement in nationalist university fraternities that were seeking German unification.[97] Like Diederich in Heinrich Mann's novel *Man of Straw,* most members of *Burschenschaften* viewed their participation in a duel as the defining moment of their lives: a coming-of-age ritual that ensured their acceptance by the fraternity and provided physical evidence of their devotion to the cause of national reunification. Along with hazing rituals, duelling was a codified and ritualized practice that helped to keep the fraternities exclusive. By literally marking their members with facial scars, the fraternities established networks of influence that lasted well past members' university years.

German duelling fraternities saw themselves as preparing their members for the fight that they foresaw ahead of them to unify Germany as a liberal state. This 'exercise in aggression checked by accepted rules' was accompanied by the type of behaviours that are still familiar in many university fraternities: hazing rituals, alcohol abuse and nepotism. Though German fraternities would eventually become sites of much more conservative (and even fascist) rituals,[98] they initially justified their existence with recourse to the ideals of political republicanism. Fraternities as a site of opposition to autocratic rule were also evident elsewhere in Europe. The Russian Decembrists (a secret society that launched an unsuccessful uprising against Tsar Nicholas I in 1825) also viewed duelling as a way of establishing a form of honour distinct from monarchical rituals. By the late nineteenth century, and particularly in St Petersburg, university fraternities in Russia were following the German example in setting up strict honour codes of behaviour with disputes settled in ritualized duels. These societies provided venues for enduring friendships while also fostering opposition to the monarchical regime.[99]

For the middle classes, then, fraternities and duelling offered arenas where valour and deservingness could be demonstrated. Perhaps this is best understood as a reaction to the fact that the political process put in motion by the French Revolution had held out the promise of 'universal' rights but had then quickly retracted this universality. It was necessary, in other words, to prove that one was worthy of being equal. Duelling was a dramatic way of demonstrating one's willingness to stand and die as an honourable citizen. The practice was largely confined to members of elite institutions (like universities, secret societies, special military units and fencing clubs). Simply being a member of an organization where the practice could be honourably conducted in accordance with strict duelling codes was already an indication of having been accepted into a self-regulating and powerful group. Women were by definition excluded from this group. But it is perhaps even more important to notice that duelling and fraternities were the quintessential cultural expressions of a new martial definition of masculinity. The aggressive exclusion of women that had arisen out of the French Revolution was routinized further over the course of the nineteenth century through these male arenas of elite citizenship.

Conclusion

Democratic activists across Europe in the revolutionary era proclaimed 'Liberty, Equality and Fraternity' as their main political goals. In each case, their victories were temporary, but they were not meaningless. The seeds of future change had been sown.

The concept of liberty that was developed in the American and French Revolutions had a lasting impact on the politics of Europe. It did not immediately or permanently transform political systems everywhere, but it provided a new language – a set of concepts and rhetorical weapons – that could not henceforth be banished from the vocabulary of those seeking political change. Even the new autocrat Napoleon described his quest for European hegemony in terms of liberty and encouraged the use of the word in the statutes and constitutions of the European states that fell under his yoke. The relationship between the individual and the state had changed, and all European nations were affected by the shift in terminology. From the French Revolution forward, to be declared a loyal citizen meant more than simply obeying the will of rulers above; it required individual commitment to the state and personal choice. Rousseau's prescriptions to women were exemplary of this new ideal of liberty. In granting women just enough rationality to make the choice to be subordinated to man's will, Rousseau perfectly described the limitations that were built into the concept of liberty from the start. As radical as the concept may have appeared when it was first uttered, Alexis de Tocqueville knew at the time that the 'real object of the [French] Revolution was less a new form of government than a new form of society; less the achievement of political rights than the destruction of privileges'.[100] Liberty had less to do with democracy than it had to do with building a new kind of political consensus. This consensus depended upon the existence of free will in the population, but it did not require absolute equality.

'Equality' stood as an unassailable tower in the rhetoric of the revolution. The Declaration of the Rights of Man and Citizen insisted: 'All citizens being equal in the eyes of the law, are equally eligible to all dignities and to all public positions and occupations, according to their abilities, and without distinction except that of their virtues and talents.' But as we have seen, 'equal' never applied to women and 'virtues and talents' could be used in such a way as to exclude many men. Neither the revolutionaries nor their successors were immune from the pressures of economic competition and social disruption, and they were quick to temper their political promises when social turmoil and violence threatened. The fact that the revolution had initially held out the promise of improved social conditions (the King had promised bread to the female marchers on Versailles and accepted grievances from the population) empowered the hungry masses to assume they too could use the language of liberty to seize what they needed to survive. But the chaos and violence that resulted sent the new republic in search of moral certainties. One convenient path to stability appeared to be the taming of women, whose involvement in bread riots and other public disturbances was particularly disruptive of the traditional sense of order. Women, it seemed clear, needed to be domesticated. Following Rousseau, advocates of women's rights like de Gouges and Wollstonecraft insisted that this domestication should occur only through women's individual and educated choice. But as the events of the Terror proved, removing this choice from them and imposing a ban on their political participation proved a convenient way of demonstrating that a society wracked by violence could be returned to a semblance of order. Inequality quickly became the preferred path to orderly, rational politics.

To the extent that liberty and equality had been achieved, they had emerged through violence that was, if not unprecedented, then certainly of a particularly public nature. The guillotine's blade spilled blood in the streets of Paris in the name of 'public safety' and the good of the collective. When men sought sole control over this violence, declaring female participation illegitimate, they were codifying gender relations in the name of the public good. 'Fraternity' appeared to be the only guarantee of liberty and equality. Controlled masculine violence was the antidote to the chaos of the uncontrolled (feminized) mob and the path to social advancement for the middle-class citizen. The debates over conscription in the Napoleonic state and in the nations trying to defend themselves from French invasion, along with the popularity of duelling in nineteenth-century Europe made the centrality of disciplined male violence especially clear. As war consumed the continent, this connection between the martial code and citizenship was only further reinforced.

Notes

1. Isabel de Madariaga, *Russia in the Age of Catherine the Great* (New Haven, CT and London: Yale University Press, 1981), 8–9.

2. Ibid., 27.

3. Ibid., 32–37.

4. There is speculation that she may in fact have married Grigory Potemkin, her most trusted advisor and greatest love, in a secret ceremony. But the desire for that secrecy just underlines Catherine's political need to remain unwed. On Potemkin and his relationship with Catherine, see: Simon Sebag Montefiore, *Prince of Princes: The Life of Potemkin* (London and New York: St. Martin's Press, 2000). See also: Douglas Smith, ed., *Love and Conquest: Personal Correspondence of Catherine the Great and Prince Grigory Potemkin* (DeKalb, IL: Northern Illinois University Press, 2004).

5. Prince M. M. Shcherbatov, *On the Corruption of Morals in Russia*, trans. A. Lentin (Cambridge: Cambridge University Press, 1969).

6. Ibid., 115.

7. Ibid., 159, 247.

8. Ibid., 235.

9. Ibid., 259.

10. Norman Davies, *Europe: A History* (Oxford and New York: Oxford University Press, 1996), 596.

11. Geneviève Fraisse, *Reason's Muse: Sexual Difference and the Birth of Democracy* (Chicago and London: University of Chicago Press, 1994), xiv.

12. See: Dena Goodman, *The Republic of Letters: A Cultural History of the French Enlightenment* (Ithaca, NY and London: Cornell University Press, 1994); and Daniel Gordon, *Citizens without Sovereignty: Equality and Sociability in French Thought, 1670–1789* (Princeton: Princeton University Press, 1994). Goodman argues that Rousseau had a lasting impact on later interpretations of the salons that underrated their influence in the mid-eighteenth century (pp. 62–63). The salons eventually did lose their power, however, and 'when the literary public sphere was transformed into the political public sphere in 1789, it had already become masculine' (p. 280).

13. Lieselotte Steinbrügge, *The Moral Sex: Woman's Nature in the French Enlightenment*, trans. Pamela E. Selwyn (Oxford and New York: Oxford University Press, 1995), 3.

14. The most modern translation is Jean-Jacques Rousseau, *The Collected Writings of Rousseau*, 9 vols, vol. 6, eds Roger D. Masters and Christopher Kelly (Hanover, CT: Published for Dartmouth College by University Press of New England, 1990).

15. Ibid., 17–18.

16. Mary Seidman Trouille, *Sexual Politics in the Enlightenment: Women Writers Read Rousseau* (Albany: State University of New York Press, 1997), 4.

17. The argument in this paragraph is derived largely from Steinbrügge.

18. Quoted from Condorcet, *Fragment sur l'Atlantide* (posthumous reprint Paris: G. F. Flammarion, 1988), 326, in Fraisse, *Reason's Muse*, 51.

19. Quoted from Condorcet, 'On Admission of Women to the City', in *Oeuvres de Condorcet* (1847 edn, vol. X, 122) in Siân Reynolds, 'Marianne's Citizen? Women, the Republic and Universal Suffrage in France', in *Gender and History in Western Europe*, eds Robert Shoemaker and Mary Vincent (London: Arnold, 1998), 310.

20. Ibid., 308.

21. Compare the rather optimistic view of Darline Gay Levy and Harriet B. Applewhite, 'A Political Revolution for Women? The Case of Paris', in *Becoming Visible: Women in European History*, 3rd edition, eds Renate Bridenthal, Susan Mosher Stuard and Merry E. Wiesner (Boston and New York: Houghton Mifflin Co., 1998), 279 to Olwen H. Hufton, *Women and the Limits of Citizenship in the French Revolution* (Toronto: University of Toronto Press, 1992). An overview of the debate is provided in Karen Offen, 'The New Sexual Politics of French Revolutionary Historiography', *French Historical Studies* 16, no. 4 (1990): 909–22.

22. Joan B. Landes, *Women in the Public Sphere in the Age of the French Revolution* (Ithaca, NY and London: Cornell University Press, 1988), 18–20.

23. Joan B. Landes, *Visualizing the Nation: Gender, Representation, and Revolution in Eighteenth-Century France* (Ithaca, NY: Cornell University Press, 2001), 57. For an extended account of the importance of imagery of the body during and after the French Revolution, see: Dorinda Outram, *The Body and the French Revolution: Sex, Class and Political Culture* (New Haven, CT: Yale University Press, 1989).

24. Leora Auslander, *Taste and Power: Furnishing Modern France* (Berkeley: University of California Press, 1996), 1–34.

25. Landes, *Women in the Public Sphere*, 21.

26. Simon Schama, *Citizens: A Chronicle of the French Revolution*, reprint edition (New

York: Vintage, 1990), 61–62.

27. Ibid., 40.

28. Meyer Kestnbaum, 'Citizenship and Compulsory Military Service: The Revolutionary Origins of Conscription in the United States', *Armed Forces and Society* 27, no. 1 (2000): 11.

29. For a clear discussion of this process, see: ibid.

30. Schama, *Citizens*, 43.

31. Georges Lefebvre, *The French Revolution: From its Origins to 1793*, trans. Elizabeth Moss Evanson (New York: Columbia University Press, 1962), 12.

32. Ibid., 359.

33. The classic account of the revolution in the countryside is Georges Lefebvre, *The Great Fear of 1789: Rural Panic in Revolutionary France*, trans. Joan White (New York: Schocken Books, 1973).

34. Landes, *Women in the Public Sphere*, 232, n. 10.

35. Ibid., 107.

36. 'Petition of Women of the Third Estate to the King' (1 January 1789) at Liberty, Equality, Fraternity: Exploring the French Revolution, City University of New York and George Mason University, available from http://chnm.gmu.edu/revolution/d/473/ (accessed February 2005).

37. Levy and Applewhite, 'A Political Revolution for Women?', 272.

38. Quoted in Landes, *Women in the Public Sphere*, 112.

39. Dominique Godineau, *The Women of Paris and Their French Revolution* (Berkeley and Los Angeles: University of California Press, 1998).

40. Available online at the Avalon Project at Yale Law School, http://www.yale.edu/lawweb/avalon/rightsof.htm (accessed June 2006).

41. William H. Sewell, 'Le Citoyen/La Citoyenne: Activity, Passivity, and the Revolutionary Concept of Citizenship', in *The French Revolution and the Creation of Modern Political Culture*, vol. 2, ed. Colin Lucas (New York: Pergamon, 1988), 114.

42. The Declaration is reprinted in its entirety, including the letter to the Queen, in Darline Gay Levy, Harriet Branson Applewhite and Mary Durham Johnson, eds, *Women in Revolutionary Paris, 1789–1795: Selected Documents* (Urbana, IL: University of Illinois Press, 1979), 87–96, quotation p. 91.

43. Landes, *Women in the Public Sphere*, 123.

44. The concept of republican motherhood developed in dialogue with American feminists. See: Linda Kerber, *Women of the Republic: Intellect and Ideology in Revolutionary America* (Chapel Hill, NC: University of North Carolina Press, 1980); and Jane Rendall, *The Origins of Modern Feminism: Women in Britain, France, and the United States 1780–1860* (Basingstoke: Macmillan, 1985), esp. Ch. 2.

45. Ibid., 4.

46. Landes argues that 'She ultimately fails to appreciate the contradictions resulting from the applications of masculine ideology to women.' See: Joan B. Landes, *Women in the Public Sphere*, 134.

47. On the early development of this group, see: Gary Kates, *The Cercle Social, the Girondins, and the French Revolution* (Princeton: Princeton University Press, 1985).

48. For a detailed account, see: Landes, *Women in the Public Sphere*, 118–21.

49. David Andress, *The Terror: The Merciless War for Freedom in Revolutionary France* (New York: Farrar, Straus and Giroux, 2005), 6.

50. Colin Lucas, 'The Theory and Practice of Denunciation in the French Revolution', *The Journal of Modern History* 68, no. 4 (Dec. 1996): 774.

51. Quoted in Landes, *Women in the Public Sphere*, 142.

52. Levy and Applewhite, 'A Political Revolution for Women?', 285.

53. Schama, *Citizens*, 221.

54. Ibid., 226–27.

55. Bonnie G. Smith, *Changing Lives: Women in European History since 1700* (Boston: Houghton Mifflin Co. College Division, 1989), 93.

56. For a comprehensive collection of these rumours, see: Antoine de Baecque, *The Body Politic: Corporeal Metaphor in Revolutionary France, 1770–1800* (Stanford, CA: Stanford University Press, 1997).

57. Joan Wallach Scott, *Only Paradoxes to Offer: French Feminists and the Rights of Man* (Cambridge, MA: Harvard University Press, 1996), 3.

58. Ibid., 3–4.

59. Offen, 'The New Sexual Politics', 910. As Offen points out, seventeenth-century England provides some parallels.

60. On 'the social' as a category, see: Hannah Arendt, *The Human Condition* (Chicago and London: University of Chicago Press, 1958). See also the discussion in Hannah Arendt, *On Revolution* (London: Penguin Books, 1963), 29. For an extended debate on the relationship between gender and the emergence of the public sphere see the contributions by Daniel Gordon, David A. Bell and Sarah Maza to 'Forum: The Public Sphere in the Eighteenth Century', *French Historical Studies* 17, no. 4 (1992): 882–956.

61. Quoted in Karen M. Offen, *European Feminisms, 1700–1950: A Political History* (Palo Alto, CA: Stanford University Press, 1999), 70.

62. Ibid., 72.

63. The account to follow relies on Wayne Ph. te Brake, Rudolf M. Dekker and Lotte C. van de Pol, 'Women and Political Culture in the Dutch Revolutions', in *Women and Politics in the Age of the Democratic Revolution*, eds Harriet B. Applewhite and Darline G. Levy (Ann Arbor: University of Michigan Press, 1990), 109–46. Quotation from p. 130.

64. Ibid., 116.

65. Brake, Dekker and van de Pol, 'Women and Political Culture in the Dutch Revolutions', 119.

66. Ibid., 136. The Batavian definition of citizenship also included a provision that active (enfranchised) citizens had to pay a minimum of direct tax. This also effectively excluded women, who were considered dependents.

67. Ibid., 139.

68. J. G. A. Pocock, *The Machiavellian Moment: Florentine Political Thought and the Atlantic Republican Tradition* (Princeton: Princeton University Press, 1975).

69. For a discussion of the question of military force in the context of the Scottish Enlightenment, see: Richard B. Sher, 'Adam Ferguson, Adam Smith, and the Problem of National Defense,' *Journal of Modern History* 61, no. 2 (1989): 240–68.

70. Alan Forrest, 'Conscription as Ideology: Revolutionary France and the Nation in Arms', *The Comparative Study of Conscription in the Armed Forces* 20 (2002): 99.

71. Clarence J. Munford, 'Conscription and the Peasants of the Morvan District of Chateau-Chinon, 1792–1794', *Canadian Journal of History/Annales candiennes d'histoire* 4, no. 2 (1969): 7–9.

72. Cited in Forrest, 'Conscription as Ideology', 103.

73. Peter Paret, *Understanding War: Essays on Clausewitz and the History of Military Power* (Princeton: Princeton University Press, 1992), 62.

74. Munford, 'Conscription and the Peasants of the Morvan District of Chateau-Chinon', 14.

75. For a ground-breaking study of revolutionary fraternity, see: Lynn Hunt, *The Family Romance*.

76. On the exclusion of women from the social contract of revolutionary France, see: Carol Pateman, *The Sexual Contract* (Stanford, CA: Stanford University Press, 1988); and Fraisse, *Reason's Muse*.

77. For an extended discussion of the proposition that what fraternity meant in the French Revolution was the younger generation of 'brothers' destroying their father-king, see: Lynn Hunt, *The Family Romance*.

78. Cited in Jennifer Ngaire Heuer, *The Family and the Nation: Gender and Citizenship in Revolutionary France, 1789–1830* (Ithaca, NY and London: Cornell University Press, 2005), 77.

79. Ibid., 129–30.

80. Fraisse, *Reason's Muse*, 3.

81. Forrest, 'Conscription as Ideology', 104; Isser Woloch, *The New Regime: Transformations of the French Civic Order, 1789–1820s* (New York and London: W. W. Norton & Company, 1994), 418.

82. David M. Hopkin, 'Sons and Lovers: Popular Images of the Conscript, 1798–1870', *Modern & Contemporary France* 9, no. 1 (2001).

83. Paret, *Understanding War*, 66–72.

84. Cited in Karen Hagemann, 'Female Patriots: Women, War and the Nation in the Period of the Prussian-German Anti-Napoleonic Wars', *Gender & History* 16, no. 2 (2004): 403.

85. Ibid.

86. John Lawrence Tone, 'Spanish Women in the Resistance to Napoleon, 1808–1814', in *Constructing Spanish Womanhood: Female Identity in Modern Spain*, eds Victoria Lorée Enders and Pamela Beth Radcliff (Albany, NY: State University of New York Press, 1999), 276.

87. John Lawrence Tone, 'The Virgin of the Pillar and Agustina Zaragoza', paper delivered at the Annual Meeting of the American Historical Association (Philadelphia: 2006). Many thanks to Professor Tone for allowing us to use and cite this manuscript.

88. Cited in Tone, 'Spanish Women in the Resistance to Napoleon', 263.

89. Hagemann, 'Female Patriots', 408–9.

90. Tone, 'The Virgin of the Pillar'.

91. This is not to say that the duel was a new phenomenon. France was the 'leading dueling nation' by the seventeenth century, with 10,000 deaths by duel between 1589 and 1610 alone. Wolfgang Schivelbusch, *The Culture of Defeat: On National Trauma, Mourning and Recovery* (New York: Picador, 2003), 131.

92. The literature on duelling has grown apace in recent years. To provide just a brief selection: Robert A. Nye, *Masculinity and Male Codes of Honor in Modern France* (New York: Oxford University Press, 1993); Peter Gay, 'Mensur – the Cherished Scar', in *The Bourgeois Experience, Victoria to Freud*, III: The Cultivation of Hatred (New York and London: W. W. Norton & Company, 1993), 9–33; James Kelly, *'That Damn'd Thing Called Honour': Duelling in Ireland, 1570–1860* (Cork: Cork University Press, 1995); Istvan Deak, 'Latter-Day Knights: Officers' Honor and Duelling in the Austro-Hungarian Army', *Oesterreichische Ostheft* 28, no. 3 (1986): 311–27; Irina Reyfman, *Ritualized Violence Russian Style: The Duel in Russian Culture and Literature* (Palo Alto, CA: Stanford University Press, 1999); Robert B. Shoemaker, 'The Taming of the Duel: Masculinity, Honor and Ritual Violence in London, 1660–1800', *Historical Journal* 45, no. 3 (2002): 525–45; Ute Frevert, *Men of Honour: A Social and Cultural History of the Duel*

(Cambridge: Polity Press, 1995); and Kevin McAleer, *Dueling: The Cult of Honor in Fin-de-Siècle Germany* (Princeton: Princeton University Press, 1997).

93. Robert A. Nye, 'Fencing, the Duel and Republican Manhood in the Third Republic', *Journal of Contemporary History* 25, no. 2/3 (1990): 366–67.

94. Nye, *Masculinity and Male Codes of Honor*, 9–11.

95. Schivelbusch, *Culture of Defeat*, 131.

96. Rolland Ray Lutz, 'The Burschenschaft: Reformist Movement or Conformist Movement?', *Consortium on Revolutionary Europe 1750–1850* 19, part 1 (1989): 357–77; Gary D. Stark, 'The Ideology of the German Buschenschaft Generation', *European Studies Review* 8, no. 3 (1978): 323–48.

97. Gay, 'Mensur – the Cherished Scar', 11 and 21.

98. Hitler did not approve of the duel, but its culture was so engrained that even high-ranking SS members engaged in it. See: William Combs, 'Fatal Attraction: Duelling and the SS', *History Today* 47, no. 6 (June 1997): 11–16.

99. Rebecca Friedman, *Masculinity, Autocracy and the Russian University, 1804–1863* (Basingstoke and New York: Palgrave Macmillan, 2005), 12. See also pp. 53ff.

100. Quoted from Alexis de Tocqueville, *'The European Revolution' and Correspondence with Gobineau* (Garden City, N.Y.: Doubleday, 1953), 160 in Arno J. Mayer, *The Furies: Violence and Terror in the French and Russian Revolutions* (Princeton: Princeton University Press, 2000), 38.

–2–

Gendered Capitalism and its Discontents

The political revolutions of the late eighteenth century transformed discourses about gender and sexuality in intellectual, political and scientific circles. But abstract notions of 'rights' or theories of sexual difference had very little impact on the everyday lives of the vast majority of Europeans, who had little or no access to this realm of sophisticated discourse or to social or political power. While the French Revolution marked a political and intellectual transition of enormous significance and therefore also affected conceptions of gender and sexuality, the economic transformations of the nineteenth century had a much more immediate effect on public attitudes towards gender roles, on patterns of family life and on the actual conditions of sexual behaviour in Europe. Industrialization brought many changes to European society over the course of the nineteenth century. New technologies had a profound impact on all aspects of society. But nowhere were the changes more deeply transformative of everyday relationships and the patterns of daily life than in the sphere of labour. Industrialization changed not only how people worked and how they earned money, but also how they related to others socially and sexually. As European countries industrialized, transformations in labour changed the norms and practices of family life. In some cases (as in the South and the East) these changes took place very gradually, sometimes even imperceptibly. In central and northern Europe, the changes were much more sudden, dramatic and socially disruptive. But wherever the Industrial Revolution took hold, wage labour entrenched a new separation of the working lives of men and women.

It must be admitted at the outset that the term 'Industrial Revolution' is contested.[1] The word 'revolution' generally applies to a hectic and quickly completed process, and it often has connotations of positive progress. Europeans often did perceive industrialization in these terms. Norman Davies has described the nineteenth century as an era in which 'Europe vibrated with power as never before: with technical power, economic power, cultural power, intercontinental power'.[2] But Davies also argued that this was the perspective only of the minority of Europeans who were involved in or benefited from technological innovations. For a majority of the population in industrializing countries, the process of transformation from agrarian to industrial societies was drawn out, uneven and filled with social disruption, turmoil and suffering. Industrialization also accelerated international competition and created many losers, especially among peasants, artisans and colonized peoples.

The technological aspect of industrialization was only one component of a larger process of social, cultural and economic modernization.[3] It took more than technology for European societies to transition from economic systems in which most people directly worked the land and clothed themselves to a society in which most people worked for wages that could then be used to buy food and clothing. It was necessary for norms of family life and social interaction to change before the factory system could take hold, and resistance to industrialized production was often justified with reference to the desire to preserve traditional family structures. This was a complex and long-term process. Nevertheless, the term 'Industrial Revolution' remains a powerful historical metaphor, because it suggests how important economic changes were in driving social and political change and hints at the ruptures that industrialization produced in the lives of Europeans.

As the struggles of developing nations today still demonstrate, industrialization is most likely and most rapid when conditions permit a stable political system, a sophisticated system of education and training, and the accumulation of capital. These conditions were present in England by the latter half of the eighteenth century, and British industry had rocketed ahead of all competitors by 1840. In Germany, conditions necessary for industrialization only started to become established in the middle of the nineteenth century, but the German economy, particularly after the end of the wars of reunification in 1870/71, then industrialized more quickly than any other in Europe. In France, industrialization progressed more gradually over the course of the nineteenth century. Industrialization did not, however, affect all parts of these countries equally. Life in cities like Paris, Vienna, Berlin and London, or in Rotterdam, Marseilles and Manchester looked nothing like it did in rural, traditional Ireland, Sicily or Galicia. Life on the margins of Europe remained relatively untouched by these processes: a growing gap emerged between the industrializing North and West and the rural South and East. Even in the more dynamic West and North, the early phases of industrialization rarely increased people's wages, and the rising price of goods often offset any gains. Productivity (the amount of 'product' able to be created in a given time period) increased, but these gains only slowly trickled down to workers, who still struggled to survive.

Even when wages rose, standards of living could stagnate. Although real wages in Great Britain increased after 1815, levels of food consumption were lower in 1840 than they were in 1760.[4] Historians who explore the economic transitions from early modern to modern Europe must rely on insufficient and spotty statistical data, and there is heated debate about whether or not industrialization improved living conditions over the short and long terms.[5] There is very little debate, however, that many of the people who lived through these tumultuous economic times felt that the anxiety produced by the shift to wage labour overshadowed the limited financial gains they saw. Infant mortality can be taken as a measure of this psychological suffering. Wherever there was a large influx of poor people into cities, infant mortality soared, primarily because working mothers could no longer breastfeed their infants.[6]

Nevertheless, improvements in agriculture (first in Holland, then in Great Britain and elsewhere) curtailed the cycle of famine that had long kept the growth of populations in check. In north-western Europe, population density doubled over the course of the eighteenth century.[7]

These changes affected men and women in different ways but ultimately combined to transform family life for all Europeans. The Industrial Revolution created new patterns of marriage and new relationships between community, family, the individual and the state. This chapter will outline these changes, pointing to the intersection of labour patterns, gender roles and the boundaries that economic organization and structure can set on sexual behaviour. On the one hand, the transformation of labour and the emerging system of capitalism provided the social conditions and the ideological justification for the argument that male and female life should be viewed as operating in separate spheres. But the reverse is also true. Gender norms and understandings of appropriate forms of work for men and women also had an impact on the form that capitalism took in Europe and on the tripartite relationship between the individual, the family and the state.[8]

The Transformation of Labour and the Family

In 1919, Alice Clark, a Quaker activist for women's rights, wrote a book entitled *The Working Life of Women in the Seventeenth Century*. In a careful and path-breaking economic history, Clark argued that before the Industrial Revolution women and men worked together cooperatively as part of a family unit. Tasks were divided into gender-specific categories (women spun the wool for weaving and men worked the looms, for instance), but it was the sum total of work performed by all members of the family that guaranteed its material and social survival. This system was transformed when factories tempted individual family members away from family industry with the lure of higher, individualized wages. Women's contributions to family income were diminished by this turn to wage labour, Clark argued, since their domestic (or later industrial) work no longer functioned as a crucial cog in the wheel, but only as a supplement to the husband's income.[9] Sixty years later, Joan Scott and Louise Tilly supported Clark's assessment, supplementing it with demographic and social data that provided much richer detail about women's lives in the pre-industrial era.[10] Tilly and Scott argued against the notion that women only gained access to work after modern cultural values changed and women's rights became integral to 'modern individualist ideology'. Women had always worked.[11] Only if one restricted one's view to the history of urban middle-class women, they insisted, and excluded the vast majority of the population who lived in the countryside or who were working class, could one come to the conclusion that the history of women's work was a process of evolution from the home to the workplace spurred on purely by a shift in cultural values. Tilly and Scott (and many historians after them) emphasized that work in pre-industrial Europe centred around the family as the main unit of production. Individuals worked or earned money not for themselves alone but to ensure the survival and maintenance of their families.

The impact of the Industrial Revolution on gender relations must therefore be understood – in part – as a progressive dismantling of what Bonnie Smith has called the 'complementarity of the subsistence family'.[12] This transition from a social structure where most families worked together as a unit on farms to societies in which each individual member earned wages and worked in separate locations irrevocably transformed gender relations in Europe. Numerous factors both close to home (on the farms and in the cities) and farther away (in the seats of political power and on the routes of international trade) combined to bring about these far-reaching social changes, but for the moment we will concentrate on how changes in work patterns affected the relationship between family members.

What did pre-industrial families look like? In a Europe still largely rural, all family members worked, either on the farm, within the household or in nearby towns. Individuals who were left alone (after the death of a spouse, for instance) quickly remarried, since the work required to feed and clothe oneself while still bringing in some income for incidental needs was too much for any one person to manage. As David Sabean has so vividly demonstrated in his micro-history of the German town of Neckarhausen, quarrelling married couples who separated often found a way of reconciling when the reality of economic survival apart from the family unit sunk in.[13] Decisions about when to marry, whom to marry and whether to continue to live within a difficult marriage generally depended not only on bonds of affection, but also (particularly in times of economic insecurity) on the desire to survive or to preserve one's economic and social status.

Outside pressures on one's choice of marriage partner were particularly intense for members of guilds. Guilds were predominantly (though not exclusively) male organizations that controlled access to individual trades (carpentry, shoemaking, cabinet-making, stonemasonry, etc.) and established and protected the rights and privileges of their members.[14] Unlike unions today, they were less interested in increasing wages than they were in ensuring an equitable distribution of work between members. Guild membership was therefore something that had to be earned and was a carefully protected privilege. But guilds also determined the social lives of their members, setting rules and restrictions on marriage and providing the site for community celebrations, rituals and charitable support.[15] The 'familial' relationship between the master and his apprentice could produce warm bonds of belonging, but this did not change the fact that the guild system was part of a broader system of control over the marriage and sexual practices of young adults.

Guilds, along with many other small-scale institutions of social discipline in early modern towns and villages, slowly weakened and disappeared with industrialization. Many historians have described this process as an effect of the dramatic scale of economic change transforming family and sexual life in modern Europe. In the late

1960s, historians influenced by modernization theory (such as Edward Shorter and William Goode) argued that industrialization transformed marriage patterns by breaking down traditional pressures on couples to marry for economic reasons.[16] Shorter postulated an early 'sexual revolution' that followed industrialization, which, he argued, brought young people independence, the desire to be free from traditional structures, and the ability to rely on their own wage labour to choose partners more independently.

These theories have since been soundly criticized by historians eager to demonstrate that, despite pressures from local communities, pre-industrial European family patterns had long allowed for individual choice. The practice of 'bundling', common in Scandinavia and central Europe, had provided young couples with some control over the choice of future mates. Ritualized overnight visits from boys in girls' bedrooms were carefully monitored by the peer group and only partially controlled by parents. Any resulting premarital pregnancy was only considered scandalous if the couple did not follow through by getting married.[17] By the same token, as one study of Sweden has demonstrated, the decline of these practices and the increased opportunities for finding mates outside the village in the nineteenth century did not entail an end to parental control or a sudden 'burst of sexual energy and romantic love blast[ing] the walls of tradition defended by elders and parents'.[18] So even though marriage was crucially important to individuals' material well-being and survival in the early modern period, love was not a creation of the Industrial Revolution. Historians relying on the records of marital complaint are now uncovering considerable evidence that the hope for love was always present in early modern marriage, and that material interests were generally pragmatically balanced with the desires of each partner to fulfil emotional needs.[19]

Nonetheless, changing economic circumstances and the need to move away from an exclusively agricultural and rural existence greatly complicated married and family life. Families found it necessary to diversify their means of bringing in income, because a slow transition in agricultural production began to affect most of Europe in the mid-eighteenth century. Ironically, the impoverishment of many rural families was a result of agricultural innovations that spread across western and central Europe (we will return to the East and the South shortly) between the 1760s and the mid-nineteenth century. New strategies of crop rotation and organic fertilization increased crop yields. Many European regions also followed the lead of Frederick the Great of Prussia, who imported the potato from South America in 1760 and eventually convinced (and sometimes forced) his peasants to cultivate it to guard against famine. Potatoes, turnips and beets proved much more resilient to unpredictable European weather patterns than wheat, while legumes added an important nutritional component to European diets. All this helped to break cycles of famine that had plagued Europe since the Middle Ages. But these new crops also changed the division of labour in the countryside, because they were most often worked by women, who were given the time-consuming tasks of hoeing, weeding and staking.

But the agricultural productivity gains were not passed on to agricultural workers. Rather than paying farmhands more or allowing them to work less, landlords on the large estates tended to extract the same amount of labour from fewer individuals, pocketing the increased financial rewards or reinvesting them in industry. This both spurred on industrialization (since it created new sources of capital) and produced an oversupply of agricultural labour across large swathes of rural Europe by the nineteenth century. The first areas to industrialize were those where structural changes in agriculture coincided with a general growth in the population. Between 1700 and 1800, the population of Great Britain rose from six million to nine million, with most of the increase occurring in the second half of the eighteenth century.[20] This oversupply was exacerbated by specific policy decisions and systems of land ownership.

In England, agriculture was progressively transformed by the process of enclosures, which began in the sixteenth century and accelerated in the nineteenth. Enclosure was the process of consolidating strips of agricultural land that had previously been farmed separately (originally by serfs who owed service to the lord and later by peasants who paid a landlord rent) into larger, continuous units of land, controlled directly by the landlord. The process was initially resisted by the early modern British monarchy, since dispossessing peasants of the land and livelihood created great social disorder. But the success of the larger estates eventually quelled this resistance, and by 1700, Acts of Parliament were used to legally regulate the process of enclosure.[21] Legislation now also made it possible for landlords to control what had previously been common lands, whose use was governed by local custom. New enclosure acts in 1801, 1836 and 1845 further rationalized and accelerated the process, with special government commissioners overseeing the transition and reporting back to Parliament. By the early 1800s, the percentage of Britons employed in agriculture decreased to 33 per cent (compared to 60 per cent in the late seventeenth century), and enclosure had forced a growing number of rural families to become dependent upon wage labour.[22] There were, however, various transitional stages.

Families reacted to the pressure of an oversupply of rural labour in various ways. The first response was often to supplement agricultural income with small-scale manufacturing in the home or with itinerant labour outside of the home. Rural families in economic hard times sent their older children to work as itinerant farm labourers or domestic servants. The experiences of Tess in Thomas Hardy's novel *Tess of the D'Urbervilles* (1891) vividly symbolized the choices available to young rural women and the harsh conditions under which they laboured in the fields and in the homes of the upper classes. At various points, Tess works as a keeper of hens, a milkmaid and a labourer on a beet farm. The young lord of an estate takes advantage of her, she returns to her parents' house and gives birth to a baby, who soon dies. Later, her true love discovers the secret of Tess's girlhood indiscretion and abandons her, setting the stage for her ultimate downfall. Tess's tragedy was so powerful as a novel because it symbolized the experiences of scores of young women, whose tenuous economic and social existence left them vulnerable to sexual exploitation. Rural poverty also often forced men (both fathers and sons) into itinerant work away from home, though their choices were more diverse. Expanding cities meant a demand for labour in construction, railway and road building. These jobs separated men from their families and left women home alone to tend garden plots and animals. Since work outside of the household was paid in cash, it could be tracked in economic statistics and was understood as a vital part of the national economy. Domestic chores, on the other hand, were not quantified in this way, and they were thereby rendered virtually invisible as a form of economic production. Much of women's labour, in other words, was not part of the 'wealth of nations'.

But not all rural families moved directly from agriculture to wage labour. Many also reacted to the agricultural revolution and the pressures that it put on rural life by resorting to cottage industry of various kinds. 'Cottage industry' or 'the putting-out system' were terms used to describe small manufacturing enterprises within the home. As capitalism developed in eighteenth-century towns, merchant capitalists wishing to expand their markets and increase their profits began to understand that they could circumvent the high wages of guild members by farming out small-scale manufacturing to rural families.[23] The most well-known form of cottage industry was weaving. During times when agricultural work was lighter, families took in wool and divided up the tasks of washing, spinning and weaving it. Families purchased or rented equipment like the spinning jenny (invented by James Hargreaves in 1764) and sold their finished products (often under contract) to middlemen. Many areas of Europe had specialized forms of cottage industry. Handmade lace often supplemented or constituted the income of rural families, particularly in parts of France, Spain and Italy. In the early nineteenth century, lace machines were developed in Nottingham, England, and cottage industries of machine-made lace sprang up in the St Gall area of Switzerland, Plauen in Saxony and Calais in France. These complicated and expensive machines required considerable skill and investment, so that more complex hierarchies of family labour developed, with the head of the household (the father) performing the most complex tasks and all other family members being assigned jobs according to their age and gender. Similar divisions of labour occurred in the homes of artisans, such as glassmakers in Bohemia.

The example of rural weavers demonstrates that the transition of labour from a predominance of family-based rural agriculture to a more urban, industrialized and wage-labour oriented economy was by no means immediate or uniform across Europe, nor did it instantaneously transform social norms concerning marriage. There were long periods in each European country during which family life was characterized by what Olwen Hufton has called the 'economy of makeshift' – a combination of agricultural work with various forms of manufacturing (including cottage industry), building or itinerant labour for wages that pieced together a meagre survival for early modern families.[24] The 'complementarity of the subsistence family' was thus already disappearing in the eighteenth century and was being replaced with a phase of 'proto-industrialization'.[25] In Neckarhausen, a town of only eighty adult males, thirty were engaged in handicrafts of goods for sale in a larger market.[26] Historians have tended to assume that men's more frequent access to income from crafts or work outside of the village increased the likelihood that they would abandon their families in times of economic distress. But newer research has tended to show that divorce was most often provoked by women and that women were not averse to using the various laws describing the duties of husbands and wives to their advantage.[27] In England, for instance, laws of coverture gave women the right to make purchases 'suitable to the couple's situation in life' and provided women with a sense of entitlement to support from their husbands. Even though men generally owned the property and produced most of the cash income in the early modern family, they were dependent upon wives, who kept the family household running smoothly.[28] We can speak therefore of relationships of codependency in which the husband's patriarchal authority was kept in check by community standards and specific laws that circumscribed his duty to his family.

Changes in how goods were produced and how individuals earned their living inevitably placed strains upon and transformed patterns of marriage. 'Marriage is, after all', Sabean writes, 'an exchange relationship, composed of, if not reducible to, a property settlement, a labor contract, sexual privileges and duties, and reproductive claims and responsibilities. All of these elements are under constant renegotiation as conditions change.'[29] As increasing percentages of the European population moved from agricultural production to manufacturing (or found ways of combining these two modes of making a living) the division of labour within families and the relative value placed on each family member's work inevitably changed. The work of rural European women had generally centred on the home. But in farming communities, these activities (which in many regions of Europe included the management of the household or shop's finances) were so essential to the family's survival that it is extremely misleading to categorize them as housework. It makes more sense to think about these women as contributors to 'smallholdings': rural farming households, practising diversified agriculture and other forms of income generation (including sale in markets, cottage industries and work in rural or urban factories) in areas of dense population.[30] But the more common it became for individual family members to find work in factories, the more separate the daily experiences of men and women became. It is important to remember that smallholders often continued to maintain their farms even as family members began earning money in industry or other forms of wage labour. In some cases, such as on the dairy farms in the Swiss alps, this coexistence of smallholding and work in industry or the tourist trade persists to this day.[31] But when entire families or individual family members moved permanently to the cities, the separation between men's work and women's work tended to become more pronounced. We will return to this process of urbanization shortly. First, however, it is necessary to contrast the Western patterns of work and family that we have described above with circumstances in other parts of Europe.

Family and Work on the Periphery of Europe

The patterns of work and family life that we have described for the industrializing western areas of Europe bear little relationship to the experiences of eastern and southern Europeans. A description of life on an estate in the Baltics will demonstrate the degree to which a different economic system and different patterns of work provided different boundaries for family life and the relationship between the genders.

Andrejs Plakans's description of life on an estate in Kurland (a Russian Baltic province now part of Latvia) in the 1790s provides a graphic illustration of the variety of conditions under which European families laboured in the early modern period. Peasants, who made up about 85–90 per cent of the region's population, were tied to the land under a system of serfdom that included the obligation to provide unpaid labour to the lords who owned the grand estates of this region. Central governments and their policies played very little role in life on the estates, which was governed by the landowner. While the peasants were Latvian and Estonian, the upper classes (landowners) were the descendants of the Teutonic Order that had conquered this region in the thirteenth and fourteenth centuries. These nobles still considered themselves German. This system of land ownership stayed in place until well into the mid-nineteenth century. Indeed, as the estate owners faced international competition and decreasing profits, they increased the dues that peasants owed to their lords. On the estates, peasants lived in extended family units that included several generations and some non-family members. These units were somewhat like the *zadruga* of the Balkan lands, where fathers lived together with their married sons and their families. Plakans provides a detailed description of how this system worked in the Daudzwas estate, a large agricultural estate with a population of 924.[32]

The owner of Daudzwas did not live on the estate itself, which was managed by an unmarried overseer. The estate housed one doctor, six German-speaking managers and several artisans, tradesmen and innkeepers, who provided their services to all those living on the estate. Each artisan hired a farmhand to work his household's land. Almost 72 per cent of the population on the estate were serfs, meaning they were tied to the land, were considered the landowner's property and were obligated to perform agricultural and other services for the landowner. Those whom the landlord considered suitable headed their own farms, while the others worked on yearly contracts for a *Wirth* (a peasant manager of a portion of the lord's land). A large percentage of landless peasants roamed from job to job within the estate. Their family lives were never stable, and their children seldom stayed with them past the age of ten. All this meant that people's daily lives were not governed by a family unit but by a farmstead (or commune), headed by a *Wirth* who might or might not be related to his underlings. Only the *Wirth* and his wife, and perhaps some older relatives, had a room of their own in the farmhouse. Others shared cramped quarters with makeshift sleeping arrangements or, when the weather was warmer, slept out in the haylofts and barns. This farmstead worked as a unit to provide food for its inhabitants and to provide the demesne labour service required by the lord.

The agricultural estates of the Baltic Littoral provide only one example of the organization of agricultural life in eastern Europe. Nonetheless, the stark conditions of life on the Daudzwas estate are symbolic of the struggles that eastern European families faced in the transition towards industrialization. The multigeneration household was typical of pre-industrialized eastern Europe.[33] Even after serfs were emancipated during the nineteenth century (1816–19 in Russia's Baltic provinces, 1848 in Austria and the Habsburg Empire, 1853 in Hungary, 1861 in Russia proper), impoverished rural individuals had few alternatives but to continue working on the estates, since they either did not have the means to own property or were heavily indebted for its purchase. The opportunities for wage labour in the cities grew only slowly and unpredictably. In many cases the obligatory labour was simply renamed 'rent'.[34] These developments contrasted with the process that Max Weber observed on Prussian estates, where the Junker class's preference for cheap, seasonal wage labour and the lure of more rapidly growing German cities led to a depopulation of the East Elbian countryside. Indeed, many impoverished peasants from Baltic and Russian lands came to work for these meagre wages on Prussian estates.[35] Nonetheless, the freedom to move off the estate meant that younger brothers could go in search of their own headship rather than be forced to live as a subordinate in an older brother's household. In many areas of the Russian Empire, however, the freedom to leave could only be granted by a decision of the commune, which was collectively indebted for the purchase of land from the lord after emancipation. Given that the loss of a debtor meant an increase in everyone else's debt, requests for permission to move were not always granted. Emancipation also removed the lord's right to control the marital choices of peasants, but commune elders managed to take over authority in these matters for a time. Emancipation, in other words, did not immediately increase individual freedom. But it did provide for a dramatic transformation in individual identity. Peasants – who were now expected to sign contracts with landowners – were given surnames for the first time.

Industrialized Labour and Gender Conflict

European countries industrialized at different times and followed quite different patterns. Great Britain capitalized on a strong banking system, abundant natural resources, agricultural reorganization and access to foreign markets acquired through colonial possessions in North America, India and Africa, to be the first country to achieve the level of investment necessary to build large factories and raw-material processing plants. In France, the process was slowed by an agricultural system dominated by small-landholders and (by the mid-nineteenth century) a declining birth rate, both of which diminished the supply of labour to new industry. A weak banking system and the damage to investor confidence wreaked by the Napoleonic and the revolutionary wars of the late eighteenth and mid-nineteenth century also thwarted investment in capital industry. Cottage industry thus prevailed far longer than in Britain. Meanwhile, German industrialists had to contend with a myriad of tariffs, at least until the creation of the *Zollverein* (a free-trade zone encompassing most of the future German Empire) in 1834. Industrialization, particularly in coal and steel, began in earnest after German unification in 1871, but cottage industries remained prominent there much longer than in Britain. Despite these differences, the process of industrialization across Europe affected the gendered division of work in similar ways. Wherever industrial production grew, cottage industry and factories transformed the rhythms of work, the kind of work performed and the forms of work discipline for both men and women.[36]

Home manufacturing had allowed families to work together, but under factory conditions, parents worked separately from their children (at least after legislation banned child labour around mid-century) and from each other. The daily rhythms of family life were now governed by the factory whistle, and the clock replaced the rooster and the sun as the family's temporal point of reference. 'Those who are employed experience a distinction between their employer's time and their "own" time ... Time is now currency; it is not passed but spent.'[37] This division of life between family time and work time and the geographical separation of work and home (workers often had to travel considerable distances to get to their jobs) had a significant impact on gender relations and was 'by and large, experienced as a calamity' by individuals more accustomed to the flexibility and cooperative possibilities of work within the home.[38] Skilled artisans were more able to resist stringent forms of discipline than unskilled workers and women. In specific crafts, they successfully organized, resisted moving to factories or maintained some independence within the factory system. Those who did move to factories were eventually forced to succumb to stricter time management and control of their communication with each other. The strongly patriarchal attitudes of most factory managers were particularly onerous for women, who often endured various forms of harassment.[39] At the same time, male workers and male factory managers increasingly defined manliness in terms of skill, reinforcing a gender division of labour and a hierarchy between working men.[40] Increasingly, factory work was gendered, with the more highly skilled and lucrative jobs being reserved for men. A specific monetary value was now placed on each family member's contribution to the household income. The task of raising children and performing housework fell to women, who inevitably earned less than men, even if they worked long hours outside of the home. These untenable circumstances led to various conflicts within the family and on the shop floor.

In some areas of Europe, the industrialization of production was contested precisely because of its dramatic influence on family life. In the 1840s, the handloom weavers of the Pays des Mauges (also known as the Choletais) in France successfully resisted the efforts of local mill owners to mechanize production.[41] After the 1860s, power looms eventually triumphed, but for a time the handloom weavers protected their identities as individual artisans in control of their own working lives and the destinies of their families. Given that handloom weaving was increasingly becoming less lucrative, the practice survived only because wives and daughters supplemented family incomes with underpaid factory jobs. Men protected their status as independent heads of households only with the help of female income. The resulting source of cheap female labour helped spur on new industries in the region, particularly in the shoe and garment industry. But the weavers clung to their trade as being vital to their identities as men and fathers, resorting to living off food 'pilfered from farmers by moonlight' rather than accepting jobs in the shoe industry.[42] As poverty eventually forced at least some of the weavers into the factories, the weavers, like their daughters before them, fed an industry that relied on cheap labour. Having hung onto their dignity so long by forcing their daughters into cheap labour, they had set off a 'negative spiral' that drove wages down and eventually exacted its price on both sexes.[43]

As the English example shows, the gendering of work and skill continued on the factory floor. As steam-driven looms replaced handlooms in the 1840s, highly skilled male weavers were driven out of their jobs. They were often replaced by women, who were believed to possess more dexterous hands that could better operate the often dangerous spinning frames, but who were paid considerably less than men.[44] By the 1830s, this process of 'deskilling' (the replacement of skilled artisans with unskilled wage labourers using industrial forms of production) had produced an unsustainable social and economic situation, since families who had lost the income of an artisan head of household could now no longer make enough money to survive. An emerging trade union movement started to place pressure on government, and in 1847 the Ten-Hours Act limited the working day to ten hours for women and younger workers.

Factory legislation, though explicitly targeted at the concerns of the working class, was also an expression of middle-class values. Bourgeois commentators had become increasingly scandalized by the fact that men and women were working together on the same factory floor and had begun pushing for a clearer separation of men's and women's work. The ultimate effect was to further exclude women from the more skilled trades.[45] The more mechanized that industrial production became, the more 'skill' came to be defined in terms of gender rather than ability or training.[46] As disparity between women's and men's wages increased, women's double burden of work and domestic chores (including child-rearing) became more onerous and apparent. But most women did not protest the disparity in wages. To the contrary, by the late nineteenth century, female labour leaders in Britain were arguing that a 'woman's job' should get a 'woman's wage' and that improvements of conditions for working women could not come at the expense of working men.[47] The idea of a family wage (where the man alone could earn enough money to support the entire family) looked increasingly attractive to both sexes. Men hitched their sense of masculine identity to their role as primary wage earner, and women sought relief from the double burden of work and domestic chores.[48] The move to the family wage not only further separated the labour of men and women, but it also provided an even stronger justification for male dominance within the family. As Friedrich Engels commented in 1891: 'In the great majority of cases today, at least in the possessing classes, the husband is obliged to earn a living and support his family, and that itself gives him a position of supremacy, without any need for special titles and privileges.'[49] The ideal of the family wage ensured that women continued to be excluded from the higher-skilled and higher-paid jobs, since they otherwise represented competition for male 'breadwinners'. A tradition that had begun with guilds, which had protected artisans from the control of capitalists in the early modern era, continued to ensure a gendering of work in the nineteenth century.[50]

Utopian Responses

The pressures that wage labour placed on families prompted some Europeans to think up radical solutions to the social and familial consequences of industrialization. In France, a group of social radicals formed a new church around the ideas of Charles Fourier and Claude Henri de Rouvroy, Comte de Saint-Simon. Fourier was a rather mystical self-taught philosopher who advocated the creation of self-contained communal societies that would end the dehumanization of labour by organizing production through interdependent work groups called phalanxes. This new organization, he argued, would balance out human passions and skills. Fourier believed that society could only progress if full sexual freedom were attained and the slavery of women ended. In 1808, he famously declared that 'the extension of the privileges of women is the general principle of all social progress', thus winning him a place in the hearts of future socialist feminists like Flora Tristan.[51] Saint-Simon was a Romantic philosopher who had written utopian pamphlets on the need to reorganize economic life around moral values. On Christmas Day 1829, his followers, the 'Saint-Simonians', named Prosper Enfantin (the son of a bankrupt banker) one of their two 'popes'. The group sought harmony between the classes, the equal valuation of all work and a peaceful process towards progressive social change. They believed that this could only be achieved through a religion where men and women were equally valued, and Enfantin promised that a female messiah would come to take the position of the second pope in the movement. He argued that social harmony could only be produced if male and female principles were brought into balance. In theory, he praised 'female' emotion over 'male' reason, but the movement continued to be governed by men despite the increased involvement of the movement's 'mother', Claire Bazard, who began to officiate at ceremonies in 1833. The Saint-Simonians also advocated free love and argued that sexual relationships should occur only on the basis of love, rather than with reference to considerations of family, class or socio-political needs. As Claire Moses has shown, however, these ideals provided only a thin cloak for what remained a sexual double standard that tolerated male promiscuity while tending to portray women as sexual temptresses.[52]

While the Saint-Simonians rapidly ran into legal problems and charges that their thought endangered public morals, they had a lasting influence in the inspiration they provided for early French feminism. In 1832, a group of Saint-Simonian women under the leadership of the working-class feminist Suzanne Voilquin founded a newspaper, *Tribune des femmes*. The paper was meant to represent a wide range of female experience and covered topics such as religion, work, sexual morality, marriage, economics and politics. To a far greater extent than Enfantin's mystical religion, the women of the *Tribune* attempted to blend 'sex consciousness' with 'class consciousness'.[53] While drawing inspiration from the communal living projects and the socialist critique of the early Saint-Simonian movement, these women recognized that Enfantin's preaching of sexual freedom made no sense to women who could be impoverished by single motherhood under the conditions of early capitalism. 'Saint-Simonian women emancipated themselves from male tutelage and created an independent women's movement, the first in history.'[54] They tried to convince women that they had a collective interest in fighting against male tutelage and in bringing about far-reaching social changes that would ensure women's material and emotional well-being.

The conflict between the interests of men and women, and the ability of early socialist movements to generate ideas about female emancipation, was also apparent in English Utopian Socialism. After 1829, groups inspired by the thinking of factory reformer Robert Owen began forming Communities of Mutual Association, utopian communities that promised to create a 'world turned upside down' by giving the 'productive classes a complete dominion over the fruits of their own industry' and eliminating all relationships of power and subordination.[55] The capitalist should no longer dominate the worker, the parent the child, or the man the woman. The Owenites argued that capitalists had purposely intensified gender conflict in order to further subdue the working classes and thwart their struggle against exploitation. Social radicals began to argue that only a change in the material circumstances of European society could alter the subordinated status of women. 'Under the withering influence of competition for wealth, mammon worship and an aristocracy of birth', wrote an Owenite woman in 1839, 'very little progress can be made in the attainment of true liberty for women ... . The only way left ... is to organize small societies on a better system, as examples and patterns to the rest of the world.'[56] The Owenites published hundreds of books, tracts and newspaper articles and travelled the country giving lectures in support of this new collective, egalitarian society. By the 1840s, London groups were delivering three lectures a week on 'women's rights' to large audiences.[57]

Owen believed that society could only be transformed if the 'human character' itself could be encouraged to nourish more harmonious relations. This meant reshaping sexual relations that subordinated women and creating a system of collectivized (though still exclusively female) housework and childcare. In his 1835 tract *Lectures on the Marriages of the Priesthood in the Old Immoral World*, Owen called for 'marriages of nature', formed out of affection rather than economic need. Owen's advocacy for 'free love' prompted one detractor to lament that his ideas would lead to the creation of 'one vast brothel' in every Owenite community. Women members of the movement also pointed out that free love could only benefit women if they had already achieved economic, social and political equality. Nonetheless, his ideas were extremely influential. They inspired Catherine Barmby and her husband Goodwyn to co-found the short-lived 'Communist Church' in 1841, which preached the doctrine of the coming of a 'Female Messiah' who would bring Owenite ideas on female equality to fruition.[58]

In February 1834, individual Owenite cooperatives merged to form a 'General Union of all Trades'. Although this organization was rent by conflicts between the different trades and lasted only seven months, it was feared by governments and attracted considerable female participation. Gender tension within this movement was symbolic of the larger tensions created by deskilling; women workers began to form their own unions as a defence against male resentment of the tendency of factory owners to replace skilled male labour with cheaper female unskilled labour.[59] While this direct conflict between male and female unionists was only a brief flare-up in the short-lived history of the General Union, it displayed underlying gender tensions of the capitalist system. As soon as Owen and his followers began suggesting a universal commitment to eliminating divisions between workers and accepting the principles of sexual egalitarianism, the distinctly gendered nature of early capitalism was exposed.[60] As the emergence of these utopian projects demonstrates, the twin disruptions of political revolution and massive economic change were creating the possibility for novel visions of social order and political practices. Those possibilities became even clearer in the middle of the nineteenth century, when a new wave of unrest crashed across the continent.

Revolution and New Political Ideas

As the historian James Sheehan has written, 'Revolutions are rare because they require an unusual conjunction of suffering and hope, a sense of outrage and an act of faith.'[61] Just such a situation prevailed in several European countries in the spring of 1848. Poor harvests since 1845 had fuelled an economic recession and financial panics, particularly where banks were still weak (as they were virtually everywhere outside of England). The Irish Potato Famine of the late 1840s, which caused a million deaths, was the most extreme case among many across Europe. A string of bankruptcies threw workers into the streets, and soldiers were frequently dispatched to quell urban riots. Fears were heightened by the Swiss Civil War (1847–48) and insurrections in Palermo, Sicily, and Naples in early 1848. But once again, the spark of pan-European revolution was ignited in Paris, where rioting had prompted soldiers to construct barricades and King Louis-Philippe was forced to abdicate. A new French Republic was declared on 24 February 1848. The unrest spread eastward right up to the Russian border. While specific political demands varied in each national case, a revolutionary atmosphere across the continent prompted many critiques of existing social, economic and political structures. In Germany, liberal student groups met at banquets and proclaimed the need to unify the nation. In Austria too, intellectuals signed petitions and demanded an end to repressive censorship laws. But the driving force behind the growing violence came from below.

Romantic political ideas about nationhood were not particularly relevant to the masses of hungry Europeans who gathered in the major cities in 1848 to protest their destitute state. Skyrocketing food prices sent people – often crowds of women – into the streets to scream at merchants who had upped their prices yet again or to storm potato stands (as in Prussia in 1847) to steal what they could not afford to buy. As news of events in Paris spread, workers and even domestic servants organized themselves into unions and began to demand higher wages and other improvements to their working conditions. Women were almost always involved in the strikes and political protests and were particularly active in food riots. In Germany, the experience led women like Louise Aston, Mathilde Anneke and Louise Otto-Peters to found women's newspapers and set up clubs and organizations dedicated to improving the plight of women in general and the plight of female workers in particular. The radicalizing experience of the 1848 revolution also spurred women like Anna Skimborowicz, Kazimiera Ziemiecka and Wincentyna Zablocka in Poland to form political organizations and publish reformist pamphlets and newspapers. In England, female members of the Chartist movement fought alongside their husbands and brothers for electoral reform. The Chartists fought for universal manhood suffrage and the removal of property requirements for elected officials. By the time the Chartists' third petition to Parliament was rejected in 1848, female membership had grown into the thousands and there were over 100 separate female-only Chartist groups. While they made some demands for women's rights, these groups mostly lobbied for working-class male political representation and a decent 'family wage' to sustain families without female and child labour. Nevertheless, activism within Chartism was a training ground for women who would later form their own organizations.[62] Others, like the Saint-Simonian women in France, broke away from their larger organization and used the revolutionary violence to underline the need for attention to specifically female concerns.[63] In April 1849, Jeanne Deroin, editor of a feminist newspaper, made history by standing as a candidate in a by-election, though she and Pauline Roland were later arrested and spent six months in a prostitute's prison for organizing a teachers' union.[64]

The revolutions brought some tangible political changes: the Second Republic was declared in France; limited constitutional reforms and moves towards parliamentary government were achieved in the German and Habsburg lands; and the Hungarians, under Louis Kossuth, got concessions from the Habsburg Empire. New constitutions were written in Naples, Piedmont-Sardinia, Tuscany and the Papal states. But the revolutions of 1848 left many regions virtually untouched, and political changes in central Europe were quickly reversed. The Hungarian revolutionaries were eventually defeated by the combined imperial forces of Austria and Russia. By 1851, soldiers loyal to their monarchs had defeated revolutionary aspirations in Austria, Prussia, Italy and France. Though monarchies were faltering and definitions of citizenship and soldierly duty were transforming in the middle of the nineteenth century, older forms of loyalty had not yet been replaced by broad-based class consciousness or bonds of solidarity that stretched beyond rather immediate and local concerns. As Eric Hobsbawm has argued, middle-class theorists of democratic revolution were careful to avoid unleashing the full fury of the masses, since doing so threatened their own property and livelihoods. Meanwhile, the labouring poor were 'strong enough to make the prospect of social revolution look real and menacing, [but] they were too weak to do more than frighten their enemies'.[65] Nevertheless, the experience of revolution fuelled the search for unifying ideologies of social change that went beyond the sealed-off communities of Chartism or Saint-Simonianism.

Above all, the revolution provided a venue for younger men to voice their concerns about new forms of patriarchy that were changing the social hierarchy and making it more difficult for them to establish themselves as heads of households. Journeymen were particularly numerous on the barricades in Berlin and Vienna, and they protested the growing gap in wages between various trades and their steadily decreasing chances of becoming a master. These arguments had a long history, particularly in France, where journeymen's complaints had led to special laws to protect the familial relationship between apprentices and their masters during the First Republic.[66] In the early nineteenth century, the pressures of the transition to wage labour and the disruption that this caused to patterns of family organization provided a significant impetus for the formation of radical democratic organizations based on the ideals of fraternalism.[67]

In France Pierre-Joseph Proudhon (1809–65) developed a brand of socialism that sought the return of male dignity damaged by the factory work of women and the diminishing role of artisans. 'Women's place is in the home [*la femme au foyer*]', Proudhon proclaimed, receiving support from socialists in other countries, like Ferdinand Lassalle in Germany.[68] The initial inspiration for socialist ideology in the mid-nineteenth century was thus the goal to create a brotherhood of male workers to revolt against patriarchy in the workplace. But Proudhon's 'mutualism' (as his socialist ideas came to be called) was quickly outshone by a theory that portrayed industrialization as having emancipatory potential for both men and women. Karl Marx (1818–83) developed an analysis of mid-century European capitalism directly out of his experiences as a political radical during the revolutionary years before and after 1848. Unlike the socialist utopians before him, Marx argued that true social progress could not be achieved by setting up isolated communities. Instead, he sought to demonstrate to European workers that they had to transform the exploitative property relations that stood at the heart of the capitalist system.

In 1859, Marx argued that the economic system under which goods in any society are produced determines how the members of that society perceive the world. 'The mode of production of material life', he argued, 'determines the general character of the social, political and spiritual processes of life.'[69] It followed from this that modern European societies depended upon a specific type of property relations (private property being held by the wealthy, who also owned the means of production – the factories), which also determined the types of social interaction and created a social hierarchy of classes. For those who laboured in the factory, this system of production and property ownership created new fetters – new types of oppression that the strikes and social revolutions of the mid-nineteenth century were beginning to fight against. Under capitalist conditions as Marx observed them at mid-century, workers were 'alienated' from their labour since both how they worked and what they produced were now completely controlled by the employer. It was the bourgeois – the owner of the factory – who reaped the financial and material rewards of the workers' labours.

Together with his long-time collaborator Friedrich Engels (1820–95), Marx also insisted that marriage represented a similar kind of exploitative property relationship. Relying on Marx's notes after his death, Engels concluded in *The Origin of the Family* that 'Within the family [the husband] is the bourgeois and the wife represents the proletariat.'[70] Both Marx and Engels believed that this oppressive power of men over women would only end when capitalist relations of production were destroyed. Only the revolution of the proletariat and the abolishment of private property relations could end women's slavery. Marx and Engels acknowledged that women's lot in nineteenth-century capitalism was more dire than men's. They were subjected to a 'double oppression', because they received half the wages of men. Employers justified this lower pay with the argument that women were supported by their husbands, yet lower wages also kept women dependent upon a male primary wage-earner.[71] Marx and Engels argued that in a capitalist system women could only create a political space outside of the domestic sphere by engaging in wage labour. Economic equity would have to come before political equality.[72]

The intervention of Marx and Engels definitively transformed socialist discussions of gender relations. In 1891, the German socialist August Bebel revised his previously published book *Woman and Socialism* to reflect Engels's arguments. Bebel argued for women's rights to vote, to property, to dress comfortably and to personal sexual satisfaction. Bebel in turn inspired a generation of socialist feminists in Germany, the most prominent of whom – Clara Zetkin (1857–1933) – went on to become a founder of the German Communist Party in 1918 and a delegate to the German parliament in 1920. Marxism also inspired feminists in France, such as Hubertine Auclert (1848–1914) and Madeleine Pelletier (1874–1939), and in Russia, particularly Aleksandra Kollontai (1873–1952), who in 1917 was elected Commissar for Social Welfare in the Soviet government.

All over Europe, socialist feminists grappled with the problem of how to achieve both sexual equality and a proletarian revolution. No dilemma better demonstrates how gendered oppression was intertwined with and often inseparable from class oppression in the era of industrialization.[73] Having aligned themselves with the socialist movement, feminists adopted an identity – that of the worker – whose imagery ran counter to the dominant imagery of womanhood, which continued to be linked to motherhood in all European societies. Despite the fact that women had worked as wage labourers since the very beginning of industrialization, they were always marginal to the symbolic language of workers' movements. In fact, women's involvement in socialist movements often provided rhetorical fuel to conservatives, who took it as a sign of danger and decadence. '*L-ouvrière* [female worker]!', French historian Jules Michelet (1798–1874) sputtered, 'impious, sordid word that no language has ever known, that no age ever understood before this age of iron, and that holds in the balance all our supposed progress!'[74] In cases where groups of female workers did manage to assert a specific public identity, they had to operate within the framework of existing cultural stereotypes and were rarely granted a public voice to assert identities of their own making. For instance, when 5,000 female tobacco workers created a media sensation by rioting in Seville in 1896, their communications with journalists were coloured by the image of the strong-willed yet intensely feminine *cigarrera* (female tobacco worker) made famous by Georges Bizet's opera *Carmen* (1875). Journalists, in other words, relied on stereotypes of fiery country girls and tended not to take women seriously as political actors.[75]

The imagery of the worker as male became even more ubiquitous as socialist movements gained momentum across Europe, and particularly after the Russian Revolution in 1917. Communism became closely identified with masculine strength; both the armed soldier and the muscular worker provided the iconic symbols of a movement that hoped to bring about world revolution.[76] Socialist feminists like Clara Zetkin in Germany did hope that socialism would bring about equal rights for women when she argued that 'the liberation struggle of the proletarian woman ... must be a joint struggle with the male of her class against the entire class of capitalists'.[77] But the strength of masculine imagery in communist propaganda greatly complicated efforts to rhetorically link the struggle of the worker with the struggle for women's rights. In practice, feminist priorities generally took a back seat to socialist priorities, and socialist feminists were influenced and constrained by the common argument that socialist revolution had to precede the granting of equal rights to the sexes. This meant that socialist feminists who campaigned too single-mindedly for women's rights were often accused by their ideological brethren of being counterproductive or even seeking to delay the proletarian revolution.

Liberal feminists had an easier time reconciling their politics with their feminism. Despite the failures of the revolutionary era to instil the conviction that 'human rights' also implied 'women's rights', liberals who sought the improvement of women's political position in European society could appeal directly to the most basic tenets of liberal belief. The most influential liberal to do so was John Stuart Mill (1806–73). In close cooperation with his wife, Harriet Taylor Mill (1807–58), Mill built on the liberal theories outlined in *Principles of Political Economy* (1848) and *On Liberty* (1859) to advocate for the inclusion of women in the liberal defini-tion of rights. Mill (a member of Parliament) brought petitions in favour of women's suffrage before the British Parliament, though they were voted down in 1867. In 1869, Mill wrote his *On the Subjection of Women*, in which he argued that many of society's social problems could be traced back to the unequal treatment of men and women.[78] The essay was immediately translated into many languages (including Danish, Polish, French and Spanish) and helped to inspire liberal feminists across Europe. But most nineteenth-century (and many twentieth-century) liberals con-tinued to believe that the right to participate in politics should be tied to the right to own property. Since European women rarely owned property or were legally excluded from the right to do so, liberal arguments about equal rights also came up against economic and social realities. It was not only the working classes, in other words, whose gender relations were structured by economic change and industrial-ization.

Separation of Spheres

We have already taken note of the separation of home and working lives among the working classes of industrializing Europe. This separation was perhaps even more pronounced among the middle classes – the property owners, civil servants, profes-sionals and managers of the new capitalist economy. As these classes benefited from their role in driving industrialization and urbanization, their homes ceased being sites of production (such as the making of clothes, which could now be bought) and became places of relaxation and contemplation. Improvements in public transporta-tion also made it possible for the wealthy to remove themselves from increasingly crowded and filthy industrial cities and to build comfortable homes on the outskirts of town.

This separation of work and home reinforced and was made possible by class dis-tinctions. Middle- and upper-class families relied on domestic servants to perform any dirty, demeaning or laborious domestic chores. The 'unhygienic' homes of the lower classes were looked down upon, which intensified class prejudice. Cleanliness was thus a marker of middle-class values and the lack of it an 'obstacle to equality and improvement'.[79] The homes of the wealthy (and those striving to improve their social standing) were thus consciously organized to contrast with lower-class mayhem and mess. Houses were divided into 'living' areas for the primary inhabitants and 'domestic' areas for the servants. Doors and individual bedrooms, a luxury previously only enjoyed by the aristocracy, became a standard feature of bourgeois homes in the nineteenth century, thus vastly increasing individual privacy and the ability to withdraw in solitude.[80] The middle classes treated bodily functions of any kind as vulgar and unmentionable, and they used their class prerogatives and economic power to pass these nasty tasks to the lower classes whenever possible. Even nursing one's own baby was considered a job better suited to a lower-class wet nurse. The term 'back passages' came to refer both to the halls and doorways used only by servants in the mansions of the rich and to 'unmentionable' parts of the anatomy associated with waste.[81]

For some, the association between servants and bodily functions provided titillation. Middle-class men often sought out lower-class women for casual sexual liaisons. Lingering memories of physical warmth from lower-class nannies and nursemaids explain part of the attraction. Sigmund Freud was certainly not alone in remembering that his first sexual feelings had been for his nursemaid. But, as Leonore Davidoff has persuasively argued in her account of the relationship between Arthur J. Munby (a minor poet, writer and civil servant, who was supported mostly by his wealthy family) and Hannah Cullwick (a scullery maid), crossing the class boundary provided a thrill in itself.[82] Munby spent most of his time between 1859 and 1898 studying the lives of women who toiled at the most physically demanding forms of labour (in homes, mines and factories). He sketched them, took dozens of pictures of them and recorded his thoughts about their lives in his diaries. He eventually married Cullwick, with whom he had a decades-long secret affair. Davidoff argues that the fact that he was completely uninterested in women of his own class and instead equated 'dirt and degradation with female strength and love' reveals a fundamental contradiction of Victorian society. 'The sheltered lives that middle-class ladies were supposed to lead depended directly on the labor of working-class girls and women, who through their service created the material conditions necessary to maintain a middle-class life-style for men and women alike.'[83]

Middle-class women, unlike working-class women, could generally afford to stay out of the paid labour force. Indeed, having a 'woman of leisure' at home became an important indication of status for middle-class families.[84] Women were also responsible for navigating the increasingly complex selection of consumer goods, selecting clothing and home decorations that would best signal the bourgeois status of the family.[85] In late nineteenth-century Germany, families scrambling their way up the social ladder (or those fearing that they were falling down it) often scrimped on groceries rather than give up their domestic servant. Even with this domestic help, the woman was expected to spend the majority of her time caring for her family within the home. Images of the 'angel of the house' who protected the safe haven of the home from the harshness of the outside world proliferated in the novels, advice manuals and political rhetoric of late nineteenth-century Europe.[86] An 1877 Spanish pedagogical pamphlet defined the woman's role as being 'an angel of love, consolation to our afflictions, defender of our merits, patient sufferer of our faults, faithful guardian of our secrets, and jealous depository of our honor'.[87] An 1889 Swedish housekeeping manual preached a similar ideology to its readers when it observed that

> A man who spends his day away from the family, who has to work outside the home, counts on finding a restful and refreshing atmosphere when he returns home, and sometimes even a little merriment and surprise. A good man who … provides for his family … has the right to expect this, and it is his wife's duty to ensure that he is not disappointed in his expectation … [S]he can thus continue to keep her influence over him and retain his affection undiminished.[88]

This 'domestic ideology' was part of a conscious effort to set middle-class values apart from both working-class mores and the 'immoral' values of the aristocracy. While the argument that women were predestined for domestic duties was certainly not new (Aristotle argued that 'A good wife should be the mistress of her home', and insisted that her only goal should be 'to obey her husband; giving no heed to public affairs'), the ideology of separate spheres was a particularly forceful organizing concept in the lives of middle-class families in the nineteenth century.[89] Domestic ideology drew on Enlightenment thinkers like Rousseau and was further reinforced by critics like John Ruskin. Ruskin insisted that men and women were entirely different, though infinitely compatible: 'Each has what the other has not: each completes the other, and is completed by the other: they are nothing alike, and the happiness and perfection of both depends on each asking and receiving from the other what the other only can give.'[90]

The importance of a separation of spheres was reinforced by the growth of various Christian movements across Europe. Evangelical movements in Great Britain, pietism in Germany and a revival of strict Catholicism in France reinforced a strict code of moral values within the middle classes and sought to instil a self-reflective moral code into everyday behaviour. Groups like the Clapham sect (a group that wanted to reform the Church of England from within) sought to encourage a new national morality through pamphlets, sermons, manuals and travelling preachers. Influential preachers of this message, like William Wilberforce and Hannah More, insisted that God's will could only be carried out by Christians who subjected themselves to constant self-criticism and who interpreted the political and social questions of the day in strictly moral, Christian terms. Sin, they argued, was a grave threat to the family that could only be combated if women stood steadfast as the protectors of the private sphere.[91] Hannah More directly countered Mary

Wollstonecraft's idea that education would elevate women so that they could demonstrate that they deserved legal and political equality with men. For evangelicals, the 'natural' division between the sexes was a rule of nature that had to be reinforced rather than undermined if the family was to survive the social changes of industrialization. While strict followers of such beliefs remained in the minority, their influence cannot be underestimated. By the 1830s and 1840s, the language of these evangelical preachers had begun to colour government reports and made it easier for middle-class commentators to preach a mode of living that only the wealthy could attain.[92]

Separate spheres ideology affected not only European working practices and religious sensibilities, but the practice of politics as well. As political life expanded in the wake of democratic revolutions, theorists and politicians alike began to see the 'public sphere' or the space 'made up of private people gathered together as a public and articulating the needs of society with the state' as a central political arena in which political opinions could be formulated and political progress achieved.[93] European women's exclusion from clubs and associations that were the venues of social discussion and places of debate limited their abilities to influence the shape of politics and society even after they had achieved the right to vote over the course of the twentieth century.[94]

But we must point out that domestic ideology, like any ideology, had its cracks and could never entirely describe or control lived reality. The vision of the home as a haven hid the fact that for many it was the site of abuse, mistrust and unhappiness.[95] 'The sweetness of home depended upon the drudgery of numerous servants',[96] and when budgets did not allow for them, middle-class wives and daughters toiled to live up to the exacting standards of bourgeois etiquette and decorum. Along with these servants, many women and men never married at all. Out of choice or because they were excluded, they spent their lives without the lived experience, though still under the social influence, of domestic ideology.[97] While formally excluded from political life, some women had access to the public sphere through their activities as writers, charity organizers and – particularly in England – Methodist preachers and Anglican deaconesses.[98]

Finally, not all married individuals convinced of the ideology actually followed its dictates. Many married men were quite involved in domestic life. Take, for instance, the case of Edward Benson, a teacher at Rugby School and Wellington College in the mid-nineteenth century. With his family life based very close to his place of work, Benson involved himself deeply in the moral and intellectual lives of his wife and children. In families like this, the genders were separated more by temperament and emotion than by space and time.[99] Benson's wife did not experience her role in the family as personally fulfilling, and the emotional development of his sons also suffered from their father's insistence on maintaining a strict form of almost public decorum at home. All three of his sons turned away from the family ideal and associated themselves with the 'Uranians', an influential group of writers interested in 'the aesthetic and spiritual appeal of younger and adolescent men'.[100] The ability of the Benson children to abandon the domestic order instituted by their father and to explore alternative and (for the time) scandalous sexual identities was the other side of the story of gender and the Industrial Revolution.

Urbanization, Sexual Danger and the Creation of Sexual Identities

The late nineteenth and early twentieth centuries witnessed the transformation of many towns into cities and many cities into full-scale metropolitan areas. In 1800, London was the only city in Europe with a population of more than one million. By 1900, five more cities gained the status of metropolis: Paris, Vienna, Berlin, Moscow and St Petersburg. Whereas only twenty-two European cities had populations of more than 100,000 before 1800, by 1900 there were eighty cities with populations over 100,000.[101]

Industrialization and urbanization provided Europeans with unprecedented possibilities for social and physical mobility. By 1902, London, Budapest, Glasgow, Paris and Berlin all had systems of rapid transportation, with some underground railway lines. Also by the turn of the century, advances in metallurgy had helped make possible the mass production of bicycles, which provided women in particular with a socially acceptable means of transporting themselves unchaperoned across urban and rural spaces.[102] The spectacle of women racing across towns on mechanized vehicles wearing modified and 'masculine' clothing greatly worried conservative observers. Doctors and hygienists in France and elsewhere launched campaigns to try to restrict women's access to cycling on the grounds of protecting their reproductive health and social propriety.[103] But the bicycle (and women on them) became an accepted feature of modern cities, where people could move relatively anonymously and quickly.

Cities provided an escape from the constraints of kinship networks and tight-knit communities that had carefully regulated sexual behaviour and courtship rituals. People with similar interests and sensibilities could more easily gather in spaces outside of the control of disapproving family members and other upholders of traditional norms. In cities like London and Berlin, networks of 'inverts', 'Uranians' and 'mannish' women were established. These networks, and the stories behind them, have only recently become visible to historians, thanks to the labours of scholars inspired by the lesbian and gay rights movements of the 1970s and 1980s.[104] Their initial research set out to find traces of 'authentic' sexualities of the past that had been repressed by political policy and social taboo and suppressed by traditional histories that relegated these stories to the margins or discussed them only in terms of perversity. But viewing the past as providing 'legitimating antecedents to the present' has its pitfalls, as Ludmilla Jordanova has convincingly pointed out.[105] While it is undeniably true that cities provided space for alternative sexual expression that was simply not possible in claustrophobic villages, it would be misleading to presume that what we are finding are 'authentic' sexualities, released from their closets. A closer look at these sexual subcultures reveals that sexual gay and lesbian identities were created in a symbiotic relationship with the larger culture. These subcultures and the very identity of being 'homosexual' or 'lesbian' surfaced at different times across Europe. Randolph Trumbach has argued that identifiable homosexual subcultures arose in the larger European cities (Paris, Amsterdam and London) around 1700.[106] But other historians have pointed out that the existence of a community of men who only wanted to have sex with men is not identical to the existence of what we would today call homosexual identities. The idea that one is either innately and unchangeably homosexual or heterosexual seems to have solidified in Europe and North America only in the late nineteenth and early twentieth centuries.[107] Even after middle-class 'inverts' started thinking of themselves as homosexuals, working-class men were still viewing their sexual activities with other men in a more pragmatic way.

Jeffrey Weeks's exploration of male homosexual prostitution in late nineteenth-century England demonstrates that homosexual identities did not inevitably emerge from homosexual behaviours in this period. As early as the 1720s, a homosexual subculture was developing in Britain's larger cities, centred around 'Molly houses', pubs, public parks and lavatories. These centres of sexual exchange were known as 'markets'. All classes came together in these spaces, and the 'cash nexus' dominated – in other words, sex took place after an exchange or a promise of money or 'gifts'. By the last decades of the nineteenth century, the word 'trade' was in common use to describe any male homosexual act, whether or not a cash exchange took place.[108] The upper-class participants in this subculture, most of whom led 'respectable' family lives and sought out the markets in secret, were often searching for the thrill of crossing the class divide by having sex with lower-class men. These 'rough trade' recipients of their gifts, on the other hand, did not consider themselves to be homosexuals and often saw their prostitution as an expedient means of survival. Thus what we would today call a homosexual subculture was created that depended upon and was nurtured by the class divides of the industrializing city and the economic inequalities that it produced.

The most famous example of how this kind of cross-class relationship could lead to ruin was the case of the playwright Oscar Wilde. Wilde pushed the boundaries of public decorum, subtly (and later openly) calling attention to his sexual predilections. In 1892, he and several associates wore green carnations to the opening of his play, *Lady Windermere's Fan*. He insisted that this was simply a symbol of 'subtle artistic temperament', but others noted that the wearers of the green carnation all had the same 'waggle', and these observers took this as an emblem of homosexuality.[109] In 1895, Wilde took the Marquess of Queensbury (the father of his lover Lord Alfred Douglas) to court on libel charges for having called him a 'Somdomite' (*sic*). At the trial in April, the defence named several boys whom Wilde had solicited, and Wilde's case collapsed. Soon after, he was arrested for gross indecency under

Section 11 of Criminal Law Amendment Act of 1885. Two criminal trials eventually led to Wilde's conviction. He died of meningitis in November 1900, having sustained an ear infection while serving a two-year prison sentence. Wilde's fame, and even his witty rejoinders at his trials, guaranteed a new appreciation of the presence of homosexual subcultures in Europe. Having made use of the new public spaces and opportunities for sexual adventure that the modern metropolis afforded, Wilde was undone by the glaring light that this new public sphere shed upon private behaviours.

By the 1920s, the big cities of Europe were increasingly looked upon as dens of sexual vice. The Austrian essayist Stefan Zweig described the scene in Berlin:

All values were changed, and ... Berlin was transformed into the Babylon of the world. Bars, amusement parks, honky-tonks sprang up like mushrooms ... along the Kurfürstendamm powdered and rouged young men sauntered and they were not all professionals; every high school boy wanted to earn some money and in the dimly lit bars one might see government officials and men of the world of finance tenderly courting drunken sailors without any shame. Even the Rome of Suetonius had never known such orgies as the pervert balls of Berlin, where hundreds of men costumed as women and hundreds of women as men danced under the benevolent eyes of the police. In the collapse of all values a kind of madness gained hold particularly in the bourgeois circles which until then had been unshakeable in their probity.[110]

Similarly, urban lesbian subcultures sprang up in Berlin and Paris. Unlike their male counterparts, lesbians could rely on a tolerance for female 'romantic friendships' that had been widespread in Europe for centuries.[111] In the early twentieth century they could also rely on the cloak of fashion to obscure their activities. With 'mannish' clothes all the rage in the roaring twenties, they did not immediately mark women as having same-sex desires.[112] Prominent actresses like Marlene Dietrich played with the new possibilities for individual expression offered by the image of the 'new woman' with her boyish dress and hairstyles. Radclyffe Hall's semi-autobiographical novel *The Well of Loneliness* (1928) described the life of a female 'invert' who dressed and acted like a man. Hall was somewhat successful in gaining sympathy for lesbians by describing their condition as congenital.[113] Her novel was banned soon after publication but became an underground success. Films of the 1920s also helped to publicize the gender-bending of metropolitan culture, while generally emphasizing its dangers.[114]

The new public spaces that the city afforded created new venues for enacting gendered identities. The most iconic representative of the modern male urbanite was the *flâneur*, a character made famous by the French lyric poet Charles Baudelaire. Resembling the English dandy, the flâneur strolled through the newly built arcades of Paris and other metropolitan cities, seeing and being seen in the new public spaces of the modern city. This cosmopolitanism was 'a bourgeois male pleasure' not open to women (who could not walk so freely without danger to their reputations or their physical well-being) or to the underprivileged (who would not have been socially accepted in all spaces).[115] In their great attention to clothing and decoration, dandies and flâneurs set themselves apart from 'masculine' men and from those who could not afford their attention to style. 'They made a morality of the aesthetic of the everyday.'[116] Only men of privilege had the means to observe the city from a safe place and record its dangers and allures. The eye of the journalist recording sensational scandals, Arthur Munby's prurient interest in the lives of working women and Baudelaire's flâneur all had something in common: the city for them was a venue for voyeurism.

Baudelaire described the flâneur in his famous 1863 essay 'The Painter of Modern Life': 'The crowd is his domain, just as the air is the bird's, and water that of the fish. His passion and his profession is to merge with the crowd.'[117] The practice became fashionable after Louis Napoleon put Baron Georges Hausmann in charge of modernizing Paris. Hausmann reorganized the city: he straightened out roads, created long thoroughfares, tore down slums and began installing gas lamps in the 1850s. The goal was to modernize and make the city less susceptible to rebellions and revolution. But the reconstruction displaced thousands and further separated the poor from the areas, lit by gas lamps, where those with means could comfortably stroll. Baudelaire's 1857 collection of poems *Les Fleurs du Mal* described the possibilities for decadence and eroticism that this new city offered. The book was censored by the French government: six poems were removed on 'moral' grounds, and Baudelaire and his publisher were fined. But the obscenity trial only served to increase Baudelaire's fame. The collection contained several poems dedicated to the theme of lesbian love. His poem 'Lesbos', which incorrectly associated an island in classical Athens with female same-sex intercourse (in reality the island was famous for the practice of oral sex in general), helped bring the word 'lesbian' into European languages.

Walter Benjamin, the famous German philosopher and social critic, recognized that Baudelaire's poems presented 'woman as allegory of the modern'. On the one hand, the urban prostitute was modern because she represented the ultimate commodification of the female sex, whose specific characteristics had already been blurred by wage labour and work in industrial factories.[118] Lesbians, on the other hand, represented both a protest against modernity through their unwillingness to be commodified, and a testament to the new social conditions created in large urban areas.[119] Baudelaire's association between lesbians and the modern city would continue to influence French ideas about female same-sex love. In the 1920s, the tendencies of flâneurs to use the public spaces of the city to flaunt their sexuality were often juxtaposed against lesbians' more secretive practices.[120] But both flâneurs and lesbians showed how the modern city created spaces for alternative sexualities.

The image of the metropolis as a place of sexual sin was accentuated by the increasingly visible presence of prostitution. Prostitution was, of course, nothing new. But urbanization in the era of industrialization produced social conditions that were particularly conducive to the growth of commodified sex. Rural women who sought domestic service in the homes of the urban middle classes proved to be in a particularly vulnerable situation. If they continued to follow the courtship rituals of their rural villages, they could easily be left pregnant and abandoned by their suitors, who were now no longer acting under the watchful eyes of a small community. Employers often presented another danger, since the man of the house could rely on his unquestioned authority and his maid's innocence and vulnerability to assert 'rights' to sexual access. If these acts resulted in pregnancy or were discovered by the lady of the house, the girl was inevitably fired and left to fend for herself in the harsh city. Having 'fallen' she was likely to avoid the shame of returning to her rural home. Under these circumstances, prostitution often provided the only means of survival. Others resorted to prostitution only 'unprofessionally' as a way of attaining some small luxuries or as a supplement to wages that were too low for subsistence.[121] It is important to note that the line between professional and casual prostitution is difficult to draw. To understand who the prostitutes of turn-of-the-century Europe were and why they resorted to renting their bodies, one must understand all the aspects of prostitution as a social institution. This also means understanding that the *demand* for prostitution was growing at this time. The Victorian ideology of sexual restraint (which we will discuss in more detail in Chapter 5) encouraged men to believe that sexual satisfaction (as opposed to the sober production of children) could not be found in the home. The ritual visitation to a brothel indeed became a rite of passage for the middle-class male.[122]

The growth of prostitution prompted a feminist response, particularly in Great Britain and Germany. After 1869, Josephine Butler's Ladies National Association fought single-mindedly against the Contagious Diseases Acts passed by the English Parliament in 1864, 1866 and 1869. The 'Acts' were originally motivated by the desire to protect soldiers from venereal infection. They called for the mandatory examination of prostitutes for venereal disease, while leaving male customers entirely uncontrolled.[123] They followed a pattern already established by French authorities, who had drawn on the theories of Alexandre Jean-Baptiste Parent-Duchatelet's 1836 book *De la Prostitution dans la ville de Paris* to create a system of regulation for the prostitutes of the city of Paris.[124] Butler and her followers were outraged at the double standard implied by regulation. Worse, after being 'registered' by authorities, women had a much harder time leaving a life of prostitution for more respectable work. The abolitionists – or 'repealers' as they were known in Britain – sought to protect 'fallen' women by campaigning for the repeal of the Acts.[125] They inspired similar movements across Europe and North America, particularly in Germany.[126] But the repealers' tactics often produced unintended consequences. Playing up the imagery of under-age girls being entrapped and forced into prostitution, the repealers consistently represented women involved in prostitution as 'innocent victims of male lust'. They downplayed the agency of the prostitutes themselves and reinforced patriarchal values by calling on working-class men to protect 'their' women.[127] Although they succeeded in getting the Acts suspended in 1883, Butler and her followers also helped to reinforce the prevalent gender stereotypes of the day; the passive, asexual and vulnerable female and the lustful, powerful and patriarchal male. They inspired a string of sensationalistic newspaper articles in the *Pall Mall Gazette* (W. T. Stead's 'Maiden Tribute of Modern Babylon series') that detailed 'true' accounts of girls being sold into sexual slavery. The Maiden Tribute essays prompted the passage in 1885 of the Law Amendment Act (mentioned above), which raised the age of consent for girls from thirteen to sixteen, but also gave police far-reaching controls and made consenting sexual acts between men a crime.[128] In trying to combat the sexual dangers of the cities, Butler and other abolitionists reinforced gender norms that further restricted the possibilities for individual sexual choice.

Nonetheless, these anti-vice campaigns were enormously successful in raising questions about sexual violence and unequal power relations between the genders. They helped to inspire more broad-based feminist movements everywhere in Europe. A vast network of women's organizations sprang up across Europe at the close of the nineteenth century. While some were engaged in active political campaigns to gain women equal political rights with men, most were primarily occupied with the search for social policies that would allow urban women to live more secure and fulfilling lives within industrial society. The word 'feminist' is often attributed to Charles Fourier, but was in fact first used in French medical textbooks of the 1870s and popularized by the novelist Alexandre Dumas. In its original medical form, 'feminism' referred to a feminization of the male body. In Dumas' anti-feminist usage it described the 'virilization of women', or women who acted like men. In both cases, the word connoted a confusion between the sexes: 'Feminism is the appearance of man in woman or of woman in man.'[129] The word spread into other European languages in the 1890s, and unsurprisingly found little favour with activist women.

Middle-class activists in particular took the word 'feminism' (and sometimes used it) as a slur, feeling that it did not describe their efforts to better the lot of women of various classes through reform rather than revolution.[130] Rather than concentrating on achieving equality with men (as the current usage of the word usually implies) liberal feminist movements on the continent (particularly in Germany and France) tended to devote themselves primarily to welfare work with the underprivileged or to the promotion of education for middle-class girls. These movements arose, in other words, as a reaction to the pressures of industrialization, its social dangers and new challenges. Leaders of the bourgeois movements, like Helene Lange (1848–1930) and Gertrud Bäumer (1873–1954) in Germany, or Maria Deraismes (1828–94) in France, were intent upon working within their respective political systems to improve social conditions for women. Bäumer openly rejected the word feminist, and long after women had gained the right to vote in Germany in 1918, she kept insisting that the true goal of the women's movement had never been formal equality or the outward trappings of political power, but rather to engender 'feminine-civil responsibility ... for the preservation and improvement of the biological substance of her people'.[131] Like their socialist counterparts, bourgeois feminists in Europe were often more focused on economic and social conditions – the negative consequences of rapid industrialization – than on abstract principles and rights. They tended to remain closely wedded to male political parties (particularly in France, where they feared for the survival of the fragile liberal republic), and they dreaded being viewed as unpatriotic or lacking in propriety.[132]

There were, of course, exceptions. Hubertine Auclert was prepared to be declared unladylike when she began overturning voting urns and making radical speeches that made her more moderate feminist colleagues blanch. After the 1890s, Millicent Garrett Fawcett's National Union of Women's Suffrage Societies (NUWSS) set out to use constitutional means and steady, but non-violent, tactics to achieve the vote for British women. In Germany, Anita Augsburg and Lida Gustava Heymann formed the German Union for Women's Suffrage in 1902, organized a meeting of the International Woman Suffrage Alliance meeting in Berlin in 1904, and continued to work tirelessly for women's political rights up to the Nazi era. But by far the most visible campaign to achieve female suffrage was waged by British members of the Women's Social and Political Union. Members of the WSPU were by no means typical of other European feminists in terms of their strategies and convictions.[133] But the publicity accorded to their struggle produced such strong reactions across Europe that this particular moment in the history of feminism can be taken as evidence of a striking shift in European discourse about women's relationship to the public sphere.

The WSPU was founded in 1903 by Emmeline Pankhurst (1858–1928) and her daughters Christabel (1880–1958) and Sylvia (1882–1960). Having been forced to provide for herself and her daughters after her husband's early death, Emmeline was moved by the plight of working women and found other feminist groups too timid and compliant with male wishes. She became disillusioned with the socialist movement and its continued exclusion of women. Inspired particularly by the ideas of Christabel, she began to insist that men only understood violence. She and her daughters set about bringing attention to the cause of women's suffrage in extremely public ways. They certainly succeeded. Through various acts of violence and public protest (firebombing, breaking windows, chaining themselves to railings, disrupting political meetings, and hunger strikes) the 'suffragettes' – as the press soon dubbed members of the WSPU – drew attention to their cause and created public furore. In a brilliant public relations move later emulated by other activist groups, the women seized a word used to demean them – suffragette – and made it their own, turning a slur into an identity. After Herbert Asquith, who was adamantly against women's suffrage, became Prime Minister in 1908, Emmeline and her followers led seven processions to Hyde Park in London, where they attracted crowds of up to 300,000.[134] When jailed and force-fed for their hunger strikes in 1909, the suffragettes made sure that their depiction of this indignity as a kind of sexual assault made it into the press. On 18 November 1910 (a day later called Black Friday), police stopped a group of 300 suffragists from marching to Parliament. The women faced physical assault: their arms were twisted; their throats were grabbed; their breasts were pinched; they were thrown to the ground and kicked. The authorities made it very clear that these women, by taking charge of public space, had overstepped the boundaries of their gender. In return, they were treated like 'public' women – a euphemism for prostitutes.[135] On 4 June 1913, Emily Wilding Davison (1872–1913) drew attention to the suffragette cause by attempting to grab the reins of the King's horse, Anmer, at the Epsom Derby. She died a few days later of a fractured skull. While it was unclear whether she had meant to commit suicide, and while she was viewed by the WSPU leadership as a reckless militant, fellow suffragettes decided to turn her rash act into a martyrdom, and at her funeral they marched in white dresses in front of large crowds, giving the coffin a military salute.[136] The suffragettes only gave up their militant tactics when the First World War made such violent protest seem unpatriotic and self-defeating.

The suffragettes epitomized the new possibilities for political organization that urbanization and mass communication provided. Their extremely public protests were attempts to turn the public spaces of densely populated cities into a battleground of the sexes. Since their campaign was interrupted by the war, we cannot today determine whether their visible protests advanced the cause of female suffrage. It is tempting to view their strategies as publicity stunts. But theirs was an original insight. They recognized that modern cities provided new venues for gender conflict and for the manipulation of gender stereotypes. In forcing men (policemen) to assert masculine rights through physical violence and in refusing to portray 'respectable' ladies who demurely ceded public spaces to male power, the suffragettes both exposed the physical violence that lurked behind separate spheres ideology and challenged the confinement of women to the private sphere. They relied on society's understandings of proper male and female behaviour in order to tear down these categories. They performed gender roles in order to subvert them.[137] Davison's dramatic protest was immortalized on film and shown in newsreels across the country.[138] A new era of publicity had arrived.

Conclusion

We have seen throughout this chapter that the transformation of labour and the processes of urbanization wrought by the Industrial Revolution fundamentally changed gender relations and discourse about the public roles of men and women. The introduction of wage labour destroyed the traditional family economy, leading to the massive disruption of traditional patterns of family and community life. It placed a premium on forms of labour that directly earned a wage and devalued 'women's' work done in the home. The harsh conditions of early capitalism, the oversupply of labour in industrializing areas and the social vulnerability and isolation of country folk who had only recently made their way to the cities, all helped fuel arguments that a single 'family wage' earned by a male head of the household was the best way to protect the interests of wives and children, who were increasingly viewed as dependants. Class distinctions were intensified as middle-class women sought to establish social status and shield themselves from dirt by employing domestic servants. Religious revivals across the continent helped reinforce the image of woman as the angel of the household, whose primary role was to provide emotional support for her family. Unlike the various 'domestic goddesses' who would succeed her, however, this nineteenth-century homemaker was primarily a phenomenon of the wealthier classes. The vast majority of women toiled – either in wage labour, in the shops and small businesses of their husbands, on the streets and in the bawdy houses of the urban centres or in the homes of the wealthy – simply to ensure their survival. Their working lives became more complex than they had been in small rural communities, since they were often removed from family networks and community cooperatives that could help to raise children or pool resources for the preparation of food and clothing. For these women, the Industrial Revolution could hardly have seemed like progress.

And yet, the city did extend opportunities to women and to marginalized men. Wage labour could lead to independence from strict family control, and the cities provided unprecedented possibilities for mobility, entertainment and individual choice. Despite the dangers of anonymity, cities also provided spaces for the development of new subcultures. Individuals interested in same-sex relationships could find each other in cities and remain relatively free from the intervention of their families and tight community norms. For these individuals, public space among the masses in urban centres provided a welcome respite from the strictures of tradition, even if – as Oscar Wilde found to his pain – it also created the conditions for much more public scandal and opprobrium.

The effects of industrialization and urbanization on individual men and women and their family and career choices can only be described as ambivalent. The city both reinforced and contradicted separate spheres ideology. Industrial wage labour brought about a gendering of women's and men's work that was at times stricter than traditional models of labour and the old ideal of complementarity within the family. At the same time, mechanization destroyed artisanal production and the guild system, thus undermining traditional assumptions about who could produce different types of goods. Politicians, religious authorities and social commentators scrambled to cope with the confusing changes and they developed complex philosophies and scientific theories to buttress arguments meant to preserve the gender status quo. As we shall see in the next chapter, they were aided in this task by racial and economic theories that encouraged the projection of European power abroad. Imperialism and industrialism both worked to produce the new gender system of the nineteenth century.

Notes

1. The causes of the Industrial Revolution are also contested. A classic argument, which continues to prompt debate, is provided in: David S. Landes, *Unbound Prometheus: Technological Change and Industrial Development in Western Europe from 1750 to the Present*, 2nd edition (Cambridge: Cambridge University Press, 1969).

2. Davies, *Europe*, 759.

3. Ibid., 764.

4. Robert Lee, 'Demography, Urbanization, and Migration', in *A Companion to Nineteenth-Century Europe, 1789–1914*, ed. Stefan Berger (Malden, MA and Oxford: Blackwell Publishing, 2006), 64.

5. For an overview of some of these debates, see: John Komlos, 'Stature and Nutrition in the Habsburg Monarchy: The Standard of Living and Economic Development in the Eighteenth Century', *American Historical Review* 90, no. 5 (1985): 1,149–61. See also: Lee, 'Demography, Urbanization, and Migration', 64.

6. Lee, 'Demography, Urbanization, and Migration', 65.

7. Ivan T. Berend, *History Derailed: Central and Eastern Europe in the Long Nineteenth Century* (Berkeley: University of California Press, 2003), 9.

8. For a summary of the debates among historians about the proper role of gendered analysis in labour history, see: Laura L. Frader, 'Labor History After the Gender Turn: Transatlantic Cross Currents and Research Agendas', *International Labor and Working Class History* 63 (2003): 21–31.

9. Alice Clark, *The Working Life of Women in the Seventeenth Century*, new edition (London: Routledge, 1992).

10. Louise Tilly and Joan W. Scott, *Women, Work and Family* (New York: Holt, Rinehart and Winston, 1978).

11. Louise Tilly and Joan W. Scott, 'Women's Work and the Family in Nineteenth-Century Europe', *Comparative Studies in Society and History* 17, no. 1 (1975): 36–64.

12. Bonnie G. Smith, *Changing Lives*, 141.

13. David Warren Sabean, *Property, Production, and Family in Neckarhausen, 1700–1870* (Cambridge: Cambridge University Press, 1991).

14. For a useful case study of women's participation and eventual exclusion from guilds, see: Jean Quataert, 'The Shaping of Women's Work in Manufacturing: Guilds, Households, and the State in Central Europe, 1648–1870', *American Historical Review* 90, no. 5 (1985): 1,122–48. Quataert argues that women were increasingly excluded from guilds in the mid-seventeenth century as part of the process of guilds trying to defend their monopolies in a period of early industrialization.

15. James J. Sheehan, *German History, 1770–1866* (Oxford: Oxford University Press, 1989), 108.

16. William Joshiah Goode, *The Family* (Englewood Cliffs, N.J.: Prentice Hall, 1964), 108–9; Edward Shorter, *The Making of the Modern Family* (New York: Basic Books, 1975), esp. 19–20.

17. For a detailed description of these rituals in rural Sweden, see: Marco H. D. Leeuwen and Ineke Maas, 'Partner Choice and Homogamy in the Nineteenth Century: Was There a Sexual Revolution in Europe?', *Journal of Social History* 36, no. 1 (2002): 105–7.

18. Ibid., 119.

19. Joanne Bailey, *Unquiet Lives: Marriage and Marriage Breakdown in England, 1660–1800* (Cambridge: Cambridge University Press, 2003).

20. David Landes, *Unbound Prometheus*, 46.

21. The exact periodization of these developments is the subject of some dispute among economic historians. See: Robert C. Allen, 'Tracking the Agricultural Revolution in England', *Economic History Review* 52, no. 2 (1999): 209–35.

22. Berend, *History Derailed,* 11; and Paul Carter, 'Enclosure, Waged Labour and the Formation of Class Consciousness: Rural Middlesex *c.* 1700–1835', *Labour History Review* 66, no. 3 (2001): 269–93.

23. William H. Sewell, 'Artisans and Factory Workers, 1789–1848', in *Working Class Formation*, eds Ira Katznelson and Aristide R. Zolberg (Princeton: Princeton University Press, 1986), 50.

24. Olwen Hufton, *The Poor of Eighteenth-Century France, 1750–1789* (Oxford: Clarendon Press, 1974), 69ff., 25–43 and 108–9.

25. For an overview of this transition, see: Maxine Berg, *The Age of Manufactures: Industry, Innovation, and Work in Britain, 1700–1820* (Oxford: Basil Blackwell Ltd., 1985), esp. 69–77.

26. Sabean, *Property, Production, and Family in Neckarhausen*, 156.

27. On divorce, see: ibid., 157.

28. Joanne Bailey, *Unquiet Lives*, 57 and 83.

29. Sabean, *Property, Production, and Family in Neckarhausen*, 161–62.

30. Robert McC. Netting, *Smallholders, Householders: Farm Families and the Ecology of Intensive, Sustainable Agriculture* (Stanford, CA: Stanford University Press, 1993), 2.

31. Ibid., 10. It is, in other words, incorrect to assume that these smallholdings are a phenomenon that disappeared with industrialization.

32. Andrejs Plakans, 'Peasant Farmsteads and Households in the Baltic Littoral, 1797', *Comparative Studies in Society and History* 17, no. 1 (1975): 36–64.

33. Andrejs Plakans, 'Agrarian Reform and the Family in Eastern Europe', in *Family Life in the Long Nineteenth Century, 1789–1913*, eds David I. Kertzer and Marzio Barbagli (New Haven, CT and London: Yale University Press, 2002), 77.

34. Ibid., 86.

35. Max Weber, 'National Character and the Junkers', in *From Max Weber: Essays in Sociology*, eds H. H. Gerth and C. Wright Mills (Oxford and New York: Oxford University Press, 1946), 386–95.

36. Laura Frader, 'Doing Capitalism's Work: Women in the Western European Industrial Economy', in *Becoming Visible: Women in European History*, 3rd edition, eds Renate Bridenthal, Susan Mosher Stuard and Merry E. Wiesner (Boston and New York: Houghton Mifflin Co., 1998), 298–99.

37. E. P. Thompson, 'Time, Work-Discipline, and Industrial Capitalism', *Past and Present* 38 (1967): 61.

38. Jürgen Kocka, 'Problems of Working-Class Formation in Germany: The Early Years, 1800–1875', in *Working Class Formation*, eds Ira Katznelson and Aristide R. Zolberg (Princeton: Princeton University Press, 1986), 319.

39. Daniel E. Bender has argued that late nineteenth- and early twentieth-century female American garment workers were subjected to harassment as a form of enforcing the sexual segregation of work and the women's lower pay scale. See: Daniel E. Bender, '"Too much of Distasteful Masculinity": Historicizing Sexual Harassment in the Garment Sweatshop and Factory', *Journal of Women's History* 15, no. 4 (2004): 91–116.

40. Anne Phillips and Barbara Taylor, 'Sex and Skill: Notes Towards a Feminist Economics', in *Feminism and History*, ed. Joan W. Scott (New York: Oxford University Press, 1996), 317–30.

41. Tessie P. Liu, 'What Price a Weaver's Dignity? Gender Inequality and the Survival of Home-Based Production in Industrial France', in *Gender and Class in Modern Europe*, eds Laura L. Frader and Sonya O. Rose (Ithaca, NY and London: Cornell University Press, 1996), 57–76.

42. Ibid., 61–62.

43. Ibid., 76.

44. Frader, 'Doing Capitalism's Work', 299.

45. Michele Barrett and Mary McIntosh, 'The "Family Wage": Some Problems for Socialists and Feminists', *Capital and Class* 11 (1980): 51–72.

46. See: Gerjan de Groot and Marlou Schrover, 'Between Men and Machines: Women Workers in New Industries, 1870–1940', *Social History* 20, no. 3 (1995): 279–96; and Phillips and Taylor.

47. Jane Lewis, 'The Working-Class Wife and Mother and State Intervention 1870–1940', in *Labour and Love: Women's Experience of Home and Family 1850–1940*, ed. Jane Lewis (London and New York: Basil Blackwell, 1986), 105.

48. Sonya O. Rose, 'Gender Antagonism and Class Conflict: Exclusionary Strategies of Male Trade Unionists in Nineteenth-Century Britain', *Social History* 13, no. 2 (1988): 191–208, esp. 202.

49. Excerpted from Friedrich Engels, *The Origin of the Family. Private Property and the State in the Light of the Researches of Lewis H. Morgan* (a translation of the 1891 edition of the original German text) in *Women, the Family and Freedom: The Debate in Documents*, eds Susan Groag Bell and Karen Offen (Stanford, CA: Stanford University Press, 1983), 81.

50. Deborah Simonton, 'Women Workers; Working Women', in *The Routledge History of Women in Europe since 1700*, ed. Deborah Simonton (London and New York: Routledge, 2006), 157–58.

51. Quoted in Charles Sowerwine, 'Socialism, Feminism, and the Socialist Women's Movement from the French Revolutionary to World War II', in *Becoming Visible: Women in European History*, eds Renate Bridenthal, Susan Mosher Stuard and Merry E. Wiesener, 3rd edition (Boston: Houghton Mifflin Co., 1998), 359.

52. Claire Moses, 'Saint Simonian Men / Saint Simonian Women: The Transformation of Feminist Thought in 1830s' France', *Journal of Modern History* 54, no. 2 (1982): 240–67.

53. Ibid., 255.

54. Ibid., 265.

55. Barbara Taylor, '"The Men are as Bad as Their Masters.": Socialism, Feminism and Sexual Antagonism in the London Tailoring Trade in the Early 1830's', *Feminist Studies* 5, no. 1 (1979): 9.

56. Quoted in ibid., from W. W. P. (pseudo.), 'Woman as She is and As She Ought to Be', *New Moral World* 5, no. 13 (26 January 1839): 210.

57. Ibid., 12.

58. Citations and summary from Joy Dixon, *Gender, Politics, and Culture in Modern Europe* (Vancouver: Access Guided Independent Study, University of British Columbia, n.d.), 55–56.

59. Barbara Taylor, *The Eve of the New Jerusalem: Socialism and Feminism in the Nineteenth Century* (New York: Pantheon Books, 1983), 92–93.

60. Ibid., 95.

61. Sheehan, *German History*, 656.

62. Dorothy Thompson 'Women and Nineteenth-Century Radical Politics: A Lost Dimension', in *The Rights and Wrongs of Women*, eds Juliet Mitchell and Ann Oakley (London: Penguin Books, 1976).

63. For an overview of various women's groups during the 1848 revolutions, see John Chastain's excellent website, *Encyclopedia of 1848 Revolutions*, available from http://www.ohiou.edu/~chastain/index.htm (accessed June 2006), particularly the following contributions: Ruth-Ellen B. Joeres, 'Frauen-Zeitung' and 'Otto-Peters, Louise'; Peter Mc Phee, 'Roland, Pauline'; Karen Offen, 'D'Hericourt, Jenny P.'; S. Joan Moon, 'Women's Rights in France'; Leszek Kuk, 'Women in Poland During the 1848 Revolution'; Isabelle Naginski, 'Sand, George'; Dorothy Thompson, 'Women Chartists'; and Robert B. Carlisle, 'Saint-Simonians'; Rüdiger Hachtmann 'Journeymen (Germany)'.

64. Sowerwine, 'Socialism, Feminism, and the Socialist Women's Movement', 364.

65. E. J. Hobsbawm, *The Age of Capital 1848–1875* (New York: Charles Scribner's Sons, 1975), 17.

66. Auslander, *Taste and Power*, 152.

67. Rüdiger Hachtmann, 'Journeymen (Germany)', in *Encyclopedia of 1848 Revolutions*. See also: Jonathan Sperber, *The European Revolutions, 1848–1851* (Cambridge: Cambridge University Press, 1984), 43–47.

68. Quoted in Sowerwine, 'Socialism, Feminism, and the Socialist Women's Movement', 365.

69. Karl Marx, *Selected Writings in Sociology and Social Philosophy*, trans. T. B. Bottomore (London: McGraw-Hill, 1964), 51.

70. Friedrich Engels, *The Origin of the Family*, excerpted in Bell and Offen, *Women, the Family and Freedom*, 81.

71. Marx and Engels's argument is summarized in: Sowerwine, 'Socialism, Feminism, and the Socialist Women's Movement', 366.

72. Quoted in ibid., from Karl Marx, *Capital: A Critique of Political Economy*, vol. 1, trans. Ben Fowkes (Harmondsworth: Penguin Books, 1976), 620–21.

73. Biographies of key socialist feminists and historical accounts of their movements testify to the difficulty of balancing these two convictions. See: Alfred G. Meyer, *The Feminism and Socialism of Lily Braun* (Bloomington: Indiana University Press, 1985); Taylor, *The Eve of the New Jerusalem*; Jean H. Quataert, 'Unequal Partners in an Uneasy Alliance: Women and the Working Class in Imperial Germany', in *Socialist Women: European Socialist Feminism in Nineteenth and Early Twentieth Century Europe*, eds Marilyn Boxer and Jean Quataert (New York: Elsevier, 1978); Karen Honeycutt, 'Clara Zetkin: A Socialist Approach to the Problem of Women's Oppression', *Signs* 3, no. 3/4 (1976): 131–44; Charles Sowerwine, *Sisters or Citizens: Women and Socialism in France Since 1876* (Cambridge and New York: Cambridge University Press, 1982).

74. Quoted in Judith F. Stone, 'Republican Ideology, Gender and Class: France, 1860s–1914', in *Gender and Class in Modern Europe*, eds Laura L. Frader and Sonya O. Rose (Ithaca, NY and London: Cornell University Press, 1996), 239.

75. D. J. O'Conner, 'Representations of Women Workers: Tobacco Strikers in the 1890s', in *Constructing Spanish Womanhood: Female Identity in Modern Spain*, eds Victoria Lorée Enders and Pamela Beth Radcliff (Albany, NY: State University of New York Press, 1999), 151–72.

76. Eric D. Weitz, 'The Heroic Man and the Ever-Changing Woman: Gender and Politics in European Communism, 1917–1950', in *Gender and Class in Modern Europe*, eds by Laura L. Frader and Sonya O. Rose (Ithaca, NY and London: Cornell University Press, 1996), 313.

77. From a speech given to the Party Congress of the Social Democratic Party of Germany, 16 October 1896. Clara Zetkin, 'Only in Conjunction With the Proletarian Woman Will Socialism Be Victorious', in *Clara Zetkin: Selected Writings*, ed. Philip Foner,

trans. Kai Schoenhals (New York: International Publishers, 1984), transcribed at: http://www.marxists.org/archive/zetkin/1896/10/women.htm (accessed May 2006).

78. For an excellent critical edition of Mill's key texts, including *On Liberty* and *On the Subjection of Women*, see: John Stuart Mill, *Mill: Texts, Commentaries,* ed. Alan Ryan (New York: W. W. Norton, 1997).

79. Jonas Fryman and Orvar Löfgren, *Culture Builders: A Historical Anthropology of Middle-Class Life* (New Brunswick, NJ: Rutgers University Press, 1987), 175. Fryman and Löfgren concentrate on conditions in Sweden, but their arguments hold true for other areas of Europe.

80. Ibid., 127.

81. Leonore Davidoff, 'Class and Gender in Victorian England: The Diaries of Arthur J. Munby and Hannah Cullwick', *Feminist Studies* 5, no. 1 (1979): 97.

82. Ibid., esp. 130.

83. Ibid., 130.

84. Bonnie G. Smith, *Ladies of the Leisure Class: The Bourgeoises of Northern France in the Nineteenth Century* (Princeton: Princeton University Press, 1981).

85. Auslander, *Taste and Power*, 145.

86. Catherine Hall, 'The Early Formation of Victorian Domestic Ideology', in *Gender and History in Western Europe*, eds Robert Shoemaker and Mary Vincent (New York and London: Arnold, 1998), 181.

87. Julián López Catalán, *Breves reflexiones sobre la educación doméstica: Discurso leído el día 1 de mayo de 1877 en la sesión pública que celebró la Sociedad Barcelonesa de Amigos de la Instrucción* (Barcelona: Librería de Juan y Antonio Bastinos, Editores, 1877), 10–11, quoted in Mary Nash, 'Un/Contested Identities: Motherhood, Sex Reform and the Modernization of Gender Identity in Early Twentieth-Century Spain', in *Constructing Spanish Womanhood: Female Identity in Modern Spain*, eds Victoria Lorée Enders and Pamela Beth Radcliff (Albany, NY: State University of New York Press, 1999), 28.

88. Quoted in Fryman and Löfgren, *Culture Builders*, 134.

89. Amanda Vickery, 'Golden Age to Separate Spheres? A Review of the Categories and Chronology of English Women's History', in *Gender and History in Western Europe*, eds Robert Shoemaker and Mary Vincent (New York and London: Arnold, 1998), 197. The quotation is from Aristotle, *The Politics & Economics of Aristotle*, trans. Edward English Walford and John Gillies (London: G. Bell & Sons, 1908). It is also available online at Paul Halsall's *Ancient History Sourcebook*, 'Aristotle: On a Good Wife, from Oikonomikos, c. 330 BCE', http://www.fordham.edu/halsall/ancient/greek-wives.html (accessed June 2006).

90. John Ruskin, *Sesame and Lilies*, ed. Deborah Epstein Nord (New Haven, CT: Yale University Press, 2002 [1865]), 77.

91. Hall, 'The Early Formation of Victorian Domestic Ideology', 183.

92. Ibid., 195.

93. Jürgen Habermas, *The Structural Transformation of the Public Sphere: An Inquiry into a Category of Bourgeois Society* (Cambridge, MA: MIT Press, 1991 [1989]), 176.

94. On the gendering of public spaces and the division between male/public and female/domestic identities see: Leonore Davidoff and Catherine Hall, *Family Fortunes: Men and Women of the English Middle Class, 1780–1850* (Chicago: University of Chicago Press, 1987), esp. 13, 211, 229 and 409.

95. Statistics on this are notoriously difficult to come by, but it is instructive that incest did not come to be thought of as a form of child abuse in England until the late 1880s. After a Royal Commission study in 1906 found that incest between men and young girls in their family was common, the Punishment of Incest Act was passed in 1908. See: Adam Kuper,

'Incest, Cousin Marriage, and the Origin of the Human Sciences in Nineteenth-Century England', *Past & Present* 174 (2002): 159–83, esp. 180–81.

96. Fryman and Löfgren, *Culture Builders*, 127.

97. Some percentage of men and women who never married were what we would today call homosexual. But there is considerable debate about the extent of same-sex sexual activity. Lillian Faderman prefers to document 'romantic friendship' between women without exploring in detail whether these friendships involved sexual contact or not. See: Lillian Faderman, *Surpassing the Love of Men: Romantic Friendship and Love between Women from the Renaissance to the Present* (New York: William Morrow and Company, Inc., 1981). Others, such as George Chauncey Jr. in *Gay New York: Gender, Urban Culture, and the Making of the Gay Male World, 1890–1940* (New York: Basic Books, 1994), 12–13, insist that self-definition is crucial. For an overview of the debate, see: Martin Bauml Duberman, 'Reclaiming the Gay Past', *Reviews in American History* 16, no. 4 (1988): 515–25. Unmarried celibacy was, however, also common, particularly in regions with high emigration, such as Ireland. See: Timothy Guinnane, 'Coming of Age in Rural Ireland at the Turn of the Twentieth Century', *Continuity and Change* 5, no. 3 (1990): 443–72.

98. See: Robert B. Shoemaker's balanced conclusions on the usefulness of 'separate spheres' in *Gender in English Society, 1650–1850: The Emergence of Separate Spheres* (London and New York: Longman, 1998), esp. 305–18. On female preachers, see: Susie Steinbach, *Women in England, 1760–1914: A Social History* (New York: Palgrave Macmillan, 2004), 154–58; and Deborah Valenze, *Prophetic Sons and Daughters: Female Preaching and Popular Religion in Industrial England* (Princeton: Princeton University Press, 1985).

99. John Tosh, 'Domesticity and Manliness in the Victorian Middle Class: The Family of Edward White Benson', in *Manful Assertions: Masculinities in Britain since 1800*, eds Michael Roper and John Tosh (London and New York: Routledge, 1991), esp. 49–50.

100. Ibid., 66.

101. Robin W. Winks and R. J. Q. Adams, *Europe, 1890–1945: Crisis and Conflict* (New York: Oxford University Press, 2003), 2.

102. Bicycle riding for women was controversial. See: Patricia Vertinsky, *The Eternally Wounded Woman: Women, Exercise and Doctors in the Late Nineteenth Century* (Manchester: Manchester University Press, 1990), 76–83.

103. Christopher Thompson, 'Un Troisième sexe? Les bourgeoises et la bicyclette dans la France fin de siècle', *Mouvement Social* 192 (2000): 9–39.

104. Martin Duberman, Martha Vicinus and George Chauncey Jr., eds, *Hidden from History: Reclaiming the Gay and Lesbian Past* (New York: Meridian, 1989).

105. Ludmilla Jordanova, *Sexual Visions: Images of Gender in Science and Medicine between the Eighteenth and Twentieth Centuries* (Madison: University of Wisconsin Press, 1989), 11.

106. See: Randolph Trumbach, 'The Birth of the Queen: Sodomy and the Emergence of Gender Equality in Modern Culture 1660–1750', in Duberman *et al.*, eds, *Hidden from History*, 129–40.) Before 1700, Trumbach argues, men who had sex with other men did not risk their reputations as masculine as long as they were the penetrative partner in the sexual act and as long as they also married and had children with a woman.

107. George Chauncey, *Gay New York*, 12–13.

108. Jeffrey Weeks, 'Inverts, Perverts, and Mary-Annes: Male Prostitution and the Regulation of Homosexuality in England in the Nineteenth and Early Twentieth Centuries', in Duberman *et al.*, eds, *Hidden From History*, 202.

109. George Mosse, 'Masculinity and Decadence', in *Sexual Knowledge: Sexual*

Science: The History of Attitudes to Sexuality, eds Roy Porter and Mikulas Teich (Cambridge and New York: Cambridge University Press, 1994), 257.

110. Quoted in Otto Friedrich, *Before the Deluge: A Portrait of Berlin in the 1920s* (New York: Harper Perennial, 1995 [1963]), 128–29.

111. See: Faderman, *Surpassing the Love of Men*.

112. Laura Doan, 'Passing Fashions: Reading Female Masculinities in the 1920s', *Feminist Studies* 24, no. 3 (1998): 663–700.

113. Faderman, *Surpassing the Love of Men*, 320.

114. Richard W. McCormick, 'From Caligari to Dietrich: Sexual, Social, and Cinematic Discourses in Weimar Film', *Signs* 18, no. 3 (1993): 640–68.

115. Judith R. Walkowitz, *City of Dreadful Delight: Narratives of Sexual Danger in Late-Victorian London* (Chicago: Chicago University Press, 1992), 16. Of course many middle-class women resisted these restrictions. See for example: Deborah Cherry, 'Going Places: Women Artists in Central London in the Mid-Nineteenth Century', *London Journal* 28, no. 1 (2003): 73–96; and Leslie Choquette, 'Paris-Lesbos: Lesbian Social Space in the Modern City, 1870–1940', *Proceedings of the Western Society for French History* 26 (1999): 122–32.

116. Auslander, *Taste and Power*, 248–49.

117. Quoted in Keith Tester, ed., *The Flâneur* (London and New York: Routledge, 1994), 2.

118. Christine Buci-Glucksmann, 'Catastrophic Utopia: The Feminine as Allegory of the Modern', *Representations*, no. 14 (Spring 1986): 220, 222.

119. On the juxtaposition of images of prostitutes and lesbians, see: Leslie Choquette, 'Degenerate or Degendered? Images of Prostitution and Homosexuality in the French Third Republic', *Historical Reflections/Réflexions historiques* 23, no. 2 (1997): 205–28.

120. Carolyn J. Dean, 'Lesbian Sexuality in Interwar France', in *Connecting Spheres: European Women in a Globalizing World, 1500 to the Present*, eds Marilyn J. Boxer and Jean H. Quataert, 2nd edition (New York and Oxford: Oxford University Press, 2000), 290.

121. Historical work on prostitution continues to grow. Here is a representative sample: Lynn Abrams, 'Prostitutes in Imperial Germany, 1870–1918: Working Girls or Social Outcasts?', in *The German Underworld*, ed. Richard Evans (London and New York: Routledge, 1991), 189–209; Alain Corbin, *Women for Hire: Prostitution and Sexuality in France after 1850* (Cambridge, MA: Harvard University Press, 1990); Mary Gibson, *Prostitution and the State in Italy, 1860–1915*, 2nd edition (Columbus, OH: Ohio State University Press, 2000); and Linda Mahood, *The Magdalenes. Prostitution in the Nineteenth Century* (New York: Routledge, 1990).

122. Konrad H. Jarausch, 'Students, Sex and Politics in Imperial Germany', *Journal of Contemporary History* 17 (1982): 285–303.

123. For an overview of recent historical literature on prostitution and extensive citations to scholarly work see: Timothy J. Gilfoyle, 'Prostitutes in History: From Parables of Pornography to Metaphors of Modernity', *American Historical Review* 104, no. 1 (Feb. 1999): 117–41.

124. Although Parent-Duchatelet's book was only published after his death, he was considered the foremost authority on prostitution all over Europe. See: Jill Harsin, *Policing Prostitution in Nineteenth Century Paris* (Princeton: Princeton University Press, 1985), esp. 97–129; and Corbin, *Women for Hire*, 1–29.

125. For a general account, see: Frank Mort, *Dangerous Sexualities: Medico-moral Politics in England since 1830* (London and New York: Routledge and Kegan Paul, 1987), 65–99.

126. See: Richard J. Evans, 'Prostitution, State, and Society in Imperial Germany', *Past and Present* 70 (1976): 106–209.

127. Judith R. Walkowitz, 'Male Vice and Female Virtue: Feminism and the Politics of Prostitution in Nineteenth Century Britain', in *Powers of Desire: The Politics of Sexuality*, eds Ann Snitow, Christine Stansell and Sharon Thompson (New York: Monthly Review Press, 1983), 423–4. Walkowitz gives a fuller account of the Maiden Tribute affair in *City of Dreadful Delight*, where she also details the panic surrounding Jack the Ripper.

128. Ibid., 427.

129. Fraisse, *Reason's Muse*, 194.

130. The German word *Feminismus* was, up until the 1960s, used to describe men who displayed female qualities. See: Richard J. Evans, 'The Concept of Feminism', in *German Women in the Eighteenth and Nineteenth Centuries*, eds Ruth-Ellen B. Joeres and Mary Jo Maynes (Bloomington: Indiana University Press, 1986), 247–48.

131. Cited from Gertrud Bäumer, *Die Frau im deutschen Staat* (Berlin: Junker & Dunnhaupt, 1932) in Reinhard Opitz, *Der Deutsche Sozial-Liberalismus 1917–1933* (Cologne: Pahl-Rugenstein, 1973), 256.

132. Stephen Hause and Anne R. Kenney, *Women's Suffrage and Social Politics in the French Third Republic* (Princeton: Princeton University Press, 1984); Stephen C. Hause and Anne R. Kenney, 'The Limits of Suffragist Behavior: Legalism and Militancy in France, 1876–1922', *American Historical Review* 86, no. 4 (1981): 781–806.

133. The literature on feminist movements in Europe is too comprehensive to cite here. For an overview see: Offen, *European Feminisms*.

134. A good summary of the activities of the suffragettes can be found in: June Purvis, 'Deeds not Words', *History Today* 52, no. 5 (2005): 56–63. For useful primary sources, see: Cheryl R. Jorgensen-Earp, ed., *Speeches and Trials of the Militant Suffragettes: The Women's Social and Political Union, 1903–18* (Cranbury, NJ: Associated University Presses, 1999).

135. Susan Kingsley Kent, *Sex and Suffrage in Great Britain* (Princeton: Princeton University Press, 1987), 200.

136. June Purvis, *Emmeline Pankhurst: A Biography* (London and New York: Routledge, 2002), 223.

137. For a theoretical exploration of gender as performance, see: Judith Butler, *Gender Trouble: Feminism and the Subversion of Identity* (New York: Routledge, 1990).

138. The event was captured on film. See: 'Vintage Video: Death of Suffragette at Epsom Derby, 1913'. FirstWorldWar.com. Available from http://www.firstworldwar.com/video/epsomsuffragette.htm (accessed February 2006).

...erial Drive and the Colonial World

On the face of it, the developments of the Age of Revolution seemed to augur badly for European empires. The political upheavals of the era had begun with the revolt of a remarkably large coalition of thirteen American colonies against a British Empire that had just won the Seven Years' War against France (1756–63) and seemed to have cemented its place as the premier global empire. The victory of those colonies emboldened a generation of the politically dissatisfied. In addition to the dramatic events of the French Revolution that were discussed in Chapter 1, Haiti saw a successful slave revolt and independence movement between 1791 and 1803, and the Spanish Empire succumbed to the pressures of colonial uprisings and military defeat at home. By 1825, only Canada and a few island and coastal territories remained as European territories in the Western Hemisphere.

In Africa, though, European influence had increased in the Mediterranean territories north of the Sahara Desert during the Napoleonic era, the presence south of the Sahara still mostly consisted of strips along the ocean that were fortified for defence of the trading activities that Europeans had been conducting with relish since the fifteenth century. In Asia, China loomed large as the dominant imperial power in the region, though European incursions in the early modern period had established European commercial and military influence in many of the most strategic areas of the continent. In India, the East India Company (the chartered company granted both economic rights and the responsibility for governing Indian dependencies from 1757 to 1857) had established itself as a political and military power to be contended with, and the Seven Years' War had removed French power from the equation on the subcontinent. Dutch and Portuguese traders and sailors had established themselves in Indonesia; French merchants and colonists continued to deepen their involvement in Southeast Asia; British explorers had claimed Australia and New Zealand; and Russian soldiers, explorers and officials continued to acquire prestige and territory throughout central and northern Asia.

Still, the vast majority of people living in Africa, Asia and in the Pacific had no contact with European traders, much less European states. The web of early modern imperialism had transformed economic production and relations in many areas of the world, but most people were still governed by indigenous elites and maintained traditional social and cultural practices. The great empires and kingdoms in central Africa ruled unchecked; the early modern Islamic empires that stretched from

North Africa to India still retained a significant amount of power; and the massive Chinese Empire remained relatively unimpressed by the arrival of seaborne Europeans into the political ecosystem of East Asia. For rulers around the world and intellectual critics in Europe, it was still very much an open question whether modest numbers of European migrants to the south and the east would continue to grow or whether the great anti-imperial revolts and revolutions of the late eighteenth and early nineteenth centuries had shaken the ideological basis of European expansion as well as the social and political power necessary to extend European influence.[1] Meanwhile, the economic changes associated with the Industrial Revolution had undermined the very basis of colonial economic policy. The mercantilist policies that had stressed the importance of the imperial state's regulation of commerce had come under severe attack (most famously in the Scottish political economist Adam Smith's 1776 *Wealth of Nations*), and new economic entrepreneurs now began to stress the slogan of 'Free Trade' in their dealings with the state. Even in the realm of the globalizing economy, the imperial state appeared to have lost its justification.

It turned out, however, that the era of empires had not yet passed. As the events of the next century would demonstrate, the imperial decline that many thought they were witnessing in the first years of the nineteenth century was illusory. In fact, those very same revolutionary forces that challenged the form of the early modern empire made possible a much stronger, more expansive and ultimately more destructive form of modern empire. By the end of the nineteenth century, virtually the whole world had been conquered or reduced to dependence by the great European empires. The only states that seemed able to resist were those very settler states in North and South America that had been so successful in breaking free during the Age of Revolution. By 1900, the chance that one would find a white man sitting in the governor's chair of virtually any province on the face of the earth was very good. Indeed, the global face of power was so white and so male that scientists and politicians alike came to believe that this manifestation of racial and gender superiority was natural rather than circumstantial.

Nor was this a thin layer of control, as it had been earlier. The wave of European emigration to the rest of the world crested in the nineteenth century, as the adventurers, the ideologues, the opportunists, the dispossessed and the disaffected sought their fame and fortune. Great Britain alone saw 22.6 million people emigrate to the colonies over the course of the century between the Congress of Vienna in 1815 and the outbreak of the First World War in 1914.[2] The percentage of ethnic Europeans living outside of Europe jumped from about 4 per cent to over 20 per cent over the course of the same century.[3]

Economically too, the intrusion of European power was much more significant. The new form of empire was increasingly geared towards changing the way export goods were produced rather than towards simply extracting goods through unequal trade. Hunter-gatherers were forced into land cultivation, while new European enterprises expanded dramatically enough to push indigenous peoples into wage labour in many areas. The extraction of rubber expanded exponentially in many tropical regions, scarce minerals were systematically mined in Africa, and enormous cotton plantations with extensive irrigation systems flowered from Uzbekistan to Egypt, destroying pastureland and traditional economies in the space of a few short years.

The increased presence of European demographic and economic forces in the colonial world was enough to justify greater intervention on the part of European imperial states. As land was fenced off and tilled, and as mines began churning out wealth, European colonists rushed to introduce their form of law and the primacy of private property in the regions they controlled. Much to the dismay of local peoples, these institutional importations, though clothed in the language of the law, had little to do with justice. White newcomers usurped property worked by local people who had laid claim to it for generations, and then insisted that this form of property arrangement was both fair and part of a superior civilization that indigenous peoples were simply too ignorant to comprehend fully. When natives rebelled or protested against the colonial order, the Europeans brought out their guns. So, as European diplomats scrambled for new territories, local peoples scrambled to adjust to this much more intrusive new order, which came not only to rule and to profit, but also to legislate, to instruct and to lecture these new subjects on why they should learn to love their new positions. These powerful new men (and at the outset nearly all of the colonists were male), previously on the distant periphery of the lives of most Asians and Africans, were now much more intimate and much more present.

Our argument in this chapter is that the impact of this intimacy ran both ways. Just as local societies were forever transformed by the European invasions, so too were European societies deeply affected by their imperial ventures. When nineteenth-century Europeans thought about their own civilization, those musings were comparative in nature. Europeans were only 'civilized' because there was a world full of the 'uncivilized'. These comparisons were not value-neutral; one form of social order was considered better than the other. Needless to say, most Europeans saw their 'civilization' as superior to the 'barbarism' that existed in wilder societies, but this was always a judgement that was tinged with anxiety. Civilization meant in part the ability to objectify nature so as to better control it, a process that was most clearly seen in the rise of man-made urban centres throughout Europe that further distanced city dwellers from 'nature'. This creation of a civilized artifice troubled men and women who suspected that important things had been lost when 'natural' ties had been severed. The colonies served a paradoxical purpose in this regard. On the one hand, they were the arena for the daily demonstration of the superiority of the European way of life, a superiority felt not only in the smug quarters of colonial governors, but perhaps even more deeply and importantly among people who had never left the home country. On the other, the colonies were also the space to which those frustrated or troubled by domestic social norms and practices fled. In a sense, Europeans sent their 'savages' to perform the 'civilizing' mission.

These notions of superiority and feelings of anxiety were evident in the realm of gender and sex. Indeed, imperial relationships between Europe and the rest of the world provide a striking example of how political change was both predicated upon and helped to transform norms and relations of gender in Europe. The imperial project exposed Europeans to new forms of family relationships and to new expressions of sexuality. This exposure forced them to understand their own practices in a comparative light and eventually to construct an entire cultural, scientific, military and political edifice to codify and to justify their gendered visions, their sexual fantasies and their understanding of a proper social order. The engine that drove this process forward was the growing sense that there was a contradiction between one's primal sexual urges and the needs of an orderly, civilized society. As we have seen, this was a contradiction that had been explored earlier by figures like Rousseau in their discussions of proper gendered behaviour of upstanding men and women. Over the course of the nineteenth century, this question of the relationship between passion and control grew ever more important, finally culminating in the work of Sigmund Freud, who argued in his famous *Civilization and Its Discontents* (1930) that the development of civilization from its earliest stages was based on the control of sexual urges.[4] In order to develop civilization, and with it global power, women had to control their urges by submitting obediently to their husbands, and men had to exercise iron self-control. Few individuals actually lived up to these ideals, but hardened and restrictive gender norms had an enormous impact on the ways in which Europeans thought about their world.

Gender and the Culture of Empire

European explorers, social commentators and general publics were deeply fascinated by the places and peoples that the process of empire building opened up to them. This attraction to the exotic was present from the beginning of the age of exploration straight through to the present day, as readers, music fans and museum-goers picked up hints of cultural difference and let their imaginations run wild. Those imaginations did not run free, however, for they were bounded by the constraints of their own cultures and by the concerns of their own lives. All human beings develop certain mental and behavioural patterns that condition the ways that they think and act in the world, and even the most novel experiences must be understood within those dynamic and changing patterns that we call 'cultures'. As a result, when Europeans described and imagined encounters with the foreign, they were reflecting as much upon themselves as upon the 'exotic' people they purported to describe.

Michel de Montaigne's essay 'On Cannibals' (1580) was an early example of this sort of colonial encounter. Montaigne was a well-informed and highly placed French nobleman who kept abreast of news from the Americas and made sure to interrogate three Native Americans who had been taken back to Europe for a tour and a meeting with the French King. His essay described the culture of one of the peoples living in what is now Brazil. Montaigne had learned that these people killed and ate the prisoners they took in war, that they liked to dance nearly naked and that men took many wives. Nevertheless, Montaigne contended that these native Brazilians had much to teach his French compatriots. 'I do not believe', he argued, 'that there is anything barbarous or savage about them, except that we all call barbarous anything that is contrary to our own habits.' They were only barbarous 'in the sense that they have received very little moulding from the human intelligence, and are still very close to their original simplicity. They are still governed by natural laws and very little corrupted by our own'. This was a people, he continued, 'in which there is no kind of commerce, no knowledge of letters, no science of numbers ... The very words denoting lying, treason, deceit, greed, envy, slander, and forgiveness have never been heard.'[5]

One might see in this idealized description of American 'savages' an ethic of cultural tolerance, as indeed there was, but we should also note that this was a stance as surely based upon fantasies of the exotic as the simultaneous condemnations of barbarous cannibals. The figure of the 'uncivilized' native, closer to nature and natural desires for sex and violence, held certain attractions for writers like Montaigne (and many more that would follow), but it portended visceral danger to many others. As a result, priests, soldiers and state officials frequently demanded that this danger be erased through forced assimilation via religious conversion, educational programmes, land settlement and other markers of European civilization. Montaigne's essay was not really 'on cannibals' at all; it was a critique of his own society, a critique that he shrewdly made through the voice of the colonized, who even explained in the conclusion of the essay (at Montaigne's urging) what they found strange about sixteenth-century France.

There are two important points to make about this debate between Montaigne and those who urged the mass conversion of cannibal tribes. The first is that this was a debate *within* Europe and *about* Europe. The natives themselves are barely known and serve only as surrogates for European positions (Montaigne, for instance, admits that he grew frustrated with the interpreter, that little real communication took place and that he could only remember two of the Brazilian observations of France). This is not to say that the colonized people had no historical agency; as we shall see shortly, they did. But it is to stress that the dynamics of exotic fantasies and imperial projects were part of the core of European identities, policies and practices in the modern era. Empires and colonies were not something external to Europe. They were constitutive of it. There was, as a result, a complicated interaction between fantasies of the colonial world and those actual places and peoples. As Edward Said has argued, the imperial project as a whole depended heavily on the creation of an 'Orient' (an 'East' that stretched from Europe's border with the Ottoman Empire to Japan). This Orient, which was constructed both by cultural and by political figures, was necessary in order for the 'West' to define itself and to assert its political dominance and cultural superiority. With so much at stake, there was considerable pressure to maintain the internal consistency of European fantasies about the Islamic world, regardless of what facts emerged from the actual study of and interaction with those people and places. It was 'finally Western ignorance which [became] more refined and complex, not some body of positive Western knowledge which [increased] in size and accuracy. For fictions have their own logic and their own dialectic of growth or decline.'[6]

The second thing to note is that exposure to different peoples and different cultures created an opportunity for Europeans to see their own institutions and practices in new ways. Frequently, this cultural comparison led to proclamations of superiority and dreams of civilizing missions. Many, for instance, thought it better that Europeans did not eat their prisoners of war and believed it was their responsibility to prevent others from doing so as well. But the imperial nature of European states in the modern era also meant that there was a permanent source of social criticism always waiting to be tapped. For Montesquieu, Rousseau, Flaubert, Tolstoy, Conrad and many others, engagement with the colonial world allowed critics to condemn everything from European monarchies to European fashions.

One of the most prominent themes of these probing criticisms and the response of the conservative defenders of European civilization was the question of desire and the regulation of desire. What attracted and repelled European commentators on foreign societies was the perceived lack of restraint shown by colonial peoples. This lack of self-control, they observed, was manifested in violent cycles of blood vengeance, thoughtless crime and wanton expressions of sexuality. These images of savages following their 'natural' instincts were constantly condemned, and yet Europeans could not seem to look away, in part because so many longed to be free, at least temporarily, from the self-discipline that they felt marked their own lives. Put another way, the colonial encounter came to stand in for a tension that many Europeans felt within themselves between their 'lustful' desires and their desire for social order and civilization. Since constructions of gender lie precisely at this intersection between desire and order, gender ideas in Europe both inflected the imperial project as a whole and were transformed by it. But this was no straightforward process. Instead, there was always a deep ambivalence about the colonial project, precisely because there was a deep ambivalence about European gender upon which imperialism shone a bright light.

These dualities of attraction and repulsion, freedom and anarchy, passivity and vigour were always present. The 'oriental' woman, for instance, was often portrayed by European authors as submissive, sensual and available, outside of the sexual and moral restraints placed upon European women. But this picture was always complicated by the simultaneous picture of the colonial woman as a source of treachery and manipulation and, further, one even *more* constrained by social norms than European women were. This was particularly the case when Europeans considered the place of the Muslim woman, subordinated in a patriarchal system that seemed despotic even to the grey patriarchs of Europe. There were ways in which these two images could be partially reconciled, most notably through the sexual fetishization of the markers of the Islamic patriarchal domination such as the harem and the veil, but this reconciliation was never total, either for authors or for colonists.

In a similar fashion, colonized men were seen as both emasculated and hyper-masculine. On the one hand, the very fact of European military victory and imperial domination suggested that colonized men had been stripped of core aspects of their masculinity. Unable to defend their lands and their families successfully, they were now forced into rituals of humiliating submission to foreign invaders, and this very humility suggested to European observers that they were somehow unmanly, weak and impotent. On the other hand, the same notion that natives were closer to nature meant that indigenous men were often portrayed as being somewhat more 'pure' in their sexuality and in their violence. This unchecked virility was thought to account for many of the 'barbarous' practices that repelled and fascinated European inter-lopers, but it also held a great deal of attraction. The thought that these pure men were manlier than the men who had conquered them troubled European masculine consciousness. The thought that European women might feel the same way and seek out the strong embrace of the colonized man drove European men to distraction. What if conquest had merely been the result of better tools? What if the men abroad were, man for man, better fighters and better lovers?

It is perhaps useful to examine this dynamic at play in the realm of literature. The revolutionary era was in some ways a culmination of Enlightenment trends that stressed the orderliness of the world and the usefulness of reason in understanding human behaviour and human progress, but it also witnessed a challenge to this sort of systematic approach. The last years of the eighteenth century and the first years of the nineteenth century saw a variety of new approaches to humanistic investiga-tion that historians and art critics have subsequently grouped under the label of Romanticism. Naturally, an impulse rooted in the rejection of system-building was not expressed in a fully coherent and unified movement. Still, there was a group of artists and associated thinkers who liked reading each other's work and shared many outlooks and principles of behaviour. Romantic icons like England's Lord Byron and Russia's Aleksandr Pushkin liked to flaunt the vibrancy and pathos of their lives, and they tended to die young and dramatically. Their 'natural' vitality was heedless and ostentatiously unconventional. They flouted the principles of monogamy and took daring risks for their ideals that both surprised and titillated their rather more cau-tious and prudent compatriots. In addition, a valorization of the natural world played an important role in the movement throughout Europe, and the wilder the nature the better. This impulse drove English poets like William Wordsworth to the fields around Tintern Abbey for inspiration just as, in the United States, it drove Henry David Thoreau to the woods of Walden. Painters like the Swiss Arnold Böcklin turned to landscapes; ethnographers like the German Grimm brothers paid close attention to tales of big, bad wolves; and musicians like the Czech Antonin Dvorak sought folk themes and exotic melodies.

In this important way, Romantic artists, if not themselves 'savages', were at least interested in tapping into the attraction of the 'natural' men and women in the wilds of the European countryside, the European past and the colonial present for their own personal and literary purposes. As a result, Romantics were among the most important and visible commentators on the cultural and political issues that imperial expansion raised for Europeans in the first half of the nineteenth century. One such figure was Mikhail Lermontov (1814–41). Lermontov was one of Russia's premier Romantic writers, and he had been exposed to the colonial world through military service in the Caucasus Mountains, the imposing range that separates the Russian steppe from what is now a string of small countries (Georgia, Armenia and Azerbaijan) and a ring of much larger ones (Turkey, Iraq and Iran). Throughout the nineteenth century, the Russian Empire was actively engaged in conquering Islamic mountain peoples like the Chechens and Dagestanis and attempted to press its influence ever further into the Islamic world. This point of contact with the 'Orient' served as a formative experience for many Russian artists and intellectuals, including both Pushkin (b. 1799) and the slightly younger Leo Tolstoy (b. 1828). Like Pushkin, Lermontov acquired a reputation for his sexual escapades as well as his poetry, and both poets died young in duels.

Lermontov's most famous work was a short collection of stories entitled *A Hero of Our Time* set in the Caucasus and largely concerned with the critical examination of the contrast between 'civilized' Europeans and the 'savage' mountain dwellers.[7] The protagonist of the work was a disaffected Russian army officer named Pechorin whose destructive exploits deeply offended both the other characters in the book and his readers. Over the course of the story, Pechorin steals a native woman named Bela from her tribe and seduces her, only to abandon her in every sense of the word and consign her to a grisly fate. For sport, he also seduces and discards a young Russian debutante named Mary, encourages a fellow officer to attempt suicide in order to win a bet, and treats old friends with cold indifference. He does not seem much like a 'hero' of his time, and this apparent contradiction has served as the main spur to literary commentary on the work ever since. Clearly, he was not intended to be a hero in the sense of a model character, and early furious criticism along these lines exasperated Lermontov to no end.[8] The more sensible reading of Pechorin as an anti-hero and his outrages as a critique of Russian society has dominated ever since. Still, Lermontov cast significant doubt on the proposition that Pechorin was thoroughly reprehensible in an authorial aside in the text itself: 'Perhaps some readers will want to know my opinion of Pechorin's character. My answer is the title of this book. "But this is wicked irony!" they will say. I wonder.'[9]

If we examine Pechorin's character solely from within the context of domestic Russian society and dominant Russian masculine norms, it is difficult to see what Lermontov might be wondering. Either cynical callousness, the dishonourable treatment of women and an utter disregard for human life and the norms of respectable society are heroic or they are not. Vladimir Nabokov, a noted author in his own right and a sensitive commentator, touched on this issue but was unable to resolve it: 'Lermontov was singularly inept in his descriptions of women. Mary is the generalized young thing of novelettes, with no attempt at individualization except perhaps her "velvety" eyes, which however are forgotten in the course of the story ... Bela, an Oriental beauty on the lid of a box of Turkish delight. What then makes for the everlasting charm of this book?'[10] Nabokov has two answers. First, he says, the text has an energy and beauty despite Lermontov's choice of hackneyed phrases and cardboard characters. Second, readers have sensed that Lermontov somehow identifies deeply with Pechorin. These sharp observations are deeply suggestive but also troubling. How can it be that the text holds lasting interest if the descriptions of place are orientalist clichés and if the treatment of women, so central to the work as a whole, relies on stereotype of the crudest sort?

The answer to Nabokov's question is twofold. The first answer is that many readers *like* oriental clichés and continue to do so. As a result, the formulaic treatment of Chechens and of women was likely the key to the commercial success of the work. The first story, 'Bela', begins with Russian officers admiring the beauty of the natural setting, disparaging the natives for being both 'robbers and paupers' and sermonizing that the mountain tribes 'don't know how to do anything and are incapable of education'. The native men are portrayed as hot-headed, reckless and murderous figures who treat women as chattels to be traded for horses or slaughtered in fits of jealous rage. Native women, as Nabokov pointed out, are oriental cut-outs. Bela is stunningly beautiful, fully passive and the object of the struggle in the story rather than a subject. The same pattern recurs in the other tales in the book. In 'Taman', the lead figure (other than Pechorin) is a wild teenage girl who entices Pechorin to the sea with the prospect of some beach loving but in fact simply wants to lure him to his death so that her smuggling activities are not discovered. The 'Orientals' in the text are savage, treacherous, lustful, beautiful and fully attached to nature. The beach girl, who falls out of a boat into the sea to what seems to be a sure death, instead swims swiftly and surreptitiously to the shore, while Bela's refusal to remain within the fortress and her desire to be in nature leads to her final abduction. Sexy, available and natural, it turned out, proved to be as powerful an aphrodisiac for Pechorin as it was for so many European colonists. For this reason, some scholars writing in the feminist tradition have contended that, just as Lermontov drank from the cup of imperial superiority, so too did he exploit misogynistic themes in order to titillate his male readers. They agreed with Nabokov that Lermontov was 'dangerously inept' in his treatment of women.[11]

At this level, *A Hero of Our Time* was no different from any of the other pulp exotic tales that flooded European book markets. European readers clearly liked tales of savages, of wild countrysides and military adventure, of dusky men and gorgeous, available women.[12] This attraction to the core orientalist themes on the part of mass reading publics was not politically innocent, for these artistic representations were a key, constitutive part of a broader understanding of colonized peoples and places.[13] It was only in the context of seeing the rest of the world as uncivilized that a civilizing mission of empire could be systematically forwarded and pursued. One might, therefore, see Lermontov's work as just one more prop of imperialism and argue that Europeans of his era did not, indeed could not, sense the deeply inhuman and dehumanizing consequences of their orientalist literary projects and associated schemes of imperial expansion.

But here is a case where a sustained examination of the relationship between gender and empire pays off. Recent scholarship focusing on gender and empire in the Russian literary context convincingly demonstrates that the misogynistic and imperial attitudes of Lermontov's characters are presented not to valorize them but to criticize them. Peter Scotto argues perceptively that Lermontov sets up many of the moral dilemmas in 'Bela' to reflect on the inhumanity of imperial ideology, and that the tragedy of the story unfolds not because Pechorin is corrupt but because the colonial context encourages precisely this devaluation of native lives.[14] Susan Layton, in the same vein, uses Lermontov's earlier poetry to demonstrate that his views of Caucasian masculinity in particular ran against the grain of the accepted imperial discourse, an observation that calls into question the thesis that Lermontov depicted the relationship between the sexes and his female characters 'ineptly' because he didn't know any better.[15] Indeed, Jane Costlow argues in line with Scotto that women were not presented as clichés simply to entertain but to criticize: like the natives, the female characters present the Russian male characters with moral tests that they fail precisely because they follow the dictates of the dominant imperial ideology.[16] All these authors agree that by the end of his life Lermontov was engaged in a project of challenging Russian imperial expansion and the orientalist ideology that underpinned it.

We can go further and argue that *A Hero of Our Time* precociously and systematically condemned both the despotism of colonial relations and of gender relations. Those two despotisms, moreover, were linked in a fundamental way. What distinguishes *A Hero of Our Time* is that though Lermontov entices his readers into his oriental fantasy world by deploying tired stereotypes and utterly conventional adventure plots, he then attempts to demonstrate the inhumane destructiveness of both colonial relations and normative Russian gender relations. The result is complex – a criticism of colonialism in the form of a thrilling exotic adventure in the Orient and a devastating indictment of gender relations accomplished through cardboard women.

A Hero of Our Time highlights three important facets of the way that gender intersected with imperial culture in the nineteenth century. The first is that the colonial world was of great interest to Europeans. Orientalist themes were not relegated to niche markets. Instead, virtually every notable European author tackled them at some point or another, and many long-forgotten authors made their careers peddling exotic and erotic tales of the East. The second point is that conceptions of the imperial order were tightly bound to conceptions of the European gender order. The connection drawn in literature and in political metaphor between men as conquerors and women as the conquered does not take especially intrepid research to uncover. It was everywhere, and it had deep consequences not only for life in the colonies, where many unfortunate aspects of European masculinity were grotesquely overplayed and where the notion of what we would call today 'sex tourism' inflected colonial relations in many unhealthy ways, but also within Europe itself. The third point is that, though the bulk of colonial literature served to buttress the ideology of empire, there was criticism not just of imperial policy, but also of imperialism as such, even as expansion was going on. Put another way, what we today call 'post-colonial' criticism in fact emerged alongside colonialism, not after the fact.[17] Taken together, these three observations add up to an additional conclusion: the gendered nature of imperial expansion served both to solidify the (unequal) gender order of Europe in the short term and to lay the groundwork for a form of opposition to the colonial order that was deeply imbued with feminism as well as anti-racism. Though it would take some time for this movement to develop fully, the sorts of criticisms of patriarchy and colonialism hinted at by Lermontov would enter the political realm soon enough. Within a decade of the publication of *A Hero of Our Time* in 1840 and Lermontov's death in 1841, Karl Marx and Friedrich Engels would link gender inequality and colonial inequality with what was, for them, the foundational inequality of class. They further argued in their famous *Communist Manifesto* that each ruling order inevitably sowed the seeds of its own destruction. While this was not necessarily universally true, it would soon prove to be the case for the great nineteenth-century European empires.

Race and Sex in the Colonies

As we have seen, the metropolitan culture of empire was deeply tied to the entire imperial project. Still, we should not imagine that there was any sort of direct correspondence between European fantasies (literary or not) and the actual interaction between colonizers and colonized on the ground. Though Europeans came to the colonies with scripts in their heads derived from the imperial culture 'at home', they then interacted with large numbers of people whose voices and actions were systematically excluded from domestic aesthetic cultures and political discourses. These interactions took many forms, ranging from economic to political to social, but the one that will concern us most here is the dynamic of sexual relationships in the expanding and deepening European colonies.

Until the late eighteenth century, statesmen in the European metropoles looked upon sexual contact between native women and European traders, frontiersmen, officials and other itinerants of the early modern empires with benevolence. Most of the Europeans abroad during the first centuries of empire were men, even in those parts of the empire (notably in North America) where full-scale colonization was taking place, and few expected that the rough and ready men of the frontier would observe monastic celibacy. The notion that sexual restraint would strengthen the self-control of colonizers and thereby their control over native peoples was only weakly developed at this stage. This meant that either homosexual or interracial heterosexual acts could be expected. Of the two, interracial sex was largely preferred. Homosexuality was looked upon with deep fear and concern by most colonizing powers.[18] The anxieties about sex with colonized peoples were much smaller, as miscegenation was widely accepted in many colonial situations, especially early on.[19] Indeed, though some were concerned that regularized relationships would blur the line between colonizers and colonized, many saw the enormous usefulness of the intimate cultural exchange that occurred in such cases. Virtually everywhere, a select cadre of local women served as cultural and linguistic 'translators' between the probing explorers and cautious local political leaders. In conditions of general mutual unintelligibility there was an important and powerful space for such cultural brokers, a space that was occupied not only by the women, but also by the men who teamed up with them. These couples, who were engaged in mutual linguistic and cultural immersion programmes while those around them remained rooted in their own cultural worlds, became the transmission belts and information filters for economic, cultural and political exchange.[20]

These were 'marriages'[21] based on the principle of cultural diplomacy, and the women were not always consulted about their participation in the process. More than a few younger daughters of local elites found themselves packed off by their fathers to cohabit with strange-looking, pale and hairy men who did not speak their language. These were obviously unions based on inequality. European men had no legal obligations to their colonial wives or offspring. Many native families were abandoned when the men departed for home and were left to cope with local societies that often considered them ruined or, worse still, traitorous spies. Still, bonds of true affection did often arise, not only because of growing intimacy in their personal relationships and the joys and responsibilities of child-rearing, but also because both parties were isolated from their own societies and living on the margins of another.[22]

Not all local societies encouraged or forced their young women to become cultural brokers through concubinage. Many had sexual or cultural concerns about this intermixing, and as the danger of associating too closely with the intruders became more clear, some tried to create distance rather than intimacy with ethnic Europeans. Still, overall, most colonized societies were 'remarkably accommodating' when it came to sexual and social interactions with those who came to rule them.[23] From the European perspective, though, this system of concubinage made a great deal of sense politically, economically and sexually, and it was very widely practised throughout the early modern period.

This makes it all the more surprising that it was not the native response that destroyed the system of inter-ethnic unions but policy initiatives taken by

Europeans. This shift in colonial sexual norms occurred at different times in different places, but in the British Empire the changes began in the last quarter of the eighteenth century. In 1770, it was still common for high-ranking officials in the East India Company to have a whole 'Indian' family.[24] By the turn of the century, the practice was socially unacceptable, and within only a couple more decades the East India Company formally prohibited it.[25] When the British government asserted direct control over Indian territories, it too first frowned on concubinage and then reiterated the ban in 1910.[26] In French Cambodia, the same process occurred in a more compressed period. On the eve of the twentieth century, relationships between French men and Cambodian women were commonplace. By 1920, they were considered nearly treasonous.[27]

There were many reasons why such a major shift in the patterns of cultural and sexual interaction took place. The shift from early modern imperialism, marked by thin presence and thin control, to high modern imperialism, marked by thorough colonization and more ambitious state projects, really began in the revolutionary era that we described in the first two chapters. The process of social unmixing that the sanctions against inter-ethnic marriage represented happened as part of this shift and occurred simultaneously with the great 'modernizing' developments like the creation of industrial economies and the expansion of the aims and means of state power. Put another way, one can see the rise of modern capitalism, modern nationalism, modern imperialism, modern state practices and modern racism at exactly the same time.

This simultaneous explosion of a new way of viewing and operating within the world was no coincidence. Instead, these seemingly independent phenomena were deeply interrelated. 'Modernity', the term used to describe the new order and new aspirations produced by these revolutionary shifts, was internally contradictory and thus instantly controversial. The appeal of the new vistas of wealth and power easily crossed cultural barriers. Many colonized people liked the new goods, admired the capacities of European states and European visitors and aspired to enter the circuits of power that these imperialists had opened up. Still, there was resistance on the part of many natives, who challenged both the fact of foreign rule and 'European' values.

This same split was present within European societies as well. As our discussion of Lermontov demonstrated, there were many who saw the brave new world of European acquisitiveness and European liberty as inherently morally degrading. With earlier moral and social systems in ruins, they feared that 'modern' men and women would be prone to shallow and destructive behaviour. The immediate victims of imperial and industrial destruction would be nature, tradition and the native peoples bound by that nature and tradition. Indeed, one might see the very rise of the Romantic movement as an expression of this ambivalence towards the modern world and as a crucial way that Europeans could work through the power and peril of the new system they were creating. It was no accident, in other words, that European Romantics were obsessed with pre-modern peoples in the form of historical investigations, European folk studies or Oriental tales.[28] This Romantic urge is part and parcel of 'modernity' itself. As long as there are glowing descriptions of the wonders of capitalism and technology and the historical gift that the West gave the rest of the world by bringing those wonders to them, there will be idealized nostalgia for the pure, uncorrupted and natural world that supposedly existed before the wholesale exportation of smokestacks and white bureaucrats.

This deep ambivalence concerning the relative benefits and costs associated with the world we think we have and the world we imagine we lost is the defining feature of our 'modern' era, and it is crucial to observe that it has played itself out largely in gendered terms. The worlds of the past, of nature, of the colonized, were all marked definitively as feminine, while the worlds of progress, capitalism and civic liberty were marked as masculine. This did not mean, of course, that all men were progressive industrialists or that all women were basket-weaving, illiterate repositories of tradition. Instead, it meant that imperial and industrial policies were often framed in the 'masculine' terms of profit and power and challenged in the 'feminine' ones of morality and the pre-eminence of domesticity. And despite the fact that virtually all European policy-makers were men, we should not assume that 'masculine' priorities were consistently and ruthlessly followed. Instead, what occurred following the revolutionary era was a constant tug of war and an attempt to represent the ambivalence of modernity in a stable form, an attempt to achieve progress while still retaining what was valuable in tradition, to build factories and still not destroy the countryside, to conquer and regularize the world but not to destroy its diversity.

If Romanticism was the attempt to represent and contain modernity culturally, nationalism was the effort to do so politically. On the one hand, as we saw in Chapter 1, the nation was construed as masculine and progressive, forged in battle, forward-looking and virile. On the other hand, it appealed to the past and to tradition. The modern study of history emerged to construct narratives that could express both the inherited legitimacy and youthful vigour of the national community and to clearly demarcate the cultural and territorial borders that set it off from other nations. Nationalism became a familial narrative that encompassed a tale of multiple generations and focused on the productive and reproductive union of male and female. Nations were unimaginable without masculinity and femininity, men and women. Men pushed forward and acquired, while women conserved those gains and reproduced them. In this respect, the Napoleonic conservative consensus we explored in Chapter 1 became the basis for the new model of nineteenth-century politics that saw the rise of the nation state and the expansion of European empire.

We are now in a position to understand better why mixed marriages fell from grace when they did. At the most basic level, as Europeans became more deeply entangled with the colonial world, their rather simplistic confidence in the power of their superior culture to transform local peoples was shaken. As a result, some colonial officials both on the ground and back in the metropole began to fear that in frontier conditions, intermarriage would be more likely to result in the European man 'going native' than in the native woman becoming civilized. This rather persistent imperial anxiety appeared as early as the seventeenth century in the French colonies in North America, and it encouraged colonists and colonial officials to articulate their superiority in terms of 'race' as well as of 'culture'.[29] The logical solution to this moral, sexual and political dilemma was to bring civilized white women to the frontier. They would stiffen the self-control of male settlers, provide a model of orderly domesticity and would direct the primal urges of white men away from the natives and towards upstanding Christian matrimonial sexual practices. After the great revolutions and the birth of nationalism, the pressure to reduce interracial sex gained even greater political importance. European men on their own might imperially produce, but they could not nationally reproduce. Settler colonies would require white women if the European colonial presence was to be maintained. As one French official succinctly put it: female migration was desirable because 'a man remains a man as long as he stays under the gaze of a woman of his race'.[30]

Thus the intent of this female migration was to civilize frontier men, to reproduce 'European' civilization both physically and culturally, and finally to enforce ethnic separation by placing white female bodies and disapproval between European men and local women. Needless to say, these goals were never fully attained, but the intent and effect were sufficient to transform the culture of the colonial world. More than one European man would ruefully note the change that had occurred and blame the female migrants not only for the more restrictive sexual climate, but also for the noticeably more segregated ethnic conditions. This tendency to blame European women for the intensification of racism was adopted by many subsequent historians. Recent scholarship has challenged the notion that female attitudes were the primary factor by demonstrating that there was racism in the colonies prior to the mass female migrations and by noting that it was odd for earlier historians to neglect women in their stories up to the point when it came time to apportion blame for colonial racism. But if women migrants did not invent racism, they did serve as the social enforcers of racial segregation in the realm of colonial sex, and they strove to create other segregated spaces in the colonies as well.[31]

The expanding population of white women did not logically have to reinforce sexual and racial segregationist tendencies. To the contrary, the arrival of female colonizers had the potential to call into question the gendered nature of colonialism. As we have seen, colonial ideology feminized conquered spaces and people while deeply masculinizing the figure of the white adventurer. Now the colonizers had a feminine side. Just as importantly, given the material discomforts and dangers of long-distance travel and of life in foreign climes, it was difficult to sustain the notion that all women were naturally passive, risk-averse and vulnerable. European expansion and imperialism had long served the purpose of providing enhanced opportunities for men who desired to take active part in the country's affairs and who loved novelty and the thrill of danger. It clearly contained the same possibilities for women seeking not only excitement but also relief from the constraints of domesticity.

A growing number of European women took up these new challenges, not only by personally travelling to the edges of the empire, but also by taking part in reform movements that concerned colonial issues. The most prominent early movement of this sort was the concerted campaign in Great Britain to abolish slavery, a reform effort that had its first success with the decision to forbid holding slaves on English soil in 1772 and which succeeded in extending that ban to colonial territories in 1838. Many groups had a hand in the movement, including liberals and religious organizations like the Quakers. But women activists were also prominent; indeed the period of greatest abolitionist fervour coincided with the rise of modern British feminism. Women took active part in a movement that included both male and female activists and sought to free both male and female slaves.[32] There was a good reason why women were especially active in this campaign and why they were, for the most part, welcome in it: abolitionism was above all a moral issue. As we have seen, morality was part of the female 'sphere', so women could become active in anti-slavery campaigns without challenging the established gender order. This fact gave political cover to those women who desired a public voice and who wanted eventually to obtain equal rights with men in this regard. Early feminist abolitionists would not live to see that day, however. Their very deployment of the notion that women had a special responsibility to comment on moral issues instead reinforced the system of separate spheres.

The mixture of gender politics and colonial politics resulted not in a joined movement of 'liberation of the oppressed', but in a movement in which energetic women were allowed to take prominent roles so long as they concentrated their efforts on correcting abuses abroad and on becoming the moral protectors of native women in the colonies. In part, this took the form of protecting them from the depredations of lonely white men through moral campaigns aimed at wild colonists. Increasingly, however, the campaigns that women activists in the colonies pursued were directed at ending the abuses that native women suffered from native men and their 'savage traditions'. Particularly important in this regard were the campaigns in Africa to end the widespread practice of performing clitoridectomies on pubescent girls (the removal of the clitoris and much of the labia, and the narrowing of the vagina) and the effort in India to end sati, the custom of widows burning themselves on (or being cast into) the funeral pyres of their husbands.[33] In short, women could be feminists as long as they were doing it as colonialists.

This acceptance of imperial and moral missions by active women was most obvious among female missionaries. Religious work had long been an arena in which many European women were welcome, and the expansion of empire dramatically enlarged the number of possible positions and the roles women might play in them. Many went abroad as 'missionary wives', and were expected to model not only proper Christian behaviour, but also proper (i.e. European) family norms. Missionary wives were to show obedience, of course, but they also were very active and visible in their own right. Few sat in their huts all day.[34] But even non-missionary women were expected to perform a certain 'civilizing' role – a role that was crucial not only ideologically but practically as well.

We have seen this already in the very reasons why women were encouraged to go to the colonies in the first place. Colonial planners in fact intended the intensified racial segregation that followed the arrival of white women. As Ann Stoler puts it, 'ratios of men to women *followed* from how sexuality was managed and how racial categories were produced rather than the other way around'.[35] Women were urged to reproduce a domestic environment that looked and felt European, from the furniture to the food, and in most places they did so willingly. As biological notions of race and civilization grew ever more important, this segregation extended even to practices that had long brought colonizer and colonized together, such as child-rearing. It had been commonplace for European women of a certain station to hire lower-class nursemaids and nannies. In the colonies, these servants were at first native, but the practice was increasingly curtailed, as whites feared the outcome of allowing their babes and children to drink native milk, to eat native food and to learn their first lessons from native women.[36]

Though the women who packed up and got on boats clearly had at least a little spirit of adventure and the ability to take care of themselves, their arrival also occasioned a rise of masculine protectiveness. In part this was an expression of the male anxieties described earlier. Many colonial men feared that their ability to protect themselves and their own was insufficient, and they especially feared that dark men might be enticing to white women. There is abundant evidence that this anxiety, for the British at least, intensified after the large rebellion (the so-called 'Sepoy Mutiny') in India in 1857, but it was also present elsewhere at other times.[37] By the twentieth century, these fears of interracial sexual liaisons between white women and colonized men had become something of a 'panic', leading, among other things, to assaults on black sailors in East London in 1917 and a series of race riots in 1919 in nine English port cities that had hosted colonial soldiers and mariners during the First World War.[38] These racial overreactions were nearly always based not on female complaints but on male suspicions. As one case study from Africa confirms, 'on the question of European women fearing the "sexually threatening African male," all the evidence from Nigeria throughout the colonial period points in the other direction, that women felt confident in remaining in an isolated camp for the day without any European male protection and in travelling freely on their own to remote parts of the interior'.[39] The outrage about 'black on white' sex and the proclamations of the need to defend the persons and honour of white women, in other words, came not from the women to be protected but from colonial men and from men and women at home whose imaginations tended to overheat. It served to protect the gender order and the racial order, not actual women.

In sum, the figure of the white woman in the process of imperialism is a complex one. On the one hand, it certainly opened up political and personal vistas for a great many European women over the course of the nineteenth and twentieth centuries. On the other, the condition of participating in the colonial enterprise was the acceptance of dominant gender and racial norms. As a result, women on the frontier adopted, and indeed did much to reinforce, the stereotypes that underpinned the notions of separate spheres and segregated colonies that structured European empire building in the modern era. Women had become quite politically active, often for causes that many modern readers would sympathize with. But they also played an active role in building and enforcing the structures of colonial racism that would do so much to poison the modern world.

Gender and the Science of Empire

In early modern Europe, most discussions of ethnic difference centred on questions of civilizational difference rather than biological difference. We saw this in Montaigne, and it is present in innumerable other sources well into the nineteenth century. The dominant view of human genesis and difference was based in an interpretation of the Bible that posited that all humans belonged to a single family. All had descended from Adam and Eve, and though the dramatic events of the Old Testament gave sufficient explanation for why human beings had scattered and separated culturally over the years, there was an underlying unity to the human race.[40] This biblical vision did not necessarily entail ethnic tolerance. Indeed it provided rhetorical justification for the massive and often forcible attempts at religious conversion that accompanied the spread of European empire throughout the imperial era. Nevertheless, in contrast with what came later, a fundamental baseline of humanity was preserved. Other ethnic groups might be murdered, displaced and enslaved, but their membership in the species was rarely challenged.

That view was to change in the wake of the revolutionary era. Again it is both impossible and undesirable to find a single cause for the rise of a more exclusive sense of race over the course of the nineteenth century. But much of the reason for this transformation lies in changes in state practices and scientific practices over the course of the nineteenth century. The eighteenth century had seen a great deal of systematization in both realms as scientists and bureaucrats labelled, differentiated and acted upon the objects of their enquiry. Carl Linnaeus (1707–78) sought to place all living beings within a single taxonomic system, while biologists and anthropologists like Johann Friedrich Blumenbach (1752–1840) attempted to define the constituent features of human races. Drawing on science, state officials devised methods of statistical collection and analysis in order to categorize their subjects. Having placed these groups into grids of their own making, it was easy for systematizers to ascribe essential and natural behaviours and attributes to each subgroup. Indeed, the whole point of the exercise was to create these multiple stereotypes in order to act upon diverse populations. As political action and scientific ambition became more totalizing in the modern era, some method was required that would allow both for broad vision and for detailed examination. The method of subdividing and stereotyping fit the bill perfectly.

Imperialism powerfully inflected the systematization of European knowledge. In the first place, it gave a sense of urgency to the process. As new peoples were encountered, scientists and state officials alike rushed to categorize them. Without this sense of order, the breathtaking diversity of humanity would have quickly overwhelmed even the most intellectually facile and curious scholars and politicians of the day. The result, however, was that earlier notions of humanity as a terribly large and unwieldy but single family and of nature as a single 'Chain of Being' created by a single God were discarded. They were replaced by theories that stressed diversity, but diversity of an irreconcilable sort. There were now sharp dividing lines between wolves and dogs, between Caucasians and Negroes, between Jews and Turks, between workers and peasants. Whereas previous thinkers had of course noticed and attempted to make sense of human difference, they conceptualized rather fuzzier and more permeable dividing lines. In the nineteenth century, a vast expansion of the field of scientific and social knowledge occurred, but the boundaries between the cells of knowledge that this new form of investigation was producing hardened.

Much the same process occurred in terms of gender and sexuality. As we saw in the introduction, anatomists and biologists in eighteenth-century Europe subscribed to a one-sex theory, in which men and women were simply variations on a single theme. There were theories that the clitoris was a smaller version of the penis and that testicles were ovaries that had migrated to the outside of the body.[41] Over the course of the latter part of the eighteenth century and then with gusto in the nineteenth century, this single-sex notion, which stressed that social distinctions were fundamental and biological ones peripheral, was replaced by one that posited radical biological difference and argued that social effects flowed from the biological facts.[42]

What proved toxic was that the new political technologies of state officials and the new scientific technologies of European scholars, which might have proceeded in parallel ways, became deeply intermeshed. Concerted efforts were made to link the behaviour of individuals and the attributes of entire societies to biological factors. All this was done very scientifically. Energetic scholars fanned out to the colonies and to the slums of their own cities to measure skulls and noses, to observe bone lengths, to comment on genitalia and then to correlate the differences they discovered with the evident social and political inequalities of the era. And the fact of inequality was an important one. As we shall see, much of the classificatory project was determined to challenge the revolutionary ideals of equality. It was not just that skulls and skin were different; one type was superior to the other. Thus science and imperialism developed a symbiotic relationship: the expansion of the empire opened up new vistas, new projects and new data for scientists, while the findings of those scientists served to justify the imperial project.

Throughout the whole process, gender played an important role in mediating all these disparate scientific investigations and political programmes. Gender, as we have already noted, is the social representation of sexual difference, and it provided a readily understandable model of the ways that biological difference might be deployed to justify a social system based both on inequality and complementarity. So too was sex brought to the foreground of investigation, as it represented the paradigmatic instance of the intersection between 'natural' biological practices and social structures.

Two examples might help us understand these developments a bit more clearly. In the middle of the 1850s, two important works were written that both consolidated the confusing proliferation of post-Enlightenment scholarship and served as new jumping off points for future discussions of race, sexuality, gender and human progress. The first book, *Essay on the Inequality of the Human Races*, was published in instalments between 1853 and 1855 by Joseph-Arthur de Gobineau (1816–82), a French thinker interested in bringing together new trends in historical studies and new trends in anthropology and biology. De Gobineau focused his attention on the big picture of world history, and asked why civilizations rose and fell. This had been a core historical question for most of the previous century, in large part because of the process of imperial expansion that had marked that era. The late eighteenth century was a period in which European statesmen were filled with anxiety about whether their conquests would weaken their states and about how and why previous empires and civilizations had declined.[43] Edward Gibbon (1737–94) best expressed this anxiety and the scholarly approach to this sort of macro-historical question in his famous six-volume *The History of the Decline and Fall of the Roman Empire*, published between 1776 and 1788 (precisely the period, of course, when the British Empire was rocked by the American rebellion). Gibbon's work stressed that the decline of the Roman Empire and its civilization was linked to the corruption of its morals and the corresponding weakening of its leaders and government.[44] In this respect Gibbon was firmly within the Enlightenment tradition we discussed in Chapter 1, which stressed political belonging and personal virtue far above ethnic group or biological attributes when considering forms of societies and governments.

De Gobineau rejected this argument about moral failure and started down an explicitly anti-Enlightenment road that would prove attractive to later fascists and racists. It was not, he wrote, 'generally true to say that in states on the point of death the corruption of morals is any more virulent than in those just born. It is equally doubtful whether this corruption brings about their fall; for some states, far from dying of their perversity, have lived and grown fat on it.'[45] Nor did he think that government had much to do with the rise and fall of civilizations. 'People are convinced', he wrote, 'that the good administration of good laws has a direct and powerful influence on the health of a people, and this conviction is so strong, that they attribute to such administration the mere fact that a human society goes on living at all. Here they are wrong.'[46] Instead, he argued, racial strength and racial strength alone determined the vigour and viability of any given society:

Societies perish because they are degenerate, and for no other reason ... The word degenerate, when applied to a people, means (as it ought to mean) that the people has no longer the same intrinsic value as it had before, because it has no longer the same blood in its veins, continual adulterations having gradually affected the quality of that blood. In other words, though the nation bears the name given by its founders, the name no longer connotes the same race ... He, and his civilization with him, will certainly die on the day when the primordial race-unit is so broken up and swamped by the foreign elements, that its effective qualities have no longer a sufficient freedom of action.[47]

As this selection indicates, de Gobineau linked historical progress and social survival with the purity of the racial 'stock'. A civilization could survive corrupt leaders, social anarchy and military misadventure, but it could not survive miscegenation.

This racial interpretation of history, of course, placed an enormous burden on women, who were responsible for preserving the purity of the race. Men who had sex with women of other races were wasting their racial contributions, but so long as they did not import these women into domestic societies, their own race would not be affected. Women who had sex with men of other races, on the other hand, were poisoning their own society. For people concerned with the effects of miscegenation, sexual purity (and therefore continuing social vigilance about that purity) was absolutely necessary. For strict racialists, sex was more important than any other social act that individuals could perform. Though de Gobineau himself did not spend much time discussing sex (he preferred to talk about blood), the implications were clear to later thinkers and politicians. He influenced the theories of most racist thinkers in the twentieth century, from the Nazis to present-day right-wing extremists in Europe and North America.[48]

The second writer was the British naturalist Charles Darwin (1809–82). Darwin is, of course, famous for the theory of evolution through natural selection that he outlined in detail in his 1859 work *The Origin of Species By Means of Natural Selection or the Preservation of Favoured Races in the Struggle for Life*.[49] Darwin was fully a man of the imperial age. As the title of the work indicates, he thought about biodiversity on the planet in terms of racial and species classification. His insights derived from his ability to travel far beyond Europe to collect specimens and to think about the state of the globe, and his thinking about human diversity and natural diversity were never far apart. Indeed, zoology and anthropology were pursuits that he would follow simultaneously during his trip away from 'civilization'. On the voyage to the Western Hemisphere that would provide the data for his theories, he wrote home to a friend about his adventures near Cape Horn that he had 'had an excellent opportunity of geologising and seeing much of the Savages.' After observing that the natives were in a 'miserable state of barbarism', and that their houses looked like houses built by children, he went on to note that 'I do not think any spectacle can be more interesting, than the first sight of Man in his primitive wildness. It is an interest which cannot well be imagined, untill [sic] it is experienced

… they threw their arms wildly round their heads and their long hair streaming they seemed the troubled spirits of another world.'[50] He observed the other locals he encountered with a similarly scholarly eye, commenting that in Tahiti 'the kind simple manners of the half-civilized natives are in harmony with the wild, and beautiful scenery',[51] but that the Maori in New Zealand were still savage, despite the beneficial impact of European missionaries, who 'have done much in improving their moral character and still more in teaching them the arts of civilization'.[52]

Similar categorizations were to be found regarding women, both in England and abroad. He was repelled and fascinated by the peoples he encountered in the Americas and, in a letter home, he openly admitted his attraction to the women of Lima, saying he 'could not keep his eyes off' the ladies there and that he considered them 'nice round mermaids'. In Australia, however, he found the female servants who waited on him 'abhorrent', and he observed that their 'vilest expressions' hid their 'equally vile ideas'.[53] As for women at home, he seems to have been less concerned with sexual possibilities than with the need for discipline, writing at one point that he had heard that one of his colleagues had recently married and that he hoped that he would 'teach his wife to sit upright'.[54] His fantasies of English ladies appear to have consisted of dreams of a woman who was 'angelic and good' – a type that he had 'almost forgotten' about since leaving the bosom of England.[55]

As these selections from his correspondence indicate, Darwin was a scientist who made sense of the world by classifying it, and this habit was present in his social thought as surely as it was in his biological thought. In this sense, the Darwin who went to the wilds of the world went armed with the mindset of an educated imperialist, sure of his ability to create a taxonomy of women and of races and to be able to generate knowledge from this process of labelling. His revolutionary scientific insights in many ways proceeded from this starting point. Without the grid of species in his mind, his notion of evolutionary progress would have been impossible; without the capacity as a scientist of the British Empire to be carried safely to the far side of the earth to study remote islands, the data that transformed his thinking would have been missing.

Darwin was at great pains to insist that the division of the animal world into species was a natural, and not human, phenomenon. 'From the most remote period in the history of the world', he wrote, 'organic beings have been found to resemble each other in descending degrees, so that they can be classed in groups under groups. This classification is not arbitrary like the grouping of the stars in constellations.'[56] The differences between species were more than cosmetic. Drawing on his predecessors of scientific classification, he argued that 'Expressions such as that famous one by Linnaeus, which we often meet with in a more or less concealed form, namely, that the characters do not make the genus, but that the genus gives the characters, seem to imply that some deeper bond is included in our classifications than mere resemblance. I believe that this is the case.'[57] Biology determined behaviour for both Darwin and de Gobineau, as indeed it had for Linnaeus.

Darwin made clear the impact of racial thinking on his theories early in his book, when he discussed an 1818 paper by Dr W. C. Wells that claimed that a form of natural selection took place among human beings. 'Negroes', Wells claimed, had developed resistance to tropical diseases, and therefore flourished in tropical climes, and a similar process had happened with whites in the north.[58] Still, the impact on racial thinking came not so much from the content of the text itself, which dealt primarily with the diversity of plants and animals, as from the method of classification and the insistence on the primacy of biology in the behaviour of living beings. What Darwin provided was not the theory of classification itself, but 'plausible and dynamic explanations for the long recognised affinities already enshrined in taxonomic categories'.[59] Immediately, Darwin's theories were taken up by other commentators to explain human diversity in identical terms. A group of so-called 'Social Darwinists', led by the British sociologist Herbert Spencer (1820–1903), maintained that human races were analogous to animal species. Human behaviour was determined by racial belonging, those races were in continuous competition, the fittest would survive and this racial victory would be both 'natural' and progressive. In other words, the European (now 'white') conquest of the world was natural, inevitable and all for the good. At the same time, Social Darwinists argued that this dominance was in perpetual peril and that the danger came primarily from racial degeneration. Sexual policies, therefore, were literally matters of racial or national life and death.[60]

Just as Darwin provided a justification for the continuance of racial stereotypes and inequality, so too did he provide support for the sustenance of gender stereotypes and inequality. Here the connection was perhaps less obvious, but it played an important role in the theory of natural selection as a whole. This was his theory of sexual selection: 'This form of selection depends not on a struggle for existence in relation to other organic beings or to external conditions, but on a struggle between the individuals of one sex, generally the males, for the possession of the other sex. The result is not death to the unsuccessful competitor, but few or no offspring.'[61] The theory of sexual selection was based upon the premise that sexuality was rooted in vigorous male competition for the possession of passive females. As with race, Darwin did not focus on humans, and he argued in any case that sexual selection was secondary to the more important process of natural selection. But again, the applicability of these ideas to human societies was evident, and those ideas served to reinforce the dominant gender norms of the era:

The *Origin*, seen in the wider context of Darwin's views on women, implies female subordination. The central focus on sexual reproduction, and the female's role as a vessel for the development of the next generation, meant that success in that role took on primary importance. Sexual selection forced males to become ever stronger and fitter, whilst making females progressively more passive. The female was akin to the infantile form, so different from the male as to be regarded in the light of separate species.[62]

Again, other commentators explicitly and quickly developed these implications, and Darwin later clarified his view that sexual inequality was both natural and progressive for mankind.[63] Over the next 150 years, this model that privileged the biological roots of behaviours and stressed difference and inequality would be challenged from within the scientific community again and again, just as it would be in the political realm, but it continues to exert a powerful influence today.

In science as well as in politics, the issues of sex and race were central in the Victorian era, and the trend in both was to highlight essential difference *and* fundamental inequality. These processes were deeply inflected by the experience of empire, in particular the urgency of dealing with the issue of human diversity, the desire to justify European dominance, and the intense interest in primal sexuality, exotic races and, of course, primal sex with members of exotic races. All these concerns were tied together in the notion of 'civilization', that bundle of practices and outlooks that allowed Europeans to exert dominance but also repressed many of their deepest desires.

Gender and the Politics of Empire

The concept of civilization as a higher form of social order based in the proper alignment of gender roles had tremendous implications, as it justified both the process of imperial conquest and the increasing intrusion into the daily lives of non-Europeans. That expansionist tendency had its limits, as the expense of conquering and maintaining empires called into question the economic profitability of the enterprise, and as the different European powers rapidly came into conflict with one another outside of Europe. These imperial dangers were very visible. At virtually every step of the way, politicians in the capital cities of Europe questioned whether ultra-competitive global conquest was really in anyone's best interest, and these questions became more pressing as time went on. As the British Foreign Office put it when the ambitious explorer Lovett Cameron claimed the mouth of the Congo River for the British Crown in 1875 without consulting London first, 'the last thing Great Britain needs is more jungles and more savages'.[64] The dominant political figure in Germany during the latter half of the nineteenth century, Chancellor Otto von Bismarck (1815–98), had a similarly cautious view about German interests in the Balkans at the same time, claiming that German interest in the region was 'so slight as to not be worth the bones of a Pomeranian musketeer'.[65] Similarly, when Europeans expanded into the domains of older empires like the Ottoman or the Qing, the dominant note was one of caution. This has led many historians to argue that the great European imperial conquests, far from being driven by greed or reckless militarism, were accomplished not willingly but, in the memorable phrase of Sir John Robert Seely, 'in a fit of absence of mind'.[66]

There was indeed a certain momentum of events that individual leaders and states felt unable to check, but it is going too far to suggest that there was no human agency on the part of powerful European diplomats. The question thus arises: if European statesmen increasingly doubted the financial or political gains from imperial expansion, why did they take the decision to expand? The answer is complicated, and it transcends the question of gender, but one important aspect of the decision-making process was certainly the model of white masculinity that all European politicians shared. They believed that they had a duty to protect the interests of their children and therefore did not want to lose out in the struggle for land, even if that struggle was costly in the short term. They had a duty to civilize the yellow, brown and black races of the world, to rid them of their horrid customs, to teach them the delights of property and to train them in the masculine self-control necessary for colonial obedience and future self-governance. Finally, they were firmly convinced that they had the unbreakable duty to protect what was already theirs, to allow no encroachment on the territory, property, honour or prestige that their forebears had sweated, bled and died for.

This final duty was, of course, deeply and self-consciously conservative, and it could not be upheld indefinitely in a competitive, multi-actor struggle. Not only was the potential for expansion rapidly shrinking, but new forces were also emerging to challenge the nineteenth-century imperial order. Politically speaking, three of these challenges deserve special mention here. The first challenge was the one most noted at the time and by later historians: the sudden shift in the balance of power within the club of 'Great Powers'. The new German Empire, formed in 1871 after the Prussian army thrashed French forces in the Franco-Prussian War, was proving to be a dynamic and destabilizing force in global affairs. In economic terms, in political influence, in territorial acquisition and in naval strength, Germany was threatening to establish itself as the pre-eminent power in Europe, a prospect looked on with horror by most of its neighbours and by Great Britain. The second challenge, which was clearer in hindsight than it was at the time, was that the forces of decolonization were organizing in the colonial world. By 1910, the movement for home rule in India had acquired such significant dimensions that Gandhi was able to suggest that 'all our countrymen appear to be pining for National Independence'.[67]

The third challenge was that decolonizing movements had come of age in many places in Europe itself. These movements, which universally declared themselves to be 'nationalist' and deployed the familiar rhetoric of the French Revolution as the justification for their desires for independence, were threatening to destroy the imperial order from within. They were maturing all over the continent, from Ireland to Poland, but the most significant developments were occurring in the place where imperial control had collapsed the most: in the Balkans. The standard-bearer of nationalist statehood in the region was Serbia, and it was on a collision course with the Habsburg Empire, which could not tolerate such an ambitious neighbour and such a dangerous precedent.

All three of these challenges to the Victorian system had one thing in common: they declared themselves to be young and masculine. Serbia, having only recently gained independence, was of course eager to stress its youth, but even Gandhi, who liked to stress the ancient roots of Indian civilization, called the newspaper he edited from 1919 to 1931 *Young India*.[68] German propagandists were equally fond of describing their nation as young and vigorous. Heinrich von Treitschke, one of Germany's great historians, argued that Germany had proved successful in creating a unified state and empire in the nineteenth century because 'it is, as a rule, only the virile formative energy of youthful peoples that achieves success in the fierce struggle for the beginnings of national unity'.[69] The maleness was even less in doubt. Prussia's leadership in the unification process was because of their 'vigorous will':

> There, in the marches beyond the Elbe, a new North German tribe had come into existence ... Hard were they, and weather-proof, steeled by toil on a niggardly land, fortified too by the unceasing combats of a frontier life, able and independent after the manner of colonists, accustomed to regard their Slav neighbors with the contempt of a dominant race, as rugged and incisive as was compatible with the genial and jovial solidity of the Low German character.[70]

This focus on muscular vigour was evident throughout Europe in the last decade before the Great War. It was no accident that the first years of the twentieth century saw much more intense attention paid to adolescent boys than ever before. Every hint of national or imperial decline across the continent, whether it was the British embarrassment in the Boer War (1899–1902) or the Russian humiliation in the Russo-Japanese War (1904–5), occasioned a bout of handwringing about the 'feminizing' forces of modern urban culture and the need to develop harder, manlier and healthier boys. The desperate fear of going soft was occasioned not only by specific defeats, but also by the more general sense of crisis and threat that pervaded European culture at the turn of the century.

The response to this fear was articulate and concrete. Throughout the continent, there was a wave of militarization that focused on the bodies and sentiments of boys. Programmes of gymnastics and other physical education, usually heavily nationalist and directed by military men, mushroomed in Germany, in the Czech lands and in Russia. Anxieties about the 'effeminate' decline of the nation led Robert Baden-Powell to form the Boy Scouts in a similar spirit in England in 1908, and Scouting took off almost immediately across Europe and North America. The Scout motto perfectly reflected this ethic of masculine defensiveness: 'Be Prepared!' The watchword of preparedness extended to industrial policy as well. The economies of the Great Powers, long geared to the low-intensity conflict and high-intensity foreign trade of colonialism, began the process of preparing for the high-intensity conflict and much lower intensity of trade that a European total war would produce.

This trajectory of economic and masculine escalation had a rather obvious logical conclusion: a devastating total war that would bleed the continent dry both in terms of human and economic power. Many European thinkers found it difficult to believe that such a comfortable continent would trade relative peace and prosperity for death and destruction. Jan Bloch, a Polish subject of the Russian Crown and wealthy railway magnate, thought that such a war was 'impossible'. As he noted in an interview with an English journalist, 'The very development that has taken place in the mechanism of war has rendered war an impracticable operation ... we should find the inevitable result in a catastrophe which would destroy all existing political organizations. Thus, the great war cannot be made, and any attempt to make it would result in suicide.'[71] Norman Angell quite agreed in his influential book *The Great Illusion*, in which he argued that military action, far from preserving domestic capital and allowing for its expansion abroad, so disrupted global trade that war was no longer economically feasible. It was now an 'economic impossibility for one nation to seize or destroy the wealth of another or for one nation to enrich itself by subjecting another'.[72]

These were sensible and logical conclusions, but they presupposed that material concerns were weightier than masculine ones. This was a great illusion that the Great War would do much to dispel, but even before the outbreak of war many citizens understood that a large part of the problem was the sudden rise to dominance of a particular model of military masculinity. Three groups of people recognized the danger and scrambled to avoid the looming collision by challenging the new, virulent form of European masculinity. The first group was that of feminist pacifists, who presumed along with the militarists that war came naturally to men and peace naturally to women. They argued that the only way to derail the train of war was to counterbalance the political strength of military masculinism with the political force of pacifist feminism. As Jane Addams, the internationally renowned American peace activist and feminist put it, feminism and militarism were in 'eternal opposition' and the only way to defeat militarism was to grant a political voice to women, who valued life as a result of their maternal instincts.[73] This position was extremely influential among European feminists involved in the international peace movement.[74]

The second group of people challenged the notion that war and aggression were natural parts of masculinity and sought to redefine the notion of what a 'real man' was. This group faced an uphill struggle, as the weight of scientific expertise at the time suggested that male aggression and violence were not only natural but also biologically necessary for survival. This was both a Darwinist argument that killing was genetically embedded in every man and a Social Darwinist argument that projected a species imperative onto human races, societies and nations. The emerging canon of secular historical studies argued along similar lines that warfare was endemic to human society and that it proved to be a force for progress. It was perhaps therefore not surprising that the dominant challenge to these powerful secular modernist discourses came from rather traditional, indeed fundamentalist, religious sources. The most prominent figure on the continent arguing that men were naturally peaceable was Leo Tolstoy, the famous Russian novelist and former army officer who underwent a religious conversion at the height of his literary fame and devoted the rest of his career to the cause of peace and of Christianity. His Christian radicalism earned him scorn from the established churches of the day. He was in fact eventually excommunicated from the Russian Orthodox Church for constantly arguing that true Christians must oppose modern states and modern armies. But he was enormously influential; the educated elite of Europe knew him and his work, and peace activists from around the world sought to correspond with him or meet him personally.[75]

Finally, there was a group of people convinced both that martial masculinity was natural and that peace was necessary. This was an international group that included a collective of Heidelberg professors who wrote to the German government just before the outbreak of the First World War urging it to create an 'army of public peace' which would unite different classes of German men in the spirit of shared national service while backing away from armed conflict with other states.[76] The most widely read articulation of this position came from the Harvard philosopher William James, who sought to contest military masculinism within the bounds of the dominant scientific and historical discourses.[77] He freely admitted that 'our ancestors have bred pugnacity into our bone and marrow, and thousands of years of peace won't breed it out of us'. He further conceded that the position of 'reflective apologists for war' had merit, that no 'healthy minded person' could help agreeing at least in part that the horrors of war 'are a cheap price to pay for rescue from the only alternative supposed, of a world of clerks and teachers, of co-education and zoophily, of "consumer's leagues" and "associated charities," of industrialism unlimited, and feminism unabashed. No scorn, no hardness, no valor any more! Fie upon such a cattleyard of a planet!' Yet James also agreed with Angell and Bloch that war had become 'absurd and impossible from its own monstrosity'. His solution was to redirect the aggression and to maintain military virtues in a different war by conscripting all young men into an 'army enlisted against Nature', where they would serve a tour of duty in difficult conditions, in mines, on trains or on 'fishing fleets in December'.[78]

These three counter-models of masculinity stood little chance. James was in no position to create the sort of institutions he proposed, and Tolstoy, though often admired, was seen as dangerously naïve. The feminists, from the perspective of their opponents, were much more dangerous. They were more numerous, they were building an organizational base and they were forwarding the popular notion of equality. The fear of 'feminism unabashed' led to delusions that a mass 'sex war' was in the offing, especially in Great Britain. There were genuine concerns that increased female political activism would make the nation 'effeminate' and therefore vulnerable to exploitation or conquest. But the frightened masculinists need not have worried so much. Behind the military model of masculinity stood science, the state, the entire educational establishment, the organized churches of the day and a deep attractiveness that reached down to all levels of European society. The new model of fraternal, militarized manhood had become embedded in high politics, in colonial policy, in industrial production and in the sphere of social relations. It would come to the forefront of political life in the years of the Great War, just as it had briefly during the years of revolution more than a century before. But this time, it would retain its pre-eminence and would colour gender relations until the present day.

Conclusion

At the turn of the twentieth century, England's most famous imperial writer was Rudyard Kipling (1865–1936), the author of *The Jungle Book* and many other thrilling tales about life in India. One of his most famous poems, however, had little obvious connection to overseas exploits, despite the fact that it was inspired by the pluck of British officers in the 1895 'Jameson Raid' in South Africa. It was an anthem to stoic manhood entitled 'If'.

> If you can keep your head when all about you
> Are losing theirs and blaming it on you
> If you can trust yourself when all men doubt you,
> But make allowance for their doubting too;
> If you can wait and not be tired by waiting,
> Or, being lied about, don't deal in lies,
> Or, being hated, don't give way to hating,
> And yet don't look too good, nor talk too wise;
>
> If you can dream – and not make dreams your master;
> If you can think – and not make thoughts your aim;
> If you can meet with Triumph and Disaster
> And treat those two imposters just the same;
> If you can bear to hear the truth you've spoken
> Twisted by knaves to make a trap for fools,
> Or watch the things you gave your life to broken,
> And stoop and build 'em up with wornout tools;
>
> If you can make one heap of all your winnings
> And risk it on one turn of pitch-and-toss,
> And lose, and start again at your beginnings
> And never breath a word about your loss;
> If you can force your heart and nerve and sinew
> To serve your turn long after they are gone,
> And so hold on when there is nothing in you
> Except the Will which says to them: 'Hold on';

> If you can talk with crowds and keep your virtue,
> Or walk with Kings – nor lose the common touch;
> If neither foes nor loving friends can hurt you;
> If all men count with you, but none too much;
> If you can fill the unforgiving minute
> With sixty seconds' worth of distance run –
> Yours is the Earth and everything that's in it,
> And – which is more – you'll be a Man my son![79]

We cite this poem in full because it provides a sharp description of imperial masculinity. Kipling's masculinity was a disciplined one. It encompassed cool rationality, a rejection of emotional extremes, a combination of inner confidence and humility, and above all a power of will that could overcome both physical unpleasantness and social anxieties. This set of virtues could be expressed simply: self-control is necessary before one can rule others. When that process of self-discipline was successful, immense power would be joined to strong notions of duty, and then the world would be yours, and everything that's in it. And which was 'more', both for Kipling and for his readers, one would be a man. The road to power and to a stable gender identity led through self-control.

Not every European with power was as keen on discipline and proud insularity as Kipling, a fact that our investigation of sex during this chapter demonstrated. The wild world that opened up before European colonists and adventurers was simultaneously attractive and repulsive, and it was often chaotic, escaping knowledge, representation and control. Sex was always right on the border of order and chaos. Where male dominance, restraint and religious virtue could be asserted, sex provided the basis for racial regeneration, colonial reproduction and imperial stability. But not all sex was in this, shall we say, missionary position. And as Europeans fanned out across the world – sometimes precisely to avoid this sexual repression – discipline and order in sexual affairs could and did break down. That freedom from restraint took many forms. For some it was a frankly exploitative form of what is today called sex tourism. Others took the opportunity to practise sexualities that were considered exotic at home (as the continuing fascination with the Kama Sutra and Tantric sex demonstrates) or were socially troublesome there (like homosexuality). The concerted effort of colonial states to rein in this disruptive sexuality by sending European women in to police the sexual interface in the colonies did much to cement certain sorts of femininity and masculinity in place. It did not, however, erase the association of sexual liberty with the colonial world, something amply attested to by the fact that Westerners are still prone to describing tired women stripping in windowless hovels as 'exotic dancing'.

Still, European men know what they *should* do. It remains much more respectable to have a stiff upper lip on the battlefield than other sorts of stiffness in an 'exotic' dance club, just as it was better for colonials to be buttoned up in the English club rather than unbuttoned with the natives throughout the later imperial era. And as the imperial age continued and deepened, the colonial interface was increasingly envisioned in martial terms. This imperial masculinity, rooted in racial notions of natural superiority and the duties as well as privileges of rule, owed a lot to the experience of colonial warfare, where Europeans were consistently outnumbered by local troops but continually prevailed due not only to superior weapons technology, but also to superior organizational technology.[80] Colonial troops, like colonial settlers, were formed into social organizations devoted to conquest and domination, and these ethics and practices of organization migrated back and forth between the colonial world and the European homelands.[81]

The common imperial masculinity so succinctly encapsulated by Kipling bound this discipline and violence together, and it depended fundamentally on the opportunity to conquer first oneself and then others. These rituals of dominance and discipline were practised in different geographical and social settings, most commonly in relation to women, but also in relation to lower-class subjects of their own realms and to colonized peoples. It was a masculinity that relied upon aggression and which demanded continuous contests with other men to prove one's worth. These contests might be channelled into sporting activities, which blossomed in the late imperial era, but mortal combat remained the true test, the final exam of masculinity, throughout the continent. As the twentieth century dawned, so many adolescents were girding for this battle, and so many states were eager to provide them with weapons, that war began to be seen not as a necessary evil, but as a necessary process without which boys could never find out whether they were really men.

Kipling's son John was one of those young men with 'If' in the back of their minds as they sought to unravel the mysteries of manhood through the practice of war. John was only sixteen when the First World War broke out, and though his youth and poor eyesight disqualified him from service, he entreated his father to pull strings to get him enlisted in the army. Kipling did so proudly. Within only a few weeks after his arrival in the lines, in the autumn of 1915, John disappeared, last seen attempting to limp away from a failed charge into a position defended by machine guns. At first, Kipling hoped he had been taken prisoner, but as time dragged on he became reconciled to the fact that his son was dead (John's battlefield remains were finally identified in 1992). Kipling continued to write patriotic verse to buck up the morale of the nation, but he was grieving deeply. He put on a good face in public, but privately he was working through the pain in verse: 'My son died laughing at some jest, I would I knew / What it were, and it might serve me at a time when jests are few.'[82]

In 1917, Kipling publicly attempted to reconcile his patriotism and his grief in a lament entitled 'The Children':

These were our children who died for our lands: they were dear in our sight.
We have only the memory left of their home-treasured sayings and laughter.
The price of our loss shall be paid to our hands, not another's hereafter.
Neither the Alien nor Priest shall decide on it. That is our right.
But who shall return us the children?

At the hour the Barbarian chose to disclose his pretences,
And raged against Man, they engaged, on the breasts that they bared for us,
The first felon-stroke of the sword he had long-time prepared for us—
Their bodies were all our defense while we wrought our defences.

They bought us anew with their blood, forbearing to blame us,
Those hours which we had not made good when the judgment o'ercame us.
They believed us and perished for it. Our statecraft, our learning
Delivered them bound to the Pit and alive to the burning
Whither they mirthfully hastened as jostling for honour—
Not since her birth has our Earth seen such worth loosed upon her.

Nor was their agony brief, or once only imposed on them.
The wounded, the war-spent, the sick received no exemption
Being cured they returned and endured and achieved our redemption,
Hopeless themselves of relief, till Death, marvelling, closed on them.

That flesh we had nursed from the first in all cleanness was given
To corruption unveiled and assailed by the malice of Heaven—
By the heart-shaking jests of Decay where it lolled on the wires—
To be blanched or gay-painted by fumes—to be cindered by fires—
To be senselessly tossed and retossed in stale mutilation
From crater to crater. For this we shall take expiation.
But who shall return us our children?[83]

Kipling clearly had not given up believing in the aims of British power that he had identified with throughout his life. Indeed, like many of his compatriots he was if anything even more desperate to reconfirm them in the years that followed the war. But a note of doubt had crept into his work, as it had throughout Europe. That increased uncertainty, and the wars that provoked it, is the theme of the next chapter.

Notes

1. Anthony Pagden, *Lords of All the World: Ideologies of Empire in Spain, Britain and France c. 1500–c. 1850* (New Haven, CT: Yale University Press, 1995).

2. Marjory Harper, 'British Migration and the Peopling of the Empire', in *The Nineteenth Century*, ed. Andrew Porter, vol. 3, *The Oxford History of the British Empire* (Oxford and New York: Oxford University Press, 1999), 75.

3. B. R. Tomlinson, 'Economics and Empire: The Periphery and the Imperial Economy', in *The Nineteenth Century*, ed. Andrew Porter, vol. 3, *The Oxford History of the British Empire* (Oxford and New York: Oxford University Press, 1999), 68.

4. Sigmund Freud, *Civilization and Its Discontents*, trans. James Strachey (New York: W. W. Norton, 2005).

5. Michel de Montaigne, *Essays*, trans. J. M. Cohen (New York and London: Penguin, 1958), 108–10.

6. Edward W. Said, *Orientalism*, 1st Vintage Books edition (New York: Vintage Books, 1979), 62.

7. Mikhail Lermontov, *A Hero of Our Time*, trans. Vladimir Nabokov (Ann Arbor, IL: Ardis, 1988).

8. Ibid., 1–2.

9. Ibid., 64.

10. Ibid., xviii.

11. For a brief discussion of feminist criticism on the novel, see: Robert Reid, *Lermontov's A Hero of Our Time* (London: Bristol Classical Press, 1997), 7.

12. For a fine discussion of both the Russian oriental exotica and the response by writers like Lermontov, see: Susan Layton, *Russian Literature and Empire: Conquest of the Caucasus from Pushkin to Tolstoy* (Cambridge and New York: Cambridge University Press, 1994).

13. Said, *Orientalism*.

14. Peter Scotto, 'Prisoners of the Caucasus: Ideologies of Imperialism in Lermontov's "Bela"', *PMLA* 107, no. 2 (1992): 246–60.

15. Layton, *Russian Literature and Empire*, 141.

16. Jane Costlow, 'Compassion and the Hero: Women in *a Hero of Our Time*', in *Lermontov's a Hero of Our Time: A Critical Companion*, ed. Lewis Bagby (Evanston, IL: Northwestern University Press, 2002), 101.

17. For another argument along this line in the American case, see: Geoffrey Sanborn, *The Sign of the Cannibal: Melville and the Making of a Postcolonial Reader*, New Americanists (Durham, NC: Duke University Press, 1998).

18. Philippa Levine, 'Sexuality, Gender and Empire', in *Gender and Empire*, ed. Philippa Levine, The Oxford History of the British Empire Companion Series (Oxford and New York: Oxford University Press, 2004), 151. Kenneth Ballhatchet, *Race, Sex and Class under the Raj: Imperial Attitudes and Policies and Their Critics, 1793–1905* (New York: St. Martin's Press, 1980), 10.

19. Ronald Hyam, *Empire and Sexuality: The British Experience* (Manchester and New York: Manchester University Press, 1990), 93.

20. For an excellent discussion of this process in an area where neither colonizer nor colonized was European, see: Paul D. Barclay, 'Cultural Brokerage and Interethnic Marriage in Colonial Taiwan: Japanese Subalterns and Their Aborigine Wives, 1895–1930', *Journal of Asian Studies* 64, no. 2 (2005): 323–60.

21. Few of the unions entered into on the frontier were either blessed by religious authorities or formally recognized as marriage by metropolitan states and legal systems. This system of informal sexual and social partnership was known as 'concubinage', and it allowed many European men to maintain a concubine in the colonies and a wife in the 'homeland'.

22. For an especially sensitive consideration of the affections and power potentials in play, see: Maya Jasanoff, *Edge of Empire: Lives, Culture and Conquest in the East, 1750–1850* (New York: Alfred A. Knopf, 2005), 64–71.

23. Hyam, *Empire and Sexuality*, 3.

24. Kathleen Wilson, 'Empire, Gender, and Modernity in the Eighteenth Century', in *Gender and Empire*, ed. Philippa Levine, The Oxford History of the British Empire Companion Series (Oxford and New York: Oxford University Press, 2004), 36.

25. Ballhatchet, *Race, Sex and Class under the Raj*, 2.

26. Philippa Levine, 'Sexuality, Gender and Empire', 138.; Ann Laura Stoler, *Carnal Knowledge and Imperial Power: Race and the Intimate in Colonial Rule* (Berkeley and Los Angeles: University of California Press, 2002), 49.

27. Penny Edwards, 'Womanizing Indochina: Fiction, Nation and Cohabitation in Cambodia, 1890–1930', in *Domesticating the Empire: Race, Gender and Family Life in French and Dutch Colonialism*, eds Julia Ann Clancy-Smith and Frances Gouda (Charlottesville, NC and London: University Press of Virginia, 1998), 117.

28. Saree Makdisi, *Romantic Imperialism: Universal Empire and the Culture of Modernity* (Cambridge: Cambridge University Press, 1998), 10.

29. On this see: Saliha Belmessous, 'Assimilation and Racialism in Seventeenth- and Eighteenth-Century French Colonial Policy', *American Historical Review* 110, no. 2 (2005): 322–49.

30. Cited in Stoler, *Carnal Knowledge*, 1.

31. Hyam, *Empire and Sexuality*, 119; Stoler, *Carnal Knowledge*, 34.

32. Clare Midgley, 'Anti-Slavery and the Roots of "Imperial Feminism"', in *Gender and Imperialism*, ed. Clare Midgley (Manchester and New York: Manchester University Press, 1998), 162–63. The same close connection between abolitionism and feminism was present in the United States in the same period.

33. On clitoridectomy see: Susan Pedersen, 'National Bodies, Unspeakable Acts: The Sexual Politics of Colonial Policy-Making', *Journal of Modern History* 63, no. 4 (1991): 647–80. On sati see: Gayatri Chakravorty Spivak, 'Can the Subaltern Speak?', in *Marxism and the Interpretation of Culture*, eds Cary Nelson and Lawrence Grossberg (Urbana, IL: University of Illinois Press, 1988), 271–313; and Lati Mani, *Contentious Traditions: The Debate on Sati in Colonial India* (Berkeley: University of California Press, 1998).

34. Catherine Hall, 'Of Gender and Empire: Reflections on the Nineteenth Century', in *Gender and Empire*, ed. Philippa Levine (Oxford and New York: Oxford University Press, 2004), 60.

35. Stoler, *Carnal Knowledge*, 2. Emphasis in original.

36. Nancy Rose Hunt, 'Le Bébé En Brousse: European Women, African Birth Spacing, and Colonial Intervention in Breast Feeding in the Belgian Congo', in *Tensions of Empire: Colonial Cultures in a Bourgeois World*, eds Frederick Cooper and Ann Laura Stoler (Berkeley: University of California Press, 1997), 296. Stoler, *Carnal Knowledge*, 133.

37. Penelope Tuson, 'Mutiny Narratives and the Imperial Feminine: European Women's Accounts of the Rebellion in India in 1857', *Women's Studies International Forum* 21, no. 3 (1998): 291–303. Stoler, *Carnal Knowledge*, 58.

38. Laura Tabili, 'Empire Is the Enemy of Love: Edith Noor's Progress and Other Stories', *Gender & History* 17, no. 1 (2005): 5–28. Lucy Bland, 'White Women and Men of Colour: Miscegenation Fears in Britain after the Great War', *Gender & History* 17, no. 1 (2005): 29–61.

39. Helen Callaway, *Gender, Culture and Empire: European Women in Colonial Nigeria* (Urbana and Chicago: University of Illinois Press, 1987), 235.

40. George W. Stocking, *Victorian Anthropology* (New York: The Free Press, 1987), 17.

41. Laqueur, *Making Sex*, 92–93.

42. Nancy Leys Stepan, 'Race, Gender, Science and Citizenship', in *Cultures of Empire:*

Colonizers in Britain and the Empire in the Nineteenth and Twentieth Centuries, a Reader, ed. Catherine Hall (New York: Routledge, 2000), 77.

43. On this see: Pagden, *Lords of All the World*.

44. Edward Gibbon, *The History of the Decline and Fall of the Roman Empire* (London and New York: Penguin, 1994).

45. Joseph Gobineau, 'Essay on the Inequality of the Human Races (1853–5)', in *Gobineau: Selected Political Writings*, ed. Michael D. Biddiss (New York and Evanston, IL: Harper and Row, 1970), 51.

46. Ibid., 54.

47. Ibid., 58–59.

48. On European influence, see: George L. Mosse, *Toward the Final Solution: A History of European Racism* (New York: Howard Fertig, 1978).

49. Charles Darwin, *The Origin of Species By Means of Natural Selection or the Preservation of Favoured Races in the Struggle for Life* (New York: Penguin, 1958).

50. Charles Darwin, 'Letter to J. S. Henslow (11 April 1833)', in *Charles Darwin's Letters: A Selection, 1825–1859*, ed. Frederick Burkhardt (Cambridge and New York: Cambridge University Press, 1996), 27–28.

51. Charles Darwin, 'Letter to Caroline Darwin (27 December 1835)', in ibid., 48.

52. Ibid., 49.

53. Cited in James Moore and Adrian Desmond, *Darwin* (London: Michael Joseph, 1991), 167, 179.

54. Charles Darwin, 'Letter to Susan Darwin (23 April 1835),' in *Charles Darwin's Letters*, 45.

55. James Moore and Adrian Desmond, *Darwin* (London: Michael Joseph, 1991), 168.

56. Darwin, *The Origin of Species*, 385.

57. Ibid., 387.

58. Ibid., 19.

59. Harriet Ritvo, 'Classification and Continuity in The Origin of Species', in *Charles Darwin's The Origin of Species: New Interdisciplinary Essays,* eds David Amigoni and Jeff Wallace (Manchester and New York: Manchester University Press, 1995), 52.

60. J. W. Burrow, *The Crisis of Reason: European Thought, 1848–1914* (New Haven, CT and London: Yale University Press, 2000), 92–96.

61. Darwin, *The Origin of Species*, 94.

62. Fiona Erskine, '*The Origin of Species* and the Science of Female Inferiority', in *Charles Darwin's The Origin of Species: New Interdisciplinary Essays*, eds David Amigoni and Jeff Wallace (Manchester and New York: Manchester University Press, 1995), 101.

63. Charles Darwin, *The Descent of Man and Selection in Relation to Sex* (New York: D. Appleton, 1902).

64. Cited in H. L. Wesseling, *Divide and Rule: The Partition of Africa, 1880–1914* (Westport, CT: Praeger, 1996), 81.

65. Cited in Louis Leo Snyder, *The Blood and Iron Chancellor; A Documentary-Biography of Otto Von Bismarck* (Princeton: Van Nostrand, 1967), 1.

66. John Robert Seeley, *The Expansion of England* (Chicago: University of Chicago Press, 1971), 12.

67. Mohandas Gandhi and Anthony Parel, *Hind Swaraj and Other Writings*, Cambridge Texts in Modern Politics (Cambridge and New York: Cambridge University Press, 1997), 13.

68. Ibid., 14.

69. Heinrich von Treitschke, *Treitschke's History of Germany in the Nineteenth Century*, vol. 1, eds Eden Paul and Cedar Paul (New York: McBride Nast & Company, 1915), 8.

70. Ibid., 28–29.

71. Ivan Stanislavovich Bloch and R. C. Long, *The Future of War in Its Technical, Economic, and Political Relations: Is War Now Impossible?*, trans. R. C. Long (New York: Garland Publishing, 1899; reprint, 1972), xi.

72. Norman Angell, *The Great Illusion; a Study of the Relation of Military Power in Nations to Their Economic and Social Advantage* (New York: Putnam, 1910), vii.

73. Jean Bethke Elshtain, *Women and War* (New York: Basic Books, 1987), 234.

74. Richard J. Evans, ed., *Comrades & Sisters: Feminism, Socialism & Pacifism in Europe, 1870–1945* (New York: St. Martin's Press, 1987).

75. See especially: Leo Tolstoy, *Writings on Civil Disobedience and Nonviolence* (Philadelphia: New Society Publishers, 1987).

76. Kenneth Holland, 'The European Labor Service', *Annals of the American Academy of Political and Social Science* 194 (November 1937): 152–64.

77. James had an international reputation largely connected with his theories of pragmatism, and his essay on war had a similar scope. The German theologian Adolf Deissmann, for instance, wrote an essay in 1913 urging Europeans not to adopt Social Darwinism as a guide to political practice and suggested adopting James's views as an alternative. On Deissmann see: Charles E. Bailey, 'The British Protestant Theologians in the First World War: Germanophobia Unleashed', *The Harvard Theological Review* 77, no. 2 (April 1984): 199. James's ideas appealed not only to pacifists but to fascists like Mussolini as well. William Kilborne Steward, 'The Mentors of Mussolini', *The American Political Science Review* 29, no. 4 (November 1928): 843–69.

78. William James, 'The Moral Equivalent of War', in *The Moral Equivalent of War and Other Essays*, ed. John K. Roth (New York: Harper and Row, 1971).

79. Rudyard Kipling, 'If', in *Rudyard Kipling's Verse: Definitive Edition* (Garden City, NY: Doubleday and Co., 1946), 578.

80. For discussions of the early development of these weapons and organizational technologies, see: Geoffrey Parker, *The Military Revolution: Military Innovation and the Rise of the West,* 2nd edition (Cambridge: Cambridge University Press, 1996).

81. See here: Isabel V. Hull, *Absolute Destruction: Military Culture and the Practices of War in Imperial Germany* (Ithaca, NY: Cornell University Press, 2005).

82. Cited in Lord Birkenhead, *Rudyard Kipling* (New York: Random House, 1978), 269.

83. Rudyard Kipling, 'The Children', in *Rudyard Kipling's Verse*, 522.

—4—

Brothers and Sisters at War

In the immediate wake of the Second World War (1939–45), it was hard to escape the impression that the great wars of the twentieth century had done more to change gender relationships in Europe than all of the political lobbying, modernist and feminist provocations, and economic changes in peacetime combined. Most European countries granted women the right to vote after the Great War (the First World War, 1914–18). Russian women, for instance, voted in 1917, British women over the age of thirty were granted suffrage in 1918, and German and Austrian women balloted in 1919. Many other states followed suit, and the other holdouts granted women the vote at the end of the Second World War. Indeed, in both France and Italy, the vote was granted even before the end of hostilities, and in Greece, where full suffrage would not come until 1952, areas controlled by resistance fighters gave women the vote in the midst of the war as well. The social changes were just as evident. Throughout the continent women had been enlisted in large numbers into urban industry, had spent time alone with men they were nursing, had donned uniforms and had generally rushed en masse into the public sphere from which they had largely been excluded in the nineteenth century. By the 1970s, there was a consensus among historians and social scientists that the wars had fundamentally transformed the gender landscape of the continent.

The reason for this transformation was also seemingly clear: the active role that women had played in the war effort had challenged the deeply ingrained nineteenth-century stereotypes about female capacities and had proved that they deserved political and social equality with men. In 1914, those hostile to equal rights for women could write that the 'full power of citizenship cannot be given to a sex which is by nature debarred from fulfilling some of the crucial duties of citizenship – enforcement of law, of treaties and of national rights, national defence, and all the rougher work of Empire'.[1] The participation of women in war industries, in the rough work of nursing and sanitation near combat zones and in the more hostile spheres of combat and espionage during the war called into question how 'natural' political and social discrimination was. Suffrage was thus presented as a gift to the women of Europe for exemplary service in one of the century's two world wars. As the Greek resistance fighters put it in 1944, 'the women of Greece participated so actively in the struggle against fascism, and so by their own efforts they won the right to debate and manage communal affairs'.[2]

131

This model of women's liberation through total war came under serious attack beginning in the 1970s with a new wave of feminist scholarship that saw with perhaps greater clarity than the previous generation had how incomplete the wartime moves towards equality had been. These historians pointed out that the wartime economic situations were extraordinary and that women lost their new jobs as soon as veterans returned to reclaim them. Indeed, in many countries the post-war situation was bleaker than it had been before the war, as women formed a smaller part of the industrial workforce than they had before it began. In Great Britain, for instance, a smaller percentage of women worked in 1921 than had done so in 1911.[3] In cultural terms too, the wars had valorized men and aggressive masculinity in ways that many feminist historians found troubling. Far from being liberated by the wars, this literature argued, women had suffered during them. They worked long hours in the war economy while still fully engaged in domestic economies, they bore the brunt of brutal occupation policies, cowered in bomb shelters and got smaller food rations than their male counterparts. When the war ended, their men victimized them in other ways. They were fired from their jobs, questioned about their wartime behaviour by jealous husbands and forced out of the public sphere. Whatever had changed during the war, the fact of male dominance and female subordination had not. Indeed, if anything, these historians argued, the situation had become even more polarized in highly militarized societies where war, in the form of the Cold War, still loomed darkly.[4]

These two positions may seem irreconcilable – either the war served the cause of women's liberation or it did not. In fact, both accounts are basically right. History does not move in a single direction. It is no contradiction to argue both that the era of total war brought about massive transformation in European gender relations and that those transformations were not all 'progressive'. We strive in this chapter to describe the gender changes that occurred over the course of the war years that may have been missed by those mainly concerned with whether war had really furthered the cause of women. One important aspect that has been largely overlooked through the focus on the mixed results in terms of liberty and equality is the dramatic 'victory' of fraternity in the first half of the twentieth century. As we argued in Chapter 1, the revolutionary era had challenged patriarchy not so much because women challenged men as because brothers challenged their fathers. Both fraternal and patriarchal systems are based on male domination, but that does not make them the same. The way that men thought about themselves and their social roles was definitively transformed; so too was the social and cultural relationship between men and women.

As we have seen, the fraternal model of masculinity recovered from the post-revolutionary backlash by attaching itself to the common European project of empire. Bellicose manliness was also present in many of the organizations that challenged the large European empires at the start of the twentieth century, certainly within the working-class socialist and communist movements, but also within the nationalist independence movements that were developing both within Europe and outside of it. There was simply too big a surplus of fighting spirit among statesmen, revolutionaries and nationalist warriors to imagine that war could be avoided indefinitely. It was not the outbreak of a global war in 1914 that was so surprising; it was the fact that it had not happened sooner.

The Great Explosion

Broad, long-term historical pressures rarely converge precisely. On 28 June 1914, however, they did. The young, fraternal, nationalist and decolonizing forces in Europe attacked the old, patriarchal, imperial and recolonizing forces with the first of what would be many shots in a long war. Gavrilo Princip was nineteen years old and a member of a fraternal revolutionary organization named 'Young Bosnia'. The members of Young Bosnia were deeply aggrieved by the recent annexation of Bosnia into the Austro-Hungarian Empire. Prior to 1878, Bosnia had been a part of the Ottoman Empire, but as that collapsed, a fierce struggle for control in the region ensued between two old empires (the Austro-Hungarian and Russian) and newly emerging national states throughout the Balkans. In 1878, Habsburg troops occupied the territory, and in 1908 Emperor Franz Joseph announced that he was annexing it outright from the Ottoman Empire. This was a blow to the Russian Empire, which had hopes of being the dominant Great Power in Balkan affairs, but it was also intended as a show of strength to intimidate the Serbian government, which the Habsburgs felt had become far too uppity. Uncomfortable with an independent young state on their borders, the Austro-Hungarian Empire had attempted in 1906 to force Serbia to become 'economically and politically dependent' upon them by imposing trade sanctions. This policy had failed.[5]

The turn from sanctions to military action on the part of Vienna prompted many Serb nationalists to seek violent solutions to the Bosnian question. Large crowds protested in the streets of Belgrade shouting 'Down with Austria!' and the Serbian government ordered a mobilization of the army before the other Great Powers successfully convinced them to adopt a course of moderation.[6] Moderation was the last thing that the volatile members of Young Bosnia wanted. Instead, they believed that Bosnia, with its large Serb population, properly belonged in an expanded Serbian state. The battlefield successes of the Serbian army against the Ottoman Empire and then Bulgaria in the first two Balkan Wars (1912–13), which led to significant territorial expansion for Serbia, only seemed to further demonstrate the viability of violence in resolving the territorial and political questions that decolonization in the Balkans had occasioned.

There was also a strong undertone of generational conflict within the revolutionary movement. Many older and more prosperous members of the Serbian elite welcomed Vienna's annexation of Bosnia, which promised greater prosperity and stability. Indeed, Evgenije Letica, the head of Sarajevo's Orthodox Church, had even arranged a public prayer for Franz Joseph in 1908 to demonstrate the loyalty of the local population. When the congregation knelt to intone the prayer, only a group of high-school boys refused to bow for the dynasty, providing a rather visual demonstration of the divide between sons and fathers. Nor was this generational divide peaceable: the outraged members of Young Bosnia resolved to assassinate Letica and three other Serb notables in Sarajevo for their collaboration with the enemy.[7]

First, however, they had larger patriarchs to attack. The Habsburg dynasty was the oldest in Europe. In 1914, it had a 73-year-old emperor who had been sitting on the throne for sixty-six years. Even the heir to the throne, the Emperor's nephew Franz Ferdinand, was old enough at fifty to be the father of nearly every member of Young Bosnia. And Franz Ferdinand had resolved to come to Sarajevo in the summer of 1914 to observe military exercises in the new Bosnian territory of the empire. On 28 June, the arrogance of age collided with the incompetence of youth. Only a series of foolish security lapses allowed the six assassins to succeed in killing Franz Ferdinand, as the first attempts to bomb or shoot the Archduke failed for lack of expertise (the bombing attempt failed when the hand-thrown bomb bounced off the rear of the car rather than land in it), or lack of nerve (four of the young men did not fire at the Archduke as he passed). It was only because Franz Ferdinand's driver literally stopped in front of a surprised Gavrilo Princip after missing the turn he had intended to take that the boy's shaking hand was able to fire the shot that would trigger the continental catastrophe.

Still, there was a moment's hesitation before war was declared. In every government across the continent, sober statesmen urged caution and restraint even as others beat the drums of war. Indeed, in most governments, the faction of caution seemed dominant throughout the month of July. Shelves of books have been written assigning various amounts of blame to the key actors in the crisis who tipped the scales for war, but the factor most important in our context is the role that masculinity played in the diplomatic decision-making process. Throughout Europe, officers and politicians alike paid close attention to their personal honour and prestige during debates; similar concern for the honour and prestige of their nations was constantly voiced. But this still does not fully explain why war was declared. After all, smaller crises had threatened war over the previous decade, and diplomatic solutions that allowed for peace with honour had been reached. This time, however, no exit strategy was found, in part because neither Austria-Hungary nor Germany was willing to countenance a diplomatic solution that did not envisage a humiliation of Serbia. The direct assault on an old Great Power by a small young country appeared to have touched a particularly sensitive nerve.

But even in countries that far preferred peace to war in 1914, such as Russia, the factor of masculinity was decisive. When the Russian cabinet met to discuss the implications of mobilizing the army, all of them knew that such a move could very well mean war, and all of them also understood what one member called the 'grave danger which Russia would run in case of hostilities'. They were right to see these possibilities. The mobilization did in the end tip the scales for war, and the empire would collapse in revolution and anarchy as a result of that war. But they decided to mobilize both because they felt that 'the honour, dignity and authority of Russia were at stake' and because they convinced themselves that a show of strength would in fact bring about a peaceful end to the crisis. As one noted, 'if we remained passive, we would not attain our object ... All factors tended to prove that the most judicious policy Russia could follow in present circumstances was a return to a firmer and more energetic attitude towards the unreasonable claims of the Central European powers.'[8]

This adoption of youthful, even reckless, masculine vigour ('firm and more energetic' rather than 'passive') by the old men of Europe led in short order not to peace but to the declaration of war. Every army on the continent had prepared for such a contingency, and they pulled their mobilization schedules off the shelves. Men were packed onto trains and hurled against one another. Russians hurried to the Polish and Ukrainian fronts; Austrians deployed to Serbia and Ukraine; Germans hustled mainly to Belgium and France, though defensive forces were left in Poland and East Prussia. Serbs, Frenchmen and Belgians dug in to defend their homelands, often in vain. In due time, most of the rest of the continent would follow down the road to war.

European society instantly changed. Over the course of the war 59,471,000 men were called up from the reserves, conscripted or volunteered for the armed forces.[9] These troop deployments produced the largest actual sexual separation in European history to that date. Unsurprisingly, mass mobilization recast the gendered spatial schemes of nineteenth-century Europe as well. Instead of the male-female divide mapping onto the public/private spheres, it now mapped onto front/home front. Just as that earlier gendered division of space was never fully reflective of reality, so too did the wartime gender division obscure the variety of ways that men and women moved, acted and lived during the war. Plenty of men, indeed the overwhelming majority of men, remained at home because of age, disability or other reasons, and thousands of women streamed to the front in official or unofficial capacities.

Still, these varieties of experience did almost nothing to change the notion that the front was masculine territory and that 'home' was feminine. The transformation was most evident and immediate for soldiers. In contrast to the situation behind the lines, a single-gender community did form in combat regions. This was a welcome development for many nationalist ideologues and military men, who cultivated an ethic of unsullied masculinity and frankly preferred the company of men to the company of women. The fantasy of a community of men pre-dated the war, but the scope of the European conflict allowed for its creation on a scale previously undreamed of. For those who valued hardness, vigour and solidity, this was better than any service in a fishing fleet in December.

These masculine communities were, of course, intentional constructs. Military leaders throughout the ages have recognized the importance of social cohesiveness to combat effectiveness, and the training techniques of every European army reflected this concern. Soldiers were taught to build small communities of trust that could be extended in concentric circles outward as far as the entire nation in arms. The most intense small-scale socialization exercises tended to take place at the level of the company (a group of roughly 100 men), though in combat practice, the platoon (about 10–20 men) was usually the group one most relied upon. As the circle of trust expanded, the ties relied more on symbolic strength and less upon personal social cohesiveness. Thus, when soldiers were taught about connections to their regiment (about 2,000 men) as much weight was placed on regimental history as on developing social ties between men of different companies or battalions. By the time one reached the identification with the armed forces as a whole (millions of men for most combatants), the procedures were almost entirely symbolic.

Within the confines of military structures, these were truly male communities, and this maleness was crucial to the way that soldiers understood their war experiences. Love between men was both encouraged and expected. These male experiences of love were quite often deeply affectionate. They were based on daily cohabitation, shared burdens, communal victories and upon mutual sacrifice. As Allen Frantzen has demonstrated, this was a love with deep roots in Christian notions of chivalry that combined Christ's own self-sacrifice with a rather less Christian warrior ethos based in vengeance and other forms of violent self-defence.[10]

Not all this male affection was quite as Christian as the chivalric model might suggest, however. There was a real strand of homoeroticism in the literature of the war, as men spent a good deal of time observing (and admiring) male bodies and feeling tragic loss when those bodies were mutilated or destroyed. There were also a good many 'crushes' that developed within the ranks, often within the context of the stylized authority relationship that was present between an officer and his men. Paul Fussell believes that most of this erotic tension was a 'sublimated (i.e. "chaste") form of temporary homosexuality' and that there was not much of the 'active unsublimated kind',[11] but it is in fact difficult to know how widespread sexual relationships were within the ranks. At least 230 British soldiers were convicted for homosexual practices during the war, but this is surely only a small percentage of the number of homosexual liaisons that occurred. It is, however, impossible to know with any degree of certainty how small.[12] Homosexuality was practised by at least some soldiers during the war years; however, the meaning of this sexual contact and its implications for soldier identity and post-war sexuality are still unclear. What we do know for certain was that the fantasy of the male community implied either a suppression of sexual relationships, homosexuality or a cycle of repression and then release with women on a short-term and likely misogynistic basis. A mixture of these three would also not be out of the question.

It is tempting to conclude that the soldiers of the Great War built their own society of men, from which women were forcibly excluded, rather like some monstrous pre-adolescent tree fort. But the situation was far more complicated. Women, with only a very few exceptions, were not allowed to serve in combat units, but as we shall see shortly, this did not mean that there was no contact between men and women during the war. Still, combat units were male fraternities. It was not simply war that built cohesion in these masculine communities, but the very fact of female exclusion. Women were seen as real dangers by military authorities charged with maintaining morale. They warned their soldiers that women were unreliable, likely to gossip and betray military secrets, that the women they would meet would be loose at best or prostitutes at worst and therefore likely to carry venereal disease. These steps were taken both because state and military leaders genuinely believed that individual women could pose serious intelligence and health risks and because the war effort required a depersonification of women and their intense symbolization.

Rightly or wrongly (probably rightly), propagandists and officers believed that the best way to motivate soldiers to risk death, to endure awful living conditions and to do so for extended periods of time was to make soldiering identical to the fulfilment of masculine duty. The equation they drew was to equate national defence (of territory, power or honour) with the masculine defence of hearth and home, of women and children and indeed the motherland itself. In this respect, the ideologies of the nation and of the community of men, which were converging upon each other with alarming speed during the war years, valued women quite highly. The purpose of the war became the defence of Woman with a capital W. They were the nurturing, passive bearers of the nation, and they were threatened by the enemy.

As this brief description of martial sexuality suggests, however, this positive and idealized symbolization of women depended in its daily practice upon sexual segregation. Women could be protected by their men only if their men could be insulated from feminine contact. Military regulations were explicit on this point in most armies of the era. In Russia, military officials at the highest levels concerned themselves with remarkably mundane questions regarding contact between their soldiers and women. They tried to prevent female members of the Red Cross and other nursing units from entering combat areas; they believed that female personnel in the rear negatively affected the morale of wounded soldiers in military hospitals; and they were positively paranoid about local civilian women.

Combined with this fear and suspicion was a widespread belief that virile young men required outlets for their sexual energy. The war represented, in a way, an end to (or at least a hiatus in) the 'civilized' repression of primal urges we discussed in previous chapters. Instead, it not only made possible, but also seemed to require a new relationship between 'natural' desires and male behaviour. It was reasonable for officials to presume that unleashing the instinct to kill would probably unleash sexual instincts as well. Many officers hoped that blocking access to sex might increase the potential for violence even more. But others believed that their boys would both need and deserve sexual release. Thus, across the armies, there was ambivalence about consorting with prostitutes. Despite official fears of venereal disease and espionage, soldiers of the Great War found ample opportunity to pay for sex with local women or camp followers. As the war dragged on, army and state officials in many combatant countries got directly involved in the sex trade by regulating the brothels that their soldiers visited. In most cases, official intervention took the form of 'authorizing' certain establishments that agreed to medical testing of their employees and that allowed officials to impose military discipline upon providers and clients alike. In a few locations, armies even operated their own brothels, taking over the positions previously held by madams or pimps.[13] Though many soldiers appreciated this access to easy sex, it would be misleading to assume that all did. As Belgian singer Jacques Brel made clear in his anti-war song 'Au Suivant', some were instead traumatized by the coldness and inhumanity of being obliged to wait in a long line of naked men at the doors for such a deeply impersonal experience. Regardless of whether the experience was positive or negative, the proximity of assembly line sex to assembly line death in the war zone led many veterans to connect sex and violence in memories of the war experience.

But there was an even darker, more hostile form of military misogyny, one that quickly came to dominate the discussion of wartime sex. As in many previous wars, soldiers raped women in territories they crossed and occupied. The extent of this behaviour is difficult to gauge for two reasons. First, both the attackers and the victims had good reasons for remaining silent about the crime, so most sources based on personal narratives systematically ignored the issue. Official records are little better, for though military justice systems would occasionally prosecute soldiers for their depredations, there is no way of telling what percentage of offences they brought to trial. Second, though we see only the tip of the iceberg at the micro-level, the issue of rape at the symbolic macro-level came into special prominence during the war years. As soon as the war began, rape became an important propaganda issue. The German invasion of neutral Belgium was instantly portrayed as a violent sexual act. The 'Rape of Belgium' became a staple of wartime mobilization for everyone who opposed the Central Powers. Posters in Great Britain decried the crime and hinted that the barbaric Germans might not stop in Belgium, patriotic directors in Russia made films on the issue, and those sympathetic to the Entente in neutral America made much of the despoiling of the innocent as they lobbied their way towards eventual entry into the war.

Describing the invasion of a country as a 'rape' was metaphoric, but journalists and state officials also argued that actual rapes were accompanying the military incursions. German officials protested that the lurid stories of predatory sex were propaganda devices of their opponents and that their troops were in fact disciplined. If anything, they argued, they were the real victims, as the savage, 'Asian' Cossacks of the Russian army were responsible for widespread sexual abuse during their short occupation of East Prussia in 1914 and their rather longer occupation of Austrian Galicia over the course of the war. Neutral observers had difficulty determining the merits of these claims and counterclaims during the war, and dispassionate neutrality became nearly impossible after the war, when war crimes and the question of war guilt became an obsession among European politicians and for generations of European historians. The most recent scholarship suggests that though the public outrage surrounding rape was less focused on the personal suffering of the women involved than it was with broader questions of the nation and the war effort, rapes did in fact occur. Belgian women were raped, French women were raped, German women were raped and Galician women were raped.[14] Some soldiers were court-martialled and executed for their violation of the laws of war and their own military discipline, but an unknown number of men went unpunished, often because their own commanders chose to look the other way and to treat rape as part and parcel of soldiering. We should not see these sexual assaults as accidental or natural, or even as part of the 'heat of battle'. Rapes almost never occurred when bullets were flying. They were instead the expression of the peculiar sexual culture of the society of men and the expression of the violent quest for dominance that was the life of the soldier. It is also important to understand that these acts of violence against women were not in opposition to the symbolic idealization of women or the motherland. To the contrary, the enemy acts of misogyny stimulated one's own masculine desire to protect mothers and the motherland, and vice versa. All the armies raped, and all promised to protect their own women. Paradoxically, the defence of civilization and the practice of rape were dependent upon one another.

Still, it is possible to make too much of this phenomenon. However widespread rape was during the war, it is clear that the vast majority of soldiers never assaulted a single woman or child. And despite the organized misogyny at the front, most soldiers also had healthier and kinder relationships with women. More than a few soldiers sought girlfriends instead of prostitutes or victims in the occupied lands, though this search generally resulted in a combined effort by military authorities and local communities to prevent such a destabilizing relationship. There were also, of course, the women that men had left behind. In armies in which leaves home were provided, it was understood that the soldier on leave would make full use of his temporary respite from the men on the front to seek sexual gratification from their wives, girlfriends or any other willing women behind the lines. Finally, and perhaps most importantly, women were present through their letters. The Great War was marked by the literacy of its soldiers. Even countries like Russia and Serbia in which literacy had grown much more slowly and recently than in the countries of western Europe, the majority of soldiers could read. At home, even though female literacy lagged behind male literacy, women who could not write would often get a literate friend or relative to do so. The letters, photos and mementoes from home were important parts of army existence, and though they did not replace physical presence, the communication between men and women meant that despite the fantasies of a purely male society, the actual army was in fact a society that included women, though mostly through the marks of their absence.

The gender situation on the 'home front' was, if anything, even more complicated. The term 'home front' itself was developed in Britain during the First World War, and it betrayed both the desire to distinguish the male and female spheres of the war and the inability to stabilize the boundary between the two.[15] On the one hand, the declaration that this was 'home' marked it as a female space, a connotation that was only strengthened by the eviction of so many men from that space during mobilization. On the other hand, it was declared a 'front', with all the military and masculine connotations that implied. The combination of the two terms raised an important but largely unarticulated question: was there such a thing as martial femininity?

The answer to this question is quite difficult. Everyone knew that women had assumed special duties during wartime throughout the course of European history, but the traditional role they played was one of support for male family members. This had meant temporary husbandry at the homestead during campaigns, taking care of the male jobs as well as the female ones on the farm. More importantly, it meant moral support. Women were expected to reassure anxious men, to remind them of their masculine and patriotic duties as warriors, and to promise continued obedience and fidelity in their absence. The sexual aspects of this particular contract were present even in ancient Greece, as the memorable sexual strike waged by the Athenian women in Aristophanes' play *Lysistrata* (411 BCE) to end the Peloponnesian War attests. But even this precocious (and fictional) peace protest only reinforced the notion that the social organization through which women were expected to work was the family. The more common phenomenon of the so-called 'Spartan Women' who told their sons to come home either 'with their shield or on it', became part of European mythology, and it too stressed the role of women within the family in times of war.

The same situation prevailed all over Europe at the beginning of the war. It was only in two neutral countries (Norway and Finland) that European women had the vote in 1914, and the explicit reason for their exclusion elsewhere was that the fundamental social unit throughout the continent remained the patriarchal family, not the individual. Women were represented by their men at the ballot box; so too would they be represented by men at the front while women tended to domestic affairs. It was therefore no surprise that belligerent states across the continent used the family as one of the devices to mobilize soldiers and the main device to mobilize non-soldiers throughout the war.

The only other institution through which women could reasonably expect to contribute to the war effort in large numbers in 1914 was the Church. Christian charity work had been one of the few areas in which women visibly acted in the public sphere in patriarchal Europe, and it seemed only natural that women eager to participate in the war effort would do so under the aegis of the cross. The most famous such cross at the time was the Red Cross, an institution that blended the Christian, the national and the feminine in a socially acceptable way. But nursing was far from the only outlet for charity that the war promised to provide. As events would show, families deprived of breadwinners would slip into poverty, refugees would fill the roads and city streets begging for assistance, and children adrift in the war-torn world would need guidance. Women would be expected to care in public ways for non-family members, and the long history of women's charitable activities within Christian churches would structure and legitimate that activity without posing any threat to the established social order.

This attempt to find a way to mobilize women in a socially conservative way found its most pure expression in the attempts of female members of Europe's royal families to take visible leadership roles in charitable fundraising and work. In Russia, Empress Alexandra took on a visible role in caring for the war wounded from the very first winter of the war, and the Tsar's second daughter served as the patron of one of the most important social relief organizations of the war, the 'Tatiana Committee for the Relief of War Victims', which began its work in September 1914 to care for war widows and children but then added care for refugees to its portfolio in 1915. In Austria, Empress Zita took on much the same role, making public stops at soup kitchens and lending her name to important charity organizations.[16] At the start, the social conservatism of these organizations even led some, like the Russian Red Cross, to insist that only educated, upper-class ladies could serve in them.[17]

The conservative dream that one could wage a massive war without significant alteration in the social order did not come true, as the fate of Alexandra's and Zita's charity work demonstrates. Both Alexandra and Zita had been members of the multinational European elite prior to their marriages. Alexandra came from Hesse-Darmstadt and spoke Russian with a strong German accent. Zita was from the house of Bourbon-Parma and thus carried the taint of a French and Italian background. These international marriages had long been the norm for the great European dynasties, as few ruling houses wished to disrupt the local aristocratic order by raising native noble families to royal status, and as each sought political gain from the wedding of their offspring. In previous conflicts, national background had not mattered very much, as monarchical political systems stressed personal fealty above ethnic loyalty. But this was a new war waged in new political circumstances. Instead of receiving love and praise for their visible wartime relief work, Alexandra and Zita were vilified for being too cosmopolitan and were rumoured to have committed treason. It turned out that the subjects of the Habsburgs and Romanovs believed that ethnic belonging counted for far more than marriage into a powerful dynasty.

This shift may seem relatively insignificant; it was not. In patriarchal systems, women were expected to assume a new social position and identity upon their marriage. When the father handed his daughter to her husband at the wedding, this entailed a shift of duties, of loyalties and of subjectivities that was understood to be complete and irrevocable. In the practical workings of international law, a woman automatically took on the citizenship status of her husband rather than her father at the moment she traded her father's last name for her husband's. This absolute shift reflected the principle of absolute control of women that was the bedrock of patriarchal ideology, and it presumed that whatever political sentiment or cultural affinity a woman might have, like a dowry, was objective and fully transferable. Given this theory of the effects of marriage on women, one might have expected Alexandra to have become totally Russian and Zita to have become totally Austrian at the moment the church bells chimed.

Despite the popular rumours to the contrary, all available evidence suggests that both did: there seems to have been little ambivalence on the part of either woman during the war. Each was a hearty patriot. But the fact that there were widespread doubts is significant. The suspicion that a woman might secretly hold onto the political beliefs of her youth and wait for the moment when she might act accordingly implied that though women might lack political rights, they did not lack political subjectivity. This was, of course, the argument that feminists had been making for years, and the very existence of feminist movements should have demonstrated that this was the case. But, more effectively in some places than others, those movements had been marginalized prior to the war. During the war, it became clear that feminine political subjectivity was a universal condition, one that extended beyond the aberrant suffragettes all the way up to the royals.

It would be easy to conclude, having seen the shift in female political subjectivity, the rapid expansion of female volunteer and paid work outside of the home, the family and the church, and the acquisition of the vote in so many countries at the end of the war, that an extremely durable patriarchal bulwark had been shattered and that a new female gender role based upon autonomy instead of dependence had now emerged. Indeed, such a transformation did happen, but the new gender archetype was not unchallenged. The spectre of the independent woman, a staple of conservative nightmares for centuries, was now more tangible, and the old patriarchal model was now fatally weakened, but a third model, which we might call the 'fraternal' model of femininity also appeared and quickly became normative.

This model, largely developed during the First World War, was based not on the destruction of the family as the context of feminine behaviour but the reconfiguration of that family. As Maureen Healy has acutely observed, one of the key dimensions of the Great War was the fact that 'the family was turned "inside out" for the purposes of war-making'.[18] Two aspects of this transformation were especially important. First, women and children became very public figures whose daily lives and daily choices were understood to be deeply political and crucial for the war effort. Second, the erasure of the civilian man from the iconography of the nation led to a real crisis of masculinity for men out of uniform. The war occasioned both of these transformations, and the main outcome was the increased visibility of the state, which was actively transforming the old patriarchal order into one of state paternalism. In the long run, this change had dramatic effects upon the family. Just as the debates over a 'single wage' focused attention on the economic institution of the family at the very moment that industrialization was undermining the model of familial complementarity, so too did the increased visibility of state 'family policies' during and after the First World War indicate that the patriarchal family was actually losing power as an autonomous political institution. As the state loomed over the economic, social and (increasingly) sexual relationships within the home, the family became above all a community of sentiment. The family was very visible in the national political ideologies, but the power of householders speaking on behalf of the family unit had actually declined as states dealt directly with individual citizens without the pesky intermediary institutions of community, caste or family.

The reconfiguration of the family during the First World War opened up new possibilities for female activity. Many European women saw the transformation of gender roles that occurred during the war as a moment of liberation. Despite the tragedies of the period, some of them even expressed a certain joy in being able to participate meaningfully in what most Europeans understood to be the defining moment of their generation.[19] Taking on 'men's' work in defence industries demonstrated their capacity to work, and tending broken soldiers as nurses showed that they could help the war effort from a position of relative power over bedridden and dependent men.

In Russia, this desire to be an active part of the war effort extended to combat participation. Several women petitioned the Tsar to allow them to become soldiers during the first three years of the war; much to everyone's surprise, the Tsar granted some of these requests, probably hoping that every bit of patriotic energy that his subjects could provide would strengthen the war effort and his own precarious position. The most famous of these women, Maria Bochkareva, noted in her memoir both how difficult the position of the woman soldier was and how exciting it was. Coming from a very dark corner of Europe's patriarchal world, Bochkareva had been abused by her father and her husband and latched rather forcefully onto patriotism as a positive and defining cause for her life. In some respects, her journey from Siberian peasant woman to soldier was a flight from the traditional world, but she portrayed and understood it as a reaffirmation of traditional Russia, as a submission to the authority and unquestioned will of the father-tsar and then to the officers who would command her.[20]

When the Tsar fell in March 1917, Bochkareva sought to invigorate this quasi-traditional, quasi-modern sentiment among other women by successfully lobbying for the creation of an all-woman 'Battalion of Death' that would fight for the Provisional Government that sought to rule Russia between Nicholas's abdication in March and the successful seizure of power by radical communists in October. This women's unit was sanctioned by the government as a way to 'shame' the men of Russia by demonstrating that many women were more ready to fight for their country than were certain draft dodgers, rebellious soldiers or deserters. Bochkareva's battalion saw combat action in the middle of 1917, but it had no more success than the rest of the Russian army, which fell apart with alarming speed after a failed offensive in June of that year. In October, the traditional aspects of the women's soldier movement became even clearer. Seeing the collapse of discipline and obedience in the army as a plague, and blaming socialists for the mess, Bochkareva and her women tried to defend the Winter Palace in Petrograd when the Bolsheviks moved in to arrest the ministers of the Provisional Government and complete their coup. They were quickly defeated, Bochkareva was arrested and her battalion was disbanded.

Bochkareva's unusual rise and fall showed both the potential and limits of 'liberation' for European women. For most, however, the war was far more burdensome than liberating. Women had new opportunities, to be sure, but there was a reason that these opportunities were pitched as duties rather than benefits. Virtually everywhere, the work that women had traditionally performed got more difficult, and the work that mobilized men had done was shifted to them as well. For every childless, excitable young lady who welcomed the war and exulted in its challenges, there were several women who worked much longer and harder in the paid sector of the economy, only to return home to deal with issues of childcare, cooking and cleaning. Women tolerated these onerous burdens out of feelings of 'sacrifice' and 'duty' to the war effort, but the effort required was often barely sustainable. Any shift in this balance could make the position of domestic women impossible.

The change that ended up breaking domestic society and overwhelming overworked women was the food crisis that Europe faced from 1916 to 1918. One of the key features of the First World War was a mutual economic blockade between the warring parties. That blockade, combined with difficulties in providing enough transportation capacity for civilian interests in many regions of the continent, led to increasingly dire food shortages. Hunger appeared in many regions, from Vienna to Berlin to Petrograd. Social breakdown loomed long before outright starvation, however, because the straw that broke the camel's back was the added burden of having to wait in line every day just for the chance to purchase basic necessities at increasingly ruinous prices. There were simply not enough hours in the day for women to add several more in bread lines, and wages by the end of the war failed to keep up with inflation. The response was one of bitterness and desperate protest. Citizens blamed the state, the rich and each other. Stories of how the wealthy dined warranted press coverage, and rumours of speculation, of hoarding and of abuse of the food system led to acute social tension between consumers and merchants, between urban residents and local farmers, between poor and rich, and between citizens and their states. Again the most notable instance of this was in Russia, where the 300-year Romanov dynasty, which had survived rebellions, coup attempts, assassinations and revolutions in its recent past, succumbed in a matter of days in late February and early March 1917 to mass demonstrations in the streets of the capital begun by outraged women standing in bread lines. But much the same was occurring elsewhere. In Berlin and Vienna in particular, the social, political and economic structure of total war fractured first among exhausted urban women.[21] In this way, even women who had eschewed politics and the public sphere in the past became openly politicized in ways that the conservative order could not effectively manage.

Remarkably little has been written about the gender transformation of home-front men during the war. As we noted earlier, the spatial order of the war made the front masculine territory and the home front feminine territory, but most men were not in fact enlisted in the armed forces, much less sent into combat.[22] This combination of forces decisively transformed European masculinity. In the first place, it normalized healthy men in their teens, twenties and thirties, and marginalized all the rest. Men not at the front were not real men. They might be boys waiting to be men, or they might have been real men in the past, or they might simply have something wrong with them. Young, old, blind, crippled or diseased, certain males were coded as dependent, perhaps even partially feminine, by the war. The situation was even less secure for those men who were not visibly dependent. The implications for healthy, hale men over forty but well short of elderly were significant. These were the sort of men who had been masculine icons of power in traditional Europe, at the peak of their working years, budding or actual patriarchs in their own right. Now, however, the masculine focus was elsewhere, with younger men away from home. Young, muscular men were visibly powerful in the visual propaganda of the war, but they also exerted an invisible influence on the hearts and minds of the women and children they had left behind. The question of generational power, which we highlighted at the outset of this chapter, became ever more acute.

For men who were of fighting age and had no visible defects, the war years were uncomfortable ones. There were a variety of legitimate and illegitimate reasons why such men stayed in civilian life. On the continent, where conscript armies were the norm (of the major European combatants, only Britain lacked a draft at the start of the war; it would institute one in 1916), one was simply told when and where to appear. It was often difficult for military officials to even deal with volunteers in these circumstances. In addition, most states allowed for occupational exemptions of one sort or another. Though the list of reserved jobs varied from place to place, skilled workers in defence industries often got to stay at the bench, and policemen, firemen, many government bureaucrats, clerics and students were among the other groups freed from military service. In addition, not all health defects were visible to the naked eye. Medical examinations at induction points checked for a wide range of ailments from infectious disease, to heart irregularities, to simple 'weakness'. Finally, there were men who simply dodged the draft, resisted the recruiter or deserted soon after induction. It is only a slight exaggeration to say that these varied and very numerous reasons why a young man might not be in the army were streamlined to only three in the public imagination: one was either 'connected' by virtue of social station or fortunate job circumstances, one was physically defective or one was a coward. Women throughout the continent dispensed white feathers to men they suspected of being too fearful, and citizens rapidly came to despise and envy privilege of all sorts as well. In any case, men at home had something wrong with them, and a masculine gap emerged within civilian society. If the real men were away, and only weak men remained, who would provide for and protect the women and the children?

The answer was the state, which sought to fill the absent shoes of men by promising order, justice and social benefits to 'helpless' women and children. The rise of this state paternalism had enormous consequences. In the short term, states across the continent became much more intimately involved with their citizens. Laissez-faire principles were abandoned as quickly in the social realm as they were in the economic policies of the warring states. The enormous social dislocation and the demands of absent soldiers made either new or much enhanced social welfare policies an essential part of virtually every wartime social system. In most combatant states, soldiers' wives received supplements, widows got death benefits and the state took on the responsibility for paying these and other welfare bills. And, while both soldiers and their families wanted this money distributed with no strings attached, the state insisted that those who received this aid be 'worthy', normally by virtue of being dependent upon an absent man and free from moral vice. In Britain the benefits women received were linked to their status as wives, so the government thought it perfectly appropriate to cease payments if women neglected their wifely duties by cheating on their husbands. The Russian state, for its part, stopped paying young wives if their husbands deserted or committed some other significant crime at the front, further reinforcing the idea that these benefits flowed through the social contract that the state had made with its men. As Susan Pedersen has argued for the cases of Britain and France, the war introduced 'a particular logic of welfare and new institutional structures', and further 'enhanced the appeal and power of particular ideologies and political groups and enabled these groups to capture the issue of family policy in the interwar period'.[23]

In simple human terms, this rise of the paternal state and of aggressive, familial propaganda for the nation is indicative of one of the most important human aspects of the war. For people all over Europe, intimacy was lost at the expense of institutions.[24] Hungry women interacted with bureaucratic states, and soldiers fought for idealized women. But the social fact of large-scale human separation defined the war years. This is evident in the poems of the war, the memoirs of the war and above all the letters of the war, which were filled with mutual expressions of loneliness between husbands and wives, sons and parents, and between good friends. Loneliness quickly led to alienation. Those at the front felt they could not communicate their experience to those who had not shared their burdens, and those at home in many instances felt the same way. By the war's end, there was a need for everyone to stress how he or she had been victimized. Hungry civilians believed they had suffered for the sake of the soldiers at the front, and soldiers believed they had suffered for the sake of those at home. No one could actually bear to receive these sacrificial gifts. As a result, the language of unredeemed hurt and loss dominated the post-war landscape.

When the war ended, then, the gender landscape of the continent had been deeply changed. First, a generational shift had occurred. The iconic male was now much younger than he had been before. Second, the sexual separation of the war led to fundamental change as well. The idea of the community of men as the basis of political and in some respects intimate life had merged extensively with the national idea, and this only strengthened the fraternal overtones of the generational change. The successful assault on patriarchy changed the place of women as well. This new military fraternal gender order was paradoxically both more inclusive and exclusive of women than had been the case in the traditional patriarchal world. There was a deep undercurrent of sexual alienation at the heart of this new order that sometimes led to unrealistic idealization and sometimes to outright misogyny, but that always hinged on a rupture of intimacy. That said, the massive institutionalization of the war years, produced in part by the fact of this alienation, did much to incorporate women into national life. Not only were they on propaganda posters and serving as symbols of the nation, but they were also active politically on the newly created 'home front' through their daily action. Indeed, state paternalism required formal female political participation in order to exist at all. Simply put, the new European welfare states required female citizens.

'Uniform Politics' and the Post-war Order

We are now in a position to understand the paradox we introduced at the beginning of the chapter. The fraternal rise to dominance meant the creation of a more aggressive and violent masculinity based, ironically enough, on an ever greater stress on male affection. This often had negative effects upon women, as we shall see. On the other hand, the overt politicization of women during this total war led to the widespread acknowledgement of female political subjectivity and the formal incorporation of female citizens in the ever more intrusive and ever more inclusive institutions of the paternal state. These twin expressions of the fraternal order, born of the sexual separation and totalization of the Great War, reconstituted the European gender order in deeply ambiguous ways.

The post-war story of gender begins with homecoming. This was a protracted and often difficult process. In the first place, many did not come home at all, and many who did found those homes empty, abandoned by families who had fled the war, had migrated to cities, or had died of disease during the war. In most cases, though, people were reunited. These reunions were often difficult. However much men and women might have hoped that they could pick up their lives and their relationships where they had left off, the fact remained that the war had changed individuals in profound ways. In some respects, these were more reintroductions than reunions. There were, of course, personal traumas and joys that had not been shared together and could not now be fully shared. Just as importantly, however, the whole context of personal relationships had been changed as a result of the shift in gender order and the rupture of intimacy that the war had produced.

The first expression of these fractures was sexual jealousy. The long absences had produced deep anxiety about fidelity on the part of spouses virtually everywhere. Some of this anxiety was expressed in letters; much more of it must have remained unsaid during the separation itself. But given that lurid stories of over-heated soldiers and randy villagers and of lonely housewives seduced by wealthy shirkers ran rampant through oral networks during the war, suspicion must have at least flitted through the minds of most separated Europeans. At some point in those first few nights home together, that doubt must have flickered across faces and through hearts as well. Some relationships survived doubt (and of course the actual infidelities that did occur). Others simply did not. More permissive divorce laws came into force in some areas, and divorce rose quickly. In Russia and Germany in particular, divorce rates in the 1920s were four or five times higher than they had been before the war.[25]

Homecoming also meant a restructuring of economic life. Most men believed that the wartime flood of women into the industrial workforce was meant to be tempo-rary, but not all women who enjoyed a regular pay cheque and a measure of eco-nomic independence from their husbands wanted to leave the jobs they had taken. In the end, the public and private pressure to abandon work and give returning vet-erans their jobs back was too great. By late 1919 in Great Britain, for instance, nearly 750,000 women had lost their jobs, and the retraining sessions they were offered focused on domestic work.[26] The reassertion of male dominance in the eco-nomic realm did not mean that European culture reverted to what had existed prior to the war. To the contrary, as Chapter 5 will show, deep changes were taking place in sexual practices and sexual identities, changes that were marked by new clothing fashions, by new standards of proper behaviour in public and above all by the con-tinued visibility of the independent and intelligent 'modern woman'.

In many ways, the most interesting gender developments in the interwar years were political. As we have seen, there had been deep anxieties even prior to the war that had focused on changes in the gender order. The upheaval of the war dwarfed those earlier hints of instability. Throughout the continent, as politicians and citizens cast about for an anchor to calm their storm-tossed lives, Europeans sought to bring order and predictability to gender relations. There were some, of course, who wanted to resurrect the past and 'return to normality', but the changes the war brought made that a futile desire. The imperial patriarchs would not be coming back. Austria's Franz Joseph had died during the war, and his successor, Karl, ruled only briefly before military defeat and the dismemberment of the Habsburg Empire brought an end to the dynasty. Tsar Nicholas II had been arrested in 1917 and executed in 1918, replaced by an aggressively fraternal band of communist brothers in the lands of the Russian Empire. Kaiser Wilhelm had abdicated and was forced into exile. In states where electoral politics dominated, veterans returned to win ballot after ballot. Now fraternal nationalism was the norm throughout the continent. The task of gender sta-bilization, therefore, was to find a way to take account of the wartime changes but still to construct a reliable and comfortable gender order. The road to stability varied depending on the political heritage of the region in question, but gender questions proved central nearly everywhere.

In Great Britain, the long battle for suffrage finally came to a close with the passage of a compromise bill in 1918 that expanded the previously limited franchise to all men of twenty-one years of age and to all women who had reached thirty. Two important aspects of this suffrage victory need to be highlighted here. In the first place, as we have already pointed out, granting women the vote was presented as a gift for noble wartime service. Ideologically, this stressed both the importance of the war to politics and the continued pre-eminence of men (who after all remained the dispensers of this gift of the vote). But we should also note that more pragmatic political concerns were at play as well. One of the reasons that conservative parties and politicians were either more muted in their opposition to suffrage or dropped it completely was that opposing suffrage now carried a significant political risk. Female political activism during the war had made eventual suffrage more likely, and no party wanted to oppose women voters only to face their wrath at the next election. In addition, now that the range of female political activity had expanded, there was reason to expect that any party could court women voters. There were also hopes that limiting the vote to older women would make electoral returns much less radical than they might otherwise be. Just as importantly, however, suffrage was grudgingly accepted by conservatives in order to pre-empt the possibility of a 'sex war' that had seemed imminent in Britain before the war and now seemed ready to re-erupt on the basis of accumulated wartime grievances.[27]

This desire for unity was also visible in other contexts. Nationalists stressed the idea that nations at war not only needed to be unified but also unitary. In Germany, conservatives reached a consensus even with socialists and feminists that a temporary political peace needed to be declared in the interests of achieving victory. As we have seen, British suffragettes also laid down their firebombs and rallied to the nationalist cause. This rejection of dissent and other forms of political or ethnic pluralism was the result, in large part, of the militarization of national politics that had developed in the early twentieth century and had intensified during the war years. When the war ended, this militarization subsided only among select groups in select places. While many European intellectuals, especially in Britain and France, had indeed blanched at the horror of the war and rededicated themselves to explicitly pacifist causes, the more common post-war experience was one of conflict and constant preparation for the next war. The armistice that ended the Great War in November 1918 had not ended combat in Europe. To the contrary, civil war washed over most of central and eastern Europe for varying lengths of time, and these wars further honed the violent practices and martial form of masculinity while establishing the new political contours of the continent. The success of the communist revolution in Russia raised the spectre not only of international war, but also of continuing class-based civil wars. While communist uprisings failed or petered out in regions outside of the Soviet Union, the 'red menace' remained a constant part of European thought throughout the 1920s and 1930s, and it contributed decisively to the rise of fascism in Germany and Italy. The antidote to communism was sought in civic solidarity and in the valorization of obedience and duty, and the suppression of individuality. This search for unity and uniformity informed the political developments in many places during the interwar period.

Bulgaria is a case in point. Even before the Great War, Bulgaria had been consumed with violent conflict as it fought first the Ottoman Empire and then its Balkan neighbours in a failed bid for regional dominance. This aggressive foreign policy was costly in treasure and blood and aroused domestic opposition, most notably from Alexander Stamboliiski's Agrarian Party. Stamboliiski felt that continuing conflict and a militarized state only served to impoverish and oppress the peasant Bulgarians he sought to represent. As a result, he called upon Bulgarians to reject 'war-lovers'[28] and campaigned against entry into the Balkan Wars of 1912–13 and into the First World War. He failed each time, though Bulgaria joined the Central Powers relatively late, in 1915.

The war effort was disastrous. Bulgaria lost a higher percentage of its troops than any other non-Balkan state during the war, runaway inflation destroyed the economy and military defeat brought about the abdication of Tsar Ferdinand in favour of his son Boris, who assumed the throne in October 1918. Less than a year later, the Agrarian Party won national elections and Stamboliiski took control of the government. Given the consistency of his anti-war stance, one might have expected a rather thorough demilitarization of Bulgarian politics. The years of war, however, had left a deep imprint. Stamboliiski did attempt to rein in the military by demobilizing many of its soldiers and officers, but other than that he did little to challenge the fundamental core of the fraternal and military nation. In the first place, the leaders were young. There were nine cabinet members in Stamboliiski's government in 1920. Five were in their thirties, and Stamboliiski was only forty-one.[29] Second, the leadership proclaimed its commitment to military virtues even as it cut the size of the army.

Most significantly, the signature initiative of Stamboliiski's government was a militarization of the economic sphere. 'Drafting' people to work was a practice that many states used during the war, and it appealed to many leaders seeking economic growth in the post-war period as well. If coercion and discipline worked in the organization of violence, the thinking went, why should it not work in the organization of the economy? The Law for Compulsory Labour Service was implemented in June 1920, and it envisioned the conscription of all men at the age of twenty for one year of service and all women at the age of sixteen for six months of service. It was a scheme not unlike the one we saw earlier from William James; like the James plan, it was as much about promoting unity and social cohesion as it was economic growth. The notion of militarized young people in uniform fulfilling their duty to the nation seemed attractive to him and his supporters in a way that would have been nearly inconceivable a decade before.

Women were part of this vision too, as Stamboliiski dearly wanted to integrate women into civic life. Stamboliiski hoped that women would eventually become voting citizens, but the Compulsory Labour Service was seen as a first, halting step towards the emergence of women into the public sphere. In practice, there were many gaps in the universality of female service. Married women were exempt; so too was Bulgaria's large Muslim population. Even those liable were not always called, and the experiment was mostly limited to urban areas and in occupations like cooking and laundering that were already gendered as female.[30]

One can see a certain sort of 'progressive' nationalism in Stamboliiski's regime. It sought the economic advancement of the poor, envisioned the eventual abolition of sex-based legal discrimination and it sought to avoid needless military confrontation. But the militarized fraternalism was just as clear. Military virtues were upheld, cross-class comradeship on the basis of masculinity was valorized and radical changes in family life or the social position of women were barely contemplated. This sort of complex political system, structured around the militarized nation, but moderate in its policies, was vulnerable, however. Many contemporaries feared that the explicit concern for the oppressed and the distrust of capitalism embedded in the peasant populist ideology meant that Bulgarian politics would shift to the left as a result.

As it turned out, the real threat was from radicals on the right. Many officers and veterans, seeing even Stamboliiski's mild populism as a communist provocation and a threat to tradition, plotted against him from the very first days of his rule. They urged the formation of 'parties of order' who would pursue policies of 'social harmony' and mimicked the fascist experiments that Benito Mussolini was pioneering in Italy at the same time by forming youth organizations, sporting clubs and other militarized organizations.[31] In response, Stamboliiski, now obviously very far removed from whatever pacifist inclinations he might have held before the war, resolved to strengthen the paramilitary organizations of his own party, the so-called Orange Guard.

These developments soon reached their logical conclusion. Political street fighting intensified, and the officers finally launched their coup in June 1923. Stamboliiski was captured, tortured and killed as a way of starting a wave of right-wing terror that would result in the murder of about 16,000 members of left-wing parties.[32] Bulgaria became a right-wing authoritarian state, as so many other European countries would in the years between the First World War and the Second World War.

In Britain and Bulgaria alike, politicians believed that the communist threat required the pre-emption of sex war and training in masculine values through mechanisms that reaffirmed male supremacy and male virtues. In the Soviet Union, by contrast, revolutionaries who had proclaimed themselves crusaders for women's equality had come to power. This commitment to the 'emancipation' and the 'enlightenment' of women was taken very seriously by Bolshevik leaders, a fact reflected in the wave of legislation that dramatically transformed the legal position of Russia's women in the space of a few short months. Women had been enfranchised during the brief period of the Provisional Government in 1917 and had cast ballots in the important elections and plebiscites of that year. With the accession of the communists to power they were, in addition, granted full civic equality, promised extensive benefits for maternity and childcare, urged to join the ranks of the Communist Party and generally exhorted to help destroy the patriarchal core of Russian society. These initiatives had mixed results. The legal changes proved lasting and important, but the efforts to transform the gendered social, economic and cultural patterns met with more difficulty. Communal kitchens and nurseries failed to materialize on a mass scale because of the lack of resources, and the domestic economy changed very little. Few men, revolutionaries or not, cleaned the house, did the shopping, cared for the children or cooked dinner. As a result, the new economic and political opportunities offered to women quickly turned into exhausting duties, and Soviet women would labour under this 'double burden' for the rest of the communist period.[33]

The double burden emerged because Russian progressives and radicals understood the main political issue to be the patriarchal oppression of women. This was the core of what they called the 'woman question' in the pre-revolutionary era. With the destruction of patriarchy and the establishment of legal equality, the stage, they felt, was set for the eventual liberation of women. What was left virtually unasked was the 'man question'. This was a serious omission. Convinced that the communist revolution had destroyed the old world, revolutionaries largely failed to notice how similar Soviet post-war masculinity was to that in the 'bourgeois' European states. That masculinity emerged from the same wartime springs. Both before and during the Great War, Russian youths had undergone the same militarization as their counterparts to the west. Veterans came home feeling the same isolation, alienation and mix of deep longing and deep suspicion for women. These veterans made up the core of the Communist Party cadres after the Russian Civil War concluded in 1921. The body type men were to emulate was the same, and so too was the moral code they were supposed to practice. As a result, despite a period of time in the 1920s when it looked like it was possible that a new socialist masculinity that would explicitly reject the notion of male supremacy would emerge, the fraternal, martial masculinity that dominated Europe held firm in the Soviet Union as well.[34] This brief period of gender uncertainty came unceremoniously to an end in the mid-1930s, when the Stalinist regime changed the family code to outlaw abortion and make divorce more difficult while reaffirming martial masculinity as the only acceptable form.

The right-wing army leaders in Bulgaria and the left-wing communist leaders in the Soviet Union were different in many ways. Still, scholars of both groups have recently stressed a key similarity between these government officials in the 1930s. Both turned towards 'neo-traditional' policies in the years leading up to the Second World War.[35] As Krasimira Daskalova notes, the neo-traditional discourse in Bulgaria was different from older brands of traditionalism because of 'the different style and argumentation of this discourse – more aggressive, pseudoscientific, consciously ideological and manipulative'.[36] Neo-traditionalism was, in essence, an anchor thrown out by European radicals of both the left and the right. The appeals to 'traditional' beliefs and identities were intended to stabilize, to unify and to give social support to the rather ambitious military and economic plans of the leaders of the interwar period.

But we should not see these programmes as purely 'manipulative'. This term implies that neo-traditionalists did not believe what they were saying. Quite the opposite is the case, especially when it came to the scientific underpinnings of neo-traditional thought. What Daskalova calls 'pseudoscience' was, of course, just called 'science' in the 1930s. Biology was especially crucial in this regard, as it served as the justification for social orders based upon sexual and racial differences. The principles of equality and social peace came into sharp contrast once more with the Social Darwinist view of difference and warfare. This ideological conflict produced a certain amount of tension within most states, as we saw in the brief treatments of Britain, Bulgaria and the Soviet Union. It was possible, however, that radicals on one side of this ideological divide would successfully destroy the other ideological position within a given state. Given the experience of the war, it was especially likely that a movement would join the aggressive and misogynistic aspects of wartime masculinity with the biological justifications for sexual and/or racial dominance and would create a system that would promote unity on the basis of the ideas of radical masculinity and the practices of violent male bonding. We have a name for this system: fascism.

It is important to recognize that fascism was not a strange, exotic disease that simply afflicted Italians and Germans who fell under the spell of Mussolini and Hitler. It might be comforting for us to believe that these modern Europeans had been brainwashed or forced by circumstance to accede to the evil wishes of their dictators, since it would allow us to distance ourselves from their experience. But the historical record shows a great deal more conscious support for fascist movements not only in Italy and Germany, but across Europe as a whole as well.[37] Explaining the attraction of fascism is a book in itself; for our purposes, however, what must be stressed is how appealing this martial, neo-traditional gender order was to so many men and more than a few women as well.

Adolf Hitler, the leader of Germany's National Socialist Party and chancellor from 1933 to 1945, was always exceptionally clear that public power should be aggressively male, indeed that it should rely on the type of soldierly community of men that he fondly recalled from the years of the First World War. Nazi women did not have to be barefoot, but it was certainly best if they were pregnant. As Hitler put it in a speech to the National Socialist Women's Organization in 1934,

If the man's world is said to be the State, his struggle, his readiness to devote his powers to the service of the community, then it may perhaps be said that the woman's is a smaller world. For her world is her husband, her family, her children, and her home ... The two worlds are not antagonistic. They complement each other, they belong together just as man and woman belong together. We do not consider it correct for the woman to interfere in the world of the man, in his main sphere. We consider it natural if these two worlds remain distinct.[38]

Hitler was not alone in his hope that German women would stay at home and produce as many little soldiers as possible. Joseph Goebbels, the director of Nazi propaganda, once declared that 'the mission of women is to be beautiful and to bring children into the world', and women were prevented from serving on juries because 'they cannot think logically or reason objectively, since they are ruled only by emotion'.[39] As one may imagine, these were positions that were not universally held by German citizens, especially German women, prior to the Nazi seizure of power. In early 1933, even as the Nazi electoral fortunes were rising dramatically, only 5 per cent of women had joined the party.[40] Nevertheless, the neo-traditional Nazi message of stable, healthy 'Aryan' families with a gendered division of labour struck a chord with many women and men in a country that had seen its share of upheaval in recent years. After the Nazis secured power and began vigorously promoting the traditional child-raising family, even more women accepted the programme. There is some dispute among historians as to the amount of voluntary adoption of Nazi tenets among women and the degree of enthusiasm they brought to the Nazi project. Some, like Claudia Koonz, argue that women, by facilitating the activity of the Nazis, were complicit in the Nazi project even if they never directed policy.[41] Others, like Gisela Bock, maintain that women were primarily victims of a suffocating, misogynistic regime.[42] Like most viable historical debates, this one derives vitality from the fact that there is evidence to support both sides, but this is in part because the question is posed so broadly. We cannot expect to make precise claims about the activities and attitudes of fully half of the population. Any determination of complicity or victimhood should be made when considering rather smaller groups of people, and historians have begun to do just that.[43]

Still, if individual women and individual men had different degrees of entanglement with the Nazi project, there can be no denying that the Nazis forwarded a gendered vision that privileged men and masculinity. From the beginning, Nazi Party leaders had appealed to young men inclined towards violence and comradeship, and that remained their power base during the entire course of the Third Reich. Soldiers and veterans of course played a significant role in both forming the social base and the mythology of the movement, but the appeal was broader. The teenage boys who entered the Hitler Youth, for instance, joined a prestigious organization that promoted ideals of self-sacrifice, fraternal care and belligerence. Through shooting drills, physical education, sports and explicit political training they were prepared for a future as fighting men in Hitler's cause. As one recent historian has remarked, the 'hallmark of HJ [Hitler Youth] socialization was militarization, with a view to a war of territorial expansion and, as its predetermined goal, the neutralization of Europe's Jews'.[44] For girls who joined the female version of the Hitler Youth – the League of German Girls or BDM – militarization meant learning how to cultivate an aura of passivity and obedience towards men and preparing oneself for motherhood. Despite these stated goals, however, the BDM also held quite different attractions for young girls. Being able to leave home to go to meetings, camps and other activities provided them with opportunities of which they could previously only dream. While instilling obedience, the BDM also gave girls an enormous sense of social and political engagement and, not least, the chance to exercise power over other girls.[45] Power for girls would prove to be an illusion, but the feelings of inclusion instilled in these youth organizations were equally strong for both genders. Through carefully orchestrated recreational activities, both male and female branches of the Hitler Youth made it fun to participate in the creation of gendered citizenship. Already counting an impressive 100,000 members in early 1933, the Hitler Youth grew rapidly, counting 5.4 million boys and girls by the end of 1936.[46] The future seemed to belong to a gender order that promised the stability of the past.

Fascist movements combined masculine aggressiveness and expansiveness with firmly bounded ethnocentrism, and fascist leaders were often able to exploit the confusion among other European leaders about which of these strands was more central. This confusion came to a head in 1938, during the crisis over the Sudetenland, when Hitler insisted that the German Reich had the right to take this territory away from Czechoslovakia because it was heavily populated by ethnic Germans. Many European leaders saw Germany's expansion in the mid-1930s for what it was: the expression of the core values and practices of a regime that loved martial uniformity, praised combativeness and sought imperial expansion. Others took Hitler's ethnic politics as central and believed that Germany would cease its adventures after it annexed the 'German' areas of Europe (and drove out the non-Germans). The anti-Semitic outrages of the Nazis may have been distasteful and the truncation of Czechoslovakia unfortunate, but if Jews and Czechs were the price to be paid for 'peace in our time', then that was a price that British, French and American politicians were more than willing to pay. The Czechs were rather less sanguine about these developments, and so too was the Soviet Union, which pressed the European powers to go to war with Nazi Germany in 1938, in no small part because the communist leadership believed, rightly as it turned out, that fascism was fundamentally aggressive and expansionist. Hitler proved more than able to split these two camps, and he did so by meeting only with the politicians who were inclined to believe that Germany would be peaceful once it became ethnically homogeneous. No representatives from Czechoslovakia or the Soviet Union attended the infamous meetings in Munich in 1938 at which Hitler was supposedly 'appeased'.

The Soviets, suspicious that the real deal at Munich had been to lay the groundwork for a Nazi assault upon the Reich's communist enemies, immediately sought to turn the tables by redirecting the inevitable Nazi aggression to the west rather than the east. This they accomplished in August 1939, with the signing of a

Nazi–Soviet non-aggression pact. The promise not to attack one another and to abstain from alliances 'directly or indirectly aimed at the other party' was supposed to be in force for ten years. Neither Hitler nor Stalin really believed that the pact would last quite that long. Both knew that the immediate impact of the agreement would be to start a European war by laying the basis for a joint invasion of Poland and the Baltic States, and both suspected that the establishment of a joint border between the two empires would be unlikely to promote long-term peace between these hostile and heavily armed parties.

'Women and Children First'

The attack on Poland proceeded as planned. The Nazis attacked on 1 September 1939, and the Soviets invaded on 17 September. It was immediately clear that this new war was different from the last. The violent tactics towards civilian populations that had been gradually and in some cases unwillingly used by army officials during the First World War had been honed and made part of strategic planning in the Second World War. In eastern Poland, the Soviets deployed the policies of mass deportation and political terror that the tsarist army had used sporadically in the First World War and that the Bolsheviks had been using regularly within the Soviet Union itself over the past decade. It turned out that practice had made perfect. Lavrentii Beria, Stalin's chief of the secret police, instructed his minions to deport as many as a million Poles eastward to the interior of the Soviet Union and ordered the execution of tens of thousands of men who the Soviets believed to be security risks. These operations proceeded ruthlessly. Deportees were locked in incredibly cramped train cars that lacked toilets, windows and heat. Many children and elderly Poles perished en route, the bodies taken away from grieving family members in bags. It was a classic case of ethnic cleansing.[47]

In western Poland, German forces demonstrated from the first days of the war that they had taken the most toxic aspects of martial masculinity to their most extreme conclusion. Not only were civilian men to be assaulted, but, in contrast to the ethos of the earlier age, women and children were to be expressly targeted as well. European military figures in the modern age had long accepted the deaths of women and children as what we would now call 'collateral damage', and they were not above killing them intentionally as an extreme punitive measure either. But the Nazis made the murder of civilians a normal part of their strategy. On the eve of the invasion of Poland, Hitler instructed his commanders to 'kill without pity all men, women, and children of Polish race or language. Only in such a way will we win the vital space we need.'[48] Though this full extermination of ethnic Poles never came to fruition, witnesses recorded that even early in September 1939 it was common to see mounds of dead children and their parents in villages and along roadsides.

There was a definite gendered aspect to the Nazi war on civilians on the Eastern Front. The Nazis drew heavily upon the most aggressive and misogynistic strands of modern militarized masculinity. In addition, as the quote above demonstrates, the war in the east was explicitly conceived of as one of racial extermination. Since women and children represented the future of the races under assault, they were not only acceptable but in many cases primary targets. Total extermination was not envisioned at first, however. The economics of warfare made it unfeasible to murder all the civilians one encountered. In the first place, such organized massacres took time and resources that the army high command wanted to use against the military forces that opposed them. In the second place, every army needs local civilian populations to provide them with goods and an economic infrastructure. This economic calculus made the labour potential of any given civilian in occupied territory the most important factor in determining his or her worth to the occupying army. These calculations disadvantaged women and children, whose prospects for labour in support of the German war effort were much less significant. Thus, in contrast to the situation in the First World War, in which young males were the most likely to be targeted for deportation, execution or other coercive practices, those males were now strangely privileged. Some women, particularly those from Ukraine, were indeed rounded up and sent into slavery in factories within the German Reich, but Nazi officials tended to choose men when seeking candidates for forced labour.

The situation was made worse by the sexual dynamic of the war zone. Sex was one of the few areas of 'labour' in which local women were seen to have more potential than local men. Sexual contact is a feature of all war zones, where it can run the gamut of levels of coercion, from voluntary to rape. Sometimes this was straight prostitution, but local women also exchanged sex for other economic and social favours (such as protection, access to scarce goods or the chance for mobility) and these motivations were even more important in the dire conditions of the Second World War. In all theatres of the war, troops were very sexually active. In Paris, German commanders appropriated brothels when they occupied the city in 1940, and the US army took control of the same buildings and women when they took the city in 1944. In occupied Italy, about 75 per cent of American soldiers admitted to having had sex with local women on an average of once or twice per month. Most paid cash in exchange, though some paid in rationed food. Some did not pay at all.[49] On the Eastern Front, German soldiers both paid for sex and acquired local 'mistresses', but they engaged in more rape than either they or their enemies did on the Western Front.[50] Part of the reason for this was the very misogyny we discussed during our account of the First World War. As in the previous war, German commanders warned troops that Russian women were nearly universally infected with venereal disease and that they were all spies. The special Nazi touch was to remind soldiers that sex with inferior peoples endangered racial purity and constituted a 'moral offense'.[51] These formal injunctions did little to stop sex in the east. In Ukraine, many observers commented upon the variety of relationships that developed between local women and occupying forces, and the German government itself estimated that Germans had fathered 10,000 children in Ukraine during the war.[52]

Though some Germans simply ignored the commands from above (largely with impunity), others took a darker lesson and resolved that no witnesses should be left alive after the racial 'crime' they were committing. Rape-murder, after all, left no possibility for long-term racial pollution, and it could be portrayed as an act of race extermination, on the one hand, and of intimidation of the men who often had to witness the violence upon their loved ones, on the other. Indeed, rape-murder represented the pinnacle of aggressive misogyny. It destroyed women, demonstrated one's own dominance and virility, and emasculated enemy men. Thus, as Omer Bartov notes, it 'was possible for at least a significant part of the German troops to fraternize with individual Russians for a while, and then to "eliminate" them and burn down their houses as part of a mass of dangerous and contemptible *"Untermenschen"* ["inferior people"] the moment this or that "security" situation called for such actions'.[53]

Rape and slaughter had thus marked life in eastern Europe since 1939, with the advancing German forces the main perpetrators. In 1943, however, the tide of war changed. At the Battle of Stalingrad, the Soviet forces finally stopped the German conquest and began rolling them back. By 1944 they had crossed pre-war borders, having reconquered their country kilometre by kilometre and having seen the devastation the Nazi invasion had wrought. When they moved into eastern Europe, however, they launched the same sort of war on civilians that they had witnessed in their own land. Though much research remains to be done to establish the extent and motivations of the atrocities, it is clear that the lurid tales of the Soviet army's penchant for rape that ran rampant in Germany in 1945 were based in fact.[54] Soviet and German witnesses alike attested to the crimes, which culminated in an almost literal rape of the German capital in the final days of the war. The screams of violated women echoed throughout the city for days on end. Estimates from local hospitals indicated that somewhere between 95,000 and 135,000 women had been raped, many by multiple attackers, in the days just before and after Hitler's suicide and the final capitulation of the German army in May 1945.[55] Thus did the gruesome war end in a gruesome way on the streets and in the shattered apartments of Berlin.

The apotheosis of this gendered race war against civilians was of course the Holocaust. The groups that the Nazis targeted for immediate and total destruction – homosexuals, Roma (Gypsies), the handicapped and above all the Jews – were all identified and abused in very gendered ways. Nazi propaganda painted Jewish men as sexual predators, constantly plotting to defile German women. But Jewish men were also feminized; the image of the Jew promoted by the Nazi state was that of the anti-male, cowardly instead of brave, weak instead of strong, duplicitous rather than forthright. In the Nazi mind, Jewish women lacked the necessary attributes of femininity as well, especially after the Holocaust began. Stripped of their clothes and dignity, starved and beaten, women became less 'feminine', not only to their tormentors, but also to themselves and their loved ones. As one survivor remembered, she had pictured throughout her captivity how beautiful her reunion with her daughter would be if they both survived the war. Instead, her child screamed 'My mommy is the one in the picture, this ugly woman isn't my mommy!' when they finally found one another back home in Austria.[56] In the camps themselves, the same dynamic in which women and children were disproportionally targeted for immediate extermination, and often made to suffer sexual assault and torture as well, was present. The Nazi genocide was not 'gender-neutral'.[57]

These Nazi actions deeply affected European gender structures. Whereas in the First World War, mutual ground-level misogyny could be translated into mutual reinforcement of masculine ideas of protection at the national level, the Nazi conquest of the continent had revealed the military notion of masculine protection to be a mirage. Soldiers had failed to protect their own wives and children, and they increasingly came to believe that in order to win the war they would have to target women and children themselves. The initial military successes of the Nazis convinced state and military officials that defeating the German Reich would require an even greater 'totalization' of war than they had envisioned before, one that would entail direct assaults upon Axis civilians as legitimate and necessary war targets. In Great Britain at the start of the war, the 'terror' bombing of civilians was seen as immoral, but this judgement changed as the war progressed. By 1942, Churchill had approved a shift of Britain's strategic bombing plan from one that focused almost exclusively on the 'precision' bombing of key military and industrial sites to one that they called a 'de-housing' campaign. This was a euphemism grotesque even for a grotesque genre; in practice the idea was to 'break the spirit of the people' by killing civilians indiscriminately. By the summer of 1943, the strategy was being fully employed. A week of firebombing in Hamburg in July and August of that year left more than a million urban residents homeless, and it killed nearly as many people (about 50,000) as all German air raids in Britain did over the course of the entire war.[58]

The response of the targeted populations to these unprecedented assaults varied from place to place, but it had important implications for the gender order everywhere. In much of occupied Europe, the response was most obvious in underground movements. These movements responded to occupation and the assault on gender roles by both incorporating women into activities more extensively than had been envisioned or practised in earlier European wars and by urgently attempting to salvage some scraps of earlier gender identities.

The most extensive and unusual developments occurred in the Soviet Union, where the state and military both used the most traditional sorts of propaganda to energize Soviet masculinity and enlisted women into combative wartime roles on a scale unseen either in Russian history or, for that matter, in the history of Europe as a whole. By 1943, roughly 8 per cent of total Soviet military personnel were women, about 800,000 women in all. When one includes partisan fighters in the mix, it is likely that more than a million Soviet women took an active military role, half of them at the front. For the most part, these women stayed in support services, but to a far greater extent than elsewhere they engaged in combat. Indeed, there were three entire female regiments in the Soviet Air Force between 1942 and 1945. Women flew more than 30,000 combat sorties.[59] Still, the iconic Soviet female war figure was not a combat soldier, but the young partisan Zoya Kosmodemianskaia, who was executed by the Germans after she was caught setting fire to a stable filled with army horses. The Soviet press reported that she was tortured and undressed by her captors but went to the gallows bravely, saying 'Don't look glum, Comrades! Be brave, fight, kill the Germans, burn them, poison them! I am not afraid to die, Comrades. It is a great privilege to die for your people.' This model of belligerent sacrifice left a lasting impression. As one future dissident intellectual remembered, she was so taken by the Zoya tale that she 'modelled' her life upon her brave example.[60]

As Soviet women flew combat missions, as masses of women joined partisan units and as millions of European men looked at the ravaged homes and ravaged families they had failed to defend, gendered practices and ideals across the continent lay in rubble, destroyed by the rise to power of the radical, aggressive, misogynistic strand of masculinity that had crystallized in the First World War, had risen to prominence in the interwar period and had come to full power during the Second World War. The fascist movements had led the continent towards apocalypse, and Europe bathed in the blood that the fascists had sought and had revelled in. When their urge for destruction resulted in their own annihilation at the hands of Soviet men and women, and then finally in a wave of Allied assaults in 1944 and 1945, it remained an open question what would be left to salvage from the wreckage. Surely one of the major question marks was what sorts of masculinity and femininity would emerge.

Conclusion: The Recovery of Masculine Heroism

In contrast to the situation after the First World War, in which so many European soldiers, citizens and politicians felt more defeated than victorious at the end of the conflict, the Allied defeat of Nazi Germany and the elevation of anti-fascist politicians to national leadership allowed nearly every European nation (with the important exception of Germany) to feel that they had won the war, even though most states had seen at least part of their country occupied by foreign powers. It was everywhere a bitter victory, of course. In the Soviet Union, where the violence had raged unchecked for nearly four years, the celebrations that came with the Nazi surrender in May 1945 were muted by the destruction. Twenty-seven million Soviet citizens had died, and an additional twenty-five million were rendered homeless. About 1,700 towns and 70,000 villages had been destroyed, and major cities like Stalingrad and Sevastopol were so gutted that virtually no buildings remained standing. In Yugoslavia, a brutal civil war had accompanied the period of Nazi occupation; there too civilians had not been protected by their armies. In Paris, in Copenhagen and elsewhere, much of the war experience had been that of submission to foreign bureaucrats and soldiers. Men in occupied Europe were not masters of their own homes, their own cities or their own nations. By any of the measures of modern masculinity, most European men had failed this enormous test. Indeed, given that the atrocities of the war had resulted from the poisonous distillation of militarized national masculinity to its most brutal elements, the case could have been made that the very core of modern masculinity had been discredited by the experience of the Second World War. Perhaps it was not men but manhood that had failed.

As we have already seen, feminist peace activists had made this exact argument about the destructiveness of modern masculinity even prior to the world wars. It would be revived again a generation after the end of the Second World War, but it was not a popular stance while smoke still wafted from rubble across the continent. Instead Europeans did their best to salvage masculinity from the wreckage of fascism, total war and social apocalypse. Rather than on masculine failure, a great deal of public attention was focused on incidents of masculine heroism. In propaganda posters and in interpersonal exchanges alike, the fighting men of Europe were thanked for their service. The war was transformed into a Manichean battle between good and evil. There was a brief period of retribution right after the war's end that saw the girlfriends of German soldiers, particularly in France and Norway, taunted and abused,[61] local quislings assaulted or killed, the cleansing of ethnic German populations in Poland and Czechoslovakia and the remnants of quasi-fascist paramilitary forces in places like Croatia and Ukraine annihilated. But within only a few years, the fascist sympathizers, the collaborators and the wise 'cowards' who kept their heads down during the catastrophe faded into the silent background. The trials of Nazi war criminals at Nuremberg, which placed blame directly at the top of the political and military chain while tacitly excusing the millions of men in the lower ranks, contributed to this post-war 'reconstruction'. It was as if a couple of potent icons like the swastika and Hitler's little moustache could be made to carry the enormous weight of Europe's sins.

It was perhaps understandable that the victorious nations should have accentuated the positive when they told themselves stories about the war. In these stories, the brave men of Europe saved civilization from barbarism. The defiant, stiff-backed resistance of men like France's Charles de Gaulle or Britain's Winston Churchill was taken to represent the honourable strength of their respective nations. The more lowly men in uniform were less personally recognizable, but they too got their share of the laurels. Idolized and idealized in print, the love affair with the Second World War combat soldier has been strong and shows little sign of waning, even as the survivors themselves are now succumbing to age.

More surprising was the speed with which this same generosity of memory and absolution was extended to Germany. This generosity was not universal, and it was clearly more forthcoming from countries like the United States, which had not experienced German occupation, than it was from places like the Soviet Union, where suspicion of Germans and German power lasted for another fifty years. But still, we can see the key movements in this direction quite early. In 1948, Edward Shils and Morris Janowitz, two young enterprising scholars (and former intelligence officers under General Dwight Eisenhower), wrote one of the most influential pieces in the entire history of the field of military sociology. Entitled 'Cohesion and Disintegration in the Wehrmacht', the article argued that the young conscripts in the German army had been so resolute during the war due to their loyalty to the 'primary group' of soldiers that surrounded them. The argument resurrected the notion of combat brotherhood and argued that it was precisely these 'positive' masculine attributes of loyalty, love for the men next to you, and sense of duty that motivated the *Wehrmacht*'s soldiers. They were not, in other words, really fascist: 'the unity of the German Army was in fact sustained only to a very slight extent by the National Socialist political convictions of its members'.[62] It was true that most of the soldiers were eventually to adopt a Nazi frame of mind and to revere Hitler personally, but this, in Shils and Janowitz's examination, was the result of sociological forces rather than ideological ones. Since many of their officers and junior officers had been part of the 'hard core' committed Nazis, who were 'imbued with the ideology of *Gemeinschaft* (community solidarity), were enthusiasts for the military life, had definite homo-erotic tendencies and accordingly placed a very high value on "toughness," manly comradeliness, and group solidarity',[63] they had been socialized into their roles rather than politically convinced. The article was important because it gave a systematic and compelling argument regarding the social dynamics of military units. This argument about the importance of small-scale socialization to military cohesion retains its vitality today, as our discussion of soldier society during the First World War indicated. But in this context and at this time, it also, intentionally or not, had the effect of 'rehabilitating' the millions of German men who had wielded weapons and actively destroyed the continent.

The logic of this line of reasoning reached its pinnacle in 1985, when US President Ronald Reagan agreed to visit a cemetery in Bitburg, West Germany, where forty-nine members of the Waffen SS (an elite Nazi corps responsible for many wartime atrocities) were buried. When challenged by many Holocaust survivors and by White House reporters, Reagan replied that he would not change his itinerary because the SS men and *Wehrmacht* soldiers were 'Victims of Nazism also … just as surely as the victims in the concentration camps'.[64] In case the point was missed, Reagan again made clear at Bitburg that the young men buried in the cemetery were victims of an 'ism', saying that 'today, freedom-loving people around the world must say, I am a Berliner, I am a Jew in a world still threatened by anti-Semitism. I am an Afghan, and I am a prisoner of the Gulag … I, too, am a potential victim of totalitarianism.'[65]

Reagan's comments (and the grateful welcome of them by German Chancellor Helmut Kohl) highlight two important post-war developments that help us conclude the discussion of war and gender in the twentieth century. In the first place, they show how effectively militarized masculinity had been resurrected after nearly destroying itself and the continent along with it. Soldiers were worth honouring just because they had been soldiers. While Europeans learned to look at fascists as strange and evil fanatics with whom they had nothing in common, when they looked at young men who died in uniform, they recognized them as their own. Courage, duty, hardness and valour were now the traits that marked those who 'fought for freedom', while Nazis were increasingly portrayed as social and sexual perverts.

The second point to make is how quickly and painlessly this form of masculinity was incorporated into the great conflict of post-war Europe, the Cold War. US President John F. Kennedy's proud 1963 'boast' that 'I am a Berliner' had stressed both that the Nazi past would be forgotten (or at least ignored) and that the young, virile fight for freedom was being joined once again, with true men taking sides in the contest. Reagan reminded his German listeners of Kennedy's speech in order to make the same point. By making the Holocaust and all the other atrocities of the Second World War simply episodes in the dramatic battle of freedom-loving men against totalitarianism, or, from the Soviet perspective, in the equally dramatic battle of freedom-loving men against capitalist aggression, it became possible to dust off those old uniforms and those old leather boots in order to fight the threat of the new enemy with a feeling of pride rather than painful guilt.

For better or worse, however, the conflict between the histories we would like and the histories we have are not so easily resolved in favour of the former. It was true that at least in the initial post-war period, the gender 'backlash' seemed to have succeeded. In France, a conservative focus on the traditional family was dominant and women were urged to bear lots of children to replenish the nation.[66] But too much had happened and too much had changed for this revived gender structure to remain unchallenged. Many Europeans felt a deep unease about the similarities between the militarized dynamic of the first half of the century and the militarized dynamic of the second half. It turned out that not only the swastikas reminded people of the brutalities of the past, but those leather boots and warlike speeches did too. This unease played itself out in a variety of ways. The most important one to note here was that the cultural conflicts and the widespread rejection of the status quo by young people in the 1960s and 1970s included a powerful intellectual and political challenge by feminist movements. The final success of suffrage movements in the wake of the Second World War (Italy granted women the vote in 1945 and France in 1946) had made possible this widespread political activism and had freed feminists to press ever harder on issues like social equality and peace. Scholars and organizers alike passionately criticized the dominant form of masculinity and the social order that nurtured and depended upon it. Society and gender may have been deeply militarized, but the process of total war had also helped develop the institutions and sentiments that would challenge the bellicose trend of the twentieth century.

Similarly, the rise of Holocaust studies, which emerged relatively late on the scene of Second World War scholarship, challenged both the normalization of German soldiers and the silence about fascist sympathy across the continent. New works of history convincingly rejected the view that German soldiers and citizens were unwilling accomplices of the Nazi project and that the rest of Europe had simply bowed to necessity. Most of these studies left readers with the unwelcome conclusion that fascism and genocide, far from being alien and exotic or the result of hypnotic brainwashing, were in fact an organic part of European history. 'Ordinary Men' had pulled the trigger on the civilian victims of the war, the Holocaust itself was the logical conclusion of European 'modernity' and not only Germans but also one's 'neighbours' could be the active agents of annihilation.[67] It was serendipitous but not perhaps totally coincidental that the culmination of these academic trends coincided with the end of the Cold War, which seemed to remove the necessity for the deep militarization of society. Given the enormous changes in the post-war era that we shall see in the next chapter, it seemed that the end of the Cold War might finally free Europe not only from the threat of war, but also from the harmful aspects of the militarized masculinity that accompanied that threat. This hope was not totally in vain, but neither was it fully borne out. European masculinity remains in a state of flux at the start of the twenty-first century, but the martial and fraternal form of masculinity that rose to prominence during the years of total war and that defined manhood across the continent for the duration of the bloody twentieth century remains alive and well today.

Notes

1. *Anti-Suffrage Review*, cited in Jenny Gould, 'Women's Military Services in First World War Britain', in *Behind the Lines: Gender and the Two World Wars*, eds Margaret Randolph Higonnet *et al.* (New Haven, CT and London: Yale University Press, 1987), 117.

2. Cited in Tasoula Vervenioti, 'The Adventure of Women's Suffrage in Greece', in *When the War Was Over: Women, War and Peace in Europe, 1940–1956*, eds Claire Duchen and Irene Bandhauer-Schöffmann (London and New York: Leicester University Press, 2000), 105.

3. Susan Pyecroft, 'British Working Women and the First World War', *The Historian* 56, no. 4 (1994): 708.

4. This line of reasoning is particularly pronounced in Higonnet *et al.*, eds, *Behind the Lines*. This volume has been very influential in the field and remains so today.

5. Cited in Misha Glenny, *The Balkans: Nationalism, War and the Great Powers, 1804–1999* (New York: Penguin Books, 1999), 282.

6. Bernadotte Everly Schmitt, *The Annexation of Bosnia, 1908–1909* (New York: H. Fertig, 1970), 46–47.

7. Glenny, *The Balkans*, 297.

8. All cited in D. C. B. Lieven, *Russia and the Origins of the First World War* (New York: St. Martin's Press, 1983), 143.

9. John Ellis and Michael Cox, *The World War I Databook: The Essential Facts and Figures for All the Combatants* (London: Aurum, 2001), 245.

10. Allen J. Frantzen, *Bloody Good: Chivalry, Sacrifice, and the Great War* (Chicago: University of Chicago Press, 2004).

11. Paul Fussell, *The Great War and Modern Memory* (New York: Oxford University Press, 1975), 272.

12. A. D. Harvey, 'Homosexuality and the British Army During the First World War', *Journal for the Society of Army Historical Research* 79 (2001): 313–19.

13. It is still unclear just how many of these army brothels existed and in which armies. It appears that they were most common in the German army, but much research remains to be done. See: Lutz Sauerteig, 'Militär, Medizin und Moral: Sexualität im Ersten Weltkrieg', in *Die Medizin und der Erste Weltkrieg*, eds Wolfgang U. Eckart and Christoph Gradmann (Pfaffenweiler: Centaurus-Verlagsgesellschaft, 1996), 197–226; Elisabeth Domansky, 'Militarization and Reproduction in World War I Germany', in *Society, Culture, and the State in Germany, 1870–1930*, ed. Geoff Eley (Ann Arbor, MI: University of Michigan Press, 1996), 427–63; Joshua S. Goldstein, *War and Gender: How Gender Shapes the War System and Vice Versa* (Cambridge: Cambridge University Press, 2001), 343–44.

14. The model example of a historical work that both seeks to document wartime atrocities and to account for the power of atrocity propaganda is John N. Horne and Alan Kramer, *German Atrocities, 1914: A History of Denial* (New Haven: Yale University Press, 2001).

15. Susan R. Grayzel, *Women's Identities at War: Gender, Motherhood, and Politics in Britain and France During the First World War* (Chapel Hill, NC: University of North Carolina Press, 1999), 7.

16. Peter Gatrell, *A Whole Empire Walking: Refugees in Russia During World War I* (Bloomington: Indiana University Press, 1999), 40–41; Healy, *Vienna and the Fall of the Habsburg Empire*, 187.

17. Joshua A. Sanborn, *Drafting the Russian Nation: Military Conscription, Total War, and Mass Politics, 1905–1925* (DeKalb, IL: Northern Illinois University Press, 2003), 148.

18. Healy, *Vienna and the Fall of the Habsburg Empire*, 26.

19. Sandra M. Gilbert, 'Soldier's Heart: Literary Men, Literary Women, and the Great War', in Higonnet *et al.*, eds, *Behind the Lines*, 216.

20. Maria Botchkareva, *Yashka: My Life as Peasant Officer and Exile* as set down by Isaac Don Levine (New York: Frederick A. Stokes Co., 1919).

21. Belinda Davis, *Home Fires Burning: Food, Politics, and Everyday Life in World War I Berlin* (Chapel Hill: University of North Carolina Press, 2000); Healy, *Vienna and the Fall of the Habsburg Empire*.

22. In a development that few civilians or politicians fully understood, the more 'total' war became, the lower the proportion of uniformed men in combat became, since the enormous need for military supplies and basic necessities required an equally large logistical support system. As long as the supply system functioned, a relatively small number of combat troops could launch massive amounts of metal at the enemy lines. Given that the enemy could do the same, it made sense to keep the number of front-line troops to a minimum as well.

23. Susan Pedersen, *Family, Dependence, and the Origins of the Welfare State: Britain and France, 1914–1945* (New York: Cambridge University Press, 1993), 130–31.

24. See here: Domansky, 'Militarization and Reproduction'.

25. Marcelline J. Hutton, *Russian and West European Women, 1860–1939: Dreams, Struggles and Nightmares* (Lanham, MD: Rowman & Littlefield Publishers, 2001), 148. The divorce rate was also no doubt higher because of the many 'quickie' marriages that occurred in wartime, as couples in the trial period of courtship rushed to wed (and bed) before military deployments occurred.

26. Pyecroft, 'British Working Women', 707.

27. Susan Kingsley Kent, *Making Peace: The Reconstruction of Gender in Interwar Britain* (Princeton: Princeton University Press, 1993).

28. John D. Bell, *Peasants in Power: Alexander Stamboliski and the Bulgarian Agrarian National Union, 1899–1923* (Princeton: Princeton University Press, 1977), 105.

29. Ibid., 153.

30. Ibid., 175–76.

31. Ibid., 212–13.

32. Ibid., 245.

33. Wendy Z. Goldman, *Women, the State, and Revolution: Soviet Family Policy and Social Life, 1917–1936* (Cambridge: Cambridge University Press, 1993).

34. See here: Joshua Sanborn, *Drafting the Russian Nation*, esp. ch. 4, 'The Nationalization of Masculinity'.

35. Krasimira Daskalova, 'Bulgarian Women in Movements, Laws, Discourses (1840s–1940s)', *Bulgarian Historical Review* 27, no. 1 (1999): 180–96; Terry Martin, 'Modernization or Neo-Traditionalism? Ascribed Nationality and Soviet Primordialism', in *Stalinism: New Directions*, ed. Sheila Fitzpatrick (London and New York: Routledge, 2000): 348–67.

36. Daskalova, 'Bulgarian Women', 193.

37. Michael Mann has a thoughtful discussion of the geographical and social dimensions of fascism in interwar Europe. See: Michael Mann, *Fascists* (Cambridge and New York: Cambridge University Press, 2004).

38. Jeremy Noakes and Geoffrey Pridham, *Nazism, 1919–1945: A Documentary History* (Exeter: University of Exeter Press, 1997), 449.

39. Both quotes cited in Klaus P. Fischer, *Nazi Germany: A New History* (New York: Continuum, 1995), 355.

40. Michael H. Kater, *Hitler Youth* (Cambridge, MA and London: Harvard University Press, 2004), 74.

41. Claudia Koonz, *Mothers in the Fatherland: Women, the Family, and Nazi Politics* (New York: St. Martin's Press, 1987).

42. Gisela Bock, 'Racism and Sexism in Nazi Germany: Motherhood, Compulsory Sterilization, and the State', *Signs* 8, no. 3 (1983): 400–21. For her direct response to Koonz, see: Gisela Bock, 'Die Frauen Und Der Nationalsozialismus: Bemerkungen Zu Einem Buch Von Claudia Koonz', *Geschichte und Gesellschaft* 15, no. 4 (1989): 563–79.

43. Adelheld von Saldern, 'Victims or Perpetrators? Controversies About the Role of Women in the Nazi State', in *Nazism and German Society, 1933–1945*, ed. David F. Crew (London and New York: Routledge, 1994), 141–65.

44. Kater, *Hitler Youth*, 28–29.

45. Nori Möding, '"Ich muß irgendwo engagiert sein – fragen Sie mich bloß nicht, warum." Überlegungen zu Sozialisationserfahrungen von Mädchen in NS- Organisationen', in *'Wir kriegen jetzt andere Zeiten': Auf der Suche nach der Erfahrung des Volkes in nach-faschistischen Ländern*, eds Lutz Niethammer and Alexander von Plato (Bonn: J. H. W. Dietz Nachf., 1985), 256–304; Dagmar Reese, 'Bund Deutscher Mädel – Zur Geschichte der weiblichen deutschen Jugend im Dritten Reich', in *Mutterkreuz und Arbeitsbuch: Zur Geschichte der Frauen in der Weimarer Republik und im Nationalsozialismus*, ed. Frauengruppe Faschismusforschung (Frankfurt am Main: Fischer, 1981), 163–83.

46. Kater, *Hitler Youth*, 19.

47. Katherine R. Jolluck, *Exile and Identity: Polish Women in the Soviet Union During World War II* (Pittsburgh, PA: University of Pittsburgh Press, 2002), 9–20.

48. Cited in Richard C. Lukas, *Did the Children Cry?: Hitler's War against Jewish and Polish Children, 1939–1945* (New York: Hippocrene Books, 1994), 16.

49. Goldstein, *War and Gender*, 337.

50. Birgit Beck, *Wehrmacht und sexuelle Gewalt: Sexualverbrechen Vor Deutschen Militärgerichten 1939–1945* (Paderborn: Ferdinand Schöningh, 2004).

51. Omer Bartov, *The Eastern Front, 1941–45: German Troops and the Barbarisation of Warfare* (New York: St. Martin's Press, 1986), 128.

52. Karel C. Berkhoff, *Harvest of Despair: Life and Death in Ukraine under Nazi Rule* (Cambridge, MA: Belknap Press of Harvard University Press, 2004), 182.

53. Bartov, *The Eastern Front*, 129.

54. Norman Naimark, *The Russians in Germany: A History of the Soviet Zone of Occupation, 1945–1949* (Cambridge, MA and London: Belknap Press of Harvard University Press, 1995); Atina Grossmann, 'A Question of Silence: The Rape of German Women by Occupation Soldiers', in *West Germany Under Construction: Politics, Society, & Culture in the Adenauer Era*, ed. Robert G. Moeller (Ann Arbor, MI: University of Michigan Press, 1997), 33–52. A recently rediscovered and republished diary provides a gripping account of women's experiences with rape during the Soviet invasion of Berlin. See: Anonymous, *A Woman In Berlin: Eight Weeks in the Conquered City* (New York: Metropolitan Books, 2005).

55. Antony Beevor, *The Fall of Berlin, 1945* (New York: Viking, 2002), 410.

56. Helga Embacher, 'Unwelcome in Austria: Returnees and Concentration Camp Survivors', in *When the War Was Over: Women, War and Peace in Europe, 1940–1956*, eds Claire Duchen and Irene Bandhauer-Schöffmann (London and New York: Leicester University Press, 2000), 197.

57. Ronit Lentin, '"A Howl Unheard": Women Shoah Survivors Dis-Placed and Re-Silenced', in *When the War Was Over: Women, War and Peace in Europe, 1940–1956*, eds Claire Duchen and Irene Bandhauer-Schöffmann (London and New York: Leicester University Press, 2000), 182.

58. Gordon Wright, *The Ordeal of Total War, 1939–1945* (New York: Harper and Row, 1968), 176–79.

59. Reina Pennington, *Wings, Women, and War: Soviet Airwomen in World War II Combat* (Lawrence, KS: University Press of Kansas, 2001), 1–2.

60. Liudmila Alekseeva and Paul Goldberg, *The Thaw Generation: Coming of Age in the Post-Stalin Era* (Pittsburgh, PA: University of Pittsburgh Press, 1993), 20.

61. The punishment was usually a public head shaving. See: Claire Duchen, 'Crime and Punishment in Liberated France: The Case of les femmes tondues', in *When the War Was Over: Women, War and Peace in Europe, 1940–1956*, eds Claire Duchen and Irene Bandhauer-Schöffman (London and New York: Leicester University Press, 2000), 233–50; and Kåre Olsen, *Schicksal Lebensborn: Die Kinder der Schande und ihrer Mütter* (Munich: Knauer Taschenbuch Verlag, 2004), 251–6.

62. Edward A. Shils and Morris Janowitz, 'Cohesion and Disintegration in the Wehrmacht in World War II', *The Public Opinion Quarterly* 12, no. 2 (1948): 281.

63. Ibid.: 286.

64. Ilya Levkov, *Bitburg and Beyond: Encounters in American, German, and Jewish History* (New York: Shapolsky Publishers, 1987), 39.

65. Ibid., 170–71.

66. Sylvie Chaperon, 'Feminism Is Dead. Long Live Feminism! The Women's Movement in France at the Liberation', in *When the War Was Over: Women, War and Peace in Europe, 1940–1956*, eds Claire Duchen and Irene Bandhauer-Schöffmann (London and New York:

Leicester University Press, 2000), 157.

67. Zygmunt Bauman, *Modernity and the Holocaust* (Ithaca, NY: Cornell University Press, 1989); Christopher R. Browning, *Ordinary Men: Reserve Police Battalion 101 and the Final Solution in Poland*, 1st edition (New York: HarperCollins, 1992); Jan Tomasz Gross, *Neighbors: The Destruction of the Jewish Community in Jedwabne, Poland* (Princeton: Princeton University Press, 2001).

–5–

The Long Sexual Revolution

In 1760, the Swiss physician Simon-Auguste-Andre-David Tissot (1728–97) published a treatise, *L'Onanisme*, that reflected what some eighteenth- and nineteenth-century Europeans thought of the idea of sexual pleasure for its own sake. In that work, Tissot provided a particularly vivid description of the fate of one incurable masturbator L. D.***:

> L. D.***, watchmaker, had been good, and had enjoyed good health, up until the age of seventeen; at this period, he began to masturbate, an act which he reiterated daily, and often as many as three times a day … Before a year had passed, he began to notice a great weakness after each act; this warning was not sufficient to pull him from the mire; his soul, already given over to this filth was no longer capable of other ideas, and the repetitions of his crime became daily more frequent, until he found himself in a state where he feared death was imminent … I learned of his state, I went to his home; what I found was less a living being than a cadaver lying on straw, thin, pale, exuding a loathsome stench, almost incapable of movement. A pale and watery blood often dripped from his nose, he drooled continually; subject to attacks of diarrhoea, he defecated in his bed without noticing it; there was a constant flow of semen; his eyes, sticky, blurry, dull, had lost all power of movement; his pulse was extremely weak and racing … Mental disorder was equally evident; without ideas, without memory, incapable of linking two sentences … Thus sunk below the level of the beast, a spectacle of unimaginable horror, it was difficult to believe that he had once belonged to the human race … He died after several weeks, in June 1757, his entire body covered in edemas.[1]

Masturbation, Tissot argued, was not only a sinful but also a physically harmful act. Sexual acts performed solely for individual pleasure would be punished.

The authors of the *Encyclopedia* (the foundational text of the European Enlightenment) endorsed Tissot's arguments and ensured that they found acceptance across Europe well into the nineteenth century. Indeed, the hysteria about non-reproductive sex and the dangers of unbridled sexual passion reached a height in the late nineteenth century, an era that historians have long characterized as an age of unparalleled sexual repression. Descriptions of sexuality in Victorian England often include stories about how mothers of young brides sent them off to their wedding nights with the advice to 'close your eyes and think of England' and how middle-class housewives crafted lacy doilies to hide the sensual curves of piano legs, lest they provoke lascivious thoughts. Tracts like Tissot's lent credence to the common historical argument that nineteenth-century Europeans considered sexual pleasure to be entirely sinful – an unwanted by-product of the reproductive act that needed to be countered with moral condemnation and strict rules of etiquette.

Two centuries after Tissot, it seemed clear to scholars and casual observers alike that a radical shift in the European approach to sex and its pleasures was occurring. Most believed that the key moment was a 'sexual revolution' in the 1960s, when cultural turbulence and the social impact of the birth control pill had created a new consensus that sexual pleasure was natural and that sexual 'liberation' was healthy. Since sex could be separated from reproduction, it could shed the moral strictures of past times. Sex seemed to be everywhere in the popular culture of these years: movies became much more sexually explicit; premarital sex moved out of the shadows of taboo and became a subject of public debate; and self-proclaimed sexual revolutionaries advocated 'open' marriages and 'swinging' lifestyles as a path to self-knowledge and freedom. The British poet Philip Larkin nicely summarized the atmosphere in his 1967 poem 'Annus Mirabilis'. 'Sexual intercourse began', the poem begins, 'In nineteen sixty-three'.[2] Larkin's poem joyously proclaims the end of the 'wrangling for the ring' that used to precede sexual contact and argues that new sexual freedoms made everyone happy. Everyone, that is, except for those, like himself, who had already passed through the courtship stage of life and thus could only watch all the fun from the married sidelines.

While Larkin was not alone in feeling left out, his poem nicely symbolizes the European social consensus that the boundaries of sexual behaviour had been radically altered. Soon songs like Serge Gainsbourg's sexually explicit 'Je T'aime... Moi Non Plus', sung in orgasmic moans with British actress Jane Birkin in 1969, were achieving massive commercial success across Europe and proving that there was an increased demand for frank discussions about sex. This did not occur without opposition. Gainsbourg's song was banned from radio in Italy, Sweden, Spain and the United Kingdom. But the argument that sexual activity needed to be contained within marriage to protect the interests of society had become less persuasive. Penicillin had been available as an almost infallible cure for all bacterial sexually transmitted diseases (syphilis, gonorrhoea and chancroids) since soon after the Second World War.[3] With the arrival of the birth control pill in much of Europe after 1961, age-old arguments linking sexual behaviour, reproduction and the threat of disease and/or death were definitively buried. Or so it seemed.

While Jane Birkin's moans were indeed symbolic of a new era of public frankness about sex in the 1960s, it is misleading to argue, as many sexual revolutionaries have, that an increase in sexual satisfaction was the true core of this change. The youth of the 1960s generation may have been convinced that they were having more and better sex than their parents and that this would change the world, but their historical intervention had less to do with the quality of their orgasms than with their success in manipulating long-established political discussions about sex. From the perspective of the twentieth-century history of sexuality, focusing too much attention on the famous 1960s generation gap that pitted progressive youth against their supposedly conservative, prudish, war-generation parents overemphasizes both the radicalism of the 1960s and the conservatism of the 1950s. The roots of the sexual revolution lie not in this generation gap, but in scientific, medical and political discourses and policies on sexual behaviour and gender that had developed at the beginning of the century and had even older precedents. In fact, the wishes of the sexual revolutionaries to make sex public and their conviction that sexuality and politics were intimately intertwined were actually far more compatible with previous discourses on sex than they were willing to admit.

The sexual revolutionaries of the 1960s were correct in identifying the politicization of sexual activity as a crucial sphere of social, cultural and indeed political life in twentieth-century European society. They were also correct to assume that the massive shift in the relationship between sex and politics came to full fruition in the 1960s and 1970s. They were wrong, however, in thinking that their 'revolution' would increase the influence of sexual pleasure on politics or social life. Rather than being the agents of something new, they were actually witnesses to the demise of something old. Sex played a less significant role in the political life of Europe after the intervention of the 1960s generation than it had before.[4] To demonstrate how this is true, it will first of all be necessary to explore how historians use the term sexuality. Once we have established that the concept of 'sexuality' did not always exist, it will be easier to see how late nineteenth- and early twentieth-century scientific explorations of sexual behaviour combined with political programmes to increase the birth rate and decisively affect attitudes towards sexuality during and after the two world wars.

Defining Sexuality

The account to follow relies on a definition of the term 'sexuality' that owes much to the late twentieth-century French philosopher Michel Foucault (1926–84). Foucault was and continues to be even after his death the most influential figure in the destruction of narratives of ever-increasing sexual liberation over the course of the modern period. In 1976, Foucault published a short introduction to a planned six-volume *History of Sexuality* (he completed only three volumes before his death in 1984). The first volume (originally published in English simply as *Volume One: Introduction*) riveted the attention of historians interested in the history of sexuality, and made 'well-trodden terrain suddenly unfamiliar'.[5] The book reframed the relationship between sex and society and questioned the fundamental assumptions of the field. Foucault suggested that the supposed prudery of the Victorian period was a myth that obscured the fact that there was actually an expansion of the discussion of subjects related to sex in the nineteenth century.[6] He argued further that this concern with sex was deeply connected with changes in the larger structures of power in society, but he rejected the interpretation that the ultimate result was simply sexual repression. What previous historians viewed as examples of social control (prohibitions on masturbation and calls for female chastity, for example) Foucault saw as indications that talk about sex so pervaded political culture that it took on an unprecedented importance, becoming a key conduit for relationships of power. When popularizing their own sexual norms and translating them into social policy, European property owners were less interested in controlling their inferiors than in solidifying their own growing political power. The middle classes, Foucault insisted, first examined their *own* sexual practices and made a science out of sexuality in the hopes of redefining their roles in society, setting themselves apart from previous ruling classes. In the process, a science of sexuality was created, a complex and multifaceted scientific exploration of sex that – unlike the erotic arts of other cultures – was less a search for truth in sexual pleasure than it was a quest for personal confessions about sexual experiences. Foucault argued that these confessions collectively created 'a complex machinery for producing true discourses on sex'.[7] In the process of producing new forms of knowledge, a new and reciprocal relationship of power was formed between confessing individuals and the state.

While the search for truth about sex led to obsessions with masturbation and childhood sexuality, concerns about homosexuality and sexual perversion, the mysteries of women's bodies and the need to control reproductive behaviour, Foucault also believed that it created new forms of sexual pleasures and new identities. First under the auspices of Christianity and then in the doctor's office or on the psychiatrist's couch, teasing out sexual truth through confession incited desires: there was pleasure in the quest for truth about pleasure. Though this quest involved a relationship of power, this power did not quash sexual identities, it created them. 'L. D.***' had masturbated, but Doctor Tissot made him a 'Masturbator'. Foucault argues that it was in this confessional space that the very notion of sexual identity emerged. A search for the 'truth' of sexual experience that began in the West in the eighteenth century led to the conviction that sex constitutes our individuality, that individuals possess a core sexual essence, a natural and somewhat immutable sense of themselves that is tied to their sexual desires. As individuals confessed their sexual desires, medical experts categorized modes of sexual being, implicitly or explicitly labelling some 'normal' and others perverse. Foucault's insights have led others to explore how sexual behaviour became part of the consensus about a hierarchy of the human race as it had emerged with the growing acceptance of Darwin's theories at the turn of the century.[8] How someone's sexual desires expressed themselves came to be taken as a sign of their place on an evolutionary scale. As we saw in Chapter 3, part of the European imperial project involved the use of sexual categories and hierarchies of acceptable sexual behaviour to justify European dominance and reinforce beliefs in European racial superiority.

So, what has been the effect of Foucault's intervention into the history of sexuality? Perhaps the best way to demonstrate the impact of the *History of Sexuality* is to look at how historical narratives have changed under its influence. The first generation of historians to seriously examine the history of sexual behaviour were motivated by their involvement in the liberation movements of the 1960s and 1970s: the women's liberation movement and the gay rights movement. Their books were written to uncover the 'lost' history of sexual minorities, and their arguments were formulated on the assumption that sexual identities (like homosexuality and lesbianism) always existed. Books like John Boswell's path-breaking *Christianity, Social Tolerance and Homosexuality: Gay People in Western Europe from the Beginning of the Christian Era to the Fourteenth Century* (1980) tracked the history of homosexuality backwards into previous eras, looking for mechanisms of repression or, sometimes, modes of tolerance.[9] But his assumption that these same-sex sexual practices were identical to what we now call homosexuality has since been questioned by historians inspired by Foucault's undermining of the repressive hypothesis. In contrast to John Boswell, David Halperin's explorations of ancient Greece have led him to the conclusion that 'it is not immediately evident that patterns of sexual object-choice [choice of partner] are by their very nature more revealing about the temperament of individual human beings, more significant determinants of sexual *identity*, than for example, patterns of dietary choice'. Influenced by Foucault, Halperin insists that ancient cultures (not to mention many non-Western cultures of the present) simply did not share our belief that individuals could be separated into different 'sexualities' according to their choice of partner.[10]

Despite the impact of Foucault's ideas, historians have generally been sceptical of his historical methods. They have criticized his periodization, his failure to delve very deeply into existing scholarship, his underemphasis of sexual difference and his tendency to make generalizations about massive social changes without specifically naming historical actors, events or causes.[11] Yet even as they make these critiques, historians like Halperin, Jeffrey Weeks and Joan Scott have drawn inspiration from Foucault's ideas to chart new territories of historical research. Foucault's arguments imply, even when he himself does not explain, that all forms of human sexuality – not simply those considered to be abnormal in a given time or place – are deeply conditioned by culture and society. His ideas suggest that culture also infuses 'normal' heterosexual practices. We take this suggestion seriously as we attempt to understand the history of the relationship between sexual practices and social forces in this chapter.

In this book, we have used 'sexuality' to denote something more than simply personal sexual desire, activity or fulfilment. Gender relations, we have argued, are invariably intertwined with social prescriptions on sexual behaviour and underlying assumptions about sexual propriety, the social meaning of sex and accepted standards of sexual behaviour for each gender. In other words, we have taken sexuality, like gender, to be a constructed, historically changing and socially malleable category.

This contradicts the common-sense present-day usage of 'sexuality' (and the self-understanding of most of the historical actors we have been investigating), which tends to assume that sexual desires are naturally and inherently present in each individual and that sex is (or at least should be) confined to the private sphere. As George Chauncey puts it: 'The belief that one's sexuality is centrally defined by one's homosexuality or heterosexuality is hegemonic in contemporary culture: it is so fundamental to the way people think about the world that it is taken for granted, assumed to be natural and timeless, and needs no defense.'[12] While it is common to acknowledge how social influences can cause sexual dysfunction or neurosis, there is a somewhat unacknowledged tendency to assume that each individual is born with a predetermined set of sexual desires. Society, in this definition of sexuality, acts only negatively: it represses or deforms our natural, healthy inclinations. Much of the discussion about 'sexual health' in popular culture and self-help books begins from the assumption that individuals must be protected from potential sexual dangers to ensure the healthy development of natural and pure sexual impulses. But this popular understanding of sexuality looks less tenable once we start exploring sexuality as a historical subject. What does 'natural' actually mean when it comes to human sexual behaviour, and is our understanding of 'natural' also influenced by our particular cultural viewpoint? Once we ask these questions, our view of sexual behaviour in history changes.

Sexual Difference, Politics and Evolutionary Theory

The nineteenth century saw an increasing emphasis on sexual dimorphism: the physical dissimilarity between male and female forms. The differences between men's and women's bodies were taken as a given, while those who could not easily be classified under either definition were taken as exceptions.[13] In the case of hermaphrodites, anomalous genital configurations that threatened to destabilize the binary division of genders turned around to reinforce them as medical scientists placed emphasis on specific tissues as signs of 'true' sex: the ovaries and the testes.[14] This view of physical difference did indeed generally translate into very different social roles for men and women. But historians are increasingly demonstrating that it is more instructive to explain rather than replicate this binary opposition. Historical accounts that focus solely on female experience have a tendency to repeat the very prejudices about female difference (about the importance of their bodily difference) that marginalized the historical actors under investigation.[15] They imply that masculinity is the default identity rather than unravelling how it too was constructed in relation to femininity. Scientific understandings of sexual differences between male and female bodies contributed to the tendency to understand sexual identities as innate natural qualities expressed to the outside world through bodies and gestures.

Several strands of political thought and scientific theory helped reinforce beliefs in sexual dimorphism in the mid-nineteenth century. The work of influential French historian Jules Michelet (1798–1874) provides an excellent example of how the science of sexual difference filtered down to political thinkers and influenced ideas about gender. In the late 1850s he wrote rhapsodies to women's reproductive organs, describing how they produced emotional effects equivalent to the painful/euphoric state of falling in love. Menstruation was for him a recurring wound that both proved women's weakness and allowed them insight into a higher emotional world.[16] Michelet accepted the value of women's sexual pleasure, but his main concern was to ensure that women would be encouraged to see their primary duty as child-bearing. This was a political argument as well as a sexual one, since the French state was becoming increasingly worried about falling birth rates. Sex and politics were intertwined in other ways as well. When Michelet interpreted scientific reports about the little scars left on female ovaries when they release eggs as evidence that women were permanently wounded and therefore irrational, he was influenced by his polit-ical conviction that women's primary social task was childbirth. Like other nation-alists and most medical scientists, Michelet was convinced that the declining birth rate could only be combated if sex (biological differentiation *and* social conventions about intercourse) determined how men and women interacted and how each indi-vidual viewed his or her role as a citizen.

The link between sex and citizenship was reinforced by evolutionary theory. In 1857, Bénédict-Augustin Morel (1809–73), a French asylum director, wrote his *Treatise on the Physical, Intellectual and Moral Degeneration of the Human Race*, which explained a huge array of physical, mental and social pathologies as evidence of 'the empire of the law of inheritance'.[17] Morel's theory that the bad behaviour of one generation (smoking, drinking and drugs) could permanently damage the quality of the next was well received all over Europe. It comprised an important part of the collection of evolutionary ideas that began to inform political thought on all sides of the political spectrum in the late nineteenth century. As we saw in Chapter 3, Charles Darwin's writings were especially influential in this regard. But Europeans quickly combined Darwin's explanations of evolutionary change in the plant and animal king-doms with Morel's and de Gobineau's theories about humankind. By the turn of the century a plethora of popularizers across Europe (particularly Herbert Spencer and Francis Galton in England) were emphasizing the possibility that the human race would decline in quality if science and public policy did not intervene. The theory of eugenics was born out of this combination of Darwin and theories of degeneration. Galton (who was Darwin's cousin) coined the word 'eugenics' in 1883 to describe public policies that encouraged selective breeding. He defined eugenics as 'the science of improving stock ... to give the more suitable races or strains of blood a better chance of prevailing speedily over the less suitable than they otherwise would have had'.[18] He believed that only the most 'fit' should be allowed to have children and that the human races could be ranked in a hierarchy of value. These ideas spread rapidly through Europe, and in the early twentieth century, eugenics societies were formed not only in Great Britain, but also in Sweden, Norway, Russia, Switzerland, Germany, Poland, France, Spain and Italy. By the 1920s, eugenics had gained considerable prominence in North American social policy circles and had spread to Japan and Latin America.[19]

Eugenics did not look the same everywhere. Benito Mussolini in Italy and Francisco Franco in Spain viewed a high birth rate as a path to national glory and colonial expansion.[20] These Catholic countries generally rejected the use of birth control and abortion and made the improvement of maternal and infant health care the centrepiece of their eugenic projects.[21] But in every variant, Social Darwinist thought, particularly when mixed with eugenic pronouncements on how the race as a whole could be improved through targeted social policy, provided a battle cry for those who sought to justify a variety of political programmes promising to improve European society and strengthen individual nations. As a result, evolutionary theory penetrated every sphere of medical science and social policy in the late nineteenth and early twentieth century. It provided the inspiration for the creation of new disciplines, particularly criminology, psychiatry and sexology, that sought to explore the social effects of sexual behaviour and choices.

Sexology

The development of the discipline of sexology was a crucial step towards the long sexual revolution, because it helped disseminate the idea that sexual desires are a core aspect of individual identity, personality and social motivation. The founders of the field of sexology placed themselves in competition with religion as arbiters of correct social behaviour. Like Christian moralists before them, late nineteenth- and early twentieth-century scientists of sex examined sexual behaviour for its moral content. While they avoided words like 'sin', their concern with the social effects of 'deviant' sexual behaviour had much in common with Judaeo-Christian concepts of social conformity and redemption.[22] Drawing inspiration from evolutionary theory, most sexologists viewed their task as the identification of sexual deviance for the protection of the larger social good. Categories of sexual behaviour were discovered, labelled and, when found to be abnormal (as they generally were), treated. This new strategy of treating sexual deviance as a medical issue seemed to make sex the 'problem' of individuals rather than societies. Traditional community controls were replaced with the psychiatrist's couch and with specific laws against specific acts. But the actual effect of this medicalization was to politicize sex. Particularly, though not exclusively, in the Protestant regions of Europe, the final arbiter of 'sinful' sexual behaviour was no longer one's terrestrial or heavenly confessor, but a doctor, psychiatrist or geneticist. These individuals were in turn the executors of public policies that were increasingly influenced by eugenic ideas. In the process, an entirely new public language of the social role of sex was developed, and the European understanding of sexuality was transformed.

Sexology as a named discipline did not actually exist until 1907, when the Berlin dermatologist Iwan Bloch coined the word *Sexualwissenschaft* (literally sexual science, but best translated as sexology). But steps in this direction had been taken by scientists like the Austro-Hungarian doctor Heinrich Kaan, who catalogued sexual pathologies in 1844, and the Italian anthropologist Paolo Mantegazza (1831–1910), who wrote a three-volume *Trilogy of Love* in the 1870s and 1880s.[23] In 1886, these studies were taken a step further by the publication of Richard von Krafft-Ebing's (1840–1902) *Psychopathia Sexualis*. Krafft-Ebing's definition of sexuality as a core aspect of individual identity is the foundation of today's common-sense understanding of what sexuality is. He argued that

> If the original constitution is favourable and normal, and factors injurious to the psycho-sexual personality exercise no adverse influence, then a psycho-sexual personality is developed which is unchangeable and corresponds so completely and harmoniously with the sex of the individual in question, that subsequent loss of generative organs (as by castration) or the climacterium [menopause] or senility, cannot essentially alter it.[24]

Krafft-Ebing epitomized the sexual essentialism of nineteenth-century sexology; he relied on science to prove that each individual inherits an unchangeable sexual identity and set of sexual desires. As Jeffrey Weeks has argued, early sexology's attempt 'to explain complex forms by means of an identifying inner force or truth' was wedded to Christian beliefs about the overpowering force of sexual desire in our lives and its negative impact on society and civilization.[25] The eagerness to determine the 'truth' about human sexuality in order to secure civilization led to a concentration on perversion and abnormality, rather than on 'normal' sexual pleasures. This tendency was particularly pronounced in Krafft-Ebing, whose reading of Darwin and other evolutionary theories persuaded him that sexology was part of a modern vanguard of scientific thought that would help to ensure that European social policy was based upon 'scientific' principles.[26] It is thus no accident that he employed the language of racialism, since terms like 'degeneration' implied the need for urgent action and the sovereignty of science to determine what was pathological and what was normal. As these and related ideas came to dominate European sexology into the early twentieth century, sexual identity – meaning, at this time, the labels that sexologists gave to specific spectra of sexual behaviour, but not yet the labels that individuals gave themselves – acquired increasing political importance.[27]

But Krafft-Ebing and other sexologists did not simply set out to punish sexually 'abnormal' individuals; they were also often activists for sexual rights. The Berlin physician Magnus Hirschfeld (1868–1935), for example, hoped that further research would lead to more justice and humanity. Hirschfeld's Scientific-Humanitarian Committee even began campaigning for the decriminalization of homosexual acts (they wanted to abolish section 175 of the German criminal code) in 1897. Often called the 'Einstein of Sex',[28] Hirschfeld coined the word 'transvestism' and argued for the existence of an 'intermediate' sex between male and female. In 1919, the new Social Democratic government in Germany funded Hirschfeld's Institute for Sexual Science in the embassy district of Berlin Tiergarten, which housed a large library and provided sexual counselling for homosexuals and heterosexuals.[29] The study of homosexuality helped fuse isolated research projects into the discipline of sexology. Sexologists were influenced by non-medical activists like the Austrian-born Hungarian journalist Károly Mária Benkert (1824–82), who coined the word 'homosexual', and whose campaigns against anti-homosexual laws were motivated by a tragic personal experience (the suicide of a close friend) and general concern for human rights to privacy. Once Krafft-Ebing adopted Benkert's word in *Psychopathia Sexualis*, it came into general use, eventually replacing Karl-Heinrich Ulrich's *Urning* and other words in use at the time, such as 'invert', 'pederast', 'sodomite' and their variations in other languages. The shifts in terminology reflected a diversity of attitudes towards homosexuality in sexology circles. Krafft-Ebing epitomized this ambivalence, since over the course of his career, he moved from viewing homosexuality as a form of degeneracy to accepting the reality and legitimacy of homosexual love.[30] Along with the Swiss physician Auguste Forel (1848–1931) and the British psychologist Havelock Ellis (1859–1939), Krafft-Ebing joined with Hirschfeld to campaign against laws banning homosexual sex acts. These efforts culminated in the formation of the World League for Sexual Reform in 1928. The study of homosexuality may have begun using the language of deviance, but it is difficult to imagine today's gay rights movement without the contributions of these early pioneers.

While Krafft-Ebing and Hirschfeld helped legitimate sexology as an academic discipline, it was the Viennese psychiatrist Sigmund Freud (1856–1939) who was most successful in disseminating the idea that sexuality stands at the core of human personality. Freud began his career as an anatomist, but in the late 1880s, he came under the influence of French neurologist Jean Charcot, who had used hypnotism to treat hysteria. Freud became increasingly interested in the unconscious and came to believe that humans were strongly motivated not only by observed reality, but also by their unconscious feelings and emotions. While he insisted on the ability of science to be objective and rational, he stressed that irrational forces played a significant role in human behaviour. His arguments called moral conventions into question, since they suggested that individuals were not always making rational, self-conscious choices.

In three major books between 1900 and 1905, Freud developed the theory and techniques of psychoanalysis, a method of psychological treatment that relies on free association and dream interpretation to uncover the unconscious or repressed impulses at the heart of a patient's neurotic behaviours and psychic disorders.[31] While Freud's theories were initially rejected, a series of lectures he gave in the United States in 1909 greatly advanced his fame.[32] By the mid-twentieth century his definition of psychological development as a rational process – something that can be scientifically understood according to the laws of cause and effect despite its basis in emotional conflict – was widely accepted. In the process of exploring how sexual urges and experiences caused psychological neuroses, Freud helped to define sexuality as an observable, definable and treatable aspect of the human character. More significantly, he argued for the first time that 'normal' heterosexuality was something that needed to be explained rather than simply taken for granted.[33]

We do not have space here to do justice to Freud's complex theories on sexuality. For our purposes, it is important to emphasize three key areas. Although Freud had great respect for Darwin's evolutionary theory, he insisted that adult sexuality was not biologically predetermined but could be affected by experiences in early childhood and the conflicts that they produced. Humans, he argued, are sexually malleable. It is only social stricture that eventually stops a child from finding sexual pleasure in a wide range of bodily sensations, not just phallic (genital) but also oral and anal. This belief in 'polymorphous perversity' most famously led to Freud's Oedipus theory, which he developed at the end of the nineteenth century. Named after a Greek myth, the theory explained male sexual maturation as a process of identification with and jealousy of the father and desire for the mother.[34] The Oedipus complex was part of Freud's larger seduction theory – the belief that hysteria (the name given to a wide variety of psychological neuroses at the time) was caused by a sexually traumatic experience in childhood. While the theory itself, Freud's evidence for developing it and even the degree to which he himself continued to be convinced by it have been the subject of great controversy,[35] there is no doubting the fact that Freud's emphasis on childhood sexual development as a key to adult sexual and psychological health was extraordinarily influential and endures in some fundamental ways to this day. Freud moved beyond the study of perversion that preoccupied his contemporaries and sought to focus his scientific energies on the study of 'normal' sexuality.[36] The belief that any person's sexuality is conditioned by family relationships, childhood development and underlying and not entirely controllable desires filtered down from elite investigations into public consciousness. Freudian allusions were ubiquitous in European literature, humour and even political discourse from the early twentieth century on. More than any other thinker, he changed public discourse about what sexuality means to individuals and to societies.

The most general way in which Freud's writing influenced European and North American views on the role of sex in society was his insistence that sexuality played a key role in civilization as a whole. Sexual drives, he argued, were fundamental to human behaviour and their healthy socialization is a necessary precondition for civilization. In *Civilization and Its Discontents* (1930), Freud even argued that civilization began when the first man restrained his primal, sexual urge to display sexual potency by putting out the fire with a stream of urine. Renouncing this instinct and allowing women (who lacked the appropriate equipment) to become guardians of the hearth ensured the conquest of culture.[37] Freud related libido, a strong sexual

drive that he called Eros, to human inclinations towards aggressiveness and destructiveness, which he linked to the death instinct, or Thanatos. Civilization arose out of
the struggle between these instincts. The 'pleasure principle' of human nature, Freud
argued, leads to an egoistic drive to physically satisfy ourselves, but we are quickly
forced to realize (through the 'reality principle') that society, our weak bodies and
the natural world generally combine to frustrate the quest for physical pleasure. We
learn to renounce our desires, control them and displace them into other activities.
The result – civilization – promises to free us from conflict but actually ensures that
we must forsake the satisfaction of our instinctual search for pleasure. We must sub-
limate our desires – suppress our quest for pleasure – in order to turn these energies
into the actions necessary for our survival. This permanent sense of sexual dissatisfaction, Freud believed, helped to explain the inevitability of social conflict.

Finally, Freud developed a theory of female sexuality that dramatically reinforced
the gendered norms of his day. He prized the penis as the most sexual and therefore
important organ, argued that women had 'penis envy', and averred that 'probably no
male human being is spared the fright of castration at the sight of a female genital'.[38]
He denied the importance of the clitoris as a key site of sexual pleasure (at least for
mature women) and insisted that only vaginal intercourse could provide true female
sexual satisfaction. This rejection of centuries of anatomical knowledge was linked
to Freud's belief that the sexual and marital norms of his day made European civilization possible.[39] The fact that he understood sexuality in primarily male terms
(sexual pleasure, he argued, was best achieved through the 'discharge of sexual substances') made it clear that he was swayed by cultural norms that took men's experience as the standard of comparison, invalidating or pathologizing the experience of
women. Some women were also swayed by his logic. In 1932, French sexologist
Marie Bonaparte extolled the virtues of surgery to move the clitoris closer to the
vagina so as to eliminate the problem of women remaining immaturely fixated on
the pleasure of its stimulation.[40] She was implying that Freud was right about the
dangers of allowing women to focus on an organ of sexual pleasure (the clitoris) that
had little to do with reproduction. Later feminists, particularly in the 1970s, were
less convinced. They understood that Freud's definition of 'normal' female sexuality
pathologized women who failed to live up to social stereotypes about mothers and
who sought sexual pleasure for its own sake. But these feminist commentators did
not notice Freud's most significant analytical weakness: the failure of his male-
centred theory to define masculinity. While femininity and its 'normal' function gar-
nered extensive treatment in Freud's writings, he generally took masculinity as a
given. It was something that men had and that 'abnormal' women (particularly lesbians) could have too much of.[41]

Freud's contemporaries seemed to agree with his assessment of gender roles. For
his eightieth birthday in May 1936, he received accolades from the most prominent
cultural figures of his day, including James Joyce and Albert Einstein. Thomas
Mann, the great German novelist, wrote that Freudian thought had long 'outgrown

[its] purely medical implications and become a world movement which penetrated into every field of science and every domain of the intellect'.[42] Freud's theories, in other words, hit a very raw cultural nerve. His reinforcement of traditional gender norms and their misogynistic tendencies has to be understood in the context of the cultural politics of the time. Freud's emphasis on the productive power of male sexual desire and his insistence that female sexual pleasure was bound to reproductive function were views highly compatible with prevailing political concerns about population and civilization in Europe.

Population Policy, Pronatalism and Eugenics

In the late nineteenth century, as sexologists pioneered the investigation of individual sexual drives, social and political figures anxiously followed the dramatic shift in sexual reproduction and population growth that was taking place at the same time. Between 1860 and 1910 Austria-Hungary, Great Britain and Germany added between fifteen and twenty-nine million people to their populations.[43] Up to 1880 the increase was mainly due to rising birth rates made possible by earlier marriages as industrialization changed family patterns. After 1880, the increase in population was sustained by ever more successful strategies to combat the epidemic diseases (cholera, tuberculosis, typhoid) that had attacked European populations, particularly in rapidly growing urban centres. But the poorer parts of Europe and even some of the industrialized areas also experienced increasing rates of emigration. In 1880, 500,000 people left Europe each year. From 1906 to 1910, 1,300,000 were leaving yearly. In total, between 1846 and 1932 about sixty million people emigrated from Europe to the New World. In some cases (such as during the Irish Potato Famine of the late 1840s) emigration eased social burdens by allowing poor Europeans to escape grinding poverty. But emigration also represented a dramatic loss of potential strength, and politicians increasingly worried that slow population growth would mean weakness in the international arena. As we saw in the previous chapter, the requirements of total war placed a political premium on a growing population, and European governments (particularly France and Germany) viewed their demographic statistics as a concrete indication of military strength. The massive loss of life in the First World War only intensified the relationship between population growth and war in the minds of European politicians and military leaders.[44] Policymakers in Europe were also concerned that internal migration, particularly movement to increasingly overcrowded cities, was too quickly altering the social fabric and endangering health.

The first nation to experience an actual decline in birth rates was France. Marital fertility (the number of babies born to married couples) began to decline in 1800, about seventy years earlier than in other European countries. The population still grew, but much less quickly than elsewhere in Europe. Between 1800 and 1900, the

French population increased by 38 per cent compared with 252 per cent in England.[45] This caused great concern about France's ability to remain competitive both economically and militarily, and when other European nations began to experience similar, though far less dramatic, declines in marital fertility after about 1870, they also began to share French anxieties about the future. When Prussian forces decisively beat the French in 1870, those fears appeared to have been justified. The unification of the German Reich in 1871 only intensified concerns about demographic strength. Both countries developed pronatalist policies to combat the declining birth rate, and other European countries were pulled along by the tide of concern. While rhetoric supporting such programmes as the granting of baby bonuses and tax bonuses and the creation of milk kitchens for infants generally called up images of a threatened nation, these policies were not tied to any particular political affiliation. Policies intended to promote higher birth rates through support for families were equally prevalent in socially conservative France and more-liberal states like Great Britain. Pronatalist policies even gained ground in Italy and Soviet Russia, where birth rates remained high.[46] The age of total war encouraged regimes with widely diverse ideologies to embrace the notion that a rising population would foster military and economic strength.

The slowing rates of population growth that so worried pronatalist politicians were in part the result of a dramatic increase in the use of various methods of contraception. While noble and middle-class families had begun limiting family size for financial reasons in the eighteenth century,[47] the pressures of urbanization over the course of the nineteenth century meant that even poor, formerly rural families changed their reproductive habits to conform to the economic realities they found in the cities. By the late nineteenth century, doctors and special clinics in Germany and the Netherlands were providing working-class women with cervical caps and various chemical spermicides. Douching with wall-mounted water devices or with substances like quinine was also common. Charles Goodyear's patent on the vulcanization of rubber in 1844 made the mass production of affordable condoms possible, although they remained above the budgets of most working-class families until after the First World War. Most common of all, particularly in rural areas, were nonmechanical methods like withdrawal before ejaculation. Abortion rates also soared in the late nineteenth century. Over the course of the 1880s, 100,000 women had abortions in Paris alone.[48] This was the only method of birth control that was absolutely effective at the time, though, given prevailing practices and standards of hygiene, it was also life-threatening for the woman. European countries' responses to these various efforts to limit family size varied. In some cases, contraception was viewed as an invaluable method of preventing the sick and the weak from reproducing. At other times, as in fascist Italy, it was viewed as a fundamentally antipatriotic act.[49]

Given the ideological nature of European regimes in the first half of the twentieth century, it comes as no surprise that programmes to encourage higher birth rates varied dramatically across the continent. But these differences are not easy to predict on the basis of political system alone. Democracies, for instance, could be quite different in how they approached the problem of the birth rate. In Britain and to some degree in Weimar Germany, politicians espoused goals of progressive income distribution to poorer families. In France, in contrast, pronatalist policies were more explicitly conservative and aimed to support traditional family structures. These varying ideological goals did not equate to levels of effectiveness. Traditional France, for instance, more effectively directed aid to children than progressive Britain.[50] Even the Nazis used pronatalist policies to help families in need, though only those who passed strict racial criteria and fell in line with fascist ideology.[51] But while the Nazis were most likely to discriminate between the deserving and the undeserving, no European country in the early and mid-twentieth century was immune from new scientific ideas about the connection between evolutionary theory and politics.

The science of eugenics began to inform medical and political discussions about reproduction throughout the continent. After the turn of the century, eugenics societies cropped up all over Europe, and the argument that governments and doctors needed to actively intervene to improve the quality of the race (defined either broadly as the 'human race' or much more narrowly in nationalistic racist terms) came to dominate political discussions of social policy. This had an immediate impact on public attitudes towards sexual behaviour, since the emphasis on race inevitably conjured up fears about the consequences of individual reproductive choices. These reproductive choices, the eugenicists argued, could only be made responsibly if the public were educated about their duties to conduct their sexual lives with the good of the society as a whole in mind. Eugenic theories encouraged pronatalists and social reformers to think not just in terms of quantity (numbers of babies being born) but also in terms of quality. From the turn of the century on, arguments made on the basis of eugenic thought ranged from socialist pronouncements about the need to prevent individual suffering by spreading knowledge about genetic and congenital diseases, to extremely elitist (and sometimes racist) goals to carefully breed a genetically superior human, weeding out inferiors either before or even after conception and birth. The most extreme variants of eugenics fed into justifications for forced sterilization, euthanasia and even genocide (the Holocaust). But this should not distract us from the fact that the basic argument of eugenics – that the government should attempt to influence reproductive behaviour in the interests of future generations – was almost universally accepted in Europe in the first half of the twentieth century. Eugenics thus had a profound effect on the politicization of sexual behaviour, since it argued that individual and sexual and reproductive choices were not private but extremely public matters.

One consequence of the prominence of pronatalist and eugenic rhetoric was to dramatically reinforce perceptions of gender difference. Posters extolling the female virtues of motherhood and the innate feminine ability to nurture not only valorized traditional roles for women, but also linked female sexuality even more strongly to motherhood than it had been before. Even in predominantly Catholic countries, like Spain, a modern redefinition of gender occurred with eugenic logic and scientific argumentation replacing religious discourse in definitions of female (and male) gender roles.[52] Mothers who might formerly have been informed of their spiritual duties were now exhorted to contribute to the well-being and military strength of their nations by providing a future generation of soldiers. This was a direct admonishment that non-reproductive sex was immoral, not because it was sinful, but because it ran counter to the interests of the state. Political pronatalism reinforced the distinction between female sexuality, which was connected to motherhood, and male sexuality, which was a much more free-floating and powerful force that could be harnessed and redirected into military efforts. Exactly how pronatalism fed off of or into gender roles varied in every country. In Germany, before but especially after the rise of the Nazis, mothers were the focus of most pronatalist social programmes and propaganda. In France, fathers were much more prominent as recipients of government aid. In fascist Italy, a cultural tendency to prize male virility found expression not only in government statements about Italian superiority, but also in Benito Mussolini's rather public sexual conquests with a string of mistresses.[53] In each case, public statements about birth rates and the need to increase them helped to entrench cultural perceptions about how one's reproductive function should determine one's social role. It was not uncommon, for instance, for European feminists to argue that women should gain the right to vote because their risk of death in childbirth was analogous to a soldier's risk of death on the battlefield. In each case full citizenship was to be gained through a specific contribution to the biological survival of the nation. Governments could rely on this logic when employing pronatalist policies that conveniently combined nationalistic goals with specific rewards for citizens. By mid-century, pronatalism had become a powerful tool for the legitimation of state projects.

The case of Soviet Russia is more complex in this regard. First of all, birth rates remained high in eastern Europe, so pronatalist movements were not as strong, at least before the Second World War. Soviet ideology was also highly conflicted on the subject of sexuality and the family. After coming to power in 1917, the Bolsheviks originally set out to replace the institution of marriage with state support for families. The most prominent Bolshevik feminist, Aleksandra Kollontai, argued for free love and predicted that 'the family, in its bourgeois sense, will die out'.[54] There was a brief flowering of ideas about free love, cohabitation and the emancipation of women from family duties in the early Soviet years. Youth activists in the Communist Party preached sexual liberation as evidence of political liberation. But these tolerant attitudes towards premarital sex and freer access to divorce were quickly quashed by more conservative elements in the Communist Party, including Lenin, but particularly after the rise of Joseph Stalin. Concerns about youth delinquency in urban centres directed attention towards the family as a means of social stabilization. Women also argued that allowing freer divorce simply made it easier for men to abandon their families.[55] By the 1930s, the Soviets had recriminalized abortion, made divorce much more difficult and instituted family welfare policies that began to look much like those in other European countries, even though they rejected eugenics as fascist science.[56] As Russian losses mounted in the Second World War, pronatalist measures (such as medals for women with many children) were instituted to encourage citizens to produce future soldiers.

Pronatalist policies made sexual behaviour a matter of profound state interest and led to an intensification of social controls in the sexual sphere. Eugenic ideas helped to justify forced measures that often curtailed or limited individual choices. But this is only one aspect of a complex story. Eugenics could also justify programmes (such as making birth control available to economically needy or unhealthy mothers) that many people wanted and needed. A few specific examples will serve to illustrate the ambivalence of the politicization of sex and reproduction.

In an age before penicillin, the spread of venereal disease was viewed as a profound threat to the population (since these diseases could cause infertility and/or congenital defects), and many European nations, particularly France, Great Britain, Germany and the Scandinavian countries, implemented forced examinations not only for prostitutes, but also for anyone suspected of engaging in promiscuous behaviour. These measures disproportionately affected women, who were in far more danger of being accused of engaging in 'secret' prostitution and being forced to undergo medical examinations.[57] Throughout the late nineteenth and early twentieth century (right up until the post-Second World War period) it was quite possible for a completely innocent woman to be scooped up in a police raid and forcibly examined for venereal disease just because she was walking too slowly down a dubious street or was having a drink at a 'suspicious' bar. The effects on attitudes about women's public behaviour were incalculable. In this atmosphere, prostitution, as widespread as it was, took on a highly exaggerated role in public debates about social decline, family health and the ills of urbanization. Pronatalist and eugenic rhetoric only intensified the situation. Since prostitutes were universally identified as the primary source of venereal infection, and since unaccompanied women were in constant danger of being suspected of prostitution, all non-marital female sexual activity was stigmatized. This did not stop open displays of sexuality from flourishing in the cabarets and bars of the fin de siècle and the Roaring Twenties.[58] But the seductive nude dances of Josephine Baker in Paris and the androgynous and bisexual public displays of film actresses like Marlene Dietrich in Berlin were so remarked upon at the time precisely because they were so transgressive.

On the surface, at least, male sexual promiscuity seemed much less socially problematic. At a time when men were expected to be economically established before marriage, and when women were expected to be virgins at their weddings, male visits to prostitutes were socially tolerated. In satisfying the needs of men unlikely to remain chaste, the logic went, prostitutes helped to keep virtuous women pure.[59]

Visits to prostitutes were virtually a rite of passage for many middle-class European men.[60] But there were unintended side effects to this acceptance of male promiscuity. The distribution of condoms to soldiers during wartime in some armies taught generations of men how to use them, increasing the odds that they would ignore pronatalist policies and employ condoms as birth control with their life partners.[61] Beliefs in the universally protean nature of male sexual desire also ran into conflict with the goal of improving national health. In some cases, such as in fascist Italy, masculine sexual energy embodied in the *Duce* was so critical to political symbolism that concerns about the health consequences were rarely voiced. But in Germany and elsewhere, where concerns about venereal disease ran high, policymakers were concerned that men would bring the consequences of their indiscretions home to their wives, causing infertility. It thus became impossible to ignore the social effects of male sexual desire or its relationship to respectable female sexuality and reproduction.

The ambivalent effects of pronatalism and eugenics on the lives of everyday Europeans is also evident in the larger spectrum of social welfare programmes that they helped to justify. The First World War dramatically accelerated the creation of welfare states in all European countries. Increased attention to social welfare went hand in hand with nationalistic desires to strengthen the nation in the aftermath or in the expectation of war. These nationalistic impulses even influenced progressive sex reformers who, particularly in Germany, the Netherlands and Scandinavia, argued that access to birth control was not only a path to individual happiness, but also a way for the state to prevent abortion and ensure that fewer sickly and/or unwanted babies were born. In calling for tolerance for 'normal' sexuality and the production of only 'healthy' and wanted babies, these reformers often presumed (and helped create) categories of the abnormal and the unwanted. Helene Stöcker (1869–1943) in Germany, Marie Stopes (1880–1958) in Britain, Elise Ottesen-Jensen (1886–1973) in Sweden and Aletta Jacobs (1854–1929) in the Netherlands all relied on such arguments in their campaigns for freer access to birth control. When Jacobs opened the world's first birth control clinic in 1885, American birth control advocate Margaret Sanger (1879–1966) gushed: 'So great were the results obtained that there has been a remarkable increase in the wealth, stamina, stature and longevity of the people, as well as a gradual increase in the population.'[62] But while such sentiments, based as they were on eugenic logic and the desire to increase the birth rate, might have influenced activists and convinced officials in cities like Berlin, London and Vienna to fund birth control clinics, those actually visiting the clinics were motivated by everyday struggles, poverty and the desire to control their material and bodily well-being. We cannot thus easily separate goals of preventing human suffering from nationalistic concerns about racial quality.

Campaigns for birth control and eugenic health also contained widely divergent attitudes towards sexuality. While some birth control advocates, like radical feminist Helene Stöcker, placed emphasis on the importance of female sexual satisfaction, others, like the French socialist psychiatrist Madeleine Pelletier (1874–1939), emphasized that female sexuality was the primary tool that men used to oppress women. Pelletier was one of the first to insist that sexuality as a central core of human life was a cultural construct, and she viewed this construct as fundamentally misogynist.[63] In her 1912 book *L'Emancipation sexuelle de la femme* ('The Sexual Emancipation of Woman') Pelletier argued that 'woman is only an instrument man uses for his pleasure; he consumes her like a fruit'.[64] Pelletier advocated freedom of abortion and access to birth control. But she was wracked by emotional contradictions that eventually destroyed her (she died in an asylum in 1939). In her own personal life she chose chastity and often dressed in male clothing to protect herself from exploitation. She became more and more politically isolated and considered herself a political failure. Her fate displays how controversial it was in her day to argue that sexuality was culturally constructed. While her views clearly countered conservative understandings of the family, they were no more welcome among feminists who saw more power in extolling the social importance of motherhood and employing the rhetoric of eugenics to achieve social benefits for women and families.

Much more could be said about the relationship between feminist politics, pronatalism and eugenics.[65] But for our purposes here it is enough to point out that the prominence of these subjects in the political debates of early twentieth-century Europe helped politicize all subjects related to sexuality.

Fascist regimes were particularly adept at directing this attention to sexual matters towards political purposes. The emphasis in Italy was always on male sexual potency. The mayor of Bologna was rather explicit. Attempting to curb reliance on early withdrawal and its effects on the birth rate, he called on men to 'Screw and leave it in! Orders of the Party.'[66] While promoting higher birth rates in a country that many European observers viewed as overpopulated seemed to make little sense, pronatalism proved an effective tool of political mobilization. Mussolini's 'battle for births', first announced in a 1927 speech, was also linked to his colonial aspirations. 'Fertile people have a right to an Empire', he argued, and 'those with the will to propagate their race on the face of the earth' could rely on cheap labour to achieve world prominence.[67] He instituted various measures to try to achieve this aim, including social welfare programmes, family allowances, marriage and birth loans and health-care improvements, but also a 'tax on celibacy' for bachelors, crackdowns on prostitution and the criminalization of abortion, birth control and family planning advice. Nevertheless, eugenics was not particularly strong in Italy, and truly racist measures were only instituted near the end of the regime as the association with Nazi Germany intensified.

If eugenic thinking made sex political, then no other regime provides a better example of the possible effects on individual lives than the Third Reich. When the National Socialists came to power in Germany in 1933, Helene Stöcker and other supporters of progressive ideas about sexuality were forced into exile. (Magnus Hirschfeld was already in Paris and chose not to come back.) The Nazis initially sought to project an image of extreme sexual propriety, and their propaganda campaigns extolling the virtues of motherhood and the family, not to mention their persecution of homosexuals and their categorization of prostitutes as 'asocials', seemed to suggest that only reproductive, heterosexual sex within the context of marriage would be tolerated. Laws prohibiting sexual relationships between Jews and 'Aryan' Germans explicitly linked definitions of acceptable sexual behaviour to the racist goals of the regime. Forced abortions and sterilization of the 'unfit' were justified with the same logic as euthanasia of the 'feeble-minded' and the murder of millions of Jews. Historians of sexuality have been rather quick to suggest that the Nazi case provides an extreme example of the effects of sexually repressive ideas on social policy.[68] But this is an oversimplification of Nazi policies on sex. While Nazi propagandists certainly stressed that traditional family values would be reinstated and supported by the state, and they never tired of associating the sexual decadence of the Weimar years with economic turmoil and social distress, life in the Third Reich actually provided citizens with more opportunities for pre- and extramarital sex than ever before. It was well known that the massive gatherings staged by the Hitler Youth were inevitably followed, nine months later, by hundreds of illegitimate births.[69] And while not all Nazi leaders supported him, SS leader Heinrich Himmler's call to unmarried girls to provide the Führer with babies before war robbed the nation of valuable genetic material certainly had a public effect. Maternity and increasing the birth rate might have been the goal, but the ingenious intertwining of nationalism and sexual allure provided seductive rewards for those who supported the regime. Men who did not meet the ideal of soldierly masculinity were treated with hormones to enhance their virility.[70] The Nazis even set up brothels for slave labourers and concentration camp inmates in the hopes of exacting more labour with the promise of sexual rewards.[71] The depiction of the Third Reich as an entirely sexually repressive regime thus requires some rethinking.[72]

All this demonstrates that by the mid-twentieth century sexual behaviour had become an extremely political affair. Rhetorical links between individual sexual and reproductive choices and the fate of nations encouraged citizens to relate their individual decisions in this sphere to their roles as citizens of a nation. But the dramatic failure of the fascist projects of the twentieth century changed the context for such debates. In the aftermath of the Holocaust and the massive displacement of people caused by the Second World War, eugenic language became more guarded (particularly in West Germany, where it moved into the realm of taboo), even though it did not entirely disappear. In all European (and North American) nations, the trauma of the war led to a fierce search for normality that involved a certain amnesia about the character of pre-war regimes in the interests of a focus on rebuilding families and regenerating the broken spirits of men.[73] In Hungary and Eastern Germany, the experience of mass rape made it particularly likely that political language about sex and reproduction that might call up too many painful memories should be temporarily silenced.[74] A generational shift also played an important role in changing the terms of discourse. Estimates of the number of people killed as a direct result of the Second World War range from fifty to over sixty-three million. The majority of those killed were in the prime of life. The post-war period offered many challenges in economically struggling Europe, but also opportunities for the young to take advantage of the absence of an entire generation and move into positions of responsibility very quickly. For widowed women and young family fathers, the late 1940s and early 1950s were focused on survival, recovery and material improvements in living conditions. After an initial explosion of sexual activity during the period of demobilization and occupation (and the resulting baby boom) sex retreated from public view.

Sexual Revolution: Scientific and Philosophical Origins

Historians have long commented on the prudery of the 1950s. But this view is now being challenged, and our periodization of the 1960s and the sexual revolution is being revised backwards.[75] After the traumas of the Second World War made sexology somewhat suspect in Europe, the reinvigoration of the scientific study of sex fell to an American scientist named Alfred C. Kinsey, who published the findings of a massive research project in *Sexual Behavior in the Human Male* in 1948, and *Sexual Behavior in the Human Female* in 1953. Kinsey mobilized a large research team to administer questionnaires about sexual behaviour across the United States, and his findings about the prevalence of homosexuality, premarital sex, masturbation and other adventurous and non-procreative acts caused a media sensation around the world. His research had an immediate impact in Europe, causing marriage counsellors in Germany, for instance, to rethink their attitudes towards sexuality and place more emphasis on sexual counselling as a means of preserving marriages.

American sexology continued to influence European psychologists, scientists and doctors into the 1950s and 1960s. William H. Masters and Virginia Johnson built upon Kinsey's research in *Human Sexual Response* in 1966 and *Human Sexual Inadequacy* in 1970. Masters and Johnson observed sexual behaviour in a clinical setting, developing comprehensive treatment programmes for sexual dysfunction and sophisticated equipment to measure and track human sexual response. Their research subjects performed sexual intercourse in a laboratory, with wires and cameras attached to track vaginal lubrication, heart rates and blood pressure, and the rhythmic contractions and other physiological effects of orgasm. In 1966, they 'discovered' the female ability to reach multiple orgasms and tracked various other gender differences in male and female sexual response. As had Kinsey before them, Masters and Johnson gained immediate worldwide attention for their research, and they helped to transform the landscape for medical, psychological and sociological research into sexual behaviour. Underlying each project was the conviction that medical science could increase human happiness by helping individuals to recognize and counteract the negative influence of modern, Western culture upon their innate ability to achieve sexual pleasure. Masters and Johnson became the iconic representatives of an international scientific and social movement that sought to demystify sex, employing 'objective' scientific observation along with political and philosophical debate to liberate human sexual pleasure from the shackles of political, religious and social conventions. This was the scientific side of the 1960s sexual revolution.

Scientific observations of 'natural' sexual responses were not always compatible with euphoric calls for 'free love' and the arguments of student activists that sexual repression facilitated political oppression. New sexual therapies and medicalized forms of birth control ensured the continuing authority of 'experts' in these matters, much to the chagrin of Europe's youth. While marriage counsellors and psychologists in Europe read Masters and Johnson, student activists on the battle front of the sexual revolution were more likely to turn to literary and philosophical sources of inspiration.

Because we do not have the kind of sociological data for European populations that Kinsey collected in America, we must use cultural and philosophical signposts to understand the origins of sexual revolution in Europe.[76] Shifting from the scientific data about sexual acts to the realm of cultural analysis intensifies the impression that the war experience was crucial to post-Second World War attitudes towards sexuality. But this is true in different ways for different countries, as a comparison between France and Germany will make clear. In Germany, the tone was set by Wilhelm Reich's anti-fascist conviction that 'sexual satisfaction and sadism were mutually exclusive'.[77] The French response to the horrors of the Holocaust was quite the opposite. Key literary and philosophical texts of the 1940s and 1950s returned to the teachings of the Marquis de Sade in an effort to understand the allure of fascism and the human psychology of its crimes.

The primary guru of the sexual revolution in Germany was Austrian-American psychoanalyst and sexologist Wilhelm Reich. In fact, it was the 1945 English translation of theories that Reich had developed in the 1930s, *The Sexual Revolution: Toward a Self-Governing Character Structure*, that first brought the term 'sexual revolution' into widespread use.[78] In *The Mass Psychology of Fascism*, he relied on Marxist theory to argue that economic forces had produced a form of family life in which authoritarian fathers created an atmosphere of sexual repression that encouraged submission and created the personality types likely to support fascism. An end to social constraints on sexual expression, Reich insisted, would revolutionize political life by producing happier citizens who would not so easily fall victim to the rhetoric of demagogues eager to perpetrate violence and war.

Reich's elaborations of this theory are rather difficult to take seriously today. For instance, he invented a machine that he called the Orgone Energy Accumulator, which he believed could collect energy from orgasms to be used to cure various psychological and physical illnesses.[79] But, after languishing in obscurity for decades, his theories became enormously influential when they were rediscovered in the

1960s, affecting the activism of sexual radicals and even the theories of serious scientists.[80] For progressive young intellectuals coming of age at the height of the Cold War, Reich provided both an explanation for the violence and oppression of the past – particularly its fascist variant – and a welcome prescription for the future. Immersed in what they viewed as a critical political conflict with the generation that had conducted the Second World War, European youth found Reich's arguments convincing and enticing. Particularly in Germany, his writings provided the blueprint for the political manifestos, patterns of sexual behaviour and communal-living projects that have since become almost clichéd under the slogans 'free love', 'the summer of love' and 'make love, not war'. 'Read Wilhelm Reich and act accordingly' read an inspirational slogan that appeared in Frankfurt graffiti as early as 1968.[81] Reich's disciples truly believed that love could change the world by defeating the forces of dictatorship and authoritarian power.

The popularity of Reich's argument that sexual pleasure could provide an antidote to the abuse of power was less convincing to the French. One telling indication of this difference is the popularity of *Histoire d'O* (the *Story of O*), a novel written in 1954 by Anne Desclos under the pseudonym Pauline Réage. In elegant prose, the novel tells the story of a young woman, known only as O, who is initiated into a sex cult by her lover René. Taken to a chateau in a French suburb, she is forced to don bondage-style clothing, cannot speak to any other woman and must obey the commands of the men who come to violate her. O is a willing participant in these ritualized sex acts and views her submission as evidence of her love for René. The *Story of O* was immediately banned in other countries, but won the French literature prize Priz des Deux Magots in 1955. Feminists still debate its themes of female objectification. But this novel was written in a pre-feminist mode and its author initially intended it as a private seduction of her lover and employer Jean Paulhan, whom she feared to be losing and who did not believe that women could write erotic literature. The fact that the public initially assumed that the novel must have been penned by a man indicates exactly how revolutionary the book was. It has never gone out of print, and, despite censorship measures, was read more widely outside of France in the 1960s than any other French novel.[82]

Looking back with some historical distance, one might also view *Story of O* as a way of returning to the lessons of the eighteenth-century author Marquis de Sade (1740–1814), whose erotic literature inspired the word 'sadism' – the practice of achieving sexual pleasure through the infliction of pain on someone else. In an era still wracked by the images of the victims of concentration camps and still reeling with each new piece of information about Nazi tortures, there was an urgent need to make sense of evil and explain the human ability to inflict torture. French intellectuals looked to sex as a path to understanding the most perplexing philosophical questions of the day.[83] While this enterprise risked extreme disrespect to the victims of the Holocaust (in one scene O hopes that the 'gas chambers' will never open so that René will never leave her), it can also be viewed as a somewhat courageous acceptance of the universality of the human qualities that made the crimes of the previous decades possible. It is perhaps significant that in the post-Second World War period it was often women who explored these themes. Along with Réage, Marguerite Duras's (1914–96) writings also played with the theme of female sacrifice. The fact that both women had been members of the French Resistance against the Nazi occupation of France, and that Duras's husband had been interned in a concentration camp, makes it plausible to assume that memories of the war were at least subconsciously present in their writings.

But the most prominent French writer to explore the issue of violence and sexuality in the post-Second World War period was Simone de Beauvoir (1908–86). Her path-breaking 1949 book *Le Deuxième Sexe* (translated as *The Second Sex*) is generally considered to have jump-started 'second-wave' feminism (the first wave having been the women's rights movements of the late nineteenth and early twentieth century that fought for the right to vote) and continues to influence feminist thinkers today. De Beauvoir argued that women had to have the right to choose with whom they spend their lives, and she described the history of male oppression of women through an analysis of history, literature and myth. Men, she insisted, had always been taken as the positive norm to which women – as the 'other' – had been compared. De Beauvoir argued that one is not born but becomes a woman. She thus added a significant gender dimension to Jean-Paul Sartre's existentialist view that human action, not the natural order, creates meaning.[84] De Beauvoir later explored the ethical implications of sexual choices in more detail in her 1951 essay entitled 'Must we Burn Sade?' She argued that one had to take de Sade's position on freedom seriously, suspending judgement on the tortures he inflicted on others in order to understand what humans are capable of.[85] The metaphor of burning in de Beauvoir's title called to mind the burning of books, heretics, Joan of Arc and not least, only six years after the war, Jews.[86] Yet de Beauvoir refused to associate de Sade with fascism, attempting instead to understand the Marquis's bizarre sexual 'ethics' in their own terms. Moving beyond Freud's emphasis on childhood experience, she suggested that all aspects of a person's life must be understood in order to comprehend their sexuality and that sexuality is more than an unconscious drive.[87] We must understand de Sade, she implied, because he was the product not just of an upbringing but of a society too. As Judith Butler has argued, de Beauvoir found it necessary to explore de Sade's cruelty, because she saw him 'as a definite human possibility, one that is, therefore, at least potentially ours'.[88] De Beauvoir rejected de Sade's insistence on the primacy of individual sensations and feelings, arguing instead that 'the only sure bonds among men are those they create in transcending themselves within a common world by means of a common project'.[89] In other words, sexuality may be a primary component of human interaction, but it is not outside of individual choice and it is not the foundation of all human action. In her quest to assert woman's right to avoid being simply the object of male desire, de Beauvoir rejected both de Sade's and Freud's tendency to argue that drives are more powerful than choice. She also believed that Freud was painting a picture of an amoral world when he argued that civilization was simply the product of repressed (sublimated) drives. 'To paint, to write, to engage in politics – these are not merely "sublimations"; here we have aims that are willed for their own sakes. To deny it is to falsify all human history.'[90] The power of de Beauvoir's theories derives from her success at revealing how these arguments about sexuality and civilization were themselves gendered; they relied on a specific understanding of male sexuality and its role in civilization and thus justified male domination.

A similar interest in the relationship between Eros and civilization motivated the work of the German philosopher Herbert Marcuse (1898–1979). In fact, Marcuse's work provides an interesting bridge between Reich and de Beauvoir, since he began his philosophical writing in the 1920s with the conscious intention of fusing Marxism and existentialism. He established himself as an academic in the US with a book, *Eros and Civilization* (1955), that drew inspiration from both Marx and Freud. Like Reich, Marcuse believed that sexual liberation was related to political liberation. But, like de Beauvoir, he was also aware of the possibility that sexual pleasures could be manipulated for the purposes of exercising power.

Celebrated in the 1960s as the 'father of the New Left', Marcuse was one of the founders of the Institute for Social Research in Frankfurt, famous for its critical theory and later known simply as the Frankfurt School. Marcuse's Jewish heritage forced him into exile from Nazi Germany in 1934. He joined his colleagues Theodor Adorno and Max Horkheimer at Columbia University, but spent most of his first ten years in the US working as an intelligence analyst, first for the Office of War Information and later for the Office of Secret Services (OSS). In the meantime, he continued to develop his philosophical critique of 'one-dimensional' societies – both capitalist and communist. He has been called the 'cornerstone' of the sexual revolution in the US,[91] but he continued to influence thought on sex and society in Europe as well.[92] In *Eros and Civilization* he criticized Reich for missing how sexual instincts had been fused with violence and destructive impulses in history. Marcuse was drawing on his wartime analysis of German fascism for the OSS. He had argued in the 1940s that the Nazis had skilfully manipulated the public by promising sexual pleasures in return for political compliance.[93] Marcuse rejected the idea that sexual freedom could be an end in itself, and he accepted Freud's theory of the need for some repression of sexual urges in civilized society. But he argued that the 'performance principle' in capitalist societies produced a surplus of sexual repression, because it forced people into unfulfilling work that required a subordination of physical pleasures. Countering Freud (and echoing de Beauvoir) he argued that 'Civilization arises from pleasure, we must hold fast to this thesis, in all its provocativeness.'[94] He believed that non-procreative sexual acts contained revolutionary potential that could be used to counter the regimentation of capitalist life. By the time he wrote *One Dimensional Man*, however, Marcuse was much more pessimistic about how far sexual liberation by itself could achieve change in a capitalist society that had learned to use pleasure in a repressive way.[95] Although Marcuse gave lectures on university campuses all over the United States and in Europe and is sometimes credited with having coined the most ubiquitous slogan of the sexual revolution – 'make love, not war' – he was somewhat uncomfortable with his status as the darling of sexual revolutionaries, who often underplayed his more complex Marxist critique of capitalist and consumerist society and perverted his message in order to justify sexual satisfaction at any cost and as an end in itself.

Few at the time noted the complete absence of gender analysis in Marcuse's theories or the fact that he painted feminine sexuality simply as a passive form of masculine sexuality. In constructing a total critique of capitalist theory that included (unlike Marx) an analysis of sexuality, Marcuse and Reich before him overemphasized the significance of sexual liberation without actually explaining processes of sexual repression, including the repression of female and homosexual sexualities.[96] As feminists across Europe noted in the 1960s and 1970s, there were deficiencies in the argument that freer access to sexual pleasure was universally liberating. Indeed, what later became known as second-wave feminism began in part as a very personal reaction to sexual dynamics within European student movements and the new place of sex in European popular culture.

Sexual Revolution: Politics and Popular Culture

The sexual revolution in Europe cannot be separated from the history of student activism. While a detailed description of European student rebellion is beyond the scope of this chapter, we must note the prominence of socialist student activism and youth protest on European university campuses and in the large cities of Europe. In the 1960s, left-wing students across Europe staged increasingly well-organized protests against what they saw as the primary crimes of capitalist societies: the war in Vietnam, police repression of left-wing movements, colonialism, and Western ties to Third World dictators, like the Shah of Iran. These protests had strong international currents and were fed by events like the Soviet invasion of Czechoslovakia (to put down the reform efforts of Alexander Dubček's 'Prague Spring') in January 1968 and the assassination of American civil rights activist Martin Luther King in April of the same year. In April 1968, Rudi Dutschke, the head of a nationwide, socialist organization of student activists, German Social Student Union (SDS), was shot at a political demonstration. Political demonstrations exploded across the country. In May 1968, the West German government brought in emergency laws, giving police the power to suspend civil liberties. Meanwhile, in Paris, conflicts between right-wing groups and students campaigning against the war in Vietnam had grown increasingly violent. On 3 May, a group of students met at Sorbonne University to protest the closing of Nanterre

University. The protest quickly escalated, and police used tear gas to try to disperse the growing crowds. During the week that followed, students joined with union organizers and agricultural groups in anti-government protests, and a wave of strikes, student walkouts and political demonstrations swept the country.

These protests vastly strengthened the self-confidence of students' groups across Europe and fed an atmosphere of generational revolt that soon assumed mythic proportions. With some historical distance, we can now see that the importance of this generational divide has been vastly overrated. As Kirstin Ross has argued for the French case, overemphasizing the role played by student leaders distorts the historical record, because the actions of union organizers and members of agricultural movements produced more lasting effects on French society.[97] But the students' enduring success at highlighting the importance of their historical role is instructive in itself. Having linked their cause in the public mind to earlier protests against repressive European societies, youth activists masterfully manipulated media images to strengthen their message. Their primary weapon in this endeavour was sex.

Already before the riots of 1968, sexual revolutionaries were using sex to deliver political messages. In Berlin in 1967, the group 'Commune One' advertised their anti-bourgeois lifestyle with a picture, taken from behind, of all the commune members (four men, three women and one child) standing naked and spreadeagled up against a wall. Students across the country flocked to Berlin as the centre of the 'happenings' and as the city where, due to its unique four-power status, men could avoid conscription. That same year, the Swedish film *I am Curious – Yellow* caused a sensation and was censored in Europe and North America due to its explicit conflation of sexual and political themes, its critique of the Swedish class system and its steamy sex scenes. These were of course extreme expressions of changing social attitudes towards sex outside of marriage, but while meant to provoke, they were a symptom of larger changes.

Sociological data from the period suggests that there was indeed a transformation of social values about sex taking place. In 1967, a public opinion poll asked Germans: 'When a young man and a young woman live together, without being married, do you think that this is going too far or do you think it doesn't matter?' Forty-three per cent of unmarried men and 65 per cent of unmarried women said that this was going too far. By 1973, when the same question was posed, only 5 per cent of men and 2 per cent of women thought that premarital cohabitation was unacceptable.[98] Divorce rates in Britain doubled after 1969, and, by 1977, 44 per cent of French couples had lived together before marriage (up from 17 per cent in 1968).[99] These statistics represented a widespread and international social change of attitudes and behaviours.[100]

It is common to argue that the main cause of these changes was the introduction of the birth control pill. 'The pill' became available in Germany and Britain in the early 1960s. (Birth control remained illegal in France until 1967, and prescription contraceptives were extremely difficult to obtain in eastern Europe, leading to very high abortion rates.) It received immediate and intense media attention. But it is easy to exaggerate how widespread use of the pill was in Europe and underestimate the emotional and social restrictions on acquiring the precious prescription. Some women certainly did find sympathetic doctors willing to prescribe birth control to the unmarried. But in 1970s France, for instance, only 6 per cent of women were on the pill.[101] And not all women viewed the pill as a panacea. Extremely high doses of hormones in the early formulations produced severe side effects for some women. In Germany, feminist groups actively campaigned against the medicalization of reproductive choices represented by a pill that could likely only be obtained with a prescription from a male doctor. Despite its obvious benefits, feminists argued, the pill shifted responsibility for birth control exclusively to women while also forcing them to carry any of the associated physical side effects of hormonal intake. Female members of the German SDS began to note that the pro-sex slogans of their male counterparts failed to take these factors into consideration. They complained that men were using the theory of sexual liberation along with the existence of the pill and penicillin to coerce women into bed. When, at a September 1968 meeting of the SDS in Frankfurt, female members called upon the organization to support better access to day care and more attention to issues directly facing women, they were met with bemusement and belittlement. In response, Sigrid Röger, the token woman in the SDS leadership, pelted a male leader with tomatoes. This was the end of the pre-sumption that male socialist student activists were also speaking for their female counterparts. Separate women's groups (calling themselves *Weiberraten* – or broads' councils) quickly multiplied across the country. The first, in Frankfurt, published a leaflet with the slogan 'Liberate the socialist pricks from their bourgeois dicks' and graphic drawings depicting the act of chopping off a penis.[102] Similar disillusion-ment with socialist student movements across Europe led to the formation of sepa-rate feminist groups (the contemporary term was 'women's liberation') in Italy, France and Great Britain.[103] In the West, European women's movements gradually expanded their demands to include abortion rights, pay equity, equal access to edu-cation and training, and expanded day-care services. Meanwhile, in the Eastern Bloc, communist governments argued (somewhat disingenuously) that they had already liberated women by providing them with all these things. Abortion laws varied in eastern European countries, though they were generally much more liberal than in the West (except in Romania, where abortion and birth control were strictly prohibited.)

But Eastern Bloc countries were less open to the cultural drivers of the sexual revolution, viewing the rock music anthems of the 1960s as symbols of Western imperialism. Even in the 1950s, East German authorities argued that the West was a place where 'American non-culture, nationalist-supremacist race hatred, gangster movies, trash novels, boogie-woogie, etc. are supposed to prepare the adolescents for murder, killings, and war.'[104] In 1959, party bureaucrats even recruited musicians and dance instructors to develop a 'modern' dance style to compete with decadent and overly sexualized rock 'n' roll dancing. The Lipsi, a modified waltz, never really caught on with the East German public. Meanwhile, in the Soviet Union, rock 'n' roll was perceived as a direct capitalist assault on the communist system and an attempt to undermine socialist society. These official attitudes only fed the popularity of music as a weapon of cultural, generational and political revolt. A huge black market for Western rock music existed in all eastern European countries, and occasional loosening of controls in favour of popular demand were followed in waves by harsh repressions.[105] The appeal of Elvis, the Beatles and later the Rolling Stones was also sexual. When the Stones played in Warsaw in April 1967, fans hoped to hear, among other things, the song 'Let's Spend the Night Together'. But they were prevented from buying tickets, which mostly went to Communist Party members, and 3,000 of them rioted and damaged the interior of the Palace of Culture. During the mid-1960s, the Czech underground band the Plastic People of the Universe sang songs influenced by Andy Warhol and the American beat poet Allen Ginsberg. Particularly after their arrest and the conviction of four band members on charges of 'organized disturbance of the peace' in 1976, the Plastic People became a focal point for political dissidents. Under the leadership of playwright Václev Havel, a group of Plastic People supporters formed Charter 77, an underground political organization later instrumental in the fall of communism. Politics, sex and rock 'n' roll were never so intimate.

Rock music also produced concerns about sexual propriety in the West. Female fans swooning in front of popular singers was not an invention of rock 'n' roll, but nothing before (or even since) quite matched the orgiastic moans that greeted the Beatles wherever they performed. Something in the cultural atmosphere of the 1960s induced youth to display their sexual longings more openly and loudly. University attendance reached unprecedented levels across Europe in these years, so it is certainly possible that young people were reading and being influenced by the theories we discussed above. But it is far more likely that popular and high culture were both circling around sexual themes independently; the two spheres fed off each other but did not necessarily act as cause or sole inspiration.

One final aspect of sexual liberation must be mentioned. Even before the pill encouraged people to separate sexuality from reproduction in their attitudes and behaviours and to accept the notions of private sexual freedom, attitudes towards homosexuality were beginning to liberalize. Laws against homosexuality had reached their most severe level of repression between the 1930s and 1950s. During the Cold War, sexual deviance was viewed as a sign of moral decay, or a flaw that could leave one vulnerable to persuasion or blackmail by political enemies.[106] Nevertheless, Kinsey's reports that homosexual activity was far more common than had been previously acknowledged influenced European attitudes. The Netherlands decriminalized homosexuality in 1946. In September 1957, an English government commission, the Committee on Homosexual Offences and Prostitution, published the Wolfenden Report, which declared homosexuality a medical rather than a criminal problem. Laws to this effect were eventually passed in 1968. Homosexuality was decriminalized in Hungary, Poland, Czechoslovakia and East Germany in the mid- to late 1960s. In 1968 and 1969, first East and then West Germany repealed section 175 of the German criminal code, which had made homosexual acts illegal. Conservative and repressive attitudes and practices persisted in France, prompting the formation, in 1968, of Guy Hocquenghem's Front d'Action Révolutionnaire to fight for gay rights. Following in the footsteps of women's liberation movements, this organization and others like it across Europe fought for an end to discriminatory practices. Europeans drew inspiration from their counterparts in the US, where the New York Stonewall riots of 1969 provided symbolic encouragement to actively resist police repression. France was one of the last European countries to decriminalize homosexuality in 1982. In the process of legal liberalization, gay culture also changed. Casual sex in bathhouses and other pickup venues became less common, though it did not disappear, and the political movement turned to fighting battles for the kinds of benefits (like the right to adopt children, to be the beneficiary of a partner's pension or insurance policy, and the right to marry) that still occupy it today.[107] The movement towards more stable and monogamous relationships gained additional strength as the extent and seriousness of Acquired Immune Deficiency Syndrome (AIDS/HIV) became clear in the 1980s.

The collection of illnesses identified as AIDS and later associated with underlying HIV (Human Immunodeficiency Virus) infection was first noticed by doctors in parts of San Francisco with a thriving gay subculture. It was first thought of as an exclusively 'gay' (meaning, in this context, homosexual male) disease. This impression invigorated both the gay rights movement and its enemies and still lingers today. But by 1983, it had become clear that the disease could also be passed through blood and through heterosexual sexual contact. In Europe, the disease only appeared to be primarily homosexual in West Germany, Denmark and the United Kingdom. In France and Belgium, it was more common among those with links to central Africa, where doctors were beginning to notice a massive spread of diseases associated with AIDS.[108] Very quickly, however, intravenous drug use was recognized as a primary transmission path for the disease in Europe. After the fall of communism in 1989, drug use soared in eastern Europe, and countries that had considered themselves relatively immune from the disease had to face its consequences.[109] By 2005, the UN was estimating that there were 1.6 million cases of HIV in eastern Europe. While intravenous drug use continues to be a primary source, in May 2006, delegates to an eastern European and central Asian AIDS conference in Moscow admitted that heterosexual contact, particularly through prostitution, was growing in importance as a means of transmission of the disease.[110]

But how big an effect has the AIDS epidemic had on social attitudes towards sexuality in Europe? The ultimate analysis of this question will have to await future historians and sociologists. It is, however, already certain that AIDS has powerfully influenced rhetoric, behaviours and laws. As with venereal disease in the twentieth century, knowingly infecting someone with the HIV virus that causes AIDS can lead to legal prosecution, though many European countries (Germany, France, Hungary, Italy, Denmark, Finland, Estonia, Switzerland and the United Kingdom) rely on general laws against inflicting bodily harm or assault. In many cases, this approach replaced earlier specific laws that targeted venereal diseases. Other European countries rely on laws against purposely passing on incurable or contagious diseases. Poland, Portugal, Russia, Serbia and Montenegro and the Netherlands specifically name HIV in more general laws, with punishments ranging from three (Poland) to fifteen (the Netherlands) years' imprisonment.[111] Only Georgia, Latvia, Moldova, Slovakia and Ukraine have specific HIV laws. Ukraine's 1992 law 'About the prevention of disease AIDS and social protection of the population' is by far the most detailed in Europe and looks most like measures that Great Britain and Germany took against venereal disease in the late nineteenth and early twentieth century. AIDS activists argue that these laws simply stigmatize the afflicted without providing any social benefit. But the rates of convictions are, in comparison with measures taken in the past against victims of venereal disease, extremely low. While AIDS has certainly once again raised the spectre of disease as a punishment for promiscuity, Europeans have moved well beyond allowing these fears to turn the clock back on the liberalization of sexual norms.

Conclusion: Where is Sex in Europe Today?

Efforts to repress sexual freedoms have not disappeared from the European cultural, social or political landscape. Sexual violence both within and outside of families continues to be a serious problem, as the existence of extensive networks of rape crisis centres demonstrates. In national politics, discussions about the need for sexual propriety still crop up from time to time. In 2004, Vladimir Zhirinovsky, the leader of an ultra-nationalist party in Russia's parliament, called for a law to punish homosexual acts with the death penalty.[112] While this is an extreme opinion from an extreme politician, it indicates that sexual freedoms are still hard-won in some parts of Europe and may not be permanent. The presence of minority cultures in all European countries also complicates the historical trajectory of sexual and gender norms in ways which we have not been able to fully develop here. In 2005, for example, two Turkish-German brothers were charged with the murder of their sister, who had left an arranged marriage and 'disgraced' her family with her 'sinful' lifestyle. The German legal system is being forced to retool itself to cope with the problem of 'honour killings' on its own soil. This has evoked strong statements of conviction about the necessity of maintaining gender equality and rights to freedom of sexual choice, but also serious discussions about how conflicting cultural norms can be accommodated in multicultural societies. Given that sizeable ultra-conservative and ultra-nationalist groups exist in many European countries, and that the size of religious and cultural minorities continues to grow, it is conceivable that the battleground of the sexual revolution will once again see action.

From today's vantage point the changes wrought by the sexual revolution have been real and long-lasting. Change has by no means been uniform across the continent, but a quick survey of abortion and birth control demonstrates that the trajectory, with some exceptions, has generally moved towards liberalization. Access to birth control is now easiest in western Europe and expanding in eastern Europe and Greece (where it was illegal until 1980). New forms of birth control, like the 'morning-after pill', digital instruments to track ovulation, and hormone-releasing intra-uterine devices have been developed and made widely available in recent years. Ireland remains the western European country with the strictest laws controlling birth control. It became legal for anyone over eighteen to buy condoms and spermicide in 1985, but other forms of contraception are difficult to obtain without a marriage licence and a prescription. Where birth control is hard to get or culturally spurned, abortion rates remain high (though often, as in the Irish case, women must go abroad to obtain them). Between the 1950s and 1990s, western European countries like Sweden, the Netherlands, Great Britain and (to a somewhat lesser degree) West Germany liberalized their abortion laws while also providing easier access to birth control. Where birth control and abortion are both accessible, abortion rates tend to be low. The Netherlands, which provides free birth control under state-funded medical insurance, has the lowest rate of induced abortion in the world. Such policies do not necessarily mean a low birth rate. Despite its liberal birth control laws (including the legalization of the French 'abortion pill' RU 486) Sweden's fertility rate increased into the 1990s. Access to choice, good-quality day care and generous maternity leaves has encouraged Swedish couples to have children. Despite strong rhetorical support for large families, Catholic countries like Spain and Portugal have been less amenable to these strategies. They have restricted abortion to extreme cases, where the life of the woman is threatened. In Italy, fierce opposition from the Catholic Church and the refusal of many doctors to terminate a pregnancy makes access to abortion difficult, though it remains legal.

The situation is more complex in eastern Europe, where decades of extremely limited access to birth control made abortion the most common means of limiting family size. The Soviet Union overturned Stalinist restrictions on abortion in 1955, and many eastern European countries followed suit. Bulgaria, Albania and Romania recriminalized abortion in the mid- to late 1960s in an attempt to increase the birth rate. Combined with limited access to birth control, this resulted in high rates of illegal abortions, maternal mortality and, particularly in Romania, disastrous conditions in overcrowded orphanages. East Germany, in contrast, re-*legalized* abortion in 1972, primarily as a political means of highlighting a stronger record on women's rights compared to West Germany. Most eastern European countries (except for

Poland) have greatly expanded access to abortion, but have had a more difficult time countering strong prejudices in the population against birth control.

With some exceptions, Europeans have become more tolerant of premarital sex and non-procreative sex. And yet, the optimistic hopes of the '68ers' (as those involved in the student revolts of the late 1960s and early 1970s now call themselves) that sexual liberation would bring about a dramatic change in family relationships, an end to sexual violence, world peace and an increase in individual sensual pleasure have proved illusory. Families with double careers and childcare responsibilities are simply too weighed down by daily responsibilities to follow the dictates of the make-love-not-war generation. Even the claims of the 68ers that they had more and better sex are being called into question. Historical data are demonstrating that changes in sexual behaviour (such as increases in premarital sex) were initiated by the previous generation in the 1940s and 1950s and that the popular culture of the 1960s followed rather than led social trends in this sphere.[113]

Perhaps more significantly, sex now plays a different role in public discourse than it did before the sexual revolution. Whereas it was extremely common for European politicians in the first half of the twentieth century to discuss why it was important for the government to influence people's decisions about with whom they slept and when and how they used birth control, doing so today would prompt public outcry about unjustifiable government interference in people's private lives. While there is growing concern about falling birth rates in many European countries, discussions about how to combat this problem now focus on economic and social incentives, such as support for childcare and tax breaks, rather than on teaching individuals to make sexual decisions with the good of the state in mind. The more ubiquitous sex has become – in the media, on television and on the Internet – the less political power it seems to carry. This is not to say, of course, that the social power of sex has disappeared in European society. Advertising and popular entertainment rely on sexual stereotypes and perpetuate gendered understandings of the meaning of sexual pleasure. But it has become less rather than more likely that a politician would address the issue of sexual pleasure to make a political point. Even in discussions about legalizing same-sex marriage, it is extremely rare for either side of the debate to mention sexual acts that these couples might engage in. Rather than demanding the right to sex, most European homosexuals focus their attention on gaining social, familial and economic rights. Extreme opinions about sexual morality – like Zhirinovsky's – are the exception rather than the rule. There seems to be little appetite for reintroducing a political discourse on sex, let alone making sexual pleasure the centrepiece of political change.

The story that we have told here is not one of a simple end to repression from above, nor a story of how the private finally became political in the 1960s. The repression did not always come from above but was generally the result of a complex negotiation between citizens and states. Sometimes the most repressive states even used sex to seduce new followers. Similarly, the private (the sexual) had long become political by the time the 68ers started chanting their slogans. Indeed, those slogans were only possible because sexuality – in its political and cultural sense – already existed in social discourse, and the connection between society and individual sexual desires had been carefully, scientifically analysed. The sexual revolution began long before the communards in Berlin decided to pose naked, and long before European teenagers discovered the Rolling Stones. As soon as the biological mechanisms of reproduction began to be understood, the question of how to control them and who should decide how became burning political issues. The proliferation of laws dealing with reproduction and sexual behaviour, the vast expansion of scientific discourse about sex and the close relationship between social policies in this sphere and the larger geopolitical projects of European regimes set the stage for the battles that reached their peak – but did not begin – in the 1960s.

Notes

1. Cited in Jean Stengers, *Masturbation: The History of a Great Terror*, trans. Kathryn Hoffmann (New York: Palgrave, 2001), 65–66.

2. The poem is available online at numerous sites, including at http://www. poetryconnection.net/poets/Philip_Larkin/4761 (accessed 26 May 2006).

3. Viral STDs, such as herpes, chlamydia, genital warts, only became prevalent after the 1960s and are significantly more difficult to diagnose and treat. This 'second generation' of STDs, as the World Health Organization calls them, now includes HIV/AIDS (to be discussed below). See: A. de Schryver and A. Meheus, 'Epidemiology of Sexually Transmitted Diseases: The Global Picture', *Bulletin of the World Health Organization* 68, no. 5 (1990): 639–64.

4. It should be noted that this way of viewing the 'long sexual revolution' differs from but does not contradict the argument made by Hera Cook in *The Long Sexual Revolution: English Women, Sex, and Contraception 1800–1975* (Oxford: Oxford University Press, 2004). We accept the argument that increased access to contraception was vital for the attainment of female sexual pleasure and, indeed, full political emancipation. But we concentrate here on how sexuality and politics were intertwined in the twentieth century for both men and women and on how this relationship shifted in the 1960s.

5. Jan Goldstein, 'Foucault among the Sociologists: The "Disciplines" and the History of the Professions', *History and Theory* 23, no. 2 (1984): 171.

6. Michel Foucault, *History of Sexuality*, reissue edition, vol. 1: *An Introduction* (New York: Vintage Books, 1990), 18–23.

7. Ibid., 68.

8. Sander L. Gilman, *Difference and Pathology: Stereotypes of Sexuality, Race and Madness* (Ithaca, NY: Cornell University Press, 1985).

9. For a summary of this historiography, see: Duberman *et al.*, eds, *Hidden From History*.

10. David M. Halperin, 'Is there a History of Sexuality?', *History and Theory* 28, no. 3 (1989): 270–71.

11. For general responses from historians see: Jeffrey Weeks, 'Foucault for Historians', *History Workshop Journal* 14 (1982): 106–19; Lynn Hunt, 'Foucault's Subject in the History of Sexuality', in *Discourses of Sexuality*, ed. Domna C. Stanton (Ann Arbor, MI:

University of Michigan Press, 1992), 78–93; and Jan Goldstein, 'Foucault among the Sociologists'.

12. Chauncey, *Gay New York*, 13.

13. Robert A. Nye, 'Sexuality', in *A Companion to Gender History*, eds Teresa A. Meade and Merry E. Wiesner-Hanks (Malden, MA, Oxford and Melbourne: Blackwell Publishing Ltd., 2004), 11.

14. Alice Domurat Dreger, *Hermaphrodites and the Medical Invention of Sex* (Cambridge, Mass.: Harvard University Press, 1998). For earlier attitudes to hermaphrodites, see: Lorraine Daston and Katherine Park, 'The Hermaphrodite and the Orders of Nature: Sexual Ambiguity in Early Modern France', *GLQ: A Journal of Gay & Lesbian Studies* 1, no. 4 (1995): 419–38.

15. This case is made forcefully and convincingly in: Jordanova, *Sexual Visions*. Jordanova argues that 'Retaining a belief in the validity of linking women and nature makes it excessively hard to be sufficiently critical in the process of unravelling its history' (p. 15).

16. Jules Michelet, *L'Amour* (Paris: L. Hachette & Cie, 1858).

17. Bénédict-Augustin Morel, *Traité des dégéneréscences physiques, intellectuelles et morales de l'espèce humaine* (Paris: Baillière, 1857).

18. Francis Galton, *Inquiries into Human Faculty and its Development* (Kila, MO: Kessinger Publishing, 2004 [1883]), 17.

19. Daniel J. Kevles, *In the Name of Eugenics: Genetics and the Uses of Human Heredity* (New York: Knopf, 1985), 63.

20. Maria Sophia Quine, *Population Politics in Twentieth-Century Europe* (London and New York: Routledge, 1996), 88.

21. Nancy Leys Stepan, 'Race, Gender and Nation in Argentina: The Influence of Italian Eugenics', *History of European Ideas* 15, no. 4–6 (1992): 749–56; David G. Horn, *Social Bodies: Science, Reproduction and Italian Modernity* (Princeton: Princeton University Press, 1994); Mary Nash, 'Social Eugenics and Nationalist Race Hygiene in Early Twentieth Century Spain', *History of European Ideas* 15, no. 4/6 (1992): 741.

22. Robert A. Nye, *Sexuality* (Oxford: Oxford University Press, 1999), 115.

23. Kaan argued that the sexual instinct was natural, akin to hunger, but that several types of deviation were common, such as onanism (masturbation), pederasty (love of pre-pubescents), lesbian love (by which he meant both types of same-sex union), violation of corpses and bestiality. Michel Foucault has described the publication of Kaan's book as the 'date of birth ... of sexuality and sexual aberrations in the psychiatric field'. Michel Foucault, *Abnormal: Lectures at the College de France, 1974–1975*, eds Valerio Marchetti and Antonella Salomoni, trans. Graham Burchell (New York: Picador, 2004), 282. Mantegazza's anthropological approach helped bring about a general shift from viewing sex as primarily an erotic enterprise to studying it as an important sphere of human behaviour and culture. See also: Gilman, *Difference and Pathology*, 73–74.

24. Richard von Krafft-Ebing, *Psychopathia Sexualis, with Especial Reference to the Antipathic Sexual Instinct* (London: Staples Press, 1965), 187. It should be noted that Krafft-Ebing revised and expanded *Psychopathia Sexualis* twelve times. The first edition contained only 110 pages, while the last had 437. See: Paul Kruntorad, 'Krafft-Ebing', in Richard von Krafft-Ebing, *Psycopathia Sexualis* (Munich: Matthes und Seitz Verlag, 1997), 7–13.

25. Jeffrey Weeks, *Sexuality and Its Discontents: Meanings, Myths, and Modern Sexualities* (London and Boston: Routledge and Kegan Paul, 1985), 8.

26. Ibid., 69.

27. See: Merl Storr, 'Transformations: Subjects, Categories and Cures in Krafft-Ebing's

Sexology', in *Sexology in Culture: Labelling Bodies and Desires*, eds Lucy Bland and Laura Doan (Cambridge: Polity Press, 1998), 11–25.

28. See the 2001 documentary film of this title by Rosa von Praunheim.

29. Atina Grossmann, *Reforming Sex: The German Movement for Birth Control and Abortion Reform, 1920–1950* (Oxford: Oxford University Press, 1995), 15.

30. Harry Oosterhuis, *Stepchildren of Nature: Krafft-Ebing, Psychiatry and the Making of Sexual Identity* (Chicago: University of Chicago Press, 2000).

31. *The Interpretation of Dreams* (1900); *The Psychopathology of Everyday Life* (1901); and *Three Essays on the Theory of Sexuality* (1905).

32. Published as *Five Lectures on Psychoanalysis* (1916).

33. Sigmund Freud, 'Three Essays on the Theory of Sexuality', in *Standard Edition of the Complete Psychological Works of Sigmund Freud*, vol. 7, ed. James Strachey (London: Hogarth Press, 1953), 144–47.

34. In the myth, Oedipus's parents abandoned him after hearing a prediction from the oracle. Later, as an adult, he unknowingly fulfilled the prediction by killing his real father and marrying his real mother.

35. For summaries of the controversy about Freud's 'seduction theory' see: Hall Triplett, 'The Misnomer of Freud's "Seduction Theory"', *Journal of the History of Ideas* 65, no. 4 (2004): 647–65; and Allen Esterson, 'Jeffrey Masson and Freud's Seduction Theory: A New Fable Based on Old Myths', *History of the Human Sciences* 11, no. 1 (1998): 1–21.

36. Angus McLaren, *Twentieth-Century Sexuality: A History* (Oxford: Blackwell Publishers, 1999), 111.

37. Freud, *Civilization and its Discontents*. The book was originally published in German in 1930.

38. Sigmund Freud, 'Fetishism', in *Standard Edition of the Complete Psychological Works of Sigmund Freud*, vol. 21, ed. James Strachey (London: Hogarth Press, 1953), 154.

39. Laqueur, *Making Sex*, 242.

40. Cited from Marie Bonaparte, 'Les deux frigidities de la femme', *Bulletin de la societé de sexology* 1 (May 1932): 161–70 in McLaren, *Twentieth-Century Sexuality*, 110.

41. McLaren, *Twentieth-Century Sexuality*, 117–20.

42. Thomas Mann, 'Freud and the Future', in *Essays of Three Decades* (New York: Alfred A. Knopf, 1947), 411–28.

43. Winks and Adams, *Europe*, 2.

44. This emphasis on population policy is well summarized in Quine's comparison of Germany, France and Italy. See: *Population Politics in Twentieth-Century Europe*.

45. E. A. Wrigley, 'The Fall of Marital Fertility in Nineteenth-Century France: Exemplar or Exception?', *European Journal of Population/Revue europeenne de demographie* 1, no. 1 (1985): 31–60.

46. On Italy, see: Carl Ipsen, *Dictating Demography: The Problem of Population in Fascist Italy* (Cambridge and New York: Cambridge University Press, 1996); on the Soviet Union, see: David Hoffmann, 'Mothers in the Motherland: Stalinist Pronatalism in its Pan-European Context', *Journal of Social History* 34, no. 1 (2000): 35.

47. For an overview, see: Bonnie G. Smith, *Changing Lives*, 192–95.

48. Ibid., 345.

49. Victoria de Grazia, *How Fascism Ruled Women: Italy, 1922–1945* (Berkeley and Oxford: University of California Press, 1992), 25.

50. Susan Pedersen argues that French pronatalists, unlike their British counterparts, were uninterested in income distribution. Despite these characteristics of the 'parental welfare state', French programmes were more successful in delivering aid to children who

needed it. Pedersen, *Family, Dependence and the Origins of the Welfare State*, 366, 420 and 417. See also: Marie-Monique Huss, 'Pronatalism in the Inter-War Period in France', *Journal of Contemporary History* 25 (1990): 39.

51. Annette F. Timm, 'The Politics of Fertility: Population Politics and Health Care in Berlin, 1919–1972' (Ph.D. dissertation, University of Chicago, 1999).

52. Mary Nash, 'Un/Contested Identities', 32.

53. Quine, *Population Politics in Twentieth-Century Europe*, 37. Mussolini's biographer reports that the *Duce* was reputed to have slept with 400 women. See: R. J. B. Bosworth, *Mussolini* (New York: Oxford University Press, 2002), 74.

54. Quoted in Hoffmann, 'Mothers in the Motherland', 35. For a more extensive discussion see: Goldman, *Women, the State and Revolution*.

55. On concerns about youth morality and the problem of pregnant women being abandoned, see: Anne E. Gorsuch, '"A Woman is not a Man": The Culture of Gender and Generation in Soviet Russia, 1921–1928', *Slavic Review* 55, no. 3 (1996): 636–60.

56. Sheila Fitzpatrick, *The Cultural Front: Power and Culture in Revolutionary Russia* (Ithaca, NY: Cornell University Press, 1992), 68. See also: David L. Hoffmann and Annette F. Timm, 'Utopian Biopolitics: Reproductive Policies, Gender Roles, and Sexuality in Nazi Germany and the Soviet Union', in *After Totalitarianism: Stalinism and Nazism Compared* [provisional title], eds Sheila Fitzpatrick, Michael Geyer and Terry Martin (forthcoming).

57. Judith Walkowitz, *Prostitution and Victorian Society: Women, Class and the State* (Cambridge and New York: Cambridge University Press, 1980); Abrams, 'Prostitutes in Imperial Germany'; Corbin, *Women for Hire*; and Roger Davidson and Lesley A. Hall, eds, *Sex, Sin and Suffering: Venereal Disease and European Society since 1870* (New York: Routledge, 2001).

58. Carolyn J. Dean, *The Frail Social Body: Pornography, Homosexuality, and Other Fantasies in Interwar France* (Berkeley: University of California Press, 2000); Mary Louise Roberts, *Disruptive Acts: The New Woman in Fin-de-Siècle France* (Chicago: University of Chicago Press, 2002); Mary Louise Roberts, *Civilization without Sexes: Reconstructing Gender in Postwar France* (Chicago: University of Chicago Press, 1994); and Atina Grossmann, 'Girlkultur or Thoroughly Rationalized Female: A New Woman in Weimar Germany?', in *Women in Culture and Politics: A Century of Change*, eds Judith Friedländer, Blanche Cook, Alice Kessler-Harris and Carroll Smith-Rosenberg (Bloomington, IN: Indiana University Press, 1986), 62–80.

59. Alain Corbin, 'Commercial Sexuality in Nineteenth-Century France: A System of Images and Regulations', in *The Making of the Modern Body: Sexuality and Society in the Nineteenth Century*, eds Catherine Gallagher and Thomas Laqueur (Berkeley and Los Angeles: University of California Press, 1987), 213–14.

60. Jarausch, 'Students, Sex and Politics'.

61. James Woycke, *Birth Control in Germany, 1871–1933* (London: Routledge, 1988), 51.

62. Margaret Sanger, *Woman and the New Race* (New York: Truth Publishing Company, 1920), 205.

63. Claudine Mitchell, 'Madeleine Pelletier (1874–1939): The Politics of Sexual Oppression', in *European Women's History Reader*, eds Fiona Montgomery and Christine Collette (New York: Routledge, 2002), 256–71.

64. Cited from Madeleine Pelletier, *L'Emancipation sexuelle de la femme* (Paris: M. Giard and E. Brière, 1911) in Offen, *European Feminisms*, 245.

65. For useful surveys see: Ann Taylor Allen, 'German Radical Feminism and Eugenics: 1900–1918', *German Studies Review* 11 (1988): 31–56; and Karen Offen, 'Depopulation,

Nationalism, and Feminism in Fin-de-Siècle France', *American Historical Review* 89, no. 3 (1984): 648–76.

66. De Grazia, *How Fascism Ruled Women*, 70.

67. Quoted in Horn, *Social Bodies*, 59.

68. See the otherwise very convincing arguments of Nye, 'Sexuality', 21; and McLaren, *Twentieth-Century Sexuality*, 136–42.

69. Kater, *Hitler Youth*.

70. In the year 1943 alone, 700,000 ampoules of the testosterone-based 'Testoviron' were sold in Nazi Germany. See: Hans-Georg Hofer, 'Wenn Männer altern. Ein Projekt zur Geschichte der "männlichen Wechseljahre"', *L'Homme. Europäische Zeitschrift für Feministische Geschichtswissenschaft* 17, no. 1 (2006): 101–8.

71. Christa Paul, *Zwangsprostitution: Staatlich Errichtete Bordelle Im National-sozialismus, Reihe Deutsche Vergangenheit* (Berlin: Edition Hentrich, 1995).

72. See: Dagmar Herzog, *Sex after Fascism: Memory and Morality in Twentieth-Century Germany* (Princeton: Princeton University Press, 2005).

73. See: Elizabeth D. Heineman, *What Difference Does a Husband Make? Woman and Marital Status in Nazi and Postwar Germany* (Berkeley: University of California, 1999), esp. 108–75; and Frank Biess, 'Survivors of Totalitarianism: Returning POWs and the Reconstruction of Masculine Citizenship in West Germany, 1945–1955', in *The Miracle Years: A Cultural History of West Germany, 1949–1968*, ed. Hanna Schissler (Princeton: Princeton University Press, 2000), 57–82. For an account of similar themes in East Germany, see Donna Harsch, *Revenge of the Domestic: Women, the Family, and Communism in the German Democratic Republic* (Princeton, NJ: Princeton University Press, 2001).

74. See: Andrea Peto, 'Memory and the Narrative of Rape in Budapest and Vienna', in *Life after Death. Approaches to a Cultural and Social History of Europe*, eds Dirk Schumann and Richard Bessel (New York: Cambridge University Press, 2003), 129–149; and Naimark, *The Russians in Germany*, 73–116.

75. For a very strong argument about the United States that has comparative relevance for Europe, see: Alan Petigny, 'Illegitimacy, Postwar Psychology, and the Reperiodization of the Sexual Revolutionary', *Journal of Social History* 38, no. 1 (2004): 63–79.

76. There were a couple of pioneering surveys. A radical social science group in Britain carried out 'Little Kinsey' in 1949. But its authors were dissatisfied with their analysis and did not immediately publish their research. See: Liz Stanley, *Sex Surveyed, 1949–1994: From Mass Observation's 'Little Kinsey' to the National Survey and the Hite Reports* (London and Bristol, PA: Taylor & Francis Ltd., 1995).

77. Herzog, *Sex after Fascism*, 159. This is not to say that German philosophers of this era ignored sadism and its links to totalitarianism and fascism. An analysis of de Sade's *Juliette* formed a significant part of Theodor Adorno and Max Horkheimer's argument that the crimes of the Holocaust had undermined the Enlightenment project. See: Theodor Adorno and Max Horkheimer, *Dialectic of Enlightenment: Philosophical Fragments* (New York: Verso, 2002).

78. His theory was originally published in 1930 in *Geschlechtsreife, Enthaltsamkeit, Ehemoral*. But the English version (Wilhelm Reich, *The Sexual Revolution: Toward a Self-Governing Character Structure*, 1st English edition (New York: Orgon Institute Press, 1945) was a translation of: Wilhelm Reich, *Die Sexualität Im Kulturkampf: Zur Sozialistischen Umstrukturierung Des Menschenmacher*, 2nd revised edition (Copenhagen: Sexpol-Verlag, 1936). Nicolaus Sombart argues, however, that the Austrian anarchist (later communist) psychoanalyst Otto Gross had developed this meaning of the term 'sexual revolution' (to

describe how social or political emancipation could be achieved through the freeing of individual erotic potential) twenty years before Reich. See: Nicolaus Sombart, *Die Deutschen Männer Und Ihre Feinde. Carl Schmitt – Ein Deutsches Schicksal Zwischen Männerbund Und Matriarchmythos* (Munich and Vienna: Carl Hanser, 1991), 109–10.

79. This theory still has adherents. See: www.orgonics.com and www.orgone.org and http://www.wilhelmreichmuseum.org (accessed October 2005).

80 Weeks, *Sexuality and its Discontents*, 164.

81. Herzog, *Sex after Fascism*, 159.

82. For interesting recent takes on the book see: Molly Weatherfield, 'The Mother of Masochism', *Salon* 6 August 1998, available from http://www.salon.com/books/feature/1998/08/06feature.html and 'I Wrote the Story of O', *Guardian Unlimited/The Observer* 25 July 2004, available from http://observer.guardian.co.uk/review/story/0,6903, 1268403,00.html (accessed October 2005).

83. Nancy Huston, 'Erotic Literature in Postwar France', *Raritan* 12, no. 1 (1992).

84. The two were engaged in a lifelong intimate relationship that involved bisexual and 'shared' relationships. Recent biographical accounts suggest that Sartre was more enamoured of this 'open' arrangement than de Beauvoir. For an overview see: Louis Menand, 'Stand by Your Man: The Strange Liaison of Sartre and Beauvoir', *New Yorker* 26 September 2005.

85. Simone de Beauvoir, 'Must We Burn Sade?', in *The Marquis de Sade: The 120 Days of Sodom and Other Writings*, eds and trans. Austryn Wainhouse and Richard Seaver (New York: Grove, 1966), 3–64.

86. Judith Butler, 'Beauvoir on Sade: Making Sexuality into an Ethic', in *The Cambridge Companion to Simone de Beauvoir*, ed. Claudia Card (Cambridge and New York: Cambridge University Press, 2003), 168–88.

87. Ibid., 178.

88. Ibid., 183.

89. Cited in ibid.

90. Simone de Beauvoir, *The Second Sex* (New York: Vintage Books, 1989 [1952]), 51.

91. David Allyn, *Make Love, Not War: The Sexual Revolution, an Unfettered History* (New York: Routledge, 2001), 196.

92. *One Dimensional Man* was widely read by those who participated in the student rebellions in Paris in 1968 (to be discussed below). Kristin Ross, *May '68 and Its Afterlives* (Chicago: University of Chicago Press, 2002), 193.

93. Herbert Marcuse, 'The New German Mentality', in *Technology, War and Fascism. Collected Papers of Herbert Marcuse*, vol. 1, ed. Douglas Kellner (New York: Routledge, 1998), 139–90.

94. Quoted from a 1955 lecture in Weeks, *Sexuality and its Discontents*, 166.

95. Herbert Marcuse, *One Dimensional Man: Studies in the Ideology of Advanced Industrial Society* (London: Routledge and Kegan Paul Ltd., 1964).

96. Weeks, *Sexuality and its Discontents*, 169.

97. Ross, *May '68 and Its Afterlives*, 6, 121–22, and 199–200.

98. Werner Hülsberg, *The German Greens: A Social and Political Profile* (London and New York: Verso, 1988), 71–73.

99. McLaren, *Twentieth-Century Sexuality*, 172 and 174.

100. For an examination of equivalent events in the US see: Allyn, *Make Love, Not War*.

101. McLaren, *Twentieth-Century Sexuality*, 170.

102. Dagmar Herzog, '"Pleasure, Sex and Politics Belong Together": Post-Holocaust Memory and the Sexual Revolution in West Germany', *Critical Inquiry* 24, no. 2 (1998): 419.

103. Good overviews of the development of second-wave women's liberation movements in Europe can be found in: Arthur Marwick, *The Sixties: Cultural Revolution in Britain, France, Italy and the United States* (Oxford and New York: Oxford University Press, 1998), 679–70; and Geoff Eley, *Forging Democracy: The History of the Left in Europe, 1850–2000* (New York: Oxford University Press, 2002), 366–83.

104. Quoted in Uta G. Poiger, 'Rebels with a Cause? American Popular Culture, the 1956 Youth Riots, and New Conceptions of Masculinity in East and West Germany', in *The American Impact on Postwar Germany*, ed. Reiner Pommerin (Providence, RI and Oxford: Berghahn Books, 1995), 99.

105. Timothy W. Ryback, *Rock around the Bloc: A History of Rock Music in Eastern Europe and the Soviet Union* (New York: Oxford University Press, 1990).

106. McLaren, *Twentieth-Century Sexuality*, 187. See also the story of a gay American soldier who defected to the GDR: Jürgen Dahlkamp, 'No Country more Beautiful', *Spiegel Online* 14 July 2003, available from http://service.spiegel.de/cache/international/spiegel/0,1518,257041,00.html (accessed 7 December 2005).

107. McLaren, *Twentieth-Century Sexuality*, 197. It should be noted that the shift in emphasis towards gaining family rights has neither been uncontroversial nor complete within gay rights movements in Europe. Many gays and lesbians would still agree with Guy Hocquenghem that 'homosexual love [outside of family ties] is immensely superior' and that 'Family heterosexuality dominates the whole of civilized sexuality; it is certainly no liberation to have to go through it'. See: Guy Hocquenghem, *Homosexual Desire*, trans. Daniella Dangoor (Durham and London: Duke University Press, 1993), 131 and 139. Current legal changes, by now too extensive to summarize here, have only fuelled this debate.

108. I. Weller *et al.* 'Homosexual men in London: Lymphadenopathy, immune status, and Epstein-Barr virus infection', *Annals of the New York Academy of Science*, 437, no. 1 (1984): 248–49.

109. Francoise F. Hamers and Angela M. Downs, 'HIV in Central and Eastern Europe', *Lancet* 361 (2003): 1,035–44.

110. 'Moscow Hosts Key AIDS Conference', *BBC News* 15 May 2006, available from http://news.bbc.co.uk/2/hi/europe/4771409.stm (accessed 26 May 2006).

111. See the informative website of the Terrence Higgins Trust, a leading HIV and AIDS charity in the United Kingdom: http://www.gnpplus.net/criminalisation/list.shtml (accessed 7 December 2005).

112. 'Criminal Responsibility for Homosexual Activities Likely to Be Introduced in Russia', *Pravda* 5 October 2004, available from http://english.pravda.ru/society/stories/7158-homosexual-0 (accessed February 2006).

113. Petigny, 'Illegitimacy, Postwar Psychology'.

Conclusion

In 1991, as Europe was being wholly transformed by the massive political and demographic changes associated with the end of the Cold War, an anthropologist named Miguel Vale de Almeida travelled to Pardais, a village of 659 people in the Alentejo province of Portugal, searching for 'a place where *ancien régime* structures would meet "modernity"'.[1] It was a region of significant economic change. The marble quarries in the area had been expanding, destroying much of the agricultural land in the area, and new housing developments were filling the spaces between previously separate small towns and villages, making them a single urban area. It was, in many ways, a familiar landscape in late twentieth-century Europe, one important to understand as we conclude our discussion of the gender revolution of the past 200 years.

One of the men de Almeida spoke with during his fieldwork was Beto, the 25-year-old son of a sharecropper, who worked in the local quarries. He and his wife had four children, all of them under six years of age, and when he had finished working for the day he frequented local watering holes with his friends:

> Beto often went out in the evenings. As with most men, he was hardly ever at home. When he came back from work, he would go home to wash and change his clothes, only to go straight out to the café to have his afternoon *aperitifs*. He would interrupt this activity to go home for dinner, and once this was done, be back at the café where he remained until 11 p.m. or even later. Once or twice a week and always at weekends, he would leave the village for a [larger party].

When with male companions, Beto liked to drink, to talk about women and to boast of his own sexual prowess. Alone with the anthropologist, he discussed his 'dreams and nightmares, states of soul, melancholy and sadness, dissatisfaction and impotence'. In all company, he was proud of being a good provider for his family and proclaimed his love for them.[2]

Women in Pardais had developed their own form of single-sex sociability. When de Almeida asked Beto's wife what she thought about the fact that he spent nearly all his free time drinking with his male friends, she replied that 'it was all right with her, provided that he came back home every night and shared the bed with her, since she actually preferred to have her man outside the house: men "get in our way", "make things a mess", "do not know how to behave at home" and "their place is in the streets".[3] The men and women of Pardais had truly built a society of separate spheres, one in which the idea that sexual difference was natural and biologically based was strong and in which proper gender behaviour was taught at a very tender age. Young boys were encouraged to play games that combined conflict and public performance, while young women were taught passivity and modesty and played games that 'reproduce[d] family life and motherhood by imitation'.[4] It was a fraternal system in which many nineteenth-century men (and women) would have felt quite comfortable but which came under enormous strain throughout Europe as the result of the world wars and the sexual revolutions of the twentieth century.

But this does not mean that the citizens of Pardais were somehow 'unmodern'. To the contrary, as we have endeavoured to show throughout this book, 'modern' gender relations were built not by replacing earlier beliefs about sexual difference but by layering on new interpretations and new possibilities for behaviour, a process that frequently resulted in contestation but never in total victory for one gendered ideal over another. The sort of gender ideals seen in Pardais have been present in one form or another throughout the modern era, and despite the changes that occurred in many locations during the twentieth century, they are widespread today. Change has certainly occurred. Trendlines have clearly been moving towards greater equality for women, but there are many families across the continent in which systematic male domination is alive and well. These trends, however, are not inexorable or direct. History moves in crooked ways. For most of the nineteenth and twentieth centuries, Marxists were sure that historical 'progress' was inevitable, that the workers of the world would unite to throw off their capitalist chains and build a world of justice, prosperity and harmony. Free-market ideologues were similarly convinced that unfettered capitalism would mean democracy, wealth, peace and happiness. In the wake of the collapse of the Soviet system and the devastation of Yugoslav civil wars, during which ethnic cleansing, mass rape and bloody retribution were daily fare during the 1990s, and in view of the significant cultural and political tensions that have arisen throughout the continent in the past fifteen years, these visions now seem impossibly utopian.

The potential of Europeans, both positive and negative, is determined not by logic but by historical conditions, by the remnants of the failed and successful experiments of their predecessors, and by the institutions and languages of power developed over the past two centuries. As knowledge spreads more easily, and as humans move more quickly, those historical conditions are now global in scope. Historians and biologists alike now regularly read the scholarship of colleagues across the world. Immigrants from Morocco now live in Paris, share the metro with American tourists and send their children to school with the descendants of traditional French peasants. This global context increases the fund of potential views and potential behaviours, and it complicates the model of social interaction to such a degree that it is impossible to predict the outcome of these historical processes with confidence.

It is entirely possible that those who would like the system of separate spheres that is present in Pardais to reassert itself more broadly across the continent will succeed.

But such a retrenchment seems unlikely. Pockets of patriarchy will likely persist in Europe for some time, perhaps even indefinitely. Even in the most cosmopolitan and liberalized cities, there are many families who live 'traditionally', who believe that the honour of their daughters and their families depends upon chastity and who grant the eldest male the authority to make decisions for the entire household. Fraternalist ideology is even stronger. In contrast to earlier eras, however, the institutional, cultural and legal contexts of the 'New Europe' work to undermine these traditional gender systems rather than support them. Few powerful Europeans would now openly make derogatory comments about women or would suggest that they are unfit to participate in the public sphere. Just as importantly, state institutions now affirm the right of individuals to choose their own family circumstances, to leave unhappy situations or to move to a new village, a new city, even a new country. These legal guarantees do not protect all vulnerable individuals from abuse, but they do make a difference. In Pardais, for example, de Almeida met a young woman named Manuela, who was forthright and autonomous. She was a high-school graduate and was living outside of marriage with her boyfriend. She was a census official, and de Almeida joined her for pleasant trips around the countryside as he interviewed her. Soon, the tongues of the young men in the village were wagging, and they suggested to de Almeida that he could have his way with Manuela since she was easy. He ignored them, and so, apparently, did Manuela, who married her boyfriend on her own terms the following year and had a baby.[5] It was much harder for independent women in earlier eras to deal with efforts to force them into roles they did not wish to occupy.

The statistics demonstrate that the scale of change may be even greater than this sketch of Pardais suggests. Portugal remains one of the least urban of European countries. Only 53 per cent of the Portuguese population lives in cities, the lowest rate outside of the Balkans on the continent, with the exception of Moldova and Liechtenstein. Still, literacy rates for both men and women are virtually 100 per cent, the maternal death rate is only five per 100,000 live births and fully 19 per cent of parliament is made up of women. By European standards these are modest accomplishments. In Sweden, for instance, where the urban population numbers 84 per cent, the maternal death rate is only two per 100,000 and 45 per cent of the parliament is female. But in a global comparison, the power and health of women in Portugal is remarkably high. In the United States, where 79 per cent of the population lives in cities, the maternal death rate is more than triple Portugal's (at seventeen per 100,000) and only 14 per cent of Congress is female. African and Asian countries compare much less favourably.[6]

Europeans now live in societies that have many different family forms, ideas of proper gender roles and opportunities for men and women. We have seen over the course of this book how that variety developed. Our story began in the

Enlightenment, when European scholars offered new ways of thinking about the natural world and eventually about human beings and their place in that world. These investigations were based on the supposition that one could discover natural patterns through disciplined and rational scientific enquiry and also that human beings and human societies should seek to make their own behaviour congruent with the natural order. As we saw with our discussion of Rousseau, this scientific literature tended to emphasize rather than downplay the notion of sexual difference, a tendency that only strengthened in the nineteenth century under the influence of Darwin's writings.

Still, the shift had consequences. In the first place, the very idea that 'tradition' should serve as the basis for social order came into question. In the second, placing humans in a biological context led many to assert that there was a fundamental human equality in nature that was thwarted only by ignorant and oppressive political systems. As Rousseau famously wrote in 1762, 'Man is born free, but he is everywhere in chains.'[7] The radical philosopher Thomas Paine, who was born in England and would take part in both the American and French Revolutions, made the point even more clearly in his incendiary 1776 pamphlet *Common Sense*:

> Mankind being originally equals in the order of creation, the equality could only be destroyed by some subsequent circumstance ... But there is ... [a] distinction for which no truly natural or religious reason can be assigned, and that is, the distinction of men into kings and subjects. Male and female are the distinctions of nature, good and bad the distinctions of heaven; but ... exalting one man so greatly above the rest cannot be justified on the equal rights of nature.[8]

We can see here in Paine that the conviction that sexual difference was based in nature and ought to have social and political implications meant that the rights to equality and freedom were limited to men in the minds of many Enlightenment philosophers. As our discussion of Olympe de Gouges and Mary Wollstonecraft indicated, however, the logical implication that women were also naturally equal by virtue of membership in the human species was taken up at once. Those who pressed for women's equality lost in the revolutionary era, as political figures across the continent sought stability amidst the upheaval by reaffirming the principle of male superiority within the family and society. But the logical contradiction at the heart of revolutionary political ideology remained as an irritant and a spur to action from that point forward.

The other major gendered challenge to the old order that occurred in the revolutionary era was the elaboration of the concept of 'fraternity', which was based on the idea that young men, being equal to older men, deserved a larger share of power and authority in European political and social systems. This impetus was clear in the passage from Paine, as was the implication that republican forms of governance were more likely to assure male equality than monarchies were. The initial victories of fraternal republicans in France were short-lived, as monarchy and patriarchy returned with the rise of Napoleon to the throne, but both the idea of fraternity and its most powerful state form – the establishment of universal military service for young men – would remain powerful forces throughout the nineteenth century. Nationalism, the political form that most clearly expressed the fraternal ideal, developed rapidly in Europe in that time period and soon posed a challenge to monarchies and indeed empires across the continent.

The nineteenth century saw other important political and social developments that were intimately linked with the question of gender. The two we focused on here were the social changes brought about by the new modes of work and production established by the Industrial Revolution and the cultural and political changes that occurred as the result of Europe's intensive colonization of the rest of the world. As we saw in Chapter 2, the economic changes of the nineteenth century crippled the traditional family economy. In the first place, a great many Europeans left rural villages for work and residence in the booming cities of the era. The process of urbanization definitively changed social interactions wherever it occurred, including interactions between men and women. In the second place, the nature of labour was transformed. European economies, which had previously operated largely on a non-cash basis, now recentred themselves around wage labour.

More precisely, the trends of the era led to a situation in which only those activities that produced cash were considered economically valuable. For most women, this meant a further devaluation of the sorts of labour they performed, from cooking to cleaning to child-rearing, which they did 'for free' in their own households. For wealthy women, it meant an opportunity to further reinforce their own superior class position by hiring lower-class women to do these sorts of chores for them, right down to breastfeeding their children. Proper domestic behaviour now centred not on labour but on providing emotional support to one's husband, who was, it was thought, buffeted during the day by the storms of modern economic life and who needed a safe, gentle harbour at night. Sexual relations were part of this emotional support, but here too the 'cash nexus' of the capitalist economy made itself felt. Prostitution was not new, of course, but it expanded in scope and in visibility over the course of the nineteenth century, fitting nicely with the hierarchies of sex and class that solidified over the course of the industrial era. There was ample cause for women and lower-class men to suspect that the new modern Europe was no improvement over the old, and in terms of social security might even have represented a decline.

European imperialism left an even more ambiguous legacy in terms of gender. On the one hand, as we saw in Chapter 3, the exposure to other societies allowed for even greater criticism of European cultural and political practices, including sexual ones. In addition, the very opening of new colonies allowed those who felt hemmed in by life in European countries to explore alternative paths. This was true for ambitious young men trying to get away from their fathers. It was also true for those who sought new erotic experiences with members of the opposite sex, with members of the same sex and with any number of combinations of the two. As we saw in our discussion of concubinage, European men frequently adopted polygamous practices, keeping a wife at home and a concubine in the colonies. Women too found different sorts of adventures abroad. Wives of missionaries on the frontier often lived dangerous but personally fulfilling lives, and even those white women who stayed near the governor's mansion were important participants in the affairs of their homeland, not simply by being active colonizers, but also by forwarding ambitious moral reform programmes that affected life in the colonies and in the metropole alike.

On the other hand, the fundamental organizing principle of empire was that of European superiority. This superiority required ideological work to maintain, and the core of that work was the establishment of scientifically based 'natural' hierarchies. The two main axes were those of race and sex. Both women and men worked hard to establish these distinctions, and all parties took advantage of developments in the science of biology, especially that of genetics, to substantiate their claims of difference. The principle of separate spheres was reinforced both by scientific research and by the languages used by men and women to forward political programmes. Female activists became more visible, but mainly when they claimed the right to moral superiority granted them by the nineteenth-century discourse of gender. The principle of racial division was also sustained by scholars like Joseph-Arthur de Gobineau and Charles Darwin, both of whom also reasserted that sexual difference and sexual competition were natural facts of life. A great many European women and men were convinced by this social and scientific research, and they sought (and not infrequently found) fulfilment by working within the context of these racial and sexual hierarchies.

This increasingly urbane, hierarchical and imperial European system proved both durable and powerful. By the beginning of the twentieth century, indeed, Europeans had established it (with some local variation) across the globe. But this political order was vulnerable, both because it was based on competitive and powerful individual states who were coming into more frequent conflict with one another and because it had spawned socially disaffected groups and a political language that could articulate that unrest and mobilize people to oppose the European Great Powers. Fraternal, anti-colonial nationalists increasingly opposed patriarchal imperialists, and feminists opposed the male domination at the heart of both the patriarchal and fraternal forms. The First World War began as a revolt against imperialism within Europe, as Serbia contested the claims of the Habsburg Empire to assert hegemony on the Balkan peninsula. Given that European military systems traced their organizational and ideological roots back to the fraternalism of the revolutionary, the Napoleonic and the anti-Napoleonic military systems of the period from 1792–1815, the outbreak of war strengthened the hand of the fraternal nationalists. This time, fraternity would not be dislodged. The great land empires of eastern and central Europe broke apart, and new national states dominated by young war veterans took their place. At the same time, the social pressures of the war itself had required women to break out of their 'sphere' and assume important roles in both the war effort and in the symbolic construction of the nation itself. In practical terms, as we saw in Chapter 4, this meant not only increased participation in the industrial sector, but also the establishment of state-run social welfare systems that gave assistance to women and children not on the principle of charity but on the principle that they were deserving citizens. Europe in the 1920s and 1930s thus saw the development of highly militarized and masculine states with welfare systems and public programmes that included women as civic actors. The degree of actual political influence that women were able to wield varied widely from country to country; however, the idea of 'separate spheres' had come into question, ironically, through a war marked by a physical separation of the sexes unprecedented in European history.

The Second World War would do still more to break down the idea of separate spheres. Whereas women had been granted the vote in many places in Europe after the First World War, it happened across the continent in the wake of the second war. While the fiction of a separation between front and home front could reasonably be maintained in many places in Europe during the Great War, the devastation and widespread occupation of the continent by foreign armies during the Second World War made such a neat division impossible. Indeed, as the experience of the Holocaust and other less drastic assaults on civilians would demonstrate, women and children became primary rather than secondary targets in a conflict that took the principle of total war to its logical, apocalyptic conclusion. The suffering and chaos of the war years led to two contradictory impulses. On the one hand, the desire for normality led to intensive and initially successful efforts to stabilize society by re-establishing traditional and comfortable family and gender roles. On the other hand, the connection between modern European masculinity and the great catastrophes of the twentieth century was now only too evident. Those who wished to avoid a repetition of the carnage began systematically examining ways that they might transform European social structures, gender norms and political practices.

There were many ways in which this process developed, and it is still too early to say how extensive the results of this social reappraisal might be, but it is indisputable that the change has been very significant. The area we focused on in this book was the realm of sexual relations. As we argued in Chapter 5, sex was not transformed overnight in the 1960s by a group of longhaired, freedom-seeking rebels. The 'sexual revolution' had a much longer history, going all the way back to the 'sexologists' of the late nineteenth and early twentieth century who insisted that sexual practices had political implications. If Freud had paraphrased Rousseau, he might have claimed that men and women could only be free if they were sexually in chains. Sexual revolutionaries, conscious as a result of the wars and experiences of military authoritarianism that the path of European 'civilization' did not always run through freedom, challenged Freud's premise. As early as 1936, Wilhelm Reich and his followers argued instead that the mechanisms of sexual control, oppression and repression in fact encouraged fascism and war. This view found even more fertile ground after the experience of the Second World War, which saw a grotesque sort of sexual 'liberation' through the destruction of the local communities that had previously policed sexual practices, through the privations of civilian flight, poverty and existential desperation, and finally through the normalization of various forms of coerced sex. These were experiences few wanted to repeat, but they had broken up long-standing patterns of sexual behaviour across the continent. The sexual order that would follow the war would have to be constructed rather than simply maintained.

These transformations in sexual thought and sexual practice coincided in the 1960s with technological developments like the birth control pill and with widespread social unrest based on the rejection of the 'old Europe' of colonies, capitalism and war. This conjunction of forces resulted in the social and political phenomenon we today call 'The Sixties'. 'The Sixties' began long before the decade did, reached its peak in many ways in the 1970s and continues to exert influence today. The rebels of 'The Sixties' failed to attain their goals in many respects. War is still around, and so is imperialism, though both exist now in different forms. In terms of sexual liberation, however, those rebels can rightly claim victory. Most Europeans, to the great dismay of conservatives, especially in older generations, can now have sex how they please and with whom they please without fear of legal action (as long as it is between consenting adults). This is true not only for married and unmarried heterosexual couples, but for homosexual couples as well. The victory of sexual revolutionaries was not, of course, complete. Social norms, which are in any case almost always stronger than legal ones, continue to limit sexual liberty in many areas of the continent. Homosexual practices in particular are still viewed with suspicion and denounced in many places, but homophobia too seems to be in sharp decline across Europe. As the sexologists realized decades ago, this change in sexual tolerance and sexual practices has political consequences. In particular, male dominance in its patriarchal and fraternal forms has been based upon the sexual control of women. Today's European feminists are now trying to see whether the significant gains that women have made in the realms of equality and liberty might be extended by undercutting fraternity once and for all. That is a social transformation that will occur, if it does, as much in the bedroom as in the boardroom.

In the long run, feminists who seek this change have good reason to be optimistic. In the short term, affairs can seem much more muddled. As women have successfully asserted their right to take a place in the public sphere in western Europe, they have discovered what their sisters in eastern Europe could have told them much earlier: that entering the workforce and the political world means taking on the 'double burden' of paid work outside the home and continuing to do much of the unpaid work within it.

Trying to balance career and family is a precarious act, and this struggle has rapidly come to occupy a central role in discussions of what earlier commentators would have called the European 'woman question'. For couples with children in the European Union at the start of the twenty-first century, it remains the case that men spend more time in paid labour, and women more time in unpaid labour in the household. Beyond that, significant differences exist. In the three candidate countries scheduled to join the EU in 2007 or 2008 (Bulgaria, Romania and Turkey), men who marry continue to see a reduction in their total labour (paid labour combined with domestic labour). In all current EU countries, however, both men and women see an increase in total work after marriage and children. In most of these countries, women work more overall than men, because they do more work in the home, but this difference is rapidly declining in many areas. In Estonia, women work about an hour more per day, in France about 20–30 minutes more and in Sweden the total burden is now equal.[9]

This evidence that men are now joining women in shouldering the 'double burden' alerts us to the presence of what we might call the contemporary 'man question'. Most European men now take it as a personal, even a masculine, duty to play a role in household affairs. Given that it remains the case that when couples have children, women tend to reduce the amount of time they spend working outside the home and men tend to increase that time to compensate for lost income, men have become increasingly anxious about their domestic shortcomings. In the 'old' fifteen countries of the EU, 32 per cent of surveyed men in couples with children reported that they have found it 'difficult ... to fulfil my family responsibilities because of the amount of time I spend on the job.' In the ten new member states that joined in 2004, that number jumps to 50 per cent. Both figures are higher than that reported by women (27 per cent and 35 per cent respectively). Only in the candidate states do women report that they experience difficulty more than men, and there both the numbers are high (50 per cent for women and 48 per cent for men).[10] For most Europeans, the argument that men and women should occupy separate spheres is unpersuasive. But no one appears sure what a new, equitable family model, and with it a new and equitable gender order, might look like. Most now agree that men and women should be equal, but that only goes so far. Many young Europeans are troubled by questions about how to be a good mother or a good father, to be a good partner to one's lover or to be a responsible member of one's community. Worse, they are not even sure that they will know when they have stumbled upon the answer. European gender structures are in the midst of a major realignment. It is too soon to know what will emerge, but we already know that the transition period is marked by enormous stress and uncertainty.

And what of the villagers of Pardais? Does clinging to the fraternal family form mean that they are able to avoid this anxiety, to live in harmony and to find refuge in a model they believe brought stability and happiness to their forebears? De Almeida thinks not:

It is quite common to say that men are also victims of masculine domination. Many women may feel this statement to be dishonest ... [But women] seem to be able to appropriate for themselves symbols and practices that are labeled as masculine, thanks precisely to the hierarchy that defines these as 'superior' and closer to the moral standards of personhood. Also, a process of relative 'feminisation' of social values has been occurring in the society at large, and women in Pardais are not unaware of the growing social salience of sentiments, introspection, self-reflexivity and so on. For men, however, it is rather more difficult to invent new identity forms since – following the dichotomous thought – the alternative is manifestly 'inferior.' They are like aristocrats who have 'lost everything' and no longer know who and what they are. Acknowledging that the hegemonic model probably is just a paper tiger might be the first step for the invention of new social relations and new identities relating to gender.[11]

The comparison with aristocrats is apt. The nobles and other patriarchs of the old regime did not lose power immediately as a result of the revolutionary era, but they did lose hegemony, or the capacity to completely dominate the ideological conditions in which they lived. The same is true for those who want to maintain a system of male domination based in biology and tradition today. Their days of power look to be coming to a close, and they know it.

But we have not reached the 'End of History' in gendered terms. We still think about our world both literally and metaphorically in terms of sexual difference. It would be difficult even to create meaning through language today, much less understand political or social developments, without recourse to the long and rich history of gender associations left to us by language, by literature and by our cultures as a whole. If gender has a history, it probably has a future too. Only those unaware of the past will expect that future to unfold logically according to 'Equality', 'Justice', or 'Nature'. Women and men will create it in their family rooms and their bedrooms as surely as they do in their offices and legislative chambers. And, as always, they will create it together.

Notes

1. Miguel Vale de Almeida, *The Hegemonic Male: Masculinity in a Portugese Town* (Providence, RI and Oxford: Berghahn Books, 1996), 11.

2. Ibid., 40.

3. Ibid.

4. Ibid., 50.

5. Ibid., 130.

6. *PRB Country Profiles* (Population Reference Bureau, 2006), available from www.prb.org (accessed 9 February 2006). See also: Therborn, *Between Sex and Power*.

7. Jean-Jacques Rousseau, *The Social Contract*, trans. Maurice Cranston (New York: Penguin, 1968), 49.

8. Thomas Paine, 'Selections from Common Sense', in *Reading the American Past: Selected Historical Documents*, ed. Michael P. Johnson (Boston: Bedford Books, 1998), 95.

9. Chiara Saraceno, Manuela Olagnero and Paola Torrioni, *First European Quality of Life Survey: Families, Work and Social Networks* (Dublin: European Foundation for the Improvement of Living and Working Conditions, 2005), 35.

10. Ibid., 39.

11. De Almeida, *The Hegemonic Male*, 168.

Bibliography

Abrams, Lynn. 'Prostitutes in Imperial Germany, 1870–1918: Working Girls or Social Outcasts?' In *The German Underworld*, ed. Richard Evans, 189–209. London and New York: Routledge, 1991.

Adorno, Theodor, and Max Horkheimer. *Dialectic of Enlightenment: Philosophical Fragments*. New York: Verso, 2002.

Alekseeva, Ludmila, and Paul Goldberg. *The Thaw Generation: Coming of Age in the Post-Stalin Era*. Pittsburgh, PA: University of Pittsburgh Press, 1993.

Allen, Ann Taylor. 'German Radical Feminism and Eugenics: 1900–1918'. *German Studies Review* 11 (1988): 31–56.

Allen, Robert C. 'Tracking the Agricultural Revolution in England'. *Economic History Review* 52, no. 2 (1999): 209–35.

Allyn, David. *Make Love, Not War: The Sexual Revolution, an Unfettered History*. New York: Routledge, 2001.

Andress, David. *The Terror: The Merciless War for Freedom in Revolutionary France*. New York: Farrar, Straus and Giroux, 2005.

Angell, Norman. *The Great Illusion: A Study of the Relation of Military Power in Nations to Their Economic and Social Advantage*. New York: Putnam, 1910.

Arendt, Hannah. *The Human Condition*. Chicago and London: University of Chicago Press, 1958.

Arendt, Hannah. *On Revolution*. London: Penguin Books, 1963.

Auslander, Leora. *Taste and Power: Furnishing Modern France*. Berkeley: University of California Press, 1996.

Baecque, Antoine de. *The Body Politic: Corporeal Metaphor in Revolutionary France, 1770–1800*. Stanford, CA: Stanford University Press, 1997.

Bailey, Charles E. 'The British Protestant Theologians in the First World War: Germanophobia Unleashed'. *The Harvard Theological Review* 77, no. 2 (1984): 195–221.

Bailey, Joanne. *Unquiet Lives: Marriage and Marriage Breakdown in England, 1660–1800*. Cambridge: Cambridge University Press, 2003.

Ballhatchet, Kenneth. *Race, Sex and Class under the Raj: Imperial Attitudes and Policies and Their Critics, 1793–1905*. New York: St. Martin's Press, 1980.

Barclay, Paul D. 'Cultural Brokerage and Interethnic Marriage in Colonial Taiwan: Japanese Subalterns and Their Aborigine Wives, 1895–1930'. *Journal of Asian Studies* 64, no. 2 (2005): 323–60.

Barrett, Michele, and Mary McIntosh. 'The "Family Wage": Some Problems for Socialists and Feminists'. *Capital and Class* 11 (1980): 51–72.

Bartov, Omer. *The Eastern Front, 1941–45: German Troops and the Barbarisation of Warfare*. New York: St. Martin's Press, 1986.

Bauman, Zygmunt. *Modernity and the Holocaust.* Ithaca, NY: Cornell University Press, 1989.

Beauvoir, Simone de. 'Must We Burn Sade?' In *The Marquis de Sade: The 120 Days of Sodom and Other Writings,* ed. and trans. Austryn Wainhouse and Richard Seaver, 3–64. New York: Grove, 1966.

Beauvoir, Simone de. *The Second Sex.* New York: Vintage Books, 1989 [1952].

Beck, Birgit. *Wehrmacht und Sexuelle Gewalt: Sexualverbrechen vor Deutschen Militärgerichten 1939–1945.* Paderborn: Ferdinand Schöningh, 2004.

Beevor, Antony. *The Fall of Berlin, 1945.* New York: Viking, 2002.

Bell, John D. *Peasants in Power: Alexander Stamboliiski and the Bulgarian Agrarian National Union, 1899–1923.* Princeton: Princeton University Press, 1977.

Bell, Susan Groag, and Karen Offen, eds. *Women, the Family and Freedom: The Debate in Documents.* Stanford: Stanford University Press, 1983.

Belmessous, Saliha. 'Assimilation and Racialism in Seventeenth- and Eighteenth-Century French Colonial Policy'. *American Historical Review* 110, no. 2 (2005): 322–49.

Bender, Daniel E. '"Too Much of Distasteful Masculinity": Historicizing Sexual Harassment in the Garment Sweatshop and Factory'. *Journal of Women's History* 15, no. 4 (2004): 91–116.

Berend, Ivan T. *History Derailed: Central and Eastern Europe in the Long Nineteenth Century.* Berkeley: University of California Press, 2003.

Berg, Maxine. *The Age of Manufactures: Industry, Innovation, and Work in Britain, 1700–1820.* Oxford: Blackwell, 1985.

Berkhoff, Karel C. *Harvest of Despair: Life and Death in Ukraine under Nazi Rule.* Cambridge, MA: Belknap Press of Harvard University Press, 2004.

Biess, Frank. 'Survivors of Totalitarianism: Returning POWs and the Reconstruction of Masculine Citizenship in West Germany, 1945–1955'. In *The Miracle Years: A Cultural History of West Germany, 1949–1968,* ed. Hanna Schissler, 57–82. Princeton: Princeton University Press, 2000.

Birkenhead, Lord. *Rudyard Kipling.* New York: Random House, 1978.

Bland, Lucy. 'White Women and Men of Colour: Miscegenation Fears in Britain after the Great War'. *Gender & History* 17, no. 1 (2005): 29–61.

Bloch, Ivan Stanislavovich, and R. C. Long. *The Future of War in Its Technical, Economic, and Political Relations: Is War Now Impossible?* Trans. R. C. Long. New York: Garland Publishing, 1899; reprint 1972.

Bochkareva, Maria, and Isaac Don Levine. *Yashka, My Life as Peasant, Officer and Exile.* New York: Frederick A. Stokes, 1919.

Bock, Gisela. 'Racism and Sexism in Nazi Germany: Motherhood, Compulsory Sterilization, and the State'. *Signs* 8, no. 3 (1983): 400–21.

Bock, Gisela. 'Die Frauen und der Nationalsozialismus: Bemerkungen zu einem Buch von Claudia Koonz'. *Geschichte und Gesellschaft* 15, no. 4 (1989): 563–79.

Bosworth, R. J. B. *Mussolini.* New York: Oxford University Press, 2002.

Brake, Wayne Ph. te, Rudolf M. Dekker and Lotte C. van de Pol. 'Women and Political Culture in the Dutch Revolutions'. In *Women and Politics in the Age of the Democratic Revolution,* ed. Harriet B. Applewhite and Darline G. Levy, 109–46. Ann Arbor: University of Michigan Press, 1990.

Brauner, Sigrid. *Fearless Wives and Frightened Shrews: The Construction of the Witch in Early Modern Germany.* Amherst: University of Massachusetts Press, 1995.

Browning, Christopher R. *Ordinary Men: Reserve Police Battalion 101 and the Final Solution in Poland.* 1st ed. New York: HarperCollins, 1992.

Buci-Glucksmann, Christine. 'Catastrophic Utopia: The Feminine as Allegory of the Modern'. *Representations*, no. 14 (1986): 220–29.

Burkhardt, Frederick, ed. *Charles Darwin's Letters: A Selection, 1825–1859*. Cambridge and New York: Cambridge University Press, 1996.

Burrow, J. W. *The Crisis of Reason: European Thought, 1848–1914*. New Haven, CT and London: Yale University Press, 2000.

Butler, Judith. *Gender Trouble: Feminism and the Subversion of Identity*. New York: Routledge, 1990.

Butler, Judith. 'Beauvoir on Sade: Making Sexuality into an Ethic'. In *The Cambridge Companion to Simone de Beauvoir*, ed. Claudia Card, 168–88. Cambridge and New York: Cambridge University Press, 2003.

Callaway, Helen. *Gender, Culture and Empire: European Women in Colonial Nigeria*. Urbana and Chicago: University of Illinois Press, 1987.

Carter, Paul. 'Enclosure, Waged Labour and the Formation of Class Consciousness: Rural Middlesex c. 1700–1835'. *Labour History Review* 66, no. 3 (2001): 269–93.

Chaperon, Sylvie. 'Feminism Is Dead. Long Live Feminism! The Women's Movement in France at the Liberation'. In *When the War Was Over: Women, War and Peace in Europe, 1940–1956*, eds Claire Duchen and Irene Bandhauer-Schöffmann, 146–60. London and New York: Leicester University Press, 2000.

Chastain, John. *Encyclopedia of 1848 Revolutions*. Available from http://www.ohiou.edu/~chastain/index.htm (accessed June 2006).

Chauncey, George. *Gay New York: Gender, Urban Culture, and the Making of the Gay Male World, 1890–1940*. New York: Basic Books, 1994.

Cherry, Deborah. 'Going Places: Women Artists in Central London in the Mid-Nineteenth Century'. *London Journal* 28, no. 1 (2003): 73–96.

Choquette, Leslie. 'Degenerate or Degendered? Images of Prostitution and Homosexuality in the French Third Republic'. *Historical Reflections/Réflexions historiques* 23, no. 2 (1997): 205–28.

Choquette, Leslie. 'Paris-Lesbos: Lesbian Social Space in the Modern City, 1870–1940'. *Proceedings of the Western Society for French History* 26 (1999): 122–32.

Clark, Alice. *The Working Life of Women in the Seventeenth Century*. New ed. London: Routledge, 1992.

Clark, Anna. *The Struggle for the Breeches: Gender and the Making of the British Working Class*. Berkeley: University of California Press, 1995.

Combs, William. 'Fatal Attraction: Duelling and the SS'. *History Today* 47, no. 6 (June 1997): 11–16.

Cook, Hera. *The Long Sexual Revolution: English Women, Sex, and Contraception 1800–1975*. Oxford: Oxford University Press, 2004.

Corbin, Alain. 'Commercial Sexuality in Nineteenth-Century France: A System of Images and Regulations'. In *The Making of the Modern Body: Sexuality and Society in the Nineteenth Century*, eds Catherine Gallagher and Thomas Laqueur, 209–19. Berkeley and Los Angeles: University of California Press, 1987.

Corbin, Alain. *Women for Hire: Prostitution and Sexuality in France after 1850*. Cambridge, MA: Harvard University Press, 1990.

Costlow, Jane. 'Compassion and the Hero: Women in a Hero of Our Time'. In *Lermontov's A Hero of Our Time: A Critical Companion*, ed. Lewis Bagby, 85–108. Evanston, IL: Northwestern University Press, 2002.

'Criminal Responsibility for Homosexual Activities Likely to Be Introduced in Russia'. *Pravda* 5 October 2004, available from http://english.pravda.ru/society/stories/7158-

homosexual-0 (accessed February 2006).

'Criminalisation of HIV Transmission in Europe'. Global Network of People Living with HIV/AIDS. Available from http://www.gnpplus.net/criminalisation/list.shtml (accessed 7 December 2005).

Dahlkamp, Jürgen. 'No Country More Beautiful'. In *Spiegel Online*, 14 July 2003, available from http://service.spiegel.de/cache/international/spiegel/0,1518,257041,00.html (accessed December 2005).

Darwin, Charles. *The Descent of Man and Selection in Relation to Sex*. New York: D. Appleton, 1902.

Darwin, Charles. *The Origin of Species by Means of Natural Selection or the Preservation of Favoured Races in the Struggle for Life*. New York: Penguin, 1958.

Daskalova, Krasimira. 'Bulgarian Women in Movements, Laws, Discourses (1840s–1940s)'. *Bulgarian Historical Review* 27, no. 1 (1999): 180–96.

Daston, Lorraine and Katherine Park. 'The Hermaphrodite and the Orders of Nature: Sexual Ambiguity in Early Modern France'. *GLQ: A Journal of Gay & Lesbian Studies* 1, no. 4 (1995): 419–38.

Davidoff, Leonore. 'Class and Gender in Victorian England: The Diaries of Arthur J. Munby and Hannah Cullwick'. *Feminist Studies* 5, no. 1 (1979): 86–141.

Davidoff, Leonore, and Catherine Hall. *Family Fortunes: Men and Women of the English Middle Class, 1780–1850*. Chicago: University of Chicago Press, 1987.

Davidson, Roger, and Lesley A. Hall, eds. *Sex, Sin and Suffering: Venereal Disease and European Society since 1870*. New York: Routledge, 2001.

Davies, Norman. *Europe: A History*. Oxford and New York: Oxford University Press, 1996.

Davis, Belinda. *Home Fires Burning: Food, Politics, and Everyday Life in World War I Berlin*. Chapel Hill, N.C.: University of North Carolina Press, 2000.

Deak, Istvan. 'Latter-Day Knights: Officers' Honor and Duelling in the Austro-Hungarian Army'. *Oesterreichische Ostheft* 28, no. 3 (1986): 311–27.

De Almeida, Miguel Vale. *The Hegemonic Male: Masculinity in a Portugese Town*. Providence and Oxford: Berghahn Books, 1996.

Dean, Carolyn J. 'Lesbian Sexuality in Interwar France'. In *Connecting Spheres: European Women in a Globalizing World, 1500 to the Present*, eds Marilyn J. Boxer and Jean H. Quataert. New York and Oxford: Oxford University Press, 2000.

Dean, Carolyn J. *The Frail Social Body: Pornography, Homosexuality, and Other Fantasies in Interwar France*. Berkeley: University of California Press, 2000.

'Declaration of the Rights of Man – 1789'. The Avalon Project at Yale Law School. Available from http://www.yale.edu/lawweb/avalon/rightsof.htm (accessed June 2006).

Dixon, Joy. *Gender, Politics, and Culture in Modern Europe*. Vancouver: Access Guided Independent Study, University of British Columbia, [n.d.].

Doan, Laura. 'Passing Fashions: Reading Female Masculinities in the 1920s'. *Feminist Studies* 24, no. 3 (1998): 663–700.

Domansky, Elisabeth. 'Militarization and Reproduction in World War I Germany'. In *Society, Culture, and the State in Germany, 1870–1930*, ed. Geoff Eley, 427–63. Ann Arbor: University of Michigan Press, 1996.

Dreger, Alice Domurat. *Hermaphrodites and the Medical Invention of Sex*. Cambridge, MA: Harvard University Press, 1998.

Duberman, Martin, Martha Vicinus and George Chauncey Jr., eds. *Hidden from History: Reclaiming the Gay and Lesbian Past*. New York: Meridian, 1989.

Duberman, Martin Bauml. 'Reclaiming the Gay Past'. *Reviews in American History* 16, no. 4 (1988): 515–25.

Duchen, Claire. 'Crime and Punishment in Liberated France: The Case of les femmes tondues'. In *When the War Was Over: Women, War and Peace in Europe, 1940–1956*, eds Claire Duchen and Irene Bandhauer-Schöffmann, 233–50. London and New York: Leicester University Press, 2000.

Edwards, Penny. 'Womanizing Indochina: Fiction, Nation and Cohabitation in Cambodia, 1890–1930'. In *Domesticating the Empire: Race, Gender and Family Life in French and Dutch Colonialism*, eds Julia Ann Clancy-Smith and Frances Gouda, 108–30. Charlottesville, NC and London: University Press of Virginia, 1998.

Eley, Geoff. *Forging Democracy: The History of the Left in Europe, 1850–2000*. New York: Oxford University Press, 2002.

Ellis, John, and Michael Cox. *The World War I Databook: The Essential Facts and Figures for All the Combatants*. London: Aurum, 2001.

Elshtain, Jean Bethke. *Women and War*. New York: Basic Books, 1987.

Embacher, Helga. 'Unwelcome in Austria: Returnees and Concentration Camp Survivors'. In *When the War Was Over: Women, War and Peace in Europe, 1940–1956*, eds Claire Duchen and Irene Bandhauer-Schöffmann, 194–206. London and New York: Leicester University Press, 2000.

Erickson, Amy Louise. *Women and Property in Early Modern England*. London and New York: Routledge, 1993.

Erskine, Fiona. '*The Origin of Species* and the Science of Female Inferiority'. In *Charles Darwin's The Origin of Species: New Interdisciplinary Essays*, eds David Amigoni and Jeff Wallace, 95–121. Manchester and New York: Manchester University Press, 1995.

Esterson, Allen. 'Jeffrey Masson and Freud's Seduction Theory: A New Fable Based on Old Myths'. *History of the Human Sciences* 11, no. 1 (1998): 1–21.

Evans, Richard J. 'Prostitution, State, and Society in Imperial Germany'. *Past and Present* 70 (1976): 106–209.

Evans, Richard J. 'The Concept of Feminism'. In *German Women in the Eighteenth and Nineteenth Centuries*, eds Ruth-Ellen B. Joeres and Mary Jo Maynes, 247–58. Bloomington, IN: Indiana University Press, 1986.

Evans, Richard J. ed. *Comrades & Sisters: Feminism, Socialism & Pacifism in Europe,1870–1945*. New York: St. Martin's Press, 1987.

Faderman, Lillian. *Surpassing the Love of Men: Romantic Friendship and Love between Women from the Renaissance to the Present*. New York: William Morrow and Company, Inc., 1981.

Fischer, Klaus P. *Nazi Germany: A New History*. New York: Continuum, 1995.

Fitzpatrick, Sheila. *The Cultural Front: Power and Culture in Revolutionary Russia*. Ithaca, NY: Cornell University Press, 1992.

Foner, Philip, ed. *Clara Zetkin: Selected Writings*. New York: International Publishers, 1984.

Forrest, Alan. 'Conscription as Ideology: Revolutionary France and the Nation in Arms', *The Comparative Study of Conscription in the Armed Forces* 20 (2002): 95–115.

Foucault, Michel. *History of Sexuality*. Vol. 1: *An Introduction*. Reissue ed. New York: Vintage Books, 1990.

Foucault, Michel. *Abnormal: Lectures at the College de France, 1974–1975*, eds Valerio Marchetti and Antonella Salomoni, trans. Graham Burchell. New York: Picador, 2004.

Frader, Laura. 'Doing Capitalism's Work: Women in the Western European Industrial Economy'. In *Becoming Visible: Women in European History*, eds Renate Bridenthal, Susan Mosher Stuard and Merry E. Wiesner, 295–325. Boston and New York: Houghton Mifflin Co., 1998.

Frader, Laura. 'Labor History after the Gender Turn: Transatlantic Cross Currents and Research Agendas'. *International Labor and Working Class History* 63 (2003): 21–31.

Fraisse, Geneviève. *Reason's Muse: Sexual Difference and the Birth of Democracy*. Chicago and London: University of Chicago Press, 1994.

Frantzen, Allen J. *Bloody Good: Chivalry, Sacrifice, and the Great War*. Chicago: University of Chicago Press, 2004.

Freud, Sigmund. 'Fetishism'. In *Standard Edition of the Complete Psychological Works of Sigmund Freud*. Vol. 21. Ed. James Strachey, 152–57. London: Hogarth Press, 1953.

Freud, Sigmund. 'Three Essays on the Theory of Sexuality'. In *Standard Edition of the Complete Psychological Works of Sigmund Freud*. Vol. 7. Ed. James Strachey, 135–243. London: Hogarth Press, 1953.

Freud, Sigmund. *Civilization and Its Discontents*. Trans. James Strachey. New York: Norton, 2005.

Frevert, Ute. *Men of Honour: A Social and Cultural History of the Duel*. Cambridge: Polity Press, 1995.

Friedman, Rebecca. *Masculinity, Autocracy and the Russian University, 1804–1863*. Basingstoke and New York: Palgrave Macmillan, 2005.

Friedrich, Otto. *Before the Deluge: A Portrait of Berlin in the 1920s*. New York: HarperPerennial, 1995 [1963].

Friedrichs, Christopher R. 'The City: The Early Modern Period'. In *Encyclopedia of European Social History from 1350–2000*, vol. 2, ed. Peter N. Stearns, 249–62. New York: Charles Scribner's Sons, 2001.

Fryman, Jonas, and Orvar Löfgren. *Culture Builders: A Historical Anthropology of Middle-Class Life*. New Brunswick: Rutgers University Press, 1987.

Fussell, Paul. *The Great War and Modern Memory*. New York: Oxford University Press, 1975.

Galton, Francis. *Inquiries into Human Faculty and its Development*. Kila, MO: Kessinger Publishing, 2004 [1883].

Gandhi, Mohandas, and Anthony Parel. *Hind Swaraj and Other Writings*. Cambridge and New York: Cambridge University Press, 1997.

Gatrell, Peter. *A Whole Empire Walking: Refugees in Russia During World War I*. Bloomington, IN: Indiana University Press, 1999.

Gay, Peter. 'Mensur – the Cherished Scar'. In *The Bourgeois Experience, Victoria to Freud*, III: *The Cultivation of Hatred*, 9–33. New York and London: W.W. Norton & Company, 1993.

Gibbon, Edward. *The History of the Decline and Fall of the Roman Empire*. London and New York: Penguin, 1994.

Gibson, Mary. *Prostitution and the State in Italy, 1860–1915*. 2nd ed. Columbus, Ohio: Ohio State University Press, 2000.

Gilbert, Sandra M. 'Soldier's Heart: Literary Men, Literary Women, and the Great War', In *Behind the Lines: Gender and the Two World Wars*, eds Margaret Randolph Higonnet *et al.*, 197–226. New Haven, CT and London: Yale University Press, 1987.

Gilfoyle, Timothy J. 'Prostitutes in History: From Parables of Pornography to Metaphors of Modernity'. *American Historical Review* 104, no. 1 (1999): 117–41.

Gillis, John R. *For Better, for Worse: British Marriages, 1600 to the Present*. New York: Oxford University Press, 1985.

Gilman, Sander L. *Difference and Pathology: Stereotypes of Sexuality, Race and Madness*. Ithaca, NY: Cornell University Press, 1985.

Glenny, Misha. *The Balkans: Nationalism, War and the Great Powers, 1804–1999*. New York: Penguin Books, 1999.

Gobineau, Joseph-Arthur de. *Gobineau: Selected Political Writings*. Ed. Michael D. Biddiss. New York and Evanston: Harper and Row, 1970.

Godineau, Dominique. *The Women of Paris and Their French Revolution*. Berkeley and Los Angeles: University of California Press, 1998.

Goldman, Wendy Z. *Women, the State, and Revolution: Soviet Family Policy and Social Life, 1917–1936*. Cambridge: Cambridge University Press, 1993.

Goldstein, Jan. 'Foucault among the Sociologists: The "Disciplines" and the History of the Professions'. *History and Theory* 23, no. 2 (1984): 170–92.

Goldstein, Joshua S. *War and Gender: How Gender Shapes the War System and Vice Versa*. Cambridge: Cambridge University Press, 2001.

Goode, William Joshiah. *The Family*. Englewood Cliffs, NJ: Prentice Hall, 1964.

Goodman, Dena. *The Republic of Letters: A Cultural History of the French Enlightenment*. Ithaca, NY and London: Cornell University Press, 1994.

Gordon, Daniel. *Citizens without Sovereignty: Equality and Sociability in French Thought, 1670–1789*. Princeton: Princeton University Press, 1994.

Gordon, Daniel, David A. Bell and Sarah Maza. 'Forum: The Public Sphere in the Eighteenth Century'. *French Historical Studies* 17, no. 4 (1992): 882–956.

Gorsuch, Anne E. '"A Woman Is Not a Man": The Culture of Gender and Generation in Soviet Russia, 1921–1928'. *Slavic Review* 55, no. 3 (1996): 636–60.

Gould, Jenny. 'Women's Military Services in First World War Britain'. In *Behind the Lines: Gender and the Two World Wars*, eds Margaret Randolph Higonnet *et al.*, 114–25. New Haven, CT and London: Yale University Press, 1987.

Grayzel, Susan R. *Women's Identities at War: Gender, Motherhood, and Politics in Britain and France During the First World War*. Chapel Hill, NC: University of North Carolina Press, 1999.

Grazia, Victoria de. *How Fascism Ruled Women: Italy, 1922–1945*. Berkeley and Oxford: University of California Press, 1992.

Groot, Gerjan de, and Marlou Schrover. 'Between Men and Machines: Women Workers in New Industries, 1870–1940'. *Social History* 20, no. 3 (1995): 279–96.

Gross, Jan Tomasz. *Neighbors: The Destruction of the Jewish Community in Jedwabne, Poland*. Princeton: Princeton University Press, 2001.

Grossmann, Atina. 'Girlkultur or Thoroughly Rationalized Female: A New Woman in Weimar Germany?' In *Women in Culture and Politics: A Century of Change*, eds Judith Friedländer, Blanche Cook, Alice Kessler-Harris and Carroll Smith-Rosenberg, 62–80. Bloomington: Indiana University Press, 1986.

Grossmann, Atina. *Reforming Sex: The German Movement for Birth Control and Abortion Reform, 1920–1950*. Oxford: Oxford University Press, 1995.

Grossmann, Atina. 'A Question of Silence: The Rape of German Women by Occupation Soldiers'. In *West Germany under Construction: Politics, Society, & Culture in the Adenauer Era*, ed. Robert G. Moeller, 33–52. Ann Arbor: University of Michigan Press, 1997.

Guinnane, Timothy. 'Coming of Age in Rural Ireland at the Turn of the Twentieth Century'. *Continuity and Change* 5, no. 3 (1990): 443–72.

Habermas, Jürgen. *The Structural Transformation of the Public Sphere: An Inquiry into a Category of Bourgeois Society*. Cambridge, MA: MIT Press, 1991 [1989].

Hagemann, Karen. 'Female Patriots: Women, War and the Nation in the Period of the Prussian-German Anti-Napoleonic Wars'. *Gender & History* 16, no. 2 (2004): 397–425.

Hall, Catherine. 'The Early Formation of Victorian Domestic Ideology'. In *Gender and History in Western Europe*, eds Robert Shoemaker and Mary Vincent, 181–96. New York and London: Arnold, 1998.

Hall, Catherine. 'Of Gender and Empire: Reflections on the Nineteenth Century'. In *Gender and Empire*, ed. Philippa Levine, 46–76. Oxford and New York: Oxford University Press, 2004.

Halperin, David M. 'Is There a History of Sexuality?' *History and Theory* 28, no. 3 (1989): 257–74.

Halsall, Paul. Ancient History Sourcebook: Aristotle: On a Good Wife, from Oikonomikos, c. 330 BCE. Available from http://www.fordham.edu/halsall/ancient/greek-wives.html (accessed June 2006).

Hamers, Francoise F., and Angela M. Downs. 'HIV in Central and Eastern Europe'. *Lancet* 361 (2003): 1,035–44.

Harper, Marjory. 'British Migration and the Peopling of the Empire'. In *The Oxford History of the British Empire*, vol. 3: *The Nineteenth Century*, ed. Andrew Porter, 75–87. Oxford and New York: Oxford University Press, 1999.

Harsch, Donna. *Revenge of the Domestic: Women, the Family, and Communism in the German Democratic Republic*. Princeton, NJ: Princeton University Press, 2007.

Harsin, Jill. *Policing Prostitution in Nineteenth Century Paris*. Princeton: Princeton University Press, 1985.

Harvey, A. D. 'Homosexuality and the British Army During the First World War'. *Journal for the Society of Army Historical Research* 79 (2001): 313–19.

Hause, Stephen, and Anne R. Kenney. *Women's Suffrage and Social Politics in the French Third Republic*. Princeton: Princeton University Press, 1984.

Hause, Stephen C. and Anne R. Kenney. 'The Limits of Suffragist Behavior: Legalism and Militancy in France, 1876–1922'. *American Historical Review* 86, no. 4 (1981): 781–806.

Hausen, Karin. 'Patriarchat: vom Nutzen und Nachteil eines Konzepts für Frauengeschichte und Frauenpolitik'. *Journal für Geschichte* 5 (1986): 12–58.

Healy, Maureen. *Vienna and the Fall of the Habsburg Empire: Total War and Everyday Life in World War I*. Cambridge and New York: Cambridge University Press, 2004.

Heineman, Elizabeth D. *What Difference Does a Husband Make? Women and Maritial Status in Nazi and Postwar Germany*. Berkeley: University of California, 1999.

Herzog, Dagmar. '"Pleasure, Sex and Politics Belong Together": Post-Holocaust Memory and the Sexual Revolution in West Germany'. *Critical Inquiry* 24, no. 2 (1998): 393–444.

Herzog, Dagmar. *Sex after Fascism: Memory and Morality in Twentieth-Century Germany*. Princeton: Princeton University Press, 2005.

Heuer, Jennifer Ngaire. *The Family and the Nation: Gender and Citizenship in Revolutionary France, 1789–1830*. Ithaca, NY and London: Cornell University Press, 2005.

Higonnet, Margaret R., Jane Jenson, Sonya Michel, Margaret Collins Weitz, eds. *Behind the Lines: Gender and the Two World Wars*. New Haven, CT and London: Yale University Press, 1987.

Hobsbawm, E. J. *The Age of Capital 1848–1875*. New York: Charles Scribner's Sons, 1975.

Hocquenghem, Guy. *Homosexual Desire*. Trans. Daniella Dangoor. Durham, NC and London: Duke University Press, 1993.

Hofer, Hans-Georg. 'Wenn Männer altern. Ein Projekt zur Geschichte der "männlichen Wechseljahre"'. *L'Homme. Europäische Zeitschrift für Feministische Geschichtswissenschaft* 17, no. 1 (2006): 101–8.

Hoffmann, David. 'Mothers in the Motherland: Stalinist Pronatalism in Its Pan-European Context'. *Journal of Social History* 34, no. 1 (2000): 35–54.

Hoffmann, David L., and Annette F. Timm. 'Utopian Biopolitics: Reproductive Policies, Gender Roles, and Sexuality in Nazi Germany and the Soviet Union'. In *After*

Totalitarianism: Stalinism and Nazism Compared [Provisional Title], eds Sheila Fitzpatrick, Michael Geyer and Terry Martin (forthcoming).

Holland, Kenneth. 'The European Labor Service'. *Annals of the American Academy of Political and Social Science* 194 (1937): 152–64.

Honeycutt, Karen. 'Clara Zetkin: A Socialist Approach to the Problem of Women's Oppression'. *Signs* 3, no. 3/4 (1976): 131–44.

Hopkin, David M. 'Sons and Lovers: Popular Images of the Conscript, 1798–1870'. *Modern & Contemporary France* 9, no. 1 (2001): 19–36.

Horn, David G. *Social Bodies: Science, Reproduction and Italian Modernity*. Princeton: Princeton University Press, 1994.

Horne, John N., and Alan Kramer. *German Atrocities, 1914: A History of Denial*. New Haven, CT: Yale University Press, 2001.

Hufton, Olwen. *The Poor of Eighteenth-Century France, 1750–1789*. Oxford: Clarendon Press, 1974.

Hufton, Olwen. *Women and the Limits of Citizenship in the French Revolution*. Toronto: University of Toronto Press, 1992.

Hull, Isabel V. *Absolute Destruction: Military Culture and the Practices of War in Imperial Germany*. Ithaca, NY: Cornell University Press, 2005.

Hülsberg, Werner. *The German Greens: A Social and Political Profile*. London and New York: Verso, 1988.

Hunt, Lynn. *The Family Romance of the French Revolution*. Berkeley and Los Angeles: University of California Press, 1992.

Hunt, Lynn. 'Foucault's Subject in the History of Sexuality'. In *Discourses of Sexuality*, ed. Domna C. Stanton, 78–93. Ann Arbor: University of Michigan Press, 1992.

Hunt, Margaret. *The Middling Sort: Commerce, Gender, and the Family in England, 1680–1780*. Berkeley and Los Angeles: University of California Press, 1996.

Hunt, Nancy Rose. 'Le bébé en brousse: European Women, African Birth Spacing, and Colonial Intervention in Breast Feeding in the Belgian Congo'. In *Tensions of Empire: Colonial Cultures in a Bourgeois World*, eds Frederick Cooper and Ann Laura Stoler, 287–321. Berkeley: University of California Press, 1997.

Huss, Marie-Monique. 'Pronatalism in the Inter-War Period in France'. *Journal of Contemporary History* 25, no. 1 (1990): 39–68.

Huston, Nancy. 'Erotic Literature in Postwar France'. *Raritan* 12, no. 1 (1992): 29–46.

Hutton, Marcelline J. *Russian and West European Women, 1860–1939: Dreams, Struggles and Nightmares*. Lanham, MD: Rowman & Littlefield Publishers, 2001.

Hyam, Ronald. *Empire and Sexuality: The British Experience*. Manchester and New York: Manchester University Press, 1990.

Ipsen, Carl. *Dictating Demography: The Problem of Population in Fascist Italy*. Cambridge and New York: Cambridge University Press, 1996.

James, William. 'The Moral Equivalent of War'. In *The Moral Equivalent of War and Other Essays*, ed. John K. Roth. New York: Harper and Row, 1971.

Jarausch, Konrad H. 'Students, Sex and Politics in Imperial Germany'. *Journal of Contemporary History* 17 (1982): 285–303.

Jasanoff, Maya. *Edge of Empire: Lives, Culture and Conquest in the East, 1750–1850*. New York: Alfred A. Knopf, 2005.

Jolluck, Katherine R. *Exile and Identity: Polish Women in the Soviet Union During World War II*. Pittsburgh, PA: University of Pittsburgh Press, 2002.

Jordanova, Ludmilla. *Sexual Visions: Images of Gender in Science and Medicine between the Eighteenth and Twentieth Centuries*. Madison, WI: University of Wisconsin Press, 1989.

Jorgensen-Earp, Cheryl R., ed. *Speeches and Trials of the Militant Suffragettes: The Women's Social and Political Union, 1903–18.* Cranbury, NJ: Associated University Presses, 1999.

Kater, Michael H. *Hitler Youth.* Cambridge, MA and London: Harvard University Press, 2004.

Kates, Gary. *The Cercle Social, the Girondins, and the French Revolution.* Princeton: Princeton University Press, 1985.

Kelly, James. *'That Damn'd Thing Called Honour': Duelling in Ireland, 1570–1860.* Cork: Cork University Press, 1995.

Kent, Susan Kingsley. *Sex and Suffrage in Great Britain.* Princeton: Princeton University Press, 1987.

Kent, Susan Kingsley. *Making Peace: The Reconstruction of Gender in Interwar Britain.* Princeton: Princeton University Press, 1993.

Kerber, Linda. *Women of the Republic: Intellect and Ideology in Revolutionary America.* Chapel Hill, NC: University of North Carolina Press, 1980.

Kestnbaum, Meyer. 'Citizenship and Compulsory Military Service: The Revolutionary Origins of Conscription in the United States'. *Armed Forces and Society* 27, no. 1 (2000): 7–36.

Kevles, Daniel J. *In the Name of Eugenics: Genetics and the Uses of Human Heredity.* New York: Knopf, 1985.

Kipling, Rudyard. *Rudyard Kipling's Verse: Definitive Edition.* Garden City, NY: Doubleday and Co., 1946.

Kocka, Jürgen. 'Problems of Working-Class Formation in Germany: The Early Years, 1800–1875'. In *Working Class Formation*, eds Ira Katznelson and Aristide R. Zolberg, 279–351. Princeton: Princeton University Press, 1986.

Komlos, John. 'Stature and Nutrition in the Habsburg Monarchy: The Standard of Living and Economic Development in the Eighteenth Century'. *American Historical Review* 90, no. 5 (1985): 1,149–61.

Koonz, Claudia. *Mothers in the Fatherland: Women, the Family, and Nazi Politics.* New York: St. Martin's Press, 1987.

Krafft-Ebing, Richard von. *Psychopathia Sexualis, with Especial Reference to the Antipathic Sexual Instinct.* London: Staples Press, 1965.

Kruntorad, Paul. 'Krafft-Ebing'. In *Psychopathia Sexualis*, Richard von Krafft-Ebing, 7–13. Munich: Matthes und Seitz Verlag, 1997.

Kuper, Adam. 'Incest, Cousin Marriage, and the Origin of the Human Sciences in Nineteenth-Century England'. *Past & Present* 174 (2002): 159–83.

Landes, David S. *Unbound Prometheus: Technological Change and Industrial Development in Western Europe from 1750 to the Present.* 2nd ed. Cambridge: Cambridge University Press, 1969.

Landes, Joan B. *Women in the Public Sphere in the Age of the French Revolution.* Ithaca, NY and London: Cornell University Press, 1988.

Landes, Joan B. *Visualizing the Nation: Gender, Representation, and Revolution in Eighteenth-Century France.* Ithaca, NY: Cornell University Press, 2001.

Laqueur, Thomas. 'Orgasm, Generation, and the Politics of Reproductive Biology'. *Representations*, no. 14 (1986): 24–27.

Laqueur, Thomas. *Making Sex: Body and Gender from the Greeks to Freud.* Cambridge, MA and London: Harvard University Press, 1990.

Laqueur, Thomas W. 'Sex in the Flesh'. *Isis* 94, no. 2 (2003): 300–330.

Larkin, Philip. *Annus Mirabilis.* Available from http://www.poetryconnection.net/poets/Philip_Larkin/4761 (accessed 26 May 2006).

Layton, Susan. *Russian Literature and Empire: Conquest of the Caucasus from Pushkin to Tolstoy*. Cambridge and New York: Cambridge University Press, 1994.

Lee, Robert. 'Demography, Urbanization, and Migration'. In *A Companion to Nineteenth-Century Europe, 1789–1914*, ed. Stefan Berger, 56–69. Malden, Mass., and Oxford: Blackwell Publishing, 2006.

Leeuwen, Marco H. D., and Ineke Maas. 'Partner Choice and Homogamy in the Nineteenth Century: Was There a Sexual Revolution in Europe?' *Journal of Social History* 36, no. 1 (2002): 101–26.

Lefebvre, Georges. *The French Revolution: From Its Origins to 1793*. Trans. Elizabeth Moss Evanson. New York: Columbia University Press, 1962.

Lefebvre, Georges. *The Great Fear of 1789: Rural Panic in Revolutionary France*. Trans. Joan White. New York: Schocken Books, 1973.

Lemire, Beverly. *The Business of Everyday Life: Gender, Practice and Social Politics in England, c. 1600–1900*. Manchester: Manchester University Press, 2006.

Lentin, Ronit. '"A Howl Unheard": Women Shoah Survivors Dis-Placed and Re-Silenced'. In *When the War Was Over: Women, War and Peace in Europe, 1940–1956*, eds Claire Duchen and Irene Bandhauer-Schöffmann, 179–93. London and New York: Leicester University Press, 2000.

Lermontov, Mikhail. *A Hero of Our Time*. Trans. Vladimir Nabokov. Ann Arbor: Ardis, 1988.

Levine, David. 'The Population of Europe: Early Modern Demographic Patterns'. In *Encyclopedia of European Social History from 1350–2000*, vol. 2, ed. Peter N. Stearns, 159–70. New York: Charles Scribner's Sons, 2001.

Levine, Philippa. 'Sexuality, Gender and Empire'. In *Gender and Empire*, ed. Philippa Levine, 134–55. Oxford and New York: Oxford University Press, 2004.

Levkov, Ilya. *Bitburg and Beyond: Encounters in American, German, and Jewish History*. New York: Shapolsky Publishers, 1987.

Levy, Darline Gay, and Harriet B. Applewhite. 'A Political Revolution for Women? The Case of Paris'. In *Becoming Visible: Women in European History*, 3rd ed., eds Renate Bridenthal, Susan Mosher Stuard and Merry E. Wiesner, 265–92. Boston and New York: Houghton Mifflin Co., 1998.

Levy, Darline Gay, Harriet Branson Applewhite and Mary Durham Johnson, eds. *Women in Revolutionary Paris, 1789–1795: Selected Documents*. Urbana, IL: University of Illinois Press, 1979.

Lewis, Jane. 'The Working-Class Wife and Mother and State Intervention 1870–1940'. In *Labour and Love: Women's Experience of Home and Family 1850–1940*, ed. Jane Lewis, 99–122. London and New York: Basil Blackwell, 1986.

Lieven, D. C. B. *Russia and the Origins of the First World War*. New York: St. Martin's Press, 1983.

Liu, Tessie P. 'What Price a Weaver's Dignity? Gender Inequality and the Survival of Home-Based Production in Industrial France'. In *Gender and Class in Modern Europe*, eds Laura L. Frader and Sonya O. Rose, 57–76. Ithaca, NY and London: Cornell University Press, 1996.

Lucas, Colin. 'The Theory and Practice of Denunciation in the French Revolution'. *The Journal of Modern History* 68, no. 4 (1996): 768–85.

Lukas, Richard C. *Did the Children Cry?: Hitler's War against Jewish and Polish Children, 1939–1945*. New York: Hippocrene Books, 1994.

Lutz, Rolland Ray. 'The Burschenschaft: Reformist Movement or Conformist Movement?' *Consortium on Revolutionary Europe 1750–1850* 19, part 1 (1989): 357–77.

McAleer, Kevin. *Dueling: The Cult of Honor in Fin-De-Siècle Germany*. Princeton:

Princeton University Press, 1997.

McCormick, Richard W. 'From Caligari to Dietrich: Sexual, Social, and Cinematic Discourses in Weimar Film'. *Signs* 18, no. 3 (1993): 640–68.

McLaren, Angus. *Twentieth-Century Sexuality: A History*. Oxford: Blackwell Publishers, 1999.

Madariaga, Isabel de. *Russia in the Age of Catherine the Great*. New Haven, CT and London: Yale University Press, 1981.

Mahood, Linda. *The Magdalenes. Prostitution in the Nineteenth Century*. New York: Routledge, 1990.

Makdisi, Saree. *Romantic Imperialism: Universal Empire and the Culture of Modernity*. Cambridge: Cambridge University Press, 1998.

Mani, Lati. *Contentious Traditions: The Debate on Sati in Colonial India*. Berkeley: University of California Press, 1998.

Mann, Michael. *Fascists*. Cambridge and New York: Cambridge University Press, 2004.

Mann, Thomas. 'Freud and the Future'. In *Essays of Three Decades*, 411–28. New York: Alfred A. Knopf, 1947.

Marcuse, Herbert. *One Dimensional Man: Studies in the Ideology of Advanced Industrial Society*. London: Routledge and Kegan Paul Ltd., 1964.

Marcuse, Herbert. 'The New German Mentality'. In *Technology, War and Fascism. Collected Papers of Herbert Marcuse*, vol. 1, ed. Douglas Kellner, 139–90. New York: Routledge, 1998.

Marrese, Michelle Lamarche. *A Woman's Kingdom: Noblewomen and the Control of Property in Russia, 1700–1861*. Ithaca, NY: Cornell University Press, 2002.

Martin, Terry. 'Modernization or Neo-Traditionalism? Ascribed Nationality and Soviet Primordialism'. In *Stalinism: New Directions*, ed. Sheila Fitzpatrick, 348–67. London and New York: Routledge, 2000.

Marwick, Arthur. *The Sixties: Cultural Revolution in Britain, France, Italy and the United States*. Oxford and New York: Oxford University Press, 1998.

Marx, Karl. *Selected Writings in Sociology and Social Philosophy*. Trans. T. B. Bottomore. London: McGraw-Hill, 1964.

Marx, Karl. *Capital: A Critique of Political Economy*. Vol. 1. Trans. Ben Fowkes. Harmondsworth: Penguin Books, 1976.

Marx, Karl, and Friedrich Engels. *Manifesto of the Communist Party*. 2nd revised ed. Moscow: Progress Publishers, 1977.

Mascuch, Michael. 'Continuity and Change in a Patronage Society: The Social Mobility of British Autobiographers, 1600–1750'. *Journal of Historical Sociology* 7, no. 2 (1994): 177–97.

Mayer, Arno J. *The Furies: Violence and Terror in the French and Russian Revolutions*. Princeton: Princeton University Press, 2000.

Menand, Louis. 'Stand by Your Man: The Strange Liaison of Sartre and Beauvoir'. *New Yorker* 26 September 2005.

Meyer, Alfred G. *The Feminism and Socialism of Lily Braun*. Bloomington, IN: Indiana University Press, 1985.

Midgley, Clare. 'Anti-Slavery and the Roots of "Imperial Feminism"'. In *Gender and Imperialism*, ed. Clare Midgley, 161–77. Manchester and New York: Manchester University Press, 1998.

Mill, John Stuart. *Mill: Texts, Commentaries*. Ed. Alan Ryan. New York: W. W. Norton, 1997.

Miller, Pavla. *Transformations of Patriarchy in the West, 1500–1900*. Bloomington, IN: Indiana University Press, 1998.

Millet, Kate. *Sexual Politics*. New York: Ballantine Books, 1969.

Mitchell, Claudine. 'Madeleine Pelletier (1874–1939): The Politics of Sexual Oppression'. In *European Women's History Reader*, eds Fiona Montgomery and Christine Collette, 256–71. New York: Routledge, 2002.

Möding, Nori. '"Ich muß irgendwo engagiert sein – fragen Sie mich bloß nicht, warum." Überlegungen zu Sozialisationserfahrungen von Mädchen in NS- Organisationen'. In *'Wir kriegen jetzt andere Zeiten': Auf der Suche nach der Erfahrung des Volkes in nachfaschistischen Ländern*, eds Lutz Niethammer and Alexander von Plato, 256–304. Bonn: J. H. W. Dietz Nachf., 1985.

Montaigne, Michel de. *Essays*. Trans. J. M. Cohen. New York and London: Penguin, 1958.

Montefiore, Simon Sebag. *Prince of Princes: The Life of Potemkin*. London and New York: St. Martin's Press, 2000.

Moore, James and Adrian Desmond. *Darwin*. London: Michael Joseph, 1991.

Moring, Beatrice. 'Marriage and Social Change in Southwestern Finland, 1700–1870'. *Continuity and Change* 11, no. 1 (1996): 91–113.

Mort, Frank. *Dangerous Sexualities: Medico-Moral Politics in England since 1830*. London and New York: Routledge and Kegan Paul, 1987.

'Moscow Hosts Key AIDS Conference'. *BBC News* 15 May 2006. Available from http://news.bbc.co.uk/2/hi/europe/4771409.stm (accessed 26 May 2006).

Moses, Claire. 'Saint Simonian Men / Saint Simonian Women: The Transformation of Feminist Thought in 1830s' France'. *Journal of Modern History* 54, no. 2 (1982): 240–67.

Mosse, George. 'Masculinity and Decadence'. In *Sexual Knowledge: Sexual Science: The History of Attitudes to Sexuality*, eds Roy Porter and Mikulas Teich, 251–66. Cambridge and New York: Cambridge University Press, 1994.

Mosse, George L. *Toward the Final Solution: A History of European Racism*. New York: Howard Fertig, 1978.

Munford, Clarence J. 'Conscription and the Peasants of the Morvan District of Chateau-Chinon, 1792–1794'. *Canadian Journal of History/Annales candiennes d'histoire* 4, no. 2 (1969): 1–18.

Naimark, Norman. *The Russians in Germany: A History of the Soviet Zone of Occupation, 1945–1949*. Cambridge, MA and London: Belknap Press of Harvard University Press, 1995.

Nash, Mary. 'Social Eugenics and Nationalist Race Hygiene in Early Twentieth-Century Spain'. *History of European Ideas* 15, no. 4/6 (1992): 741–48.

Nash, Mary. 'Un/Contested Identities: Motherhood, Sex Reform and the Modernization of Gender Identity in Early Twentieth-Century Spain'. In *Constructing Spanish Womanhood: Female Identity in Modern Spain*, eds Victoria Lorée Enders and Pamela Beth Radcliff, 25–49. Albany, NY: State University of New York Press, 1999.

Nash, Stanley D. 'Marriage'. In *Britain in the Hanoverian Age, 1714–1837: An Encyclopedia*, ed. Gerald Newman, 439–40. New York and London: Garland, 1997.

Netting, Robert McC. *Smallholders, Householders: Farm Families and the Ecology of Intensive, Sustainable Agriculture*. Stanford: Stanford University Press, 1993.

Noakes, Jeremy, and Geoffrey Pridham. *Nazism, 1919–1945: A Documentary History*. Exeter: University of Exeter Press, 1997.

Nye, Robert A. 'Fencing, the Duel and Republican Manhood in the Third Republic'. *Journal of Contemporary History* 25, no. 2/3 (1990): 365–78.

Nye, Robert A. *Masculinity and Male Codes of Honor in Modern France*. New York: Oxford University Press, 1993.

Nye, Robert A. ed. *Sexuality*. Oxford and New York: Oxford University Press, 1999.

Nye, Robert A. 'Sexuality'. In *A Companion to Gender History*, eds Teresa A. Meade and Merry E. Wiesner-Hanks, 11–25. Malden, MA, Oxford and Melbourne: Blackwell Publishing Ltd., 2004.

O'Conner, D. J. 'Representations of Women Workers: Tobacco Strikers in the 1890s'. In *Constructing Spanish Womanhood: Female Identity in Modern Spain*, eds Victoria Lorée Enders and Pamela Beth Radcliff, 151–72. Albany, NY: State University of New York Press, 1999.

Offen, Karen. M. 'Depopulation, Nationalism, and Feminism in Fin-De-Siècle France'. *American Historical Review* 89, no. 3 (1984): 648–76.

Offen, Karen. M. 'The New Sexual Politics of French Revolutionary Historiography'. *French Historical Studies* 16, no. 4 (1990): 909–22.

Offen, Karen M. *European Feminisms, 1700–1950: A Political History*. Palo Alto, CA: Stanford University Press, 1999.

Olsen, Kåre, *Schicksal Lebensborn. Die Kinder der Schande und Ihrer Mütter*. Munich: Knauer Taschenbuch Verlag, 2004.

Oosterhuis, Harry. *Stepchildren of Nature: Krafft-Ebing, Psychiatry and the Making of Sexual Identity*. Chicago: University of Chicago Press, 2000.

Opitz, Reinhard. *Der Deutsche Sozial-Liberalismus 1917–1933*. Cologne: Pahl-Rugenstein, 1973.

Orgonics. Available from http://www.orgonics.com/ (accessed June 2006).

Outram, Dorinda. *The Body and the French Revolution: Sex, Class and Political Culture*. New Haven, CT: Yale University Press, 1989.

Pagden, Anthony. *Lords of All the World: Ideologies of Empire in Spain, Britain and France c. 1500–C. 1850*. New Haven, CT: Yale University Press, 1995.

Paine, Thomas. 'Selections from Common Sense'. In *Reading the American Past: Selected Historical Documents*, vol. 1, ed. Michael P. Johnson, 94–99. Boston: Bedford Books, 1998.

Paret, Peter. *Understanding War: Essays on Clausewitz and the History of Military Power*. Princeton: Princeton University Press, 1992.

Parker, Geoffrey. *The Military Revolution: Military Innovation and the Rise of the West*. 2nd ed. Cambridge: Cambridge University Press, 1996.

Parr, Joy. 'Gender History and Historical Practice'. In *Gender and History in Canada*, eds Joy Parr and Mark Rosenfeld, 8–27. Toronto: Copp Clark Ltd., 1996.

Pateman, Carol. *The Sexual Contract*. Stanford, CA: Stanford University Press, 1988.

Paul, Christa. *Zwangsprostitution: Staatlich Errichtete Bordelle im Nationalsozialismus*. Berlin: Edition Hentrich, 1995.

Pedersen, Susan. 'National Bodies, Unspeakable Acts: The Sexual Politics of Colonial Policy-Making'. *Journal of Modern History* 63, no. 4 (1991): 647–80.

Pedersen, Susan. *Family, Dependence, and the Origins of the Welfare State: Britain and France, 1914–1945*. New York: Cambridge University Press, 1993.

Pennington, Reina. *Wings, Women, and War: Soviet Airwomen in World War II Combat*. Lawrence: University Press of Kansas, 2001.

Petigny, Alan. 'Illegitimacy, Postwar Psychology, and the Reperiodization of the Sexual Revolutionary'. *Journal of Social History* 38, no. 1 (2004): 63–79.

'Petition of Women of the Third Estate to the King (1 January 1789)'. At *Liberty, Equality, Fraternity: Exploring the French Revolution*. City University of New York and George Mason University. Available from http://chnm.gmu.edu/revolution/d/472/ (accessed February 2005).

Peto, Andrea. 'Memory and the Narrative of Rape in Budapest and Vienna'. In *Life after Death. Approaches to a Cultural and Social History of Europe*, eds Dirk Schumann and Richard Bessel, 129–49. New York: Cambridge University Press, 2003.

Phillips, Anne, and Barbara Taylor. 'Sex and Skill: Notes Towards a Feminist Economics'. In *Feminism and History*, ed. Joan W. Scott, 317–30. New York: Oxford University Press, 1996.

Plakans, Andrejs. 'Peasant Farmsteads and Households in the Baltic Littoral, 1797'. *Comparative Studies in Society and History* 17, no. 1 (1975): 36–64.

Plakans, Andrejs. 'Agrarian Reform and the Family in Eastern Europe'. In *Family Life in the Long Nineteenth Century, 1789–1913*, eds David I. Kertzer and Marzio Barbagli, 73–105. New Haven, CT and London: Yale University Press, 2002.

Pocock, J. G. A. *The Machiavellian Moment: Florentine Political Thought and the Atlantic Republican Tradition*. Princeton: Princeton University Press, 1975.

Poiger, Uta G. 'Rebels with a Cause? American Popular Culture, the 1956 Youth Riots, and New Conceptions of Masculinity in East and West Germany'. In *The American Impact on Postwar Germany*, ed. Reiner Pommerin, 93–124. Providence, RI and Oxford: Berghahn Books, 1995.

Population Reference Bureau. *PRB Country Profiles*. Available from www.prb.org (accessed 9 February 2006).

Public Orgonomic Research Exchange – PORE. Available from http://www.orgone.org/ (accessed June 2006).

Purvis, June. *Emmeline Pankhurst: A Biography*. London and New York: Routledge, 2002.

Purvis, June. 'Deeds Not Words'. *History Today* 52, no. 5 (2005): 56–63.

Pyecroft, Susan. 'British Working Women and the First World War'. *The Historian* 56, no. 4 (1994): 699–711.

Quataert, Jean H. 'Unequal Partners in an Uneasy Alliance: Women and the Working Class in Imperial Germany'. In *Socialist Women: European Socialist Feminism in Nineteenth and Early Twentieth Century Europe*, eds Marilyn Boxer and Jean Quartaert, 112–40. New York: Elsevier, 1978.

Quataert, Jean H. 'The Shaping of Women's Work in Manufacturing: Guilds, Households, and the State in Central Europe, 1648–1870'. *American Historical Review* 90, no. 5 (1985): 1,122–48.

Quine, Maria Sophia. *Population Politics in Twentieth-Century Europe*. London and New York: Routledge, 1996.

Reese, Dagmar. 'Bund Deutscher Mädel – Zur Geschichte der weiblichen deutschen Jugend im Dritten Reich'. In *Mutterkreuz und Arbeitsbuch: Zur Geschichte der Frauen in der Weimarer Republik und im Nationalsozialismus*, ed. Frauengruppe Faschismusforschung, 163–83. Frankfurt am Main: Fischer, 1981.

Reich, Wilhelm. *Die Sexualität im Kulturkampf: Zur Sozialistischen Umstrukturierung des Menschenmacher*. 2nd revised ed. Copenhagen: Sexpol-Verlag, 1936.

Reich, Wilhelm. *The Sexual Revolution: Toward a Self-Governing Character Structure*. 1st English ed. New York: Orgon Institute Press, 1945.

Reid, Robert. *Lermontov's A Hero of Our Time*. London: Bristol Classical Press, 1997.

Rendall, Jane. *The Origins of Modern Feminism: Women in Britain, France, and the United States 1780–1860*. Basingstoke: Macmillan, 1985.

Reyfman, Irina. *Ritualized Violence Russian Style: The Duel in Russian Culture and Literature*. Palo Alto, CA: Stanford University Press, 1999.

Reynolds, Siân. 'Marianne's Citizen? Women, the Republic and Universal Suffrage in France'. In *Gender and History in Western Europe*, eds Robert Shoemaker and Mary Vincent, 306–18. London: Arnold, 1998.

Richie, Alexandra. *Faust's Metropolis: A History of Berlin*. London: HarperCollins, 1998.

Ritvo, Harriet. 'Classification and Continuity in the Origin of Species'. In *Charles Darwin's The Origin of Species: New Interdisciplinary Essays*, eds David Amigoni and Jeff Wallace, 47–67. Manchester and New York: Manchester University Press, 1995.

Roberts, Mary Louise. *Civilization without Sexes: Reconstructing Gender in Postwar France*. Chicago: University of Chicago Press, 1994.

Roberts, Mary Louise. *Disruptive Acts: The New Woman in Fin-De-Siècle France*. Chicago: University of Chicago Press, 2002.

Rose, Sonya O. 'Gender Antagonism and Class Conflict: Exclusionary Strategies of Male Trade Unionists in Nineteenth-Century Britain'. *Social History* 13, no. 2 (1988): 191–208.

Ross, Kristin. *May '68 and Its Afterlives*. Chicago: University of Chicago Press, 2002.

Rousseau, Jean-Jacques. *The Social Contract*. Trans. Maurice Cranston. New York: Penguin, 1968.

Rousseau, Jean-Jacques. *The Collected Writings of Rousseau*. 9 vols. Eds Roger D. Masters and Christopher Kelly. Hanover, CT: Published for Dartmouth College by University Press of New England, 1990.

Rowbotham, Sheila. *Hidden from History: Rediscovering Women in History from the 17th Century to the Present*. New York: Pantheon, 1973.

Ruskin, John. *Sesame and Lilies*. Ed. Deborah Epstein Nord. New Haven, CT: Yale University Press, 2002 [1865].

Ryback, Timothy W. *Rock around the Bloc: A History of Rock Music in Eastern Europe and the Soviet Union*. New York: Oxford University Press, 1990.

Sabean, David Warren. *Property, Production, and Family in Neckarhausen, 1700–1870*. Cambridge: Cambridge University Press, 1991.

Said, Edward W. *Orientalism*. 1st Vintage Books ed. New York: Vintage Books, 1979.

Saldern, Adelheld von. 'Victims or Perpetrators? Controversies About the Role of Women in the Nazi State'. In *Nazism and German Society, 1933–1945*, ed. David F. Crew, 141–65. London and New York: Routledge, 1994.

Sanborn, Geoffrey. *The Sign of the Cannibal: Melville and the Making of a Postcolonial Reader*. Durham, NC: Duke University Press, 1998.

Sanborn, Joshua A. *Drafting the Russian Nation: Military Conscription, Total War, and Mass Politics, 1905–1925*. DeKalb, IL: Northern Illinois University Press, 2003.

Sanger, Margaret. *Woman and the New Race*. New York: Truth Publishing Company, 1920.

Saraceno, Chiara, Manuela Olagnero and Paola Torrioni. *First European Quality of Life Survey: Families, Work and Social Networks*. Dublin: European Foundation for the Improvement of Living and Working Conditions, 2005.

Schama, Simon. *Citizens: A Chronicle of the French Revolution*. Reprint ed. New York: Vintage, 1990.

Schivelbusch, Wolfgang. *The Culture of Defeat: On National Trauma, Mourning and Recovery*. New York: Picador, 2003.

Schmitt, Bernadotte Everly. *The Annexation of Bosnia, 1908–1909*. New York: H. Fertig, 1970.

Schryver, A. de, and A. Meheus. 'Epidemiology of Sexually Transmitted Diseases: The Global Picture'. *Bulletin of the World Health Organization* 68, no. 5 (1990): 639–64.

Scott, Joan W. 'Gender: A Useful Category of Historical Analysis'. *American Historical Review* 91, no. 5 (1986): 1,053–75.

Scott, Joan Wallach. *Only Paradoxes to Offer: French Feminists and the Rights of Man*. Cambridge: Harvard University Press, 1996.

Scotto, Peter. 'Prisoners of the Caucasus: Ideologies of Imperialism in Lermontov's "Bela"'. *PMLA* 107, no. 2 (1992): 246–60.

Seeley, John Robert. *The Expansion of England*. Chicago: University of Chicago Press, 1971.

Sewell, William H. 'Artisans and Factory Workers, 1789–1848'. In *Working Class Formation*, eds Ira Katznelson and Aristide R. Zolberg, 45–70. Princeton: Princeton University Press, 1986.

Sewell, William H. 'Le Citoyen/La Citoyenne: Activity, Passivity, and the Revolutionary Concept of Citizenship'. In *The French Revolution and the Creation of Modern Political Culture.* Vol. 2. *Political Culture of the French Revolution*, ed. Colin Lucas, 105–25. New York: Pergamon Press, 1988.

Sharpe, James A. *Instruments of Darkness: Witchcraft in Early Modern England*. Philadelphia: University of Pennsylvania Press, 1997.

Shcherbatov, Prince M. M. *On the Corruption of Morals in Russia*. Trans. A. Lentin. Cambridge: Cambridge University Press, 1969.

Sheehan, James J. *German History, 1770–1866*. Oxford: Oxford University Press, 1989.

Sher, Richard B. 'Adam Ferguson, Adam Smith, and the Problem of National Defense'. *Journal of Modern History* 61, no. 2 (1989): 240–68.

Shils, Edward A., and Morris Janowitz. 'Cohesion and Disintegration in the Wehrmacht in World War II'. *The Public Opinion Quarterly* 12, no. 2 (1948): 280–315.

Shoemaker, Robert B. *Gender in English Society, 1650–1850: The Emergence of Separate Spheres*. London and New York: Longman, 1998.

Shoemaker, Robert B. 'The Taming of the Duel: Masculinity, Honor and Ritual Violence in London, 1660–1800'. *Historical Journal* 45, no. 3 (2002): 525–45.

Shorter, Edward. *The Making of the Modern Family*. New York: Basic Books, 1975.

Simonton, Deborah. 'Women Workers; Working Women'. In *The Routledge History of Women in Europe since 1700*, ed. Deborah Simonton, 134–76. London and New York: Routledge, 2006.

Smith, Bonnie G. *Ladies of the Leisure Class: The Bourgeoises of Northern France in the Nineteenth Century*. Princeton: Princeton University Press, 1981.

Smith, Bonnie G. *Changing Lives: Women in European History since 1700*. Boston: Houghton Mifflin Co. College Division, 1989.

Smith, Douglas, ed. *Love and Conquest: Personal Correspondence of Catherine the Great and Prince Grigory Potemkin*. DeKalb, IL: Northern Illinois University Press, 2004.

Snyder, Louis Leo. *The Blood and Iron Chancellor: A Documentary-Biography of Otto von Bismarck*. Princeton: Van Nostrand, 1967.

Sombart, Nicolas. *Die Deutschen Männer und Ihre Feinde. Carl Schmitt – Ein Deutsches Schicksal Zwischen Männerbund und Matriarchmythos*. Munich and Vienna: Carl Hanser, 1991.

Sowerwine, Charles. *Sisters or Citizens: Women and Socialism in France since 1876*. Cambridge and New York: Cambridge University Press, 1982.

Sowerwine, Charles. 'Socialism, Feminism, and the Socialist Women's Movement from the French Revolutionary to World War II'. In *Becoming Visible: Women in European History*, eds Renate Bridenthal, Susan Mosher Stuard and Merry E. Wiesner, 357–87. Boston and New York: Houghton Mifflin Co., 1998.

Sperber, Jonathan. *The European Revolutions, 1848–1851*. Cambridge: Cambridge University Press, 1984.

Spivak, Gayatri Chakravorty. 'Can the Subaltern Speak?' In *Marxism and the Interpretation of Culture*, eds Cary Nelson and Lawrence Grossberg, 271–313. Urbana, IL: University of Illinois Press, 1988.

'Stanislas Maillard Describes the Women's March to Versailles (5 October 1789)'. At *Liberty, Equality, Fraternity: Exploring the French Revolution*. City University of New York and George Mason University. Available from http://chnm.gmu.edu/revolution/ d/473/ (accessed February 2005).

Stanley, Liz. *Sex Surveyed, 1949–1994: From Mass Observation's 'Little Kinsey' to the National Survey and the Hite Reports*. London and Bristol, PA: Taylor & Francis Ltd., 1995.

Stark, Gary D. 'The Ideology of the German Burschenschaft Generation'. *European Studies Review* 8, no. 3 (1978): 323–48.

Steinbach, Susie. *Women in England, 1760–1914: A Social History*. New York: Palgrave Macmillan, 2004.

Steinbrügge, Lieselotte. *The Moral Sex: Woman's Nature in the French Enlightenment*. Trans. Pamela E. Selwyn. Oxford and New York: Oxford University Press, 1995.

Stengers, Jean. *Masturbation: The History of a Great Terror*. Trans. Kathryn Hoffmann. New York: Palgrave, 2001.

Stepan, Nancy Leys. 'Race, Gender and Nation in Argentina: The Influence of Italian Eugenics'. *History of European Ideas* 15, no. 4–6 (1992): 749–56.

Stepan, Nancy Leys. 'Race, Gender, Science and Citizenship'. In *Cultures of Empire: Colonizers in Britain and the Empire in the Nineteenth and Twentieth Centuries, a Reader*, ed. Catherine Hall, 61–86. New York: Routledge, 2000.

Steward, William Kilborne. 'The Mentors of Mussolini'. *The American Political Science Review* 29, no. 4 (1928): 843–69.

Stockdale, Melissa Kirschke. '"My Death for the Motherland Is Happiness": Women, Patriotism, and Soldiering in Russia's Great War, 1914–1917'. *American Historical Review* 109, no. 1 (2004): 78–116.

Stocking, George W. *Victorian Anthropology*. New York: The Free Press, 1987.

Stolberg, Michael. 'A Woman Down to Her Bones: The Anatomy of Sexual Difference in the Sixteenth and Early Seventeenth Centuries'. *Isis* 94, no. 2 (2003): 274–99.

Stoler, Ann Laura. *Carnal Knowledge and Imperial Power: Race and the Intimate in Colonial Rule*. Berkeley and Los Angeles: University of California Press, 2002.

Stone, Judith F. 'Republican Ideology, Gender and Class: France, 1860s–1914'. In *Gender and Class in Modern Europe*, eds Laura L. Frader and Sonya O. Rose. Ithaca, NY and London: Cornell University Press, 1996.

Stone, Lawrence. *The Family, Sex, and Marriage in England, 1500–1800*. New York: Harper and Row, 1977.

Storr, Merl. 'Transformations: Subjects, Categories and Cures in Krafft-Ebing's Sexology'. In *Sexology in Culture: Labelling Bodies and Desires*, eds Lucy Bland and Laura Doan, 11–25. Cambridge: Polity Press, 1998.

Sundin, Jan. 'Sinful Sex: Legal Prosecution of Extramarital Sex in Preindustrial Sweden'. *Social Science History* 16, no. 1 (1992): 99–128.

Tabili, Laura. 'Empire Is the Enemy of Love: Edith Noor's Progress and Other Stories'. *Gender & History* 17, no. 1 (2005): 5–28.

Taylor, Barbara. '"The Men Are as Bad as Their Masters": Socialism, Feminism and Sexual Antagonism in the London Tailoring Trade in the Early 1830's'. *Feminist Studies* 5, no. 1 (1979): 7–40.

Taylor, Barbara. *The Eve of the New Jerusalem: Socialism and Feminism in the Nineteenth Century*. New York: Pantheon Books, 1983.

Tester, Keith, ed. *The Flâneur*. London and New York: Routledge, 1994.

Therborn, Göran. *Between Sex and Power*. New York: Routledge, 2004.

Thompson, Christopher. 'Un troisième sexe? Les bourgeoises et la bicyclette dans la France fin de siècle'. *Mouvement Social* 192 (2000): 9–39.

Thompson, Dorothy. 'Women and Nineteenth-Century Radical Politics: A Lost Dimension'. In *The Rights and Wrongs of Women*, eds Juliet Mitchell and Ann Oakley, 112–38. London: Penguin Books, 1976.

Thompson, E. P. 'Time, Work-Discipline, and Industrial Capitalism'. *Past and Present* 38 (1967): 56–97.

Tilly, Louise and Joan W. Scott. 'Women's Work and the Family in Nineteenth Century Europe'. *Comparative Studies in Society and History* 17, no. 1 (1975): 36–64.

Tilly, Louise and Joan W. Scott. *Women, Work and Family*. New York: Holt, Rinehart and Winston, 1978.

Timm, Annette F. 'The Politics of Fertility: Population Politics and Health Care in Berlin, 1919–1972'. Ph.D. dissertation, University of Chicago, 1999.

Tolstoy, Leo. *Writings on Civil Disobedience and Nonviolence*. Philadelphia: New Society Publishers, 1987.

Tomlinson, B. R. 'Economics and Empire: The Periphery and the Imperial Economy'. In *The Oxford History of the British Empire*, vol. 3., ed. Andrew Porter: *The Nineteenth Century*, 53–74. Oxford and New York: Oxford University Press, 1999.

Tone, John Lawrence. 'Spanish Women in the Resistance to Napoleon, 1808–1814'. In *Constructing Spanish Womanhood: Female Identity in Modern Spain*, eds Victoria Lorée Enders and Pamela Beth Radcliff, 259–82. Albany, NY: State University of New York Press, 1999.

Tone, John Lawrence. 'The Virgin of the Pillar and Agustina Zaragoza'. Paper delivered at the Annual Meeting of the American Historical Association (Philadelphia: 2006).

Tosh, John. 'Domesticity and Manliness in the Victorian Middle Class: The Family of Edward White Benson'. In *Manful Assertions: Masculinities in Britain since 1800*, eds Michael Roper and John Tosh, 44–73. London and New York: Routledge, 1991.

Treitschke, Heinrich von. *Treitschke's History of Germany in the Nineteenth Century*. Vol. 1. Eds Eden Paul and Cedar Paul. New York: McBride Nast & Company, 1915.

Triplett, Hall. 'The Misnomer of Freud's "Seduction Theory"'. *Journal of the History of Ideas* 65, no. 4 (2004): 647–65.

Trouille, Mary Seidman. *Sexual Politics in the Enlightenment: Women Writers Read Rousseau*. Albany: State University of New York Press, 1997.

Trumbach, Randolph. 'The Birth of the Queen: Sodomy and the Emergence of Gender Equality in Modern Culture 1660–1750'. In *Hidden from History: Reclaiming the Gay and Lesbian Past*, eds Martin Duberman, Martha Vicinus and George Chauncey Jr., 129–40. New York: Meridian, 1989.

Tuson, Penelope. 'Mutiny Narratives and the Imperial Feminine: European Women's Accounts of the Rebellion in India in 1857'. *Women's Studies International Forum* 21, no. 3 (1998): 291–303.

Valenze, Deborah. *Prophetic Sons and Daughters: Female Preaching and Popular Religion in Industrial England*. Princeton: Princeton University Press, 1985.

Vertinsky, Patricia. *The Eternally Wounded Woman: Women, Exercise and Doctors in the Late Nineteenth Century*. Manchester: Manchester University Press, 1990.

Vervenioti, Tasoula. 'The Adventure of Women's Suffrage in Greece'. In *When the War Was Over: Women, War and Peace in Europe, 1940–1956*, eds Claire Duchen and Irene Bandhauer-Schöffmann, 103–18. London and New York: Leicester University Press, 2000.

Vickery, Amanda. 'Golden Age to Separate Spheres? A Review of the Categories and

Chronology of English Women's History'. In *Gender and History in Western Europe*, eds Robert Shoemaker and Mary Vincent, 197–225. New York and London: Arnold, 1998.

'Vintage Video: Death of Suffragette at Epsom Derby, 1913'. FirstWorldWar.com. Available from http://www.firstworldwar.com/video/epsomsuffragette.htm (accessed February 2006).

Vries, Jan D. *European Urbanization, 1500–1800*. Cambridge: Harvard University Press, 1984.

W.W.P. (pseudo.). 'Woman as She Is and as She Ought to Be'. *New Moral World* 5, no. 13 (1839).

Walkowitz, Judith R. *Prostitution and Victorian Society: Women, Class and the State*. Cambridge and New York: Cambridge University Press, 1980.

Walkowitz, Judith R. 'Male Vice and Female Virtue: Feminism and the Politics of Prostitution in Nineteenth Century Britain'. In *Powers of Desire: The Politics of Sexuality*, eds Ann Snitow, Christine Stansell and Sharon Thompson, 419–38. New York: Monthly Review Press, 1983.

Walkowitz, Judith R. *City of Dreadful Delight: Narratives of Sexual Danger in Late-Victorian London*. Chicago: University of Chicago Press, 1992.

Weatherfield, Molly. 'The Mother of Masochism'. *Salon* 6 August 1998. Available from http://www.salon.com/books/feature/1988/08/06feature.html (accessed October 2005).

Weatherfield, Molly. 'I Wrote the Story of O'. *Guardian Unlimited/The Observer* 25 July 2004. Available from http://observer.guardian.co.uk/review/story/0,6903,1268403,00.html (accessed October 2005).

Weber, Max. 'National Character and the Junkers'. In *From Max Weber: Essays in Sociology*, eds H. H. Gerth and C. Wright Mills, 386–95. Oxford and New York: Oxford University Press, 1946.

Weeks, Jeffrey. 'Foucault for Historians'. *History Workshop Journal* 14 (1982): 106–19.

Weeks, Jeffrey. *Sexuality and Its Discontents: Meanings, Myths, and Modern Sexualities*. London and Boston: Routledge and Kegan Paul, 1985.

Weeks, Jeffrey. 'Inverts, Perverts, and Mary-Annes: Male Prostitution and the Regulation of Homosexuality in England in the Nineteenth and Early Twentieth Centuries'. In *Hidden from History: Reclaiming the Gay and Lesbian Past*, eds Martin Duberman, Martha Vicinus and George Chauncey Jr., 195–211. New York: Meridian, 1989.

Weitz, Eric D. 'The Heroic Man and the Ever-Changing Woman: Gender and Politics in European Communism, 1917–1950'. In *Gender and Class in Modern Europe*, eds Laura L. Frader and Sonya O. Rose, 311–52. Ithaca, NY and London: Cornell University Press, 1996.

Weller, I., D. H. Crawford, V. Iliescu, K. MacLennan, S. Sutherland, R. S. Tedder and M. W. Adler. 'Homosexual Men in London: Lymphadenopathy, Immune Status, and Epstein-Barr Virus Infection'. *Annals of the New York Academy of Science* 437, no. 1 (1984): 238–53.

Wesseling, H. L. *Divide and Rule: The Partition of Africa, 1880–1914*. Westport, CT: Praeger, 1996.

Wiesner, Merry E. *Women and Gender in Early Modern Europe*. Cambridge and New York: Cambridge University Press, 2000.

Wiesner-Hanks, Merry E. *Gender in History*. Malden and Oxford: Blackwell Publishers, 2001.

The Wilhelm Reich Museum. Available from http://www.wilhelmreichmuseum.org (accessed June 2006).

Wilson, Kathleen. 'Empire, Gender, and Modernity in the Eighteenth Century'. In *Gender and Empire*, ed. Philippa Levine, 14–45. Oxford and New York: Oxford University Press, 2004.

Winks, Robin W., and R. J. Q. Adams. *Europe, 1890–1945: Crisis and Conflict*. New York: Oxford University Press, 2003.

Woloch, Isser. *The New Regime: Transformations of the French Civic Order, 1789–1820s*. New York and London: W. W. Norton & Company, 1994.

Woolf, Virginia. *A Room of One's Own*. New York: Harcourt, Brace and Co., 1929.

World Urbanization Prospects: The 2003 Revision. New York: United Nations, 2004. Available from http://www.un.org/esa/population/publications/wup2003/WUP2003Report.pdf (accessed 27 September 2006).

Worobec, Christine D. *Peasant Russia: Family and Community in the Post-Emancipation Period*. Princeton: Princeton University Press, 1991.

Woycke, James. *Birth Control in Germany, 1871–1933*. London: Routledge, 1988.

Wright, Gordon. *The Ordeal of Total War, 1939–1945*. New York: Harper and Row, 1968.

Wrigley, E. A. 'The Fall of Marital Fertility in Nineteenth-Century France: Exemplar or Exception?' *European Journal of Population/Revue européenne de demographie* 1, no. 1 (1985): 31–60.

Wunder, Heide. *He Is the Sun, She Is the Moon: Women in Early Modern Germany*. Cambridge, MA and London: Harvard University Press, 1998.

Zinsser, Judith P. ed. *Men, Women, and the Birthing of Modern Science*. DeKalb, IL: Northern Illinois University Press, 2005.

Index